The Emil and Kathleen Sick Lecture-Book Series

in Western History and Biography

The Emil and Kathleen Sick Lecture-Book Series
in Western History and Biography

Under the provisions of a Fund established by the children
of Mr. and Mrs. Emil Sick, whose deep interest in the history and culture
of the American West was inspired by their own experience in the region,
distinguished scholars are brought to the University of Washington
to deliver public lectures based on original research in the fields
of Western history and biography. The terms of the gift also provide
for the publication by the University of Washington Press of the books
resulting from the research upon which the lectures are based.
This book is the eighth volume in the series.

The Great Columbia Plain:
A Historical Geography, 1805–1910
by Donald W. Meinig

Mills and Markets: A History of the
Pacific Coast Lumber Industry to 1900
by Thomas R. Cox

Radical Heritage: Labor, Socialism, and Reform
in Washington and British Columbia, 1885–1917
by Carlos A. Schwantes

The Battle for Butte: Mining and Politics
on the Northern Frontier, 1864–1906
Michael P. Malone

The Forging of a Black Community: Seattle's Central District,
from 1870 through the Civil Rights Era
by Quintard Taylor

Warren G. Magnuson and the
Shaping of Twentieth-Century America
by Shelby Scates

The Atomic West
edited by Bruce Hevly and John M. Findlay

Power and Place in the North American West
edited by Richard White and John M. Findlay

Power and Place

IN THE NORTH AMERICAN WEST

EDITED BY

Richard White

AND

John M. Findlay

Center for the Study of the Pacific Northwest

IN ASSOCIATION WITH

University of Washington Press

SEATTLE AND LONDON

Library of Congress Cataloging-in-Publication Data
Power and place in the North American West /
edited by Richard White and John M. Findlay.
p.   cm.—(Emil and Kathleen Sick lecture-book series
in western history and biography)
Includes index.
ISBN 0-295-97774-4 (cloth : alk. paper).
ISBN 0-295-97773-6 (pbk. : alk. paper)
1. West (U.S.)—History—Congresses.
2. Canada, Western—History—Congresses.
3. Human geography—West (U.S.)—Congresses.
4. Human geography—Canada, Western—Congresses.
5. West (U.S.)—Social conditions—Congresses.
6. Canada, Western—Social conditions—Congresses.
7. West (U.S.)—Economic conditions—Congresses.
8. Canada, Western—Economic conditions—Congresses.
9. Power (Social sciences)—West (U.S.)—Congresses.
10. Power (Social sciences)—Canada, Western—Congresses.
I. White, Richard, 1947–   .
II. Findlay, John M., 1955–   .
III. Series.
F591.P89   1999   98-31496
978-DC21   CIP

Contents

Contents

Contents

Introduction

JOHN M. FINDLAY AND RICHARD WHITE

The chapters in this anthology had their origins as papers delivered at a symposium hosted by the Center for the Study of the Pacific Northwest, Department of History, University of Washington, Seattle, in November 1994. The conference was conceived as a means of examining the power of some places over others. That is, we originally specified interest in how region had been affected by relations between capital and province, East and West, core and periphery; our initial title was "Metropolis and Hinterland." While retaining that interest, however, we significantly changed the content of the conference by broadening the title in order to consider a wider range of questions concerning not just metropolis and hinterland but rather, as we renamed the event, "Power and Place in the North American West."

The resulting symposium offered richer fare than our original focus could have provided. We did receive and welcome scholarship on the relations between city and country, core and periphery, East and West. But we were also treated to a much wider range of issues than we might otherwise have expected. Some papers, for example, focused on relations of power within specific places, rather than between places; others addressed the power of place itself, and in particular the psychological power of western places, which so often defied eastern preconceptions and helped to define regional modes of thinking.[1]

In the end, replacing "Metropolis and Hinterland" with "Power and Place" opened up many more avenues of discussion. It also made much more difficult the tasks of summarizing the conference and introducing this book. "Power" and "place," more than "metropolis" and "hinterland," are protean words. In the context of the conference the tensions, contradictions, and ambiguities of these meanings became apparent. The distinguished historical geographer D. W. Meinig tacitly commented on historians' often imprecise and inconsistent use of key terms at the end of the conference when, asked to comment on the entire program, he took it upon himself to offer brief definitions for "a few basic geographical concepts," such as place, region, environment, and landscape. These terms, he explained, had "more or less permeated this symposium"; what he so kindly did not say (at least explicitly) was that those same terms had, to his way of thinking, been used much too loosely. The task of defining certain terms, so expected by Meinig, had not seemed fundamental for the historians who presented the majority of conference papers. So we historians discovered, at the very moment the symposium ended, that we were all much better prepared to start our conversations because of Meinig's having paved the way with a few key definitions.

This book, unlike the symposium, need not suffer from the same handicap. We are in a slightly better position to offer, at the beginning, some tentative definitions. "Place," to start with, is most helpfully understood as a spatial reality constructed by people. Meinig denotes "place" as "some kind of location and ensemble of features. Such things are human creations, in the sense of perceptions, a mental imposition of order, a parcelization of the earth's surface, a transformation of space—an abstraction—into something more specific and limited." Constructing place through an "imposition" of order entails asserting some sort of control over the environment as well as over other peoples with different ideas about the same physical space; in other words, it represents the exercise of power.[2]

Having made a tentative nod in the direction of defining "place," and having employed the term "power" in that definition, we would now seem to be obligated to take the next logical step and define "power." Broadly speaking, we offer the provisional idea that power is the ability of an agent—be it a person, a corporation, the state, or some other entity—to influence either people or natural forces to act according to that agent's desire or will. Power can be exercised through force, persuasion, manipulation, and other ways. It is never evenly distributed, but it is also probably never monopolized. Among people, power implies a relationship between persons. In other words, to speak of power among people is to speak of relations of power.

To go beyond this starting point of a definition would prove difficult and unwieldy. The papers at the symposium, like the chapters that follow, rely upon too many different ideas about the meaning of "power" to enable one to denote the concept in more detail. The authors drew consciously or otherwise upon a number of more formal and theoretical conversations about the meaning of "power," but no single definition or conceptualization prevailed among them. Meinig noted that his own discipline of geography these days "is full of Foucault and Giddens and other luminaries of the moment," but added that "there is as yet more program than product from these discourses."

Western history finds itself in a similar position. At least a few of the following chapters make explicit reference to—if not always explicit use of—definitions of power rooted in social science and critical theory, but most do not. Few historians seem comfortable defining power carefully, especially in the abstract. Yet each of the following chapters tends to draw upon theories of power based on the work of such people as Michel Foucault and Anthony Giddens that, knowingly or otherwise, historians have begun to adopt and modify for their own use. Moreover, each chapter's focus on a historical example of power as exercised in one or more specific western places broadens our understanding of the variety of ways in which we might conceptualize "power" in the history of the North American West. Indeed, by way of introducing this anthology, we propose to discuss each chapter in terms of its notion of the nature of power and its connections to place.

Part I concerns relationships between Indians and non-Indians. Each of its chapters considers power as one dimension of the colonization of the North American West by Euroamerican nation-states. They trace the imposition of, and the resistance to, Euroamerican power among indigenous peoples in western places. Each chapter also provides a different perspective on the nature of power in the specific places under consideration.

"Coboway's Tale: A Story of Power and Places Along the Columbia," the symposium's keynote address by James P. Ronda, depicts power in two ways while considering relations between Indians and non-Indians from the viewpoint of the Clatsop headman Coboway and his Indian descendants at the mouth of the Columbia River. The chapter portrays power both in relation to space and in relation to time. On the one hand, and particularly at Coboway's more "local" level, power increasingly seemed an elusive and external phenomenon: "Power is always unstable, unpredictable—like the sudden currents of a river in flood," Ronda writes. "And like the river, power is always in motion, sweeping from place to place with restless energy."

On the other hand, Ronda traces two more definite and stable trajectories of how power shifted over time, accompanying the process of colonization. From Coboway's perspective, power—understood as a people's relative ability to determine its own fate—diminished as colonization from afar proceeded apace. (It is crucial to note that what Alfred W. Crosby terms "ecological imperialism" accompanied—often preceded—the economic and political imperialism brought by non-Indians; disease and other ecological changes, and the attendant demographic decline, contributed enormously to the Clatsops' loss of power.) From the perspective of a succession of Anglo-Americans arriving in the Pacific Northwest, by contrast, power increased with each new phase of their political, economic, cultural, or military mastery over place. From explorers through fur traders, missionaries, and Indian agents to settlers, the influence or power of the colonizers—their capacity to define place on their terms—grew with their ability to bring more resources to bear upon the Pacific Northwest. Ronda highlights the accretion of political power in distant places, especially Washington, D.C., over the Clatsops' homeland. He thus draws the trajectory of federal power over the century after the initial encounters of Coboway with the U.S. expedition led by Lewis and Clark.

James F. Brooks too portrays several different kinds of power in "Violence, Justice, and State Power in the New Mexican Borderlands, 1780–1880." His chapter considers the victims of a very personal, direct, and violent exercise of power—the women and children seized (along with livestock) in the course of conflicts between New Mexicans and Indians between 1780 and 1880. Sometimes adopted or enslaved by their captors and sometimes returned to their own society, captives served as objects of exchange in a "borderlands political economy" that mediated not only between New Mexicans and Indians but also between the richer and poorer members within each society. Adopting an anthropological perspective on both the retributive and redistributive power inherent in the capture and exchange of human beings, Brooks focuses less on the fate of (and the power used against) captives than on the system in which captives became commodities. "Operating within a mutually understood framework of justice, morality, and fair trade," he writes, "organized bands, both Indian and New Mexican, conducted raids and reprisals that redistributed resources from wealthy Indians and New Mexicans to the poorer elements in both societies." This system flourished until American colonizers succeeded in suppressing it during the 1860s and 1870s. Brooks argues that under Anglo rule "borderland Indians and New Mexicans accepted a form of physical security and safety that left many destitute, dispossessed, and dependent on the questionable largesse of the United States government." Many New Mexicans and Indians (but presumably not all women and children) lamented the enforced ceasefire and abolition of traffic in humans.

For Ronda, power at bottom was political and came to reside in the nation-state; for Brooks, power basically stemmed from the arrangements of political economy and depended on the systems of exchange that different regimes permitted. For John Lutz in "Making 'Indians' in British Columbia: Power, Race, and the Importance of Place," power is a product of "culture and socialization," embedded in language. Examining ideological and legal discourse about Indians in nineteenth-century British Columbia, Lutz demonstrates how race was constructed in clear-cut stages during the white colonization of western Canada. Among English-speakers, he writes, " 'race' has become a neutral, biological phenomenon and 'racism' a social one. But racism depends on a definition of race as part of a hierarchically ordered system that has been socially constructed to redistribute power." Lutz explains how that system worked over time to impose a nonnative definition and identity upon native peoples, circumscribe their freedom of action, and diminish their ability to determine their own fate. He is equally concerned with questioning our use of such terms as "race" and "Indian"—as well as the ideology underlying them—by historicizing them. In this respect Lutz joins those historians of the western United States who have challenged uncritical use of such terms as "frontier" and "nature." That which has been socially and culturally constructed, particularly in the course of colonization, can also be deconstructed—or so the argument goes. In practice, finding substitute terms and ideas has proven very difficult.

Lutz's argument offers a valuable transition to Part II, which is devoted to race in the North American West. In "Federal Power and Racial Politics in Los Angeles During World War II," Kevin Allen Leonard argues that white supremacists have long dominated the construction of race relations in the American West. By requiring the mobilization of workers of all races, the Second World War presented the West with an opportunity to challenge, or even overthrow, that racist tradition. Leonard explains how in Los Angeles federal agencies and regulations challenged discriminatory conventions, particularly in hiring practices and in the treatment of people of Japanese descent, and forced changes that broadened opportunity for nonwhites. He argues that this experience created resentment among numerous whites who, in southern California and throughout the West, not only resisted desegregation in the mid-1940s but then continued to oppose civil-rights initiatives, especially those orchestrated by the federal government. Like Ronda's Clatsops at the mouth of the Columbia River, Leonard's white westerners chafed at power as exercised over them from the nation's capital.

In "Race, Rhetoric, and Regional Identity: Boosting Los Angeles, 1880–1930," William Deverell and Douglas Flamming offer a different view of race relations in Los Angeles. They contend that race loomed large in the constructions of both white and black boosters in southern California. White boosters borrowed from what they imagined to be the Spanish past to promote their city through La Fiesta de Los Angeles and the Mission Play. Such pageantry not only demonstrated "the inexorable . . . progression from missions to merchants, from a Spanish village to an Anglo metropolis," but also suggested orderly ways for citizens to behave. White boosters' rhetoric generally ignored the city's burgeoning Mexican population and all but ignored its black residents.

African American boosters, by contrast, gave voice to black hopes and expectations for southern California in particular and for the West in general. Leonard argues that the region's white supremacy matched the South's, but Deverell and Flamming join the middle-class, African American boosters of early-twentieth-century L.A. in saying that "segregation in the West was not as severe as it was in the South, and ghettoization was not as evident as it was in northern cities." Black boosters portrayed Los Angeles in part by contrasting it favorably to conditions in the South and Northeast. At the same time, if the West marked an improvement over the South and Northeast, it nonetheless retained much of America's hierarchically ordered social structure, which reduced the power of African Americans to shape their own destiny. Black boosters consequently deployed their rhetoric to encourage changes in race relations. In the end they contrasted urban conditions both to a less satisfactory "East" and to a more satisfactory image of Los Angeles as they imagined it could and should become in the future. Powerful images of southern California were thus constructed by means of comparison and contrast to other places both real and imagined.

Deverell and Flamming illustrate how westerners made use of other places, such as "the East" and the L.A. of past and future, to shape and reshape race relations in their present-day place. Chris Friday follows a somewhat parallel path in "Recasting Identities: American-born Chinese and Nisei in the Era of the Pacific War." These two groups of second-generation immigrants demonstrated the power of place—in this case their parents' respective homelands—in the construction of ethnicity. Seattle's Nisei and San Francisco's American-born Chinese remained loyal to the countries from which their mothers and fathers had come. Keeping track of events in 1930s Asia, especially the Sino-Japanese war, they held on to their Old World roots and found themselves at odds with each other (and at times with their parents), while simultaneously struggling to become "Americans" in a nation that did not generally welcome them. When Pearl Harbor was bombed on December 7, 1941, of necessity the two groups responded differently. American-born Chinese had few problems maintaining loyalties to both China and the United States, because the two nations became wartime allies against Japan. The Nisei by contrast found themselves forced to choose between one culture and the other, and at times to suppress their Japanese "cultural nationalism" to the point where American officials and later scholars could not even recognize that it had once existed. Thus the Nisei lost both place and power in the early 1940s; the war took away the place from which their parents had come, and internment diminished their power to shape their own future.

Friday's chapter concludes Part II, which, like Part I, focuses largely on the hierarchical social ordering of the West and the contested power of some (particularly, white men) to keep others (particularly, minorities) in "place." The chapters in both Part I and Part II touch sometimes upon issues of capitalism and politics, but they tend to focus especially on the exercise of power through discourses such as law, boosterism, and ideology. The chapters of Part III adopt a different focus—the western environment and economy—and pay greater attention to the power of capital and government. They borrow more often from geographers' insights regarding power and place in order to analyze how people shaped the control of western resources, largely through economic and political dealings. Yet they do not abandon such matters as the role of language in developing regional identity.

In "Tourism as Colonial Economy: Power and Place in Western Tourism," Hal Rothman uses the resort town of Sun Valley, Idaho, to illustrate how industrial tourism has transformed western place. Whereas Ronda, Brooks, and Lutz focus on political, legal, and rhetorical colonization, Rothman emphasizes the colonizing force of modern capital in small towns and rural areas. "Tourism in the American West is at its core colonial," he explains, "grafting new sources of power and financing atop existing social structures, bringing idealistic and romantic value systems supported by outside capital to places where the majority of residents have yet to experience material prosperity, and promising an economic panacea but delivering it only to privileged segments of the public." Rothman shows how Sun Valley, Idaho, was shaped and then reshaped by successive investors catering to different customers through different plans for the resort. The process almost unthinkingly undermined existing communities and sometimes dislocated nearby residents. But locals were hardly as pure as the driven snow that attracted skiers to Sun Valley. They participated in not only the industry but also the imagery of tourism, acquiring their "local" identity partly in accordance with the public-relations efforts of "outside" investors. "When it succeeds," Rothman avers, "tourism changes the economic structure of communities and surrounding regions, redistributes power from local people to outsiders with capital, and packages and transforms the meaning of place to successive waves of people, from 'old-timers' to the newest 'neo-native' arrivals, who seek to pull the figurative door shut behind them."

Rothman, like other contributors, points to the influence of "outside" power—in the form of capital—on the West. Paul Hirt's chapter also looks at the influence of an outside power, in his case as manifest in the timber-management policies and practices of the U.S. Forest Service in southwestern Washington State. As agent of the federal government in the West, the Forest Service has functioned not just as a conduit for outside investment but as a manager of the region's capital—its natural resources—that has generally been driven in large part by interests and ideals external to the region. Hirt portrays not so much the management as the mismanagement of the Gifford Pinchot National Forest. The Forest Service deployed a conservationist rhetoric throughout the post-1940 era, but its policies resulted in the serious depletion of timber resources. The agency justified its actions in part by reference to local and state interests; the rapid cutting of trees, as state and local leaders no doubt reminded the Service, kept small-town economies afloat and reduced regional unemployment. Big timber companies also used their clout to shape federal policy, finding in the Republican presidential administrations of the 1980s, for example, strong support for further abandonment of conservationist goals. The overcutting of timber thus worsened even as the problem became more apparent. The Forest Service itself, it must be pointed out, was never simply an agent for other people's designs. Concerned about its own political power, especially its organizational stability and its congressional funding, in setting policy it attended more to its own interests than to the cause of conservation in the Gifford Pinchot National Forest.

Whereas Rothman focuses on private enterprise and Hirt on the public sector, Joseph E. Taylor III considers how a mixture of business and government determined the "spatial relations of power in Oregon salmon management" between 1870 and 1910. Government in these contexts became one tool with which a variety of non-Indian groups tried to monopolize portions of river systems. Those who wished to exploit and manage the salmon fishery competed not only against miners, loggers, farmers, ranchers, and others who threatened salmon habitat through their use of rivers, but also against one another. Gillnetters, for example, tried to limit the take of fishwheels; hatchery advocates tried to keep others away from watersheds that they coveted; recreational anglers attempted to reduce the catch of commercial fishers; and Oregonians opposed the tactics of Washingtonians. These rivals inevitably turned to politics and the courts in order to secure the power they needed to control the places they coveted. One important result of such social, economic, and political division was what Taylor calls "the disassembly of nature." Analyzing early Oregon salmon management in a spatial context "reveals the tendency of society to understand rivers not as complete systems but only according to their relevant parts," Taylor says. "As they came to associate usage with space, Oregonians fragmented water-sheds into their socially defined constituent parts, and then insisted that they be physically managed to serve those uses. Rivers ceased to operate as purely natural systems." Consequently, as with timber in the Gifford Pinchot National Forest, the fish in Oregon rivers were not so much managed as mismanaged. Today the Pacific Northwest worries about endangered species of salmon and diminishing supplies of old-growth trees; Taylor and Hirt show that these problems are nothing new.

Taylor focuses on the specific power of different groups to control specific places in Oregon. Writing about the same state in roughly the same period, William G. Robbins evokes the attitudes in the late nineteenth and early twentieth centuries toward nature and industry that underlay the thinking and decisions of those concerned with exploitation of resources. "Nature's Industries: The Rhetoric of Industrialism in the Oregon Country" explains how Oregonians' appreciation for nature was framed in large part by their vision of how nature's resources could and should be put to industrial use. Robbins returns us, then, to the realm of ideological discourse, and he conveys the power exercised by boosters over how westerners understood and used their environs. He shows us how, before either the tourist or the preservation industry had matured to the point of wanting to "protect" nature, westerners overwhelmingly valued natural resources for their ability to connect a remote region to centers of capital by enabling it to serve distant markets and attract investors and immigrants. The same impulses glorified improved modes of transport as tools for not only conquering natural resources but tightening links between Oregon and the rest of the world. Railroads brought products to Portland; steamships carried them along the lower Columbia to the ocean and beyond.

Industrial commodities extracted from nature and exported around the world promised to propel the Oregon country along the road from hinterland to metropolis. They seemed to be able to give it greater power to determine its own future, to make it into a place that really counted for something. A century after Lewis and Clark had introduced Coboway and his people to the colonizing power of the United States, white Oregonians aspired to take colonization to what they regarded as its logical conclusion. World's fairs hosted by Portland in 1905, Seattle in 1909, and San Francisco and San Diego in 1915–16 all bespoke a regionwide determination to exist no longer on the margins of, but rather as a seat of, empire. The West as place would have arrived, according to its assorted boosters, once it could wield the same kinds of power that the East had long wielded over it.

Robbins's essay concludes with a reminder of the power of discourse. Americans imported to Oregon, as part of their cultural baggage, a vivid set of beliefs and practices for transforming the region, and they then proceeded to turn rhetoric into reality. "The grand design and ambition argued in [their] proposals urged the systematic and orderly development of the region's unparalleled natural wealth. Collectively, it was word play that implied an increasingly intrusive industrial influence on the landscape of the Oregon country. The degree and magnitude of environmental manipulation suggested in that literature would be effected in the coming decades." Indeed, as Ronda points out, American settlers had already altered aboriginal ecosystems in Oregon virtually beyond recognition, and as Taylor points out, they were disassembling the state's "natural" river systems into political and economic units. Ideas imported from the East had a direct impact on the environment; the power of "discourses" and their ability to affect place were substantial. By the same token, established ideas about race—as well as the social hierarchies that they implied—had also been imported intact to the North American West, helping to define place by imposing order not only upon spaces but also upon the diverse occupants of those spaces.

Among those diverse occupants were women. In Part IV of the anthology, the final chapter called "Lighting Out for the Territory: Women, Mobility, and Western Place," Virginia Scharff explores the intersection of region and gender. She explains how mobility has been gendered in ways that have restricted women's ability to move within and across places, and illustrates the nature of gendered mobility by reference to women of the nineteenth- and twentieth-century West. Scharff explains that strictures on women's mobility have been one means to uphold hierarchy and inequality in society. "The process of making western places out of spaces thus entails the operation of gender as an ordering . . . system of beliefs and practices," she writes. "In fact, without understanding the gender relations at work, it is impossible to make substantive sense out of events in any locale that has become (or ceased to be) a place deemed western." But neither gender relations nor western places are by themselves adequate categories for circumscribing entirely the histories of women, or men. Scharff reminds us that the power of places such as "the West" as explanatory concepts is limited, just as the power of men to control the mobility of women has never been absolute.

Because the earth and its diverse inhabitants have continuously resisted being ordered or controlled, as some of the preceding chapters attest, the power entailed in creating places—while very real—has also been limited and usually contested. As several of the chapters show, women and minorities resisted the power exerted by others in attempts to confine, control, and categorize them. Moreover, as powerful as imported ideas and rhetoric were in shaping western places, they never won the day entirely. We may have driven old-growth forests and species of salmon to the brink of extinction, but the discourses of conservation and preservation—as ineffectual as they have been at times—retain a significant amount of power themselves. Finally, as the salmon and old-growth crises suggest, it becomes clearer with each passing year that the North American West could never truly have supported boosters' visions of either unlimited and unceasing "development" of natural resources or the steady upward march from hinterland to metropolis. James P. Ronda's concluding reference to the modern condition of Astoria, Oregon—"canneries gone, plywood factories gone"—reminds us that Indians were not the only western people, and their homeland not the only western place, to experience the instability of power, particularly as exercised from a distance.

NOTES

Since the chapters in this volume were first presented as conference papers in 1994, some of the authors have published book-length studies that elaborate on the same and related themes. We would like to acknowledge the overlap between Paul Hirt's chapter and his *Conspiracy of Optimism: Management of the National Forests since World War Two* (Lincoln: University of Nebraska Press, 1994); Hal K. Rothman's chapter and his *Devil's Bargains: Tourism in the Twentieth-Century American West* (Lawrence: University Press of Kansas, 1998); and William G. Robbins's chapter and his *Landscapes of Promise: The Oregon Story, 1880–1940* (Seattle: University of Washington Press, 1997).

We would like to thank James B. Morrison for creating maps for the chapters by James P. Ronda and James F. Brooks.

1. Examples of some of the other conference papers, especially those devoted to the power of place, include the contents of a special issue of *Pacific Northwest Quarterly* 87 (Summer 1996): Robert E. Walls, "Green Commonwealth: Forestry, Labor, and Public Ritual in the Post–World War II Pacific Northwest," 117–29; Marilyn P. Watkins, "Contesting the Terms of Prosperity and Patriotism: The Politics of Rural Development in Western Washington, 1900–1925," 130–40; William L. Lang, "Lewis and Clark on the Columbia River: The Power of Landscape in the Exploration Experience," 141–48; and Sherry L. Smith, "Reimagining the Indian: Charles Erskine Scott Wood and Frank Linderman," 149–58.

2. D. W. Meinig, "Commentary," Power and Place in the North American West symposium, Seattle, November 5, 1994, typescript, files of the Center for the Study of the Pacific Northwest, University of Washington.

PART I
INDIANS AND NON-INDIANS

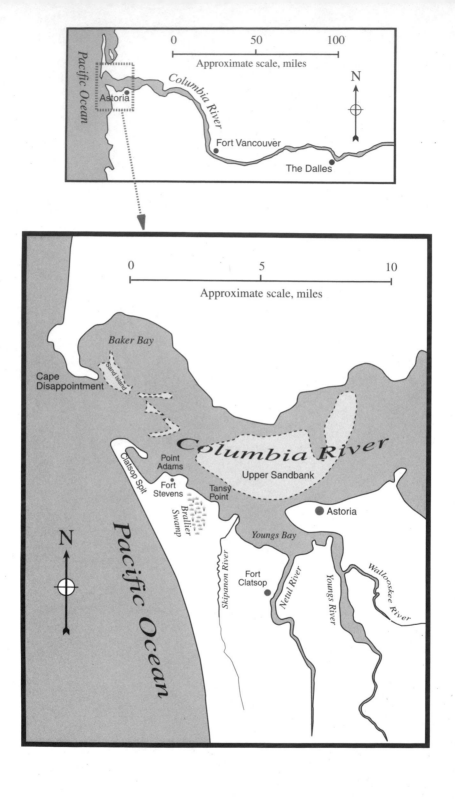

Coboway's Tale

A Story of Power and Places Along the Columbia

JAMES P. RONDA

This is a story about power and places, about what happens when power changes places, and then how those places are in turn changed. As befits the best stories, this is a tale of trust and trust betrayed, of deception and the rewards of deceit. And just like the pilgrimage to Chaucer's Canterbury, this story takes us down twisty roads, across contested borders, and into neighborhoods of what John McPhee calls suspect terrain.

The most compelling stories begin not with people but with places. Here is a geography that seems easy to triangulate. We are at the mouth of the Columbia, nearly two centuries ago. To the north looms Cape Disappointment and Baker Bay. On the south, Point Adams hooks like a bent finger seaward. This is a world of sandy shallows and pounding breakers, where weather changes by the moment and every enterprise flies the flag of uncertainty. Set one marker at the Clatsop Indian village on the tip of Point Adams. When William Clark mapped the point and the village in the winter of 1805–6, he counted eight large wood houses. Perhaps as many as a hundred Clatsops lived at the village they called "where there is pounded salmon." Most likely Coboway and his family lived there.

Pause for a moment and ask—what *is* the name of this place? If the name is "where there is pounded salmon," then the place is all about Clatsop life and labor and power drawn from the river and fish. But if it is Point Adams, then the lines of power and meaning run east to the Federal City on a very different river and to the name of an American politician. Now run a survey

Facing page: Mouth of the Columbia River (map by James B. Morrison)

line east and a little south, across the sand hills and mud flats, and into the south channel of the Columbia. Here we are in a narrow, watery trench with hazard all around. To our north is the great Upper Sandbank, sometimes bare in places at low water. To our south is Tansey Point. Mark Tansey Point on your chart. We will have reason to remember it—that point where lines of power crossed and the fortunes of some peoples slid downward. Straight ahead is Youngs Bay and the land that begins at Smith Point. We are back on land now, up over rough and densely wooded ground, and then down to what will soon be Fort Astoria. Set a second marker at Astoria and then run another line southwest across Youngs Bay to the Netul River, now Lewis and Clark River. Follow the river along its marshy, muddy banks— slippery both then and now—to the gate at Fort Clatsop. Pound a final survey stake here, at what Lewis and Clark called their "westernmost station." One last line will finish this skewed triangle. Plot it from Fort Clatsop northwest over marshy ground, across the Skipanon River, through the Brailler Swamp to the sand hills of Point Adams and the Clatsop village. Tie the line at the first post. We have marked and bounded a small world, a wedge of life and landscape.[1] Half a century after William Clark saw the mouth of the Columbia, another American explorer described it as "a perfect Indian paradise in its adaptation to canoe travel, and the abundance of scale and shell-fish."[2]

Coboway's tale was acted out inside those lines, but the meanings of the story overrun the limits of the triangle. His story happened in a world every bit as broad, every bit as intricate as the worlds of New York, Washington, Montreal, or Canton. By implication and intrusion, those places had become part of Coboway's world. We should expect a tale as surprising and as unsettling as any told in Bristol or Boston.

Just when Coboway first heard about the Lewis and Clark expedition is lost to us. As an influential man in the Point Adams village he would have been alert to the movements of outsiders. Outsiders might bring violence or chances to trade or both. Coboway's people did not live in some ancient and immense privacy at the very edge of North America. Long before Robert Gray crossed the Columbia bar in 1792, Clatsops and their Chinook neighbors across the river were part of a vast economic and social system that reached north up the coast to Nootka and south down past Cape Blanco. Most important, the trading paths ran up the Columbia to The Dalles and beyond into the Plateau. In the two decades before the arrival of Lewis and Clark, commercial life around Point Adams quickened, stimulated by the maritime fur trade. Although most traders steered toward the safety of Baker

Bay on the north shore of the river, the Clatsops did count their share in ironware, pots, and teakettles. Clatsops became intermediaries, brokers buying and selling to neighbors distant from the river marketplace. A Clatsop story from those years explains it best. A trading vessel grounded on the Columbia bar and broke up. Clatsops salvaged iron, copper, and brass from the wreck. When upriver people heard the news, they hurried to trade. As the storyteller explained, "the people [that is, the upriver people] bought this and the Clatsop became rich."[3]

When Coboway first visited Lewis and Clark's Fort Clatsop, he came as an explorer filled with questions. Who were these *pah-shish-e-ooks*, the cloth men? If they were traders, why did they come from the east instead of the west? And what about this beached ship now abuilding along the Netul River? Two generations after Coboway, a Clatsop woman named Tsin-is-tum recalled hearing that her people first feared the Americans, thinking them a party of raiders.[4] The village at Point Adams was in an exposed position, and concern about sudden attack was ever present. But for Coboway and others, fear quickly gave way to curiosity. And there was much to be curious about.

Coboway began his explorations on a windy, showery day in early December 1805, and he persisted until the very week the Americans left the mouth of the Columbia in late March 1806. What Coboway learned is part of his story. If he had written an exploration report he might have organized it under two broad headings.

First, there were the familiar things. Coboway and his neighbors knew what traders looked like, how they behaved, what they wanted, and what they had to offer. Coboway came to Fort Clatsop to trade and what he found was what he expected. Some of the earliest Clatsop stories about maritime traders described the bearded, hairy Europeans as bears. But continued contact with the "bears" proved they belonged to the human family. Coboway found men, black and white—clearly men, not bears. The woman and child in the ship-lodge along the river made less sense. Few if any trading vessels carried women and children on board. But just a glance told Coboway that they too were plainly human beings, not spirits and not bears. The things at Fort Clatsop, things that so fascinated interior tribes with less European contact, seemed quite ordinary to Coboway. Guns, pots, fishhooks, metal tools, and textile clothing—these were commonplace all along the lower Columbia. Weeks earlier, Lewis and Clark had seen European-style textiles, teakettles, pots, and pans at many river settlements. As a trader come calling, Coboway got some of those things from Lewis and Clark in exchange for wapato roots, berries, salmon, and elk. One day it was fishhooks and Shoshone tobacco; on other days it was a razor, a moccasin awl, and some thread. And once it was a pair of satin breeches. Meriwether Lewis recalled that Coboway was "much pleased" with those fancy pants. While Lewis and Clark did not master the Chinook trade jargon, Coboway and his fellow traders knew a rather select English vocabulary. "Musquit, powder, shot, nife, file, damned rascal, [and] sun of a bitch" might not have pleased some delicate ears but they did the job for trading.[5]

These were the familiar things, the expected landscape. But there was much that seemed strange and not a little unsettling. First there was time, or timing. European traders came to the Columbia first in the spring and then paid a second visit in the fall. By November they were gone. These cloth men came in December, the wrong time and from the wrong direction. Native traders from The Dalles and elsewhere often made the westward journey, but white merchants and their ships always came from the Pacific side. White traders who built lodges on land also seemed odd to Coboway. Maritime traders did business on board or immediately alongside their ships. Rarely if ever did they venture on land. But these cloth men—who came at the wrong time and from the wrong direction—seemed rooted to the ground.

Far more puzzling to Coboway was the purpose for the presence of these strangers. Clatsops understood journeys of reconnaissance as part of war or business. But a voyage of discovery launched by a distant nation, a voyage that mixed sovereignty and science, was something new for Coboway to consider. Only once before, in 1792, had Clatsops seen such an expedition, when Lieutenant William Broughton sailed the British exploring vessel HMS Chatham up the Columbia to the site of present-day Portland. The Clatsops and their neighbors looked at the American explorers and decided they must be traders. But as Coboway and others soon discovered, these cloth men did not seem to understand the rules of the trading game. The commercial system of the lower Columbia involved both the energetic accumulation of goods and the rituals of exchange. Clatsops were spirited traders who paid attention to the spirits all around them. Trading was a ceremony, a dance of offer and counteroffer that could last an hour or the day. It was both serious business and a great game. The experience itself could be as rewarding as any acquisition.

Lewis and Clark certainly understood bargaining. Whether for land or slaves, horses or tobacco, these Virginians knew firsthand about signals, bids, and breaking the price. They had seen the many ways personal relationships directed and secured commercial transactions. But Lewis and

Clark also came from an economic system on the way toward far more impersonal arrangements. Contracts, deeds, letters of credit, lawyers as intermediary negotiators—this was the direction of American capitalism. The ritual ballet of trade practiced by Coboway's people first confused and then infuriated Lewis and Clark. The same day that Coboway paid his first visit to Fort Clatsop, Clark wrote: "I can readily discover that they are close deelers, and Stickle for a very little, never close a bargain except they think they have the advantage"; Lewis agreed, calling his native neighbors "great higlers in trade."[6] These were not compliments. Lewis and Clark resented the rules and played the game reluctantly. And of course it did not help that these overland trading captains had not bothered to learn the trade jargon. But Coboway made allowances and became Fort Clatsop's most regular merchant.

Of all the unsettling things Coboway learned, none was more troubling than a new definition of space and the power to define space. First at Fort Mandan along the Missouri and now at Fort Clatsop the American explorers claimed space, squared it, walled it, and made it their own. Along the Netul, the Americans built their station, named it for their neighbors, and then constructed walls and rules to partition the neighborhood. Fort Clatsop was barely done when Lewis and Clark set about to draft their own rules—rules that marked boundaries in time and space, rules about who could come and who could stay. These were rules based not on hospitality or trade but on the captains' own notions of convenience and security. At the end of December 1805 the captains let traders like Coboway know that the rules and the spaces were changing. Clark made this note in his journal to announce the new order of things: "At Sun Set we let the nativs know that our Custom will be in the future, to Shut the gates at Sun Set at which time all Indians must go out of the fort and not return into it untill next morning after Sun Rise at which time the gates will be opened." While those Indians trading the day the rule was issued left the fort "with reluctianc," Coboway readily accepted the dawn-to-dusk business day. After all, it was not much different from the way maritime traders conducted their transactions.[7]

But two days later, on January 1, 1806, the rules changed in dramatic ways. Lewis and Clark sensed that in the first days at Fort Clatsop there had been a contest about rules—what rules and who would rule. This contest asked: Where does power live and how will it be expressed? Would it be the spoken words from the village of pounded salmon that carried the day, or would the words on paper from the lodge of the cloth men prevail? Native people exercised domain through rituals that Lewis and Clark could see only as "higle" and "stickle." Jefferson's captains were determined to impose their sense of order and authority on what seemed to them foolish whim and unbridled greed. They would define both power and the places of power. Lewis and Clark wanted to reshape the landscape of time. Days and months once measured in seasons and salmon runs were now to be calculated by calendars and journal entries. What the Americans delivered that first day of January was an elaborate machinery designed to control the roads in and out of Fort Clatsop. Drawing on their military experience, the officers established a complex arrangement of guard posts and sentries. The garrison was commanded to treat native people "in a friendly manner." But "troublesom" Indians or those who strayed into expedition living quarters without permission could be ejected by the Sergeant of the Guard, using whatever force necessary.[8]

At least in the minds of the American explorers inside Fort Clatsop, there was no question about who had power. Garrison orders made it plain. Power had changed hands and Fort Clatsop was a changed place. At one spot along the Netul, Coboway was now an outsider in his own country. He entered, traded, and occasionally stayed overnight at the sufferance of others. But even as the ground at this one place shifted, Coboway made his own adjustments. He played by the new rules and gained the grudging respect of the rule makers. Coboway's tale might end right here. Like the Mandan chief Black Cat, Coboway might have slipped off to the wings, just another bit player in a tale larger than he knew.

But the Fates and Furies were not finished with Coboway. Throughout the winter, the American explorers often found themselves on short rations. Game was scarce and expedition hunters were hard-pressed to keep the smokehouse full. In early February George Drouillard, the expedition's chief hunter, killed several elk in the country south of the fort. Having no way to transport the carcasses, Drouillard dressed the animals and cached them in the woods. But leaving so scarce a commodity worried Lewis: "We are apprehensive that the Clatsops who know where the meat is will rob us of a part if not the whole of it." For once, such worries were justified. The meat was taken, probably by some Clatsops just as hungry as their neighbors at the fort. Lewis and Clark complained to Coboway, and the chief did the appropriate thing. In mid-February he sent a man identified as the elk snatcher to the fort along with two dogs. Dog meat had become a delicacy at the post, and these dogs were meant to substitute for the missing elk. But Coboway's plan went suddenly and comically awry. The dogs ran off, perhaps sensing their destiny. Undeterred, Drouillard went to the Point Adams village, found the dogs, and returned them to the Fort Clatsop cooking pots. Rights and wrongs had been balanced. The case should have been closed. But Coboway was about to get a lesson in just how quickly power could move from one community to another.[9]

To be blunt about it, Lewis and Clark did not like their place on the Columbia. The American explorers hated the weather, loathed the food, and distrusted their neighbors. Fort Clatsop was never the home that Fort Mandan seemed to be. What danced in dreams that winter were the "fat plains of the Missouri." Lewis imagined Fort Clatsop as a prison and once wrote despairingly, "one month of the time which binds us to Fort Clatsop and which separates us from our friends has now elapsed."[10] Counting hard time along the Columbia, Lewis and Clark plotted their escape. Canoes were essential to their planned return route, and it was the search for canoes that tangled Coboway in the captains' web of deceit.

Lewis and Clark admired Northwest Coast canoes and made careful notes on the makes and varieties they saw.[11] For these captains, canoes meant one thing—safe and efficient transportation. Coboway's people invested canoes with a far greater range of meanings. They were the carriers of life. They bore the freight of trade and war. They were part of the bride price in marriage. In some places women owned trading canoes. Carriers of life, they were also bearers of death. Canoes held the remains of Columbia River peoples. They were a sign of voyages yet to come. So powerful an object as a canoe required purchase talk of equal gravity. To sell a canoe was not the work of a moment or even a day.

Such considerations were mostly lost on Lewis and Clark. Canoes were useful objects, things needed to make the homeward journey. Throughout the late winter and early spring of 1806, Lewis and Clark did their best to buy canoes. A short stock of merchandise, an even shorter set of tempers, and native reluctance to sell made the process a difficult one. In mid-March, with departure time just a matter of days away, Drouillard was sent to the Point Adams village to buy canoes. He returned to Fort Clatsop a day later accompanied by several Clatsops. One man had what Lewis called an "indifferent" canoe and would not part with it even after the captain offered his fancy lace uniform coat in trade. When Drouillard took that coat and some tobacco to a Cathlamet village, he did manage at last to purchase one canoe. Now counting down to their last days at Fort Clatsop, Lewis and Clark were both frustrated and desperate. They wanted to escape, no matter what the price. And Coboway was about to pay the price.[12]

On Monday, March 17, one of the expedition interpreters—probably Drouillard—approached Lewis and Clark with an ingenious scheme. Lewis put the outlines of this bold plan in his journal, explaining, "we yet want another canoe, and as the Clatsops will not sell us one at the price which we can afford to give, we will take one from them in lue of the six elk which they stole from us in the winter."[13] Coboway thought the case of the missing elk had been successfully settled. But now desperation and cultural arrogance worked to reopen the matter. Expediency meant more than civility. Besides, how could native ownership of a single canoe be allowed to stand in the way of so important an imperial enterprise?

The following day, March 18, a four-man detail slipped out of Fort Clatsop and headed toward Point Adams. Working unnoticed, the robbers took a canoe and went back to the fort. At their return, they discovered that Coboway was at the post for a visit. The canoe was hurriedly concealed nearby and brought out only after he left.[14]

The next day, Coboway returned to Fort Clatsop, perhaps to ask after the missing canoe. The surviving expedition journals contain no account of any exchange on that question. Instead, the written record reveals an act second in boldness only to what happened the day before. Lewis and Clark presented Coboway with a certificate of good conduct. They also handed him another document—a list of expedition members. There was something prophetic in that exchange. The American adventurers took objects—now a canoe, and later land—and gave pieces of paper in return. Lewis once characterized Coboway as "more kind and hospitable to us than any other Indian in this neighborhood." Now he was the victim of a shabby plot.[15]

But it would be a mistake to think that Coboway nursed a grudge against his sometime friends at the fort. He might have tossed away the papers, seeing them as signs of trust gone astray. But for the next eight years Coboway kept the list of expedition names—kept the paper as a souvenir, a recollection, perhaps as a connection to the bearded strangers who came and went so suddenly.

This is Coboway's tale. Some of its plot, some of the motion came from the cloth men, but this is his story, not theirs. In the years after 1806, Coboway and his people continued their trading and fishing ways. As something of an afterthought, Lewis and Clark gave Coboway possession of Fort Clatsop and its modest furnishings. At least some members of Coboway's family moved in along the Netul, spending the fall and winter seasons inside log walls. Early in April 1811, Coboway's world got a new set of tenants. John Jacob Astor's employees, having come over the bar on the ship *Beaver*, settled in and began to build Fort Astoria. This new trading post—what one contemporary called "the emporium of the west"—did not lack for diligent record keepers and scribbling journal makers.[16] Gabriel Franchère, Alexander Ross, Duncan McDougall, and Alfred Seton all put Astoria down on paper. But no one mentioned Coboway. Even though the Astorians made their closest commercial connections with the Chinooks across the river at Baker Bay, Coboway and the Clatsops must have paid at least a few calls on these new cloth men.

It was not until December 1813, some three months after Astoria was sold to the North West Company, that Coboway appears again in the surviving record. Alexander Henry the Younger, a Nor'wester who came to the Columbia a month before, noted that Coboway appeared at the post to sell some salmon and elk. And in the months that followed, "the old Clatsop chief" made an occasional trip to the place now called Fort George. Henry became his trading partner and perhaps something of a friend. In mid-May 1814, Coboway thought he knew Henry well enough to show him a possession of great value, cherished over the years. It was the list of members of the American expedition, dated March 19, 1806—the day after the canoe theft.[17]

Three days after showing Henry the prized paper, Coboway was again face to face with Astoria's new owners. There had been an argument about goods missing from the post, and Coboway was the one to recover and return them. It was the kind of conciliatory role he had played before. Henry gave Coboway some clothing as an expression of gratitude and then demanded the Lewis and Clark list. Not suspecting what would happen next, Coboway handed over the document. Henry gave the old chief a similar paper declaring the power of the North West Company. Then with great flourish Henry threw the American list—the talisman Coboway had so long cherished—into the fire. The paper blazed up, crinkled, and crumbled to ash.[18] The message in that moment was unmistakable. Assertions of power, whether between individuals or nations, were as changeable as river currents.

Coboway's own part in his tale ends here, with this trick and deception, a fire, and the claims of a new paper identity. But an expanded version of Coboway's tale, one that takes account of the Clatsop future, does not end here. Most likely Coboway did not live to see the spring and summer of 1829. In that season a fleet from the Hudson's Bay Company's Fort Vancouver bombarded and burned his village. The fire and the looting, and the bland paper explanations offered to justify the violence, are part of Coboway's story as surely as earlier moments of theft and burning.

On March 10, 1829, in bad weather and failing light, the Hudson's Bay Company ship *William and Ann* ran aground while attempting to cross the Columbia River bar. Despite Captain John P. Swan's best efforts, the ship was caught in treacherous currents. Beached on Clatsop Spit, the *William and Ann* split open and was lost with all hands. The next morning the flats around the Point Adams Clatsop village were littered with wreckage and spilled cargo. As they had done for so many years, Coboway's people busied themselves salvaging what they could. News of the wreck reached Fort Vancouver later that day. Dr. John McLoughlin, chief factor at the post, quickly sent a rescue party to Point Adams. That expedition found wreckage and cargo but no bodies.[19]

Uncertain how to proceed, McLoughlin and other company officers were ready to let the "melloncholy fate of the crew" slip away. Swan and his men would get their due in the next letter to London and that would be the end of it. But throughout the spring and early summer, rumors persisted that Swan and his crew had escaped the Columbia only to be murdered by the Clatsops. Writing a month after the wreck, company clerk Francis Ermatinger predicted that if the murder reports proved true, "we shall have more *War*."[20] The Point Adams Clatsops did have a reputation as aggressive salvagers, and relations between Point Adams and Fort Vancouver had never been friendly. But McLoughlin also recognized that the most persistent rumor monger was an Indian who seemed especially eager to stir up trouble. The chief factor bided his time, waiting for more reliable information. That information seemed to come on June 21 when an Indian trusted for his accurate accounts told McLoughlin that the crew had drowned. But, added the Indian, the Point Adams village was filled with company property. Up and down the river, word had it that the company was powerless to recover its own goods.

McLoughlin and chief trader William Connolly were determined to maintain Fort Vancouver's place of power on the river and soon set on a daring scheme. They organized a large-scale expedition, including the company ships *Cadboro* and *Vancouver*. With more than sixty armed men, Connolly and four other company officers set off toward Point Adams. A messenger was sent on ahead demanding that the Clatsops return company cargo and reveal what they knew about the crew of the *William and Ann*.

Late on the afternoon of June 21 the company flotilla reached Point Adams. A Clatsop headman hailed Connolly's raiders, telling them that all goods would be returned. At that moment the winds switched and the *Cadboro* seemed headed toward the breakers. Hurrying to escape, company men took to small boats and headed for shore. Thinking they were about to be attacked, the Clatsops opened fire. Connolly's men returned the shots, and when one Clatsop was hit, most of the other Indians fled. Connolly's men then marched to the village, where they ransacked and burned the houses. The Clatsop woman Tsin-is-tum had a starkly simple memory of the event: "My father was killed in the bombardment of the Clatsop village by the ship sent by Dr. McLoughlin."[21] Tsin-is-tum's father was not the only casualty. The attack on Point Adams killed a number of the village's most influential leaders, making recovery even more difficult. The power of a distant place had again flexed its muscle at Coboway's place.

Hard on the heels of the burning and killing at Point Adams came an attack far more deadly and with far greater consequences. From the sixteenth century on, European diseases had devastated native North America. Smallpox, influenza, measles, and a host of other afflictions not only killed millions of native people but also assaulted traditional patterns of ritual and belief. Lewis and Clark took note of such diseases on the lower Columbia. Perhaps the most destructive outbreak occurred when malaria epidemics recurred between 1830 and 1833. Native people called the illness the "cold sickness" while Europeans described it as "fever and ague" or the "intermittent fever." The disease killed as many as 85 percent of the peoples along the lower reaches of the Columbia and Willamette Rivers. Hall Jackson Kelley, who visited the mouth of the Columbia in 1834, reported that he could hear everywhere "the sighs and cries of the misery in the perishing remnants of the Clatsop and Chenook tribes."[22] In fact, the malaria afflicted peoples near the ocean much less than it did those in the vicinity of Fort Vancouver and the future site of Portland; the Chinooks and Clatsops were hardly "perishing remnants." But natives at the river's mouth were susceptible to a host of deadly diseases imported from the Old World and back east.

Encounters with explorers and traders at Fort Clatsop and Fort Astoria, the attack on the Point Adams village, and the cold sickness were all signs of things to come. They pointed toward a future filled with dispossession and death. But the events themselves, no matter how tumultuous, did not mean that Clatsops of Coboway's generation had lost either their power or their place on the Columbia. Clatsops proved resilient enough to survive in an age of troubles. When the American explorer Lieutenant Charles Wilkes visited the Point Adams village in May 1841, he saw a scene much like the one that greeted William Clark almost four decades before. There were plank houses whose interiors reminded Wilkes of ships' cabins. Once inside, he found "pieces of salmon and venison hanging up in the smoke of the fire." What most attracted his attention were "figures of men" painted on the bedsteads. The village had seemingly recovered from the 1829 attack and the recurrent impact of sickness. Wilkes found "numbers of Indians lounging about, and others gambling." But there was one highly visible reminder of the assault twelve years earlier. When Clark saw the Point Adams settlement in 1805–6, it was open to attack. Wilkes found a village surrounded by a strong palisade "made of thick planks and joists, about fifteen feet in length, set with one end in the ground."[23]

If the Clatsops thought that log walls could protect them against threats from the outside, they were badly mistaken. The decade from 1841 to 1851 saw all the hints and signs of power gone to other places come true. The first evidence appeared in the summer of 1840. Throughout the late 1830s, Protestant missionaries had busied themselves evangelizing in the Oregon country. Most of the mission activity was centered in present-day eastern Washington and Oregon from Walla Walla to The Dalles. But in 1840 the missionary invasion reached the Clatsops. In mid-July, Reverend John H. Frost, a Methodist missionary associated with Jason Lee, decided to establish a post on the Clatsop Plains south of Point Adams. While Frost was impressed with the fertility and beauty of the country, he quickly dismissed his native neighbors as "ignorant, superstitious, and barbarous."[24] Frost was soon joined by lay worker and sometime teacher Solomon H. Smith and his wife Celiast. Known to her English-speaking friends as Helen, Celiast was the second of Coboway's three daughters. Like her sisters Kilakota and Yiamust, Celiast left Point Adams early in life, lived in and around Fort Astoria and Fort Vancouver, and married a nonnative man. Later in the fall of 1840, the Frost-Smith mission was reenforced by the arrival of Reverend W. W. Kone and his family. The following year, the missionaries moved their post closer to the Columbia River at a place called New Astoria. For reasons that remain unclear, Solomon and Celiast Smith struck out on their own, building a house and store near Point Adams along the Skipanon River.[25]

While the missionary presence was not large, it was important. Frost estimated that there were about 160 Clatsops living in and around Point Adams. Like his contemporaries, Frost was convinced that native people were lost souls ready to be transformed into regenerated believers and exemplary citizens. Missionaries came armed with an evangelizing program that amounted to a direct attack on traditional practices. If Frost could have had his way, the carved ritual figures Wilkes saw would have been destroyed and replaced with Bibles and appropriate devotional literature. Unlike Astoria's traders, missionaries demanded that native people abandon the old patterns of life and thought. Whether in economy, ritual, or social relations, the model was American cultural Christianity. As one Oregon missionary put it, "We must use the plough as well as the Bible, if we would do anything to benefit the Indians. They must be settled before they can be enlightened."[26]

The threat to Clatsop cultural survival posed by the Methodist mission remains difficult to judge. Frost gained few if any converts and left the mission in disgust in 1843. He was replaced by Josiah L. Parrish, someone who spent more time as a farmer and federal Indian agent than as a missionary. The consequences of western-style agriculture, commercial fishing, and the lumber-sawmill industry were far more visible. Market capitalism was no stranger at Point Adams. The fur trade was a global enterprise and Clatsops and their Chinook neighbors across the river were deeply involved in it. But the fur trade did not have land acquisition as an essential feature of its business strategy. By 1842, farmers associated with the Methodist mission were taking up land south of Point Adams. In the following years, as the Oregon migration swelled, the Clatsop Plains drew additional farming, dairy, and livestock operations. One federal official described the lands south of Point Adams as "open level country with very rich soil." The same official reported that by 1851 "nearly or quite every acre [of the Clatsop Plains] is claimed and occupied by white people."[27] The Clatsop country also contained substantial woodlands, promising wealth to those who measured trees in board feet. Lumbering and sawmilling soon appeared, changing even further the economic face of the lower Columbia. Commercial fishing began in 1829–30, with the first cargoes sold in Boston in 1831.[28]

Point Adams Clatsops understood that these economic activities were remaking their world. Age-old patterns of fishing, hunting, and gathering now collided with farms, fences, cows, and mills. Clatsops were especially angry about the disturbing presence of steamboats and two noisy sawmills south of the point. As the Clatsops explained, the boats and the mills frightened away the fish. Without fish, they would starve and their ritual world might collapse.[29] Although most whites scoffed at such protests, at least one missionary recognized the consequences of this kind of environmental change. Pondering the future of commercial fishing on the Columbia, Henry Spalding predicted: "The Salmon will be arrested in their upward course by some measure which the untiring invention of man will find out & which is not necessary here to conjecture. That day will be the date of universal starvation of nearly all the tribes of this vast country."[30]

Missionaries, farmers, and mill owners might have been unpleasant neighbors, but they lacked the political power to push Point Adams Clatsops off their place. That power belonged to the federal government. Federal Indian policy for the lands west of the Cascades had its formal beginnings in 1848 when Oregon territorial governor Joseph Lane proposed an Indian removal plan much like the one employed against native nations in the Southeast.

Lane and his successor, John P. Gaines, were determined to remove all native people from west of the Cascades. In 1850, as U.S. Indian policy abandoned removal in favor of reservations, Oregon territorial delegate Samuel Thurston persuaded Congress to authorize treaty negotiations. Anson Dart was appointed Oregon's superintendent of Indian affairs. Once in the territory, Dart quickly realized that relocation would be devastating for the Clatsops, Chinooks, and other fishing peoples. As he explained to the federal commissioner of Indian affairs, it was bound to "insure their annihilation in a short time either from want or by the hands of their more warlike neighbors." Dart believed that "small reservations of a few sections and a portion of their fishing grounds" would guarantee Clatsop survival while achieving the goals Washington sought.[31]

When Dart and his negotiating party met with the Clatsops and other coastal Indians at Tansey Point in the first week of August 1851, he encountered native people who clearly understood their precarious position. Whites had taken up land throughout the Clatsop Plains, making hunting and gathering difficult. Commercial fishing, lumbering, and steamboat traffic all disturbed the old ways. But the most serious problem was a rapidly declining population. One federal official estimated that the number of Clatsops had dwindled to about eighty people.[32] An observer at Astoria reported that the Indian villages at the mouth of the Columbia were "mere remnants" of their former size. "It is melancholy indeed," wrote Theodore Talbot, "to witness the tremendous devastation which has here so rapidly followed in the footsteps of the strangers."[33]

Having lost so much, the surviving Clatsops were not about to abandon Point Adams. When Dart proposed moving to a small, nearby reservation, Clatsops "interposed many objections to parting with their country upon any terms." What Dart described later as "long and loud complaints" amounted in fact to a carefully reasoned analysis of the Clatsop predicament. Coboway's successors were especially angry about the consequences of the Donation Land Law of 1850. That legislation offered American citizens, or those who intended to become citizens, 320 acres without reference to Indian claims. Even before the land law, white settlers found Clatsop lands attractive. Clatsops argued that the government had "taken possession of their lands without paying them, had allowed white people—many years since—to occupy and buy and sell their country." Clatsops had watched as lands taken under the Donation Law were resold for substantial profit. Despite these complaints, Dart dismissed the Clatsop case as "very unreasonable."

Frustrated by Dart's unwillingness to discuss land issues, the Clatsops switched tactics and threatened to stop the treaty proceedings unless the Indian agent addressed the impact of steamboats and sawmills. Clatsops, known as "close deelers," had once used such delaying tactics to play out the game of trade. Now what Lewis and Clark derisively called "higle" and "stickle" came down to a larger and more consequential contest. Native negotiators repeated their fears about steamboats and the flight of the fish. When Dart told them he was powerless to halt maritime traffic and disman-tle the mills, Indian representatives again changed the agenda. They now asked for two reservations, each about ten miles square. Dart bluntly refused, and the entire negotiation dissolved in angry disagreement.

For the next two days Clatsops talked with their Chinook neighbors. While records are scanty, it does seem clear that those conversations pro-duced a new bargaining approach. The Clatsops now asked for a single reservation that encompassed both the Point Adams village and the nearby burying ground. While the request was modest and fit what Dart already had in mind, the discussion hit a sudden snag. Within the proposed reservation were lands claimed by several white farmers. Dart was not about to eject them, and proposed instead that the Clatsops "place title to *all*" their lands with the United States. When the Indians vigorously rejected this idea, Dart angrily issued an ultimatum. Clatsops could either accept the reservation treaty or face an uncertain future without any federal protection. With few alternatives, the Clatsops accepted the reservation treaty and parted with what Dart estimated was about five hundred thousand acres south of Point Adams.[34]

The Clatsops left Tansey Point believing they had escaped removal to a distant place. While the proposed Point Adams reservation was small, it did preserve a connection to ancestral places. But Coboway's people had not taken the measure of either congressional politics or the military strategies of the imperial United States. Despite Dart's best efforts, the Tansey Point treaties were not ratified by the Senate. While the reasons behind that inac-tion have never been clear, Dart believed that the potential cost of the treaties was a powerful argument for the failure to ratify them.[35] But what happened to the Clatsop treaty made little difference in the course of events either at Point Adams or in Washington. Virtually every explorer, traveler, and military observer who visited the mouth of the Columbia noted the strategic importance of Point Adams and Cape Disappointment for the de-fense of the western United States. Those two sites guarded the entrance to the River of the West. After the settlement of the Oregon Question in 1846, the War Department looked again at the Columbia and its vulnerability to attack from the Pacific. During the 1850s Washington worried about the British navy; later the concerns focused on Confederate raiders.

Because the Tansey Point treaties were not ratified, the War Department was free to act on lands at both Point Adams and Cape Disappointment. In 1852 an executive order set aside Point Adams and a portion of Cape Disappointment for the purposes of national defense. Point Adams would now be a military reservation, not an Indian one. A decade later, in the midst of the Civil War, the army began construction of Fort Stevens at Point Adams. Coboway's place now took another name change. Fort Stevens honored Isaac I. Stevens, first governor of Washington Territory. Workers under the direction of Captain George H. Elliott rearranged a portion of the Point Adams landscape, digging ditches, building gun emplacements, and putting up houses and storage sheds. When Julia Gilliss and her husband, Captain James Gilliss, moved to Fort Stevens in September 1866 they saw a settlement wholly unlike Coboway's "where there is pounded salmon." Julia Gilliss described the post as "a beautiful little earthwork bristling with guns and neat as a model, the gravel walks as precise and the grass as green as if they knew they were expected to do their best."[36] Where William Clark had found plank houses, canoes, and salmon, the Gillisses saw two-story frame houses, military equipment, canned goods, and factory-made furniture. The dispossession of Coboway's world now seemed complete.

The Clatsops had lost their place at Point Adams but they did not vanish as a people. Some went to live at the Siletz, Alsea, and Grand Ronde Reservations. Others refused to leave familiar haunts, and lived out quiet lives on remote parts of the Clatsop Plains. And a handful refused to abandon the Point Adams country. One of those who remained near Point Adams was Toston, a headman who may have played an important role in the Tansey Point treaty talks. Captain Elliott found him living at Point Adams in 1865, and reported that he had "an excellent reputation at the mouth of the Columbia." Two years later, Julia Gilliss found herself one of Toston's customers. "We have living near us," she wrote, "an old Indian named Toastern, who with his pretty daughter brings us fish and berries for sale. We were always glad to hear the musical call 'Olallies' [berries] at our door." Like Coboway at Fort Clatsop, Toston made his way as a trader calling at someone else's outpost of empire.[37]

Perhaps it would be best—certainly from the storyteller's perspective—to conclude Coboway's tale a century after he first met Lewis and Clark. Triangulating Coboway's world in 1905 takes the measure of places transformed and power even more securely in the hands of distant strangers. At the beginning of the twentieth century the U.S. Coast and Geodetic Survey mapped the mouth of the Columbia. This chart (and the British version published in 1905) starts where we began—at Coboway's village on Point Adams.[38] But in the first years of the new century the village was long gone and in its place was Fort Stevens. The imperial United States, with troops and coastal artillery, now occupied not only Coboway's village but the burial ground nearby. The long-range guns were there to repulse an armada that never came. Take note of the heft of power at Fort Stevens, with its firing pits, Vauban earthworks, and storehouses.[39] Head east and a little south, away from the guns and along the tracks of the Fort Stevens branch of the Astoria and Columbia River Railway. Strike out into the shallows beyond Tansey Point, across Youngs Bay, over the bluffs and into the city of Astoria, county seat for Oregon's Clatsop County. In 1905 Astoria was a city of ten thousand—a place where the Columbia River was put in cans and trees became lumber.[40] The Astoria of 1905 was almost as ethnically diverse as the Fort Astoria of an earlier time. Where once there had been Yankees and Scots, Hawaiians and French Canadians, now there were Finns and Chinese, Norwegians and Danes. From the city of Astoria run a line southwest back across Youngs Bay, down the banks of the Lewis and Clark River (few called it the Netul anymore) to what was once Fort Clatsop. In 1905 that place of power was a simple farm with a two-story frame house and a scattering of outbuildings. The symbols of empire—flags and guns—had moved to Fort Stevens. From what was once Fort Clatsop, walk northwest across marshy ground, over the embankment of the Lexington and Seashore Railway, and back to Fort Stevens. A century after Coboway, power was expressed in the guns at Fort Stevens, on the railroad tracks, and at Astoria's canneries and mills.

Power is always unstable, unpredictable—like the sudden currents of a river in flood. And like the river, power is always in motion, sweeping from place to place with restless energy. And as power shifts, it transforms places. The terrain, the very shape of the earth changes. Within the triangle made by Point Adams, Astoria, and Fort Clatsop the earth was shoveled, leveled, blasted, squared, made and remade. Cities, farms, forts, railroads, and canneries—these became the visible manifestations of power in the landscape. But the power that reshaped Coboway's world did not stay at the mouth of the Columbia. It moved on to Portland, San Francisco, Seattle, and back to the District of Columbia. And the reshaping continues. Fort Stevens at Point Adams is now a state park. The National Park Service superintendent at Fort Clatsop ponders problems of parking and visitor security. And—canneries gone, plywood factories gone—Astoria declines in Victorian gentility, selling a bed-and-breakfast past to travelers bound for the great Elsewhere.

Coboway's people understood, perhaps better than most, the relationship between power and places. They knew that power lives and moves and has its being in places. At the Tansey Point negotiations, Clatsops told Anson Dart that they were "fully sensible of the power of the government." Clatsops acknowledged that they could be "killed and exterminated" by that power. But they insisted that they could not be "driven far from the homes and graves of their fathers."[41] The road from Point Adams to Tansey Point was not far in miles, but walking it Coboway and his people journeyed a long way from homes and graves. Struck from their own place, they had come to feel the weight of power from other places.

NOTES

With thanks for inspiration from Robert Coles and William Cronon.

1. This survey is based on William Clark's notes and maps in Gary E. Moulton, ed., *The Journals of the Lewis and Clark Expedition*, 12 vols. to date (Lincoln: University of Nebraska Press, 1983–), Atlas, maps 82, 84; 6:475. Hereafter cited as *JLCE*. See also Charles Wilkes, *Narrative of the United States Exploring Expedition*, 5 vols. (Philadelphia: 1845), 4:322–23 and map sheet 1, "Mouth of the Columbia River . . . 1841."

2. Isaac I. Stevens to George Manypenny, 16 September 1854, in Commissioner of Indian Affairs, *Annual Report for 1854* (Washington, D.C.: Government Printing Office, 1855), 239.

3. Franz Boas, *Chinook Texts*, Bureau of American Ethnology, 20 (Washington, D.C., 1894), 277–78.

4. Olin D. Wheeler, *The Trail of Lewis and Clark, 1804–1904*, 2 vols. (New York: G. P. Putnam's Sons, 1904), 2:205–6.

5. JLCE, 6:139, 141, 162–63, 232, 384–85, and 187.

6. Ibid., 123 (Clark); 164–65 (Lewis).

7. Ibid., 146.

8. Ibid., 156–58.

9. Ibid., 275 (quotation), 299, 336, 342.

10. Ibid., 273.

11. Ibid., 262–72.

12. Ibid., 169, 272, 414, 416, 426.

13. Ibid., 426, 428.

14. Milo M. Quaife, ed., *The Journals of Captain Meriwether Lewis and Sergeant John Ordway* (Madison: Wisconsin State Historical Society, 1916), 329; *JLCE*, 6:429–30.

15. *JLCE*, 6:432 (list), 444.

16. Alexander Ross, *Adventures of the First Settlers on the Oregon or Columbia River, 1810–1813* (1849; reprint, Lincoln: University of Nebraska Press, 1986), 89.

17. Elliott Coues, ed., *New Light on the Early History of the Greater Northwest: The Manuscript Journals of Alexander Henry and David Thompson*, 3 vols. in 2 (1897; reprint, Minneapolis, 1965), 2:767–68 (Coboway), 913 (list).

18. Ibid., 915.

19. McLoughlin to Archibald McDonald, Fort Vancouver, 22 March 1829, in *Letters of Dr. John McLoughlin, 1829–1832*, ed. Burt Brown Barker (Portland: Oregon Historical Society, 1948), 6; McLoughlin to McDonald, Fort Vancouver, 17 June 1829, *Letters*, 12.

20. Francis Ermatinger to Edward Ermatinger, Fort Colvile, 13 April 1829, in *Fur Trade Letters of Francis Ermatinger*, ed. Lois Halliday McDonald (Glendale, Calif.: A. H. Clark, 1980), 123.

21. McLoughlin to the Hudson's Bay Company, Fort Vancouver, 5 August 1829, in Barker, ed., *Letters*, 19–21; McLoughlin to the Hudson's Bay Company, Fort Vancouver, 13 August 1829, in Barker, ed., *Letters*, 40–41; Wheeler, *Trail*, 2:205.

22. Fred W. Powell, ed., *Hall J. Kelley on Oregon* (Princeton: Princeton University Press, 1932), 326; Robert T. Boyd, "Another Look at the 'Fever and Ague' of Western Oregon," *Ethnohistory* 22 (Spring 1975): 135–54; Robert T. Boyd, "Demographic History, 1774–1874," in Wayne Suttles, ed., *Northwest Coast*, vol. 7 of William C. Sturtevant, ed., *Handbook of North American Indians* (Washington, D.C.: Smithsonian Institution, 1990), 139–40.

23. Wilkes, *Narrative of the United States Exploring Expedition*, 4:322–23.

24. Nellie B. Pipes, ed., "The Journal of John H. Frost, 1840–1843," *Oregon Historical Quarterly* 35 (1934): 71.

25. Robert H. Ruby and John A. Brown, *The Chinook Indians: Traders of the Lower Columbia River* (Norman: University of Oklahoma Press, 1976), 203–4.

26. Elkanah Walker, quoted in D. W. Meinig, *The Great Columbia Plain: A Historical Geography, 1805–1910* (Seattle: University of Washington Press, 1968), 125.

27. Anson Dart to Luke Lea, Oregon City, Oregon Territory, 7 November 1851, in C. F. Coan, "The First Stage of Federal Indian Policy in the Pacific Northwest, 1849–1852," *Oregon Historical Quarterly* 22 (1921): 67.

28. Pacific Northwest River Basins Commission, *Columbia's Gateway: A History of the Columbia River Estuary to 1920* (Vancouver, Wash.: Pacific Northwest River Basins Commission, 1980), 27–28, 33.

29. Dart to Lea, Oregon City, Oregon Territory, 7 November 1851, in Coan, "First Stage," 66.

30. Henry Spalding to David Greene, 2 October 1839, quoted in Meinig, *Great Columbia Plain*, 134.

31. Dart to Lea, Oregon City, Oregon Territory, 8 February 1851, quoted in Francis Paul Prucha, *The Great Father: The United States Government and the American Indians,* 2 vols. (Lincoln: University of Nebraska Press, 1984), 1:399. For additional background see Coan, "First Stage," 49–57.

32. Robert Shortess, Census of Clatsop Indians, 5 February 1851, in Ruby and Brown, *Chinook Indians,* 222.

33. Theodore Talbot to his sister, Astoria, 2 August 1850, in *Soldier in the West: Letters of Theodore Talbot During His Services in California, Mexico, and Oregon, 1845–53,* ed. Robert V. Hine and Savoie Lottinville (Norman: University of Oklahoma Press, 1972), 141.

34. Dart to Lea, Oregon City, Oregon Territory, 7 November 1851, in Coan, "First Stage," 66–67.

35. Ruby and Brown, *Chinook Indians,* 230.

36. Julia Gilliss to her parents, Fort Stevens, 30 September 1866, in *So Far from Home: An Army Bride on the Western Frontier, 1865–1869,* ed. Priscilla Knuth and Charles J. Gilliss (Portland: Oregon Historical Society Press, 1993), 99. The construction history of Fort Stevens is traced in Marshall Hanft, "The Cape Forts: Guardians of the Columbia," *Oregon Historical Quarterly* 65 (1964): 325–61.

37. Captain George H. Elliott, Construction Progress Report, April 25, 1865, in *So Far from Home,* 210, note 21. Julia Gilliss to her mother, Fort Stevens, 7 April 1867, in *So Far from Home,* 124–25.

38. U.S. Coast and Geodetic Survey, "Columbia River: Entrance to Upper Astoria, Sheet 1, 1903," Pacific Northwest River Basins Commission, *Columbia's Gateway,* map portfolio; Admiralty Office, Royal Navy, "Columbia River: Entrance to Upper Astoria 1905," ibid.

39. U.S. Army, Corps of Engineers, "Point Adams, Oregon 1885," ibid.

40. Alfred A. Cleveland, "Social and Economic History of Astoria," *Oregon Historical Quarterly* 4 (1903): 130–49; Sam McKinney, *Reach of Tide, Ring of History: A Columbia River Voyage* (Portland: Oregon Historical Society Press, 1987), 13–14, 43–50.

41. Anson Dart to Luke Lea, 7 November 1851, in Coan, "First Stage," 68.

Violence, Justice, and State Power in the New Mexican Borderlands, 1780–1880

JAMES F. BROOKS

Three years after the 1846 American conquest of New Mexico, U.S. Indian agent James S. Calhoun received a visitor in his Santa Fe headquarters. This man, a *vecino* (citizen) of the western border village of Cebolleta, reported a recent Navaho raid in which he lost four horses, one mule, sixteen oxen, and an uncounted number of sheep. Only one month before, he claimed, Navahos had struck a neighboring village, killing two men, wounding one, and "carrying off, as a captive" one New Mexican woman. When told that Calhoun could offer neither military nor financial remedies for such wrongs, the man became agitated, and proceeded to contrast "the present with the former government of the territory." He said:

> The preceding [Mexican] government permitted reprisals, which is not tolerated now; and like the Pueblo Indians, neither the Spaniards or Mexicans can see the propriety of this government interdiction unless it is the purpose of said government to make an appropriate restitution from its own treasury. The eternal state of war and reciprocal robbery under [the] former government, gave to many a pleasurable excitement, and afforded to all an opportunity of satisfying their own demands, whether founded in justice or in a mere desire to possess other peoples' property.[1]

The heated conversation in Calhoun's office reflects an era of transformation in the North American West, a time when power relations between local societies and intrusive states were changing from negotiation to confrontation. The complaint of the *vecino* indicates one man's frustration with

23

U.S. agents who sought to suppress the workings of a customary exchange economy in a multiethnic borderland, but lacked the power to replace it. The incongruous description of an "eternal state of war and reciprocal robbery" that allowed both the satisfaction of "justice" and the redistribution of "property" suggests the depth of cultural confusion among protagonists in the region. On the one hand, the particular style of *retributive* and *redistributive* justice hinted at by the angry Cebolletano reveals the quintessential local understanding of a violent and competitive exchange economy that had emerged in the region over the preceding centuries. On the other hand, Calhoun's administrative impotency illustrates one major strategic dilemma that Americans would face in the coming decades.

The following pages argue that a borderlands political economy dominated greater New Mexico between 1780 and 1880. Organized around the seizure and exchange of human captives and livestock between New Mexicans and neighboring Indians, this phenomenon constituted a political economy in the sense that through its workings these groups shared some understanding of the production and distribution of wealth, as conditioned by social relations of power. Among its myriad components existed a mutual understanding between the indigenous and colonizing men that their women and children were vulnerable and valuable objects and agents of exchange, whose seizure and adoption brought labor, knowledge, and power to the capturing society. Of course, livestock like horses, sheep, and cattle also symbolized power and prestige, but captured women and children embodied the most precious and contestable "resource" of borderland societies.

By the early nineteenth century, human exchanges within this political economy fostered "communities of interest" among certain families, factions, classes, and clans of Indians and New Mexicans within a larger atmosphere of ethnic conflict. The reciprocal capture of women, children, and livestock promoted intercultural violence while simultaneously nurturing social and economic exchanges among certain Indian and New Mexican men who aspired to power in their respective societies. Operating within a mutually understood framework of justice, morality, and fair trade, organized bands, both Indian and New Mexican, conducted raids and reprisals that redistributed resources from wealthy Indians and New Mexicans to the poorer elements in both societies. Often, however, successful raiders reproduced some of the disparities between rich and poor that had initiated their own actions, thereby perpetuating renewed cycles of brigandage. Throughout the period, these raiders elaborated complex ethnic and class interdependencies that presented real problems for state order in the region.

The borderlands economy and its practitioners flourished despite the major administrative changes historians generally use to mark the period: the transition to Mexican rule in 1821 and the American conquest of 1846. Although these events had long-term consequences, the fact that neither the Bourbon, Mexican, nor early American states exerted real military or economic control in the region allowed local groups to continue their own accommodations. Retribution through exchanges of violence, and redistribution through exchanges of people and livestock, lay at the heart of these local arrangements. Only the larger systemic conflict of the American Civil War would provide enough state power to begin dismantling the borderlands economy.

Based in a regional system of captive-seizure that provoked comparison with the American system of slavery, these intercultural networks bedeviled American territorial administrators for more than thirty years. Local attempts to codify the New Mexican institution of captive-taking into the Territorial Slave Code in 1860 were suspended by Abraham Lincoln's election. During the Civil War, Union commanders in New Mexico realized that the regional "slave trade" disrupted any progress toward pacification, and therefore sought in the 1860s to extend the eastern war against slavery into the New Mexico borderlands. Over the next two decades, the political economy of the borderlands would generally succumb to the moral and military order of free-labor capitalism. In the process, borderland Indians and New Mexicans accepted a form of physical security and safety that left many destitute, dispossessed, and dependent on the questionable largesse of the United States government.

CREATING A PASTORAL BORDERLAND

Between 1740 and 1780, kin-linked bands of Navahos and landless New Mexican families established a patchwork landscape of small farming and sheepherding in the Río Puerco–Mount Taylor region (see Map 1). Probably drawn to the area by their need for grazing lands to feed sheep flocks that had outgrown the resources of their Dinétah homeland, the Navaho bands also sought to collect on promises by Spanish priests that more sheep awaited them at the new missions of Cebolleta and Encinal.[2] New Mexican migrants also sought grazing lands. Growing families like the Bacas and Montaños found themselves "without sufficient land to raise, pasture, and maintain" their flocks, and at times so hungry that they had to resort to weeding fields and gathering firewood for their Pueblo Indian neighbors.[3]

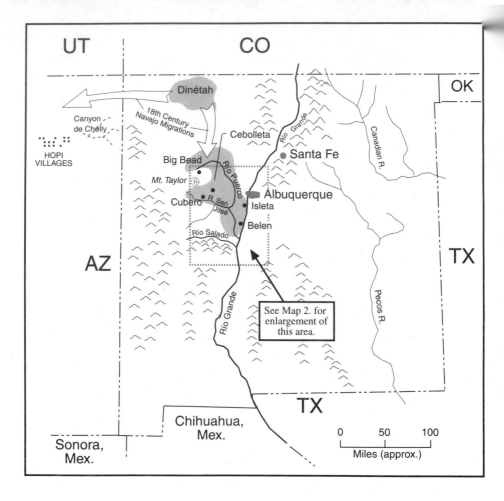

MAP 1. New Mexico in the 18th and 19th centuries (map by James B. Morrison)

New Mexican settlement began in 1754, and by 1770 Spanish governors confirmed eleven grazing grants in the area to lower-status *vecinos*, with the clear injunction that they not disturb the plantings or pasturelands of resident Navaho bands. Sharing a mixed pastoral and farming economy in a common landscape, New Mexicans and Navahos managed to coexist in the area for twenty years.[4] Coexistence included incidents of violence and some mutual captive-taking, but the borderland remained generally peaceful. On at least one occasion an informal marriage occurred between a Baca man and a Navaho woman. Their son, Francisco Baca, would later become headman of an intermediating and often vilified schismatic band, the Diné Ana'aii (Enemy Navaho).[5]

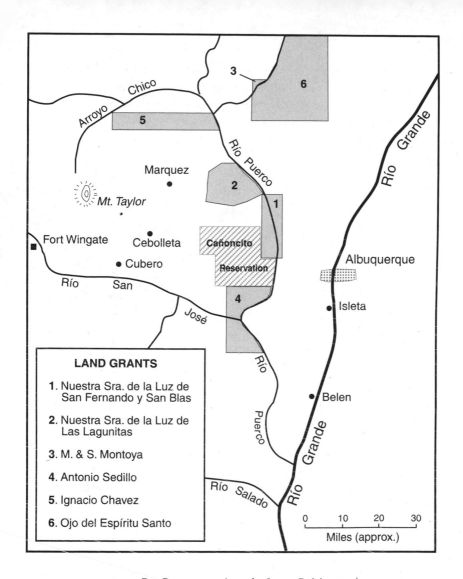

MAP 2. Rio Puerco area (map by James B. Morrison)

In 1774, however, the more numerous Navahos found the flocks and shepherds of their New Mexican and Pueblo neighbors vulnerable to capture because Comanche and Gila Apache raids in the Río Abajo had drawn Río Puerco men into militia service. In one year of raiding, Navahos seized hundreds of sheep and several young men from the scattered *poblaciones*. By December 1775 they had effectively cleared the region of New Mexican settlement. But trade relations continued between Navahos and New Mexicans along the Río Grande, evidenced by the fact that in 1785 Governor Anza proved able to bring the Navahos to the treaty table by prohibiting trade between the parties. In March 1786 some eighty Navaho headmen led by Antonio El Pinto and Don Carlos met with Anza and concluded a mutual defense alliance against the Gilas. In 1796, Lieutenant Colonel Don Antonio Cordero described local Navahos as "not nomadic like other Apaches . . . [for] they have fixed domiciles. They sow corn and other vegetables. They raise sheep and manufacture coarse cloth, blankets and other textiles of wool which they trade in New Mexico. In past times they were enemies of the Spaniards: at present they are faithful friends."[6]

In 1800, New Mexican *pobladores* (settlers) ventured again into the Río Puerco region. Although they drew upon customs of the preceding century, the nineteenth-century settlement would differ significantly from the eighteenth-century pattern. First, New Mexicans established compact, fortified *plazas* instead of scattered *poblaciones*, concentrating themselves in two major villages, Cebolleta and Cubero (see Map 2). Second, New Mexican *pastores* introduced "blanket grazing," which put huge flocks (often in the tens of thousands) on the grasslands for whole seasons. Even under the care of shepherds, they remained vulnerable to raids, but their sheer size improved the probability that a viable flock would survive most losses. These vast flocks were owned by sheep *ricos* of the Río Abajo, whose economic fortunes blossomed with new fiscal and market policies introduced in the Bourbon Reforms, and expanded with commercial opportunities attendant to open trade with the United States after 1821. The increased scale of sheep grazing would allow easier siphoning of wealth by social marginals, both New Mexican and Navaho. Third, Spanish, Mexican, and American administrators attempted to establish some semblance of military order in the region. When resources allowed, this involved garrisoning Cebolleta and Cubero with regular soldiers. More often, however, state authorities relied on civil militias who tended to pursue local objectives (sheep and captive raids) rather than the military pacification envisioned by governors. Finally, with the emergence of the Diné Ana'aii, who fought both as New Mexican auxiliaries and for their own, divergent interests, the balance of power in the pastoral borderlands became thoroughly diffused.

Among the thirty residents who petitioned Governor Fernando Chacón for a settlement grant at Cebolleta on March 15, 1800, were descendants of the eighteenth-century settlers—the Baca, Chávez, and Gallegos families.[7] Although officially they had taken shelter during the troublous 1780s and 1790s in Río Grande villages like Belén and Carnué, the fact that a lively commercial intercourse persisted during the period suggests that they so-journed as traders (often on behalf of Governor Chacón) while awaiting resettlement. Furthermore, Spanish land tenure custom required that peti-tioners hold "productive possession" of lands for three to five years prior to making a claim, so the Cebolletanos had probably returned some years earlier, in part to maintain their rights to the earlier grant.

At Cebolleta, Navahos immediately protested the new settlement, claim-ing that the New Mexicans' flocks infringed on their grazing lands. These Navahos seemed willing to accept New Mexicans as traders in their territory, but competition from large-scale sheep grazers was another matter. When Governor Chacón refused their complaint, the Navahos turned violent, strik-ing the high-walled plaza in a series of raids through the spring and summer of 1804. By August, Navahos had seized all the village livestock, killed twelve shepherds, taken several captive, and finally forced the village men to hide their dependents in a deep cave one league north of the plaza. In December, the village was briefly abandoned, then resettled on the governor's orders, with the promise that a small troop of *presidiales* would be forthcoming.[8]

The following month, Antonio Narbona's legendary winter campaign into the Canyon de Chelly resulted in 115 Navahos killed and 33 taken captive, along with 350 sheep and goats.[9] Reflecting the weakness of New Mexico's presidial garrison, Narbona's troops were largely composed of regu-lar soldiers from Sonora, as well as a company of Opata scouts from the village of Bacuachi. Narbona distributed eleven Navaho women and chil-dren to his captains as rewards, and brought the remainder to Santa Fe. In March, Navaho headmen Cristóbal and Vicente approached new governor Joaquín Real Alencaster, offering two New Mexican captives in return for the Navaho prisoners. Sixteen captives enjoyed repatriation, including the headman Segundo and his family. Alencaster now promised the Navahos permission for "commerce, stock-raising, and planting of fields and other enterprizes." But Cebolleta would remain. By October 1805, more than forty Navaho families had established themselves near the village, and although they occasionally pilfered the settlers' fields, a tenuous peace prevailed again in the region.[10]

Informal commerce between Navahos and New Mexicans subsequently became so brisk that by late 1805 it threatened to reduce formal exports in the annual *cordón* to Chihuahua. Accordingly, Governor Alencaster prohib-ited the sale of sheep to Navahos. The governor's action, coupled with even greater interference in informal commerce on the Plains, sparked a near-revolt in the province.[11] Alencaster quickly rescinded his orders and trade resumed, especially with the Navahos who lived around Cebolleta. After 1818, under the headmen "Joaquín" and Francisco Baca, they would cast their lot firmly with their Spanish neighbors.

Cebolleta remained the major New Mexican settlement in the Río Puerco region until 1833, when Juan Chávez and sixty-one neighbors from the Río Abajo established a new village at Cubero, the spring just west of the old Encinal mission of the 1740s. This grant differed from its predecessors in one important way—the lands upon which it rested were purchased the previous year from Francisco Baca, headman of the Diné Ana'aii, by Pedro Molina, then resold to the petitioners. These Navahos were emerging as key players in the borderlands by this time, and Baca's entrance into the land business signals just how thoroughly they had accommodated themselves to New Mexican norms. Cubero would henceforth serve as the pivotal trading and raiding center in the pastoral borderlands. In historian Frank McNitt's words, Cubero would become "a hell-raising military post brothel, a haven for army deserters, murderers, renegades, slavers, and thieves." But the people of the Río Puerco saw themselves in a different light.[12]

THE HEYDAY OF THE PASTORAL BORDERLANDS, 1800–1860

For sixty years, a pattern of limited local violence, occasional formal campaigns, and short-lived peace treaties came to characterize the Navaho–New Mexican borderlands. Between 1805 and 1861, Spanish, Mexican, and American administrators signed thirteen treaties with various Navaho headmen, usually broken within a few months. Scholars have generally attributed their failure to lack of formal political control on the part of both Navaho and New Mexican leaders.[13] This view seems accurate, but it does not explain why these local societies did not vest their leaders with sufficient political power to maintain peaceful stability. Historian Daniel Tyler raised this issue in 1980 when he suggested that "local arrangements" and "mutual economic needs" between village-level New Mexicans and their Indian neighbors were unanalyzed factors in borderland relations between 1786 and 1847.[14] The question becomes explicable, however, if we treat the apparently random violence of the borderlands as a system for exacting emotional retribution and redistributing wealth within and between Navaho and New Mexican societies.

The dynamic nature of the borderlands economy requires examination of how customary "slave raids and reprisals," generally deemed corrosive and debilitating to Navahos and New Mexicans alike, actually contributed to the overall growth of both societies. Without this analysis, we remain unable to explain why, if the first half of the nineteenth century was a time of unremitting warfare, the societies of the Navaho and New Mexican villagers expanded demographically, geographically, and economically throughout the period.[15] Historians like Frank D. Reeve, Lynn R. Bailey, Frank McNitt, and David M. Brugge have long recognized the existence of a slave-raiding-and-trading complex in the Southwest.[16] But they have hesitated to examine its mutually exploitable aspects that help to clarify *why* this traffic persisted as long as it did, especially those aspects involving reciprocal retribution and redistribution. These two elements of borderlands expansion worked in concert. First, the reciprocal seizure of women and children stimulated conflict between Indian groups and their New Mexican neighbors, yet it also fostered cultural and economic exchanges that produced an enmeshment of borderland interests. Second, low-grade military conflict between New Mexican and Navaho raiding bands served to redistribute resources, principally sheep but also women and children, from the wealthy to the poorer orders of both societies.

The reciprocal capture and assimilation of women and children in greater New Mexico complicated the internal character and eroded cultural boundaries in both New Mexican colonial and Navaho societies.[17] In the New Mexican case, the fact that captive women and children received baptism, and thus came at least nominally under the protection of Catholic *compadrazgo* (godparenthood) practices, suggests some nominal situation of captives in the kinship nexus.[18] Likewise, the designation of those baptized as *criadas* or *criados* (literally, those "raised up" by a family) lends support to the characterization of captives as adopted members of New Mexican households. Many such *criadas* grew to adulthood, married "Spanish" men, and bore children, who were "loved as if [they] were of our own blood."[19] In several cases, these captives appear as property, given at marriage as gifts or contested later in acrimonious divorces;[20] but *testamentos* (wills) also reveal occasions when both freedom and property were settled on *criadas* upon marriage or at the time of a *dueño*'s death.[21]

Over time, the presence of these captives contributed to subtle cultural changes in New Mexican villages. Using distinctive upright looms, captive Navaho women wove "slave blankets" that influenced later Río Grande weaving designs.[22] The residence of Navaho kinswomen in New Mexican and Pueblo villages sometimes became the pretext for peaceful trading visits.[23] Navaho captive boys likewise served as guides for both trading and raiding expeditions into Navaho country. In the 1850s, Cebolletanos had an especially favored captive boy named Kico who guided their forays against the Navahos. On these ventures, language barriers did not prevent each side from taunting the other.[24] According to oral histories, Navaho became something of a lingua franca in the borderlands, used by New Mexicans and Hopis alike. Hopi (Moqui in Spanish) captives in villages like Cubero and Cebolleta became so numerous that a surname, Moquino, appears in documentary records by the early nineteenth century, as does a village of the same name in the 1860s.[25]

Navahos also took captives from neighboring Indian groups and New Mexican villages, and in so doing enmeshed themselves in larger economic and cultural exchanges. Frederick W. Hodge reported that in the 1850s, five of nineteen Navaho clans claimed descent from Pueblo clan ancestresses, and Navahos told Washington Matthews in the 1890s that at least eight clans derived "from women of alien races."[26] The Nakaidiné (Mexican clan) may have descended from two Spanish women, Augustina de Peralta and Juana Almassan, captured near Santo Domingo in 1680.[27] Clearly, some Navaho clans had their genesis in captures or adoptions of "outsiders," and this tradition extended itself into the nineteenth century. In 1933, Curley of Chinlé described to W. W. Hill how spheres of capture and retribution expanded from intragroup competition for brides to include widespread "wars of capture":

Long ago . . . the Diné on both sides of the Lukachukai Mountains were very prosperous, while those in del Muerto and de Chelly were poor. However the people of the canyons were noted for their beautiful women. The men who had horses would sneak into the canyons and steal one or two wives from these people. The reason for this stealing was that the people of [the canyons] were originally of Pueblo stock, while those in the mountains were of the Old Navaho stock and the canyon girls were much prettier than those of the mountains. For revenge, the Canyon people would raid. First they raided the Pueblos, then the Utes, and finally the Mexicans. This drew attention to the Navaho, and raids in retaliation were sent into the Navaho country. As the Canyon people were safe in their protected location, the Navahos on the outside were forced to suffer these raids.[28]

Probably unwilling to provoke cycles of revenge with their more powerful kinsmen, poor Navahos looked beyond their wealthy cousins for retribution and expanded their raids to other Indian groups and New Mexican villages.

Generally not recognizing the sources and limitedness of these raiding groups, Utes and New Mexicans targeted Navahos in general for retribution. What Curley described was a broad intercommunity network of competitive exogamy, a "traffic in women" driven by disparities in wealth and power. Its extension to Pueblos, Utes, and Mexicans became an alternative strategy for pursuing brides in the context of a Navaho society in which wealthy men, through their ability to pay bridewealth of up to fifteen horses and other livestock, gradually acquired rights to most marriageable women.[29]

One means that younger sons of *ricos* (or *pobres* in general) employed to acquire wealth that might purchase brides came through the theft of horses, mules, and sheep. Stolen sheep were integrated into the collectively managed but individually held flocks of the clan, available for bridewealth payments when the opportunity arose.[30] These raiders might also capture New Mexican women and adopt them into Navaho clans, thereby increasing the pool of potential brides. Hence we see the emergence of two groups whose actions knit Navahos and New Mexicans in ever-tighter relations of conflict and exchange. The first, loosely termed *ladrones*, or "thieves," combined *rico* dependents and poor Navahos in raiding bands that struck New Mexican villages for sheep and captives.

The second group of borderlanders we mentioned earlier. Appearing after 1818, the Diné Ana'ii, or Enemy Navaho, under mixed-blood headmen Francisco Baca and Antonio Sandoval, maintained outfits in the Río Puerco region and formed close relations, both economically and culturally, with the valley's New Mexican settlers. Serving as guides for New Mexican military expeditions, and often acting as autonomous raiders themselves, the Diné Ana'ii functioned as entrepreneurs in the borderlands economy. Their allegiance to New Mexico increased in the 1830s, as an export market for Navaho serapes developed in northern Mexico. Antonio Barreiro reported somewhat optimistically in 1832: "Many of them speak Spanish, and entire families often come and live among us, embracing the Catholic religion. Their settlements have well-developed police and governmental regulations. Their wool manufactures are the most valuable in our province and in Sonora and Chihuahua."[31]

Although Navaho custom prohibited teaching non-Navaho captive women to weave, captive women served as "chore wives," freeing Navaho women to weave for the market. Exclusive taboos such as these may have fairly late origins, as a consequence of market forces. Retention of sacred knowledge allowed Navaho women to control one important aspect of production and to continue the concentration of wealth within matrilineal clans.[32] Likewise, excluding captives from sacred knowledge placed restrictions on their assimilation: although adopted as clan members, and married, they could not achieve complete incorporation. By the nineteenth century, female *binaalté* (slaves) in Navaho society had begun to serve as social boundary markers, institutionally marginalized in a fashion that heightened in-group identities while retaining for the slave some positive attributes of the kinship nexus.[33] On the other hand, as commercial integration increased the need for male shepherds, especially New Mexican or Mexican boys already trained to the task, we see a divergence in the *naalté* experience. Male captives could acquire sacred knowledge, as in the case of Nakai Na'dis Saal, who became a Nightway Singer.[34] These changing patterns suggest that, as commercial values came to predominate among some Navahos, the institution of Navaho slavery shaded in the direction of more rigid differentiation, especially with regard to a slave's gender.

Reciprocal retribution in captive-raiding created a pervasive sense of insecurity and anger in the borderlands. One would think, as did many Spanish, Mexican, American, and "peaceful" Navaho leaders, that truces including captive repatriation would resolve this anxiety. But social and economic inequalities in both Navaho and New Mexican societies made this difficult. Military conflict proved the quickest means for socially marginal people to compete for and acquire wealth. This low-grade military conflict in the region, which—at first glance—seems mutually destructive, fostered socioeconomic expansion among certain marginal groups. One aspect of this multifaceted dynamic derived from the role of New Mexican villagers in the defense of the province.

New Mexico seldom had more than a hundred professional troops assigned to the presidio in Santa Fe, and day-to-day defense largely depended on *milicias activas* (civil militias). But the financial troubles besetting Bourbon New Spain and, later, independent Mexico never allowed for paying these local militias, who were required to furnish their own mounts, arms, and ammunition for standard forty-five-day campaigns.[35] Their only means of compensation lay in receiving spoils of war—livestock and captives. Prior to 1821, custom had allowed for the equal distribution of captured livestock within the war band, with captured women and children going to individual captors. Although Mexican-era reforms sought to regularize this practice by making plunder the responsibility of commanders, these men generally continued customary division of spoils, after retaining the best "prizes" for themselves. In practice, volunteers stood a good chance of adding to personal wealth in a victorious campaign.[36] After several years of frustration, even American administrators like James S. Calhoun found the local militias an unfortunate necessity in Territorial defense. After 1851, governors regularly authorized and equipped militia forays over the objections of army commanders.[37]

Armed with old *escopetas* (muskets), lances, bows and arrows, and small shields termed *chimales*, the border militias entered Navaho country under the guidance of captive Navaho boys like Kico, who knew the landscape and understood Navaho night signals. Oral tradition confirms the centrality of captive-raiding in these ventures. These were "one of the greatest rewards of a campaign. . . . [because] if the captives were of average age, or young and could be domesticated and taught, then their capture bore rich fruit"— either by resale to *ricos* in the valley or by adding to the prestige of their owners as household servants or concubines. Folk memory from Cubero and Cebolleta recalls significant differences in identity between the *nacajalleses* (as New Mexican raiders were termed by Navahos) of the border villages and those they termed the *gente del rio,* or "river men," who proved timid and unskilled in border raids. Primarily pastoralists, rather than farmers, *nacajalleses* were more like their Indian neighbors than the sedentary *labradores* of the Río Grande valley. Eschewing village hierarchies, *nacajalleses* "had no leaders" but conferred authority in raids on famous fighters like Redondo Gallegos, "feared by the Navahos on account of his extraordinary strength."[38]

While these militia units ostensibly stood under the authority of Spanish, Mexican, or American governors, in practice they often existed as self-organized war bands pursuing local goals: settlement expansion, sheep herds, and captives. Since *ricos* like the Armijo, Perea, and Chávez families had consolidated their hold on the sheep industry in the Río Grande valley by the 1820s, settlers looked beyond the Río Puerco valley for all of these objectives.[39] Allied with members of the Diné Ana'aii, whose kin connections and strategic needs made conditions favorable for New Mexican forays, the *nacajalleses* pushed their control of grazing lands in a great arc to the west, as far as the borders of Zuni, Hopi, and the old Dinétah.

But acquiring sheep to graze on these lands presented a problem for New Mexicans who were short on capital. Only two possibilities presented themselves. On the one hand, New Mexican *pastores* could try to build flocks through the *partido* system, by which *partidarios* took responsibility for a flock in return for annual payments of some 20 percent of the lamb and wool crop and the long-term obligation to return the original number of ewes within three to five years. Since the annual rate of increase of sheep flocks ranges between 10 and 30 percent, the *partido* placed nearly all the speculative burden on the debtor. If all went well, the *partidario* could create a working flock of his own during this period; but if disease, bad weather, or Indian raids intervened, he could find himself deeply in debt to his *patrón*.[40]

The second avenue was quicker, but more dangerous. This involved stealing sheep indirectly from *ricos* by "rescuing" them from neighboring Navaho pastoralists. Since Navaho *ladrones* built their own flocks through raids, we can see the reciprocal and redistributive nature of the borderlands economy taking shape. By the middle years of the nineteenth century, Navaho flocks numbered some 500,000 sheep and goats. However, a mere 7 percent of Navaho families owned 40 percent of these flocks and controlled 75 percent of the horse herds. The richest of these families had forty to fifty dependent shepherds, many of them captive Hopis, Havasupais, Zunis, Apaches, or New Mexicans.[41] Lawrence Weiss and Klara Kelley estimate that fully 50 percent of Navaho households in 1850 maintained flocks of fewer than 190 sheep and goats, below the minimum to maintain both animals and owners under bad weather or stock-loss conditions.[42] These *pobres* had only two choices in pursuing security—either attach themselves as dependents to a Navaho *rico* outfit, or raid the vast flocks of New Mexican *ricos*.

New Mexicans may have held as many as three million sheep in the 1830s and 1840s. Of these multitudes, the vast majority were owned by the cartel of intermarried *rico* families in the Río Abajo.[43] While exports (both on-the-hoof and in woven goods) to Chihuahua and points south constituted much of their market, after 1830 a thriving trade with California developed as well. Returning traders brought some luxury goods like Chinese silks, but the majority of commerce was in horses and mules, many of which had been "illegally acquired" from coastal missions and ranchos by Yokuts raiders from the San Joaquin valley. Poor-to-middling entrepreneurial New Mexicans, working on speculation for the *ricos* of Río Abajo, composed most of these caravans. Many made their homes in Cebolleta, Cubero, and Abiquiu (the departure point for the Old Spanish Trail), and hence these bordermen became active in expanding the commercial circuits of the local pastoral economy. Operating in the gray area between legal trade and larcenous freebooting, they were viewed as economically important yet potentially dangerous by both Mexican and (after 1847) American authorities.[44]

Navaho raiders took full advantage of these expanding resources and proliferating networks. The numbers of sheep stolen by Navaho *ladrones* during the period are staggering: nearly 7,000 between 1800 and 1821, some 50,000 by 1846, nearly 100,000 by the end of 1859, and an additional 100,000 by 1864. In parties of four to ten men, Navaho *ladrones* swept down upon these flocks and ran them back toward the security of their deep canyons. The Navaho term for "stealing," *ansh'í*, carries no moral opprobrium and is understood more specifically as "appropriating loose property" within their cultural norms. Navaho oral histories reveal the strategic nature of this plundering. Old raiders told W. W. Hill in the 1930s that "we never burnt the villages, and always left enough sheep behind that the flocks would be good again the next year."[45]

The activities of Navaho *ladrones* played perfectly into the needs of border militiamen in Cubero and Cebolleta. Since sheep assimilate easily into new flocks, upon hearing of a *ladrón* raid in the Río Grande valley, village men could muster and ride in hot pursuit, ostensibly as a loyal civil militia. If successful in their chase, they might recapture the stolen herd. But under customary division of spoils, militiamen would not return the sheep to *ricos* in the valley; they divided the booty among themselves in compensation for their risk. If they found no Navaho flocks to raid, they might strike flocks owned by a New Mexican *rico* and claim to have taken them from Navahos. Rafael López did so in 1836, but he was caught in the subterfuge by authorities.[46] With their own flocks, and captive Navaho women as weavers, New Mexican bordermen were better able to produce commodities for the growing export trade.

The customary division of spoils provoked friction between rich and poor New Mexicans. In 1851, Ramón Luna, prefect of Valencia County, reported to Governor Calhoun: "[S]ome difficulty exists between the owners of the recovered stock and the captors. The former claim the sheep as their property, and can prove it by their brand, while the latter maintain that [the sheep] are in the same position with other goods [spoils], and should be subject to the same condition." Some 5,000 sheep, 150 horses and mules, 11 oxen, and 48 captives had been taken in this reprisal raid, a considerable reward for the militiamen's risk. Men in the western border villages along the Río Puerco considered this tradition a customary privilege associated with frontier defense. For the sheep *ricos* of the Río Grande, however, these rescues differed little from the initial Navaho raids. By 1857 they pressured the Territorial legislature into passing laws that limited militia compensation to 30 percent of the recapture, but since this accounting took place in the field, militia members still stood to profit substantially.[47]

Recapture data suggest that roughly half of the stock seized in a raid would be recovered either in the initial pursuit or in later raids on Navaho *rancherías* (although these may have been entirely different animals). Using the 30 percent compensation rate as a conservative baseline, local militias acquired through recaptures and customary divisions at least 48,000 of the 158,000 sheep taken from Navahos between 1800 and 1860. During Christopher "Kit" Carson's two-year Navaho campaign of 1862–64, several hundred thousand more sheep came into New Mexican hands.[48] Given that sheep flocks reproduce themselves in a range of 10 to 30 percent annually, it is not surprising that the *nacajalleses* of the Río Puerco found their own system preferable to that of the *partido*, since the increase would not be diluted by the 20 percent lamb and wool "interest," nor would they ever need to repay the principal.

Navaho and New Mexican *ladrones* seized more than sheep in these raids. Between 1800 and 1870, over 1,200 Navaho captives received baptism in New Mexican parishes; concurrently, Navahos seized New Mexicans by the score, retaining them either as *binaalté* (slaves), adopted kinspeople, or potential bargaining chips in hostage exchanges.[49] But this went beyond a simple two-way traffic. The internal divisions noted above worked themselves out in the captive trade as well. New Mexican *nacajalleses* might take Navaho women and children in their "reprisal" raids, but they also acquired captives by purchasing them from the schismatic Diné Ana'aii. As converted Catholics, Diné Ana'aii now had two cultural categories into which captives could be incorporated, either the Navaho *naalté* status or the *criadisma* established through baptismal godparenthood. These culturally mixed Navahos often served as scouts for organized New Mexican campaigns or freebooted themselves as sheep and captive raiders. Their quarry could be Utes, Paiutes, Hopis, or their Navaho cousins.[50] Tiana Bighorse, in her biography of her father, Gus Bighorse (born ca. 1845), notes his attitude toward these "enemies within":

> And it isn't only the other tribes we have to look out for. Even our own people work against us. That's the way it is with Ahidigishii. He is Navajo, the enemy of his own tribe, raiding upon us. With him travel several men and women. They are a tough gang. . . . [They] went raiding other tribes and made enemies against the Navajos. He made innocent people suffer and pay with their lives.[51]

Clearly, Indian captives entered New Mexican households to become *criadas* through the agency of other Indian groups, as well as through direct New Mexican slave raids. Once bartered, the women and children were either resold to *rico* families in the Río Grande valley or retained in the households of their captors. Captives served, therefore, as commodities with real market value, as weavers and laborers in the pastoral system, and as prestige items in status competition.

Kirby Benedict, chief justice of the Territorial Supreme Court in 1858, estimated Navaho captives held in bondage in New Mexico in the 1850s at 1,500 to 3,000: "the more prevalent opinion seems to be they considerably exceed two thousand." Thus Navaho slaves alone constituted at least 3.2 percent of an aggregate 1850 population of 61,525 (excluding Pueblo Indians). He noted, however, that the proportion of Navaho–New Mexican mixed-bloods was much higher, because when Navaho slave girls grew "to womanhood, they sometimes become mothers from the native of the land, with or without marriage." By the custom of the country, these mixed-descent children were "not regarded as property which may be bought and sold as had been their mothers. . . . [T]hey marry and blend with the general population."[52]

By the 1860s, an extensive network of exchange had developed in the borderlands that social marginals on all sides used to acquire the key items of wealth and prestige in Navajo and New Mexican society alike: sheep and slaves. In doing so, the marginals preyed (directly or indirectly) upon the wealth of their own societies. New Mexican villagers recaptured the sheep of their *rico patrones*, the Diné Ana'aii took captives from their wealthy cousins, while Navaho *ladrones* expanded the network to seize captives from Hopi, Havasupai, Zuni, Ute, or Apache bands on the fringes of Navaho territories. Although hurt to some degree by this redistribution, wealthy Navahos and New Mexicans lacked both the capacity and the will to interdict the traffic; their best warriors and soldiers were its principal agents, and they too received benefits, either in bridewealth payments or in a steady supply of household servants. But by 1862, a wider field of conflict around slavery and labor systems in North America would come to encompass the pastoral borderlands and begin to replace customary webs of dependency and inequality with new meanings of "freedom."

THE DISINTEGRATION OF THE PASTORAL BORDERLANDS

Federal Indian policy in the middle of the nineteenth century was a combined program of military pacification, reservation, and agricultural instruction for Indians of the western territories. In New Mexico, the settled and self-supporting Pueblos provided a model for Governor Calhoun's vision:

territorially bounded "tribes" who would "cultivate the soil, and raise flocks and herds for a subsistence." While he thought Plains groups like the Comanches too "wild" for such a solution in 1851, he felt otherwise about the Navahos: "[They are] rich in all the necessaries of life. They cultivate the soil very successfully, raise, and collect by stealing, numerous herds of sheep and goats, fine horses and mules, and make the finest blankets I have ever seen. . . . so far as the Navajoes are concerned, not one dollar would be necessary to subsist them."[53] Officials on the national level concurred and believed that gradual market dependency through connections with rail-linked commercial centers would produce salutary effects: more regular and efficient animal husbandry practices and wage employment in industry and mining for "surplus" and dangerous young men.[54] But the political economy of the borderlands had long stood as "a system of warfare that would interfere with these measures," according to Colonel Edwin V. Sumner, American military commander in New Mexico: "[T]his predatory war has been carried on for over 200 years, between the Mexican & the Indians, quite enough time to prove that unless some change is made the war will be interminable. They steal women and children, and Cattle, from each other, and in fact carry on the war in all respects like two Indian nations."[55]

But dynamics associated with the struggle over chattel slavery in the United States introduced a series of pressures that would largely eliminate this regional economy within the next fifteen years. These pressures emerged from larger issues of freedom, citizenship, and wage-labor capitalism, both in the East and in the southwestern borderlands. For if the American Civil War can be considered a racially charged economic conflict in which free-labor capitalism triumphed over slave-labor capitalism, the extension of this conflict to New Mexico meant the triumph of state-sponsored capitalist development over the exchange economy of the borderlands peoples. This campaign aimed to eliminate raids of sheep and captives as the customary system of exchange and replace kin-based subjectivity with state-sponsored tribalism and individual autonomy. Although more successful in the former than the latter, this strategy proved effective in severing the links that had bound the borderlands communities together.

But first, some Americans saw real possibilities in the New Mexican system of human bondage decried by reformers like Justice Benedict. Regularized in the Territory's Master and Servant Law of 1851, debt peonage and Indian slavery became inextricably blurred, and despite numerous attempts by reformers like Benedict to eliminate human bondage, provisions for enforcement were so ignored that involuntary servitude remained common practice.[56] Writing in 1857, U.S. Attorney W. W. H. Davis sought to assuage concerns that the Territory might enter the Union as a slave state by suggesting that the "system of Indian slavery" and associated peonage made such a decision unnecessary: "A greater barrier than climate is the cheapness of peon labor, which is less expensive to the proprietor; and even in the southern parts, where more tropical productions could be raised, their labor would fully supply the place of the negro. . . . The present labor of the country is so much cheaper than any that could be introduced, that a person would hardly be justifiable in risking his capital in slaves with so little prospect of profitable return."[57]

By the late 1850s, when some American residents of the Territory became wholesale supporters of chattel slavery's extension into the West, they sought to combine their Democratic Party's defense of slavery in the United States with an absorption of the local system. Although early administrators like James Calhoun, William Carr Lane, and David Meriwether had been Whigs with ambivalent attitudes toward slavery, by 1857 President Buchanan had appointed as governor a solid North Carolina Democrat, Abraham Rencher. An "Act Restricting the Movement of Free Negroes in the Territory" had already passed in 1856, at least in part because a few fugitive black slaves from Texas began seeking freedom by entering its borders. Two free blacks, Harriet Brown in 1859 and John Winters in 1861, suffered prosecution and expulsion from the Territory under its provisions.[58]

On February 3, 1859, the Territorial Legislature composed of three Anglo-American Democrats and thirty-four New Mexican *rico* allies passed an "Act for the Protection of Property in Slaves." Its thirty-one sections included prohibitions against slave movement and travel, denied slaves the right to testify in courts, and restricted owners' rights to arm slaves except when necessary in defending against Indian raids. The U.S. Congress attempted to disapprove the legislation in House Resolution 64, which passed 97 to 90 on May 10, 1860, but later died in committee in the Senate. In the autumn of 1860, the Territorial Legislature attempted to enlarge the scope of the earlier law to include "male or female Indians that should be acquired from the barbarous nations." Governor Rencher delayed signing the amendment, and Lincoln's election resulted in his replacement by Henry F. Connelly, a pro-Union Democrat who soon delegated all but nominal power to the military government of General James H. Carleton. In that role Connelly issued a proclamation on May 4, 1864, that prohibited "the traffic in captive Indians."[59] State resources would soon be turned to that end.

The changing role of civil militias proved crucial to the transformation that eventually dismantled the borderlands economy. With the advent of the Civil War in April 1861, and an invasion of Confederate forces from Texas, Colonel Edward R. Canby authorized the formation of two Volunteer Infantry Regiments, one under Kit Carson of Taos, the other under Miguel E. Pino of Albuquerque. Driven by a long-term antipathy toward American Texans, who had twice attempted to invade New Mexico, and drawn by the promise of wages and bounties in hard cash, more than 2,800 New Mexicans joined these and local militia units by February 1862.[60] Although they played minor roles in the defeat of Silbey's invasion, these militia units stood ready one year later, when General Carleton began his war of relocation against the Navahos.

Carson's First New Mexico Volunteers were prominent in this scorched-earth campaign. Local enthusiasm waxed warm, for the action against the Navahos conformed closely with customary practices. Carson pleaded with Carleton for the necessity of continued rewards in captives for local militias and Ute scouts, and military-census materials from 1865 bear out his successful avoidance of Carleton's prohibition: when Lafayette Head made a count of Navaho captives held in households in Costilla and Conejos Counties, Colorado Territory, 48 of the total of 112 had been acquired after the 1864 campaign commenced.[61]

In essence, however, the Carson campaign redefined the position of captives from commodities in the borderlands economy to involuntary dependents of the United States. At Bosque Redondo over 9,000 Navahos came abjectly "under the dominion of" the federal government. American administrators seized this opportunity to begin a program of assimilation that struck directly at the kin-and-clan fabric of Navaho society. Presbyterian ministers established boarding schools for Navaho children, and Indian agents denied Navaho "Big Men" access to annuities unless they disposed of "surplus" wives and "unfree" dependents.[62]

Ironically, the success of the campaign struck borderland New Mexicans as dubious. In Carson's deposition to Congress at the conclusion of his victory, he noted that "some New Mexicans now object to the settlement of Navahos at the Bosque, because they cannot prey upon them as formerly."[63] Over the next four years, two political factions argued in New Mexico's newspapers about the merits of internment. Sensing that future wealth in the new order lay with controlling land, sheep *ricos* praised the policy, perhaps in part because they could now safely graze their immense flocks on former Navaho territories. Opposing them, an odd combination of borderlanders, old Democrats, Indian traders, and philanthropists complained of local economic collapse and the immense drain that internment placed on public finance.[64]

Indeed, borderlands villagers suffered severely in the aftermath of the pacification of New Mexico. Military service under Carson, while bringing much-desired hard currency, also involved the acceptance of military discipline, an issue that grated on the borderlanders' sense of autonomy and honor. According to WPA interviews in the village of Las Huertas, submission to military discipline expressed itself symbolically in Carson's orders that they must shear their "long and braided hair. Those braids proclaimed [a man] a good and honorable citizen. . . . Short hair was a brand, a silent declaration of dishonor." Although the men "wept and begged," Carson remained adamant, and so the day of enlistment "marked the disappearance of braids from the heads of men, except for the old men. They refused to part with their braids."[65]

Military service meant wages and discipline, two key aspects of the expanding capitalist economy. But capitalist incorporation was not smooth or uncontested in greater New Mexico. In the summer of 1865, three events occurred that illustrate the tenacity with which customary relations of inequality could persist in a changing economic landscape. First, the case of an anonymous Hopi woman in the New Mexican village of Cubero shows the vulnerability of women and children in the New Mexico borderlands. Next, an executive order from President Andrew Johnson places her experience in national historical context. Finally, the response of the New Mexican Indian superintendent demonstrates how difficult the suppression of Indian slavery in the Territory would prove, given the customary practices against which emancipation would compete.

On August 12, 1865, a Hopi woman staggered into the office of Lieutenant Colonel Julius C. Shaw, commanding officer of Fort Wingate, New Mexico Territory. Her hair clotted with blood from a head wound, she declared to Shaw that while she and her nine-year-old daughter were walking the wagon road between Cubero and Fort Wingate, two men from the village overtook them, hammered her with their rifle butts, and left her stunned beside the trail. When she recovered consciousness some hours later, her daughter was missing. Retracing her steps to Cubero—where she had "lately been residing"—she discovered that the men had kidnapped her daughter and refused her requests to see the child. She then walked to Fort Wingate to plead for Shaw's intercession in the kidnapping. Shaw reported to Major Benjamin Cutler, his superior in Santa Fe, that he would dispatch First Lieutenant George McDermott to Cubero to investigate the "particulars concerning the affair."[66]

Two concurrent developments provide larger historical and cultural context for the Hopi woman's dilemma. For although discrete in certain details, the sufferings of this anonymous woman prove symptomatic of the experience of women and children caught up in larger processes of violence, exchange, and state regulation in the region.

A few months before the incident at Fort Wingate, President Andrew Johnson had issued a directive to the Secretaries of the Interior and War Departments regarding the question of Indian slavery in the Territory of New Mexico. Declaring the practice in violation of "the rights of Indians" and Territorial "organic law," he ordered his subordinates to engage in "an effective suppression of the practice."[67]

The president's letter elicited a quick response from New Mexico. Within a month, New Mexico's Superintendent of Indian Affairs Felipe Delgado wrote to Commissioner of Indian Affairs William Dole in an attempt to clarify the local practice. "Allow me to say," he replied, "that the representations made to the government upon this subject have been greatly exaggerated":

> It is true that there are among the citizens of this country a large number of Indian captives belonging to various tribes, that have been acquired through purchase from the Utahs, Navajos and some other tribes, but the object in purchasing them has not been to reduce them to slavery, but rather from a Christian piety on the part of the whites to obtain them in order to instruct and educate them in Civilization, and at the same time to leave them at full liberty whenever the Indian desires it, or—in some cases—to remain until they were twenty one years of age.

Adding more context, Delgado continued:

> This has been the practice in this country for the last century and a half and the result arising from it has been to the captives, favorable, humane, and satisfactory. When these Indians wish to marry, their guardians do not object, but rather, treat them as their adopted children, and give them pecuniary aid at the time of marriage. When the guardian dies, they usually leave something to the captives, as their adopted children.[68]

Arguing that the captive trade was a multilateral affair in which purchase from other Indian groups occurred as often as direct seizure, and that the custom had evolved over the previous centuries under the guise of the Spanish civilizing mission, Delgado's reply underscores the depth of historical and cultural processes that underlay the phenomenon. The case of the Hopi woman provides further evidence of the extent to which the system permeated local society.

Lieutenant McDermott delivered his report to Shaw within twenty-four hours. Having arrived in the village of Cubero, he interviewed several residents about the case of the Hopi woman, and discovered that one of her attackers was a local *vecino*, Filomeno Sánchez, commonly known as "Chato." This man indeed held the woman's daughter against her will, but said "he had assumed a debt which this woman contracted" and had taken both the mother and daughter as security against that debt. Soon after doing so, he claimed, the mother and child attempted to escape, so he and a *compadre* pursued the fugitives and "beat the woman on the head with his rifle until senseless, then carried the child away." Under pressure from McDermott, Chato fetched the child and returned her to her mother in the presence of the *Alcalde ordinario* (municipal magistrate), Manuel García. When asked to point out her assailant, she indicated Chato, which McDermott noted as occurring in the presence of several other witnesses. But with martial law recently suspended in the West at the end of the Civil War, McDermott could do little more, and he harbored doubts that the civil authorities would take "any steps to punish this fellow." To support this judgment, he added a postscript, noting that García himself had in his possession "two small Moqui [Hopi] Indians" which "he held as his property."[69]

When Chato Sánchez claimed that he held the woman and child as security against a debt, he probably spoke the truth as he saw it. Since at least the early eighteenth century, Spanish New Mexicans had engaged in the practice of *rescate*, or rescue and redemption, of captives held in the power of *los indios bárbaros*. In New Mexico, *rescate* served as the artifice by which legal and moral sanctions against Indian slavery could be subverted. Once redeemed from the horrors of captivity among the heathen, and situated within the civilizing embrace of a Christian family, the rescued Indians were expected to work off the expense of their redemption, usually for a period not to exceed twenty years. (Virtually no evidence exists that self-redemption occurred in New Mexico.) By 1865 the price of "a likely girl, not more than eight years old, healthy and intelligent," could reach "four hundred dollars or more," and the "debt" for which the Hopi woman was responsible approached $1,000. Her bondage might well be considered perpetual.[70]

The custom of *rescate*, and its amendments following the American conquest, provide the likely explanation of how the Hopi woman had come to reside in Cubero, in the household of Chato Sánchez. David Brugge's analysis of baptismal records in New Mexico reveals some 360 Hopis receiving baptism in local *parroquias* between 1740 and 1870; 37 of these occur after 1800, and Brugge deems them "definitely servants acquired by purchase or capture." Navaho raiders had struck the Hopi mesas several times in the 1860s, taking corn and captives, and this may be when the woman became a commodity in the system.[71]

Furthermore, the case of Chato Sánchez's Hopi woman and child reveals how extensive and customary the local form of slavery had become by the 1860s. In its farthest reaches, the system extended from Sonora and Chihuahua in northern Mexico to California in the west, to say nothing of its extensions in the eastern plains and northern mountains. Violent, competitive, and based in tangible transfers of culture through intercommunity alliances, the political economy of captivity in the borderlands articulated with larger economic systems, but remained almost entirely under the control of the local people. As such, it posed a viable alternative and substantial barrier to free-labor capitalism in the Southwest.

The case of the Hopi woman illustrates the general ineffectiveness of President Johnson's proclamation. Local resistance to emancipation, and Carleton's belief that "enslavement was an effective method for punishing Indians for their depredations," contributed to the de facto persistence of slavery and peonage for another decade and a half. Stronger moral and military sanctions did subdue the continuing traffic in captives after William Tecumseh Sherman took control of Indian affairs in 1868. His position reflected the consensus that had formed among the victorious liberal modernizers at the end of the Civil War, a policy of pacification and economic development that had long been debated but not implemented due to the disruptions of the sectional conflict.[72]

Yet the legacy of the captive trade lingered. While the military and legal arms of the American state succeeded in suppressing the traffic, emancipation itself was hindered by the persistence of customary kin and culture bonds. In early 1868, Special Commissioner for Indian Affairs William W. Griffen, a confirmed Radical Republican, prepared nearly 600 cases against New Mexicans who still held Indian slaves for presentation to a local grand jury. But the jury, composed of prominent citizens, found few of his charges compelling and ruled that unless the victims would swear to their "forcible restraint or ill-treatment," indictments would not be issued. Griffen succeeded in freeing 146 persons in Río Arriba and Sante Fe Counties, but hundreds more remained with their masters.[73] In 1872, General Oliver O. Howard of the recently defunct Freedmen's Bureau arrived in New Mexico to facilitate the repatriation of several hundred Navaho slaves held in New Mexican households. Some, especially women with children, refused the offer.[74] Although we can only speculate, the intimate bondages of kinship may have seemed preferable to a "freedom" without the protection of family.

Likewise, ten years later Navaho Agent Dennis Riordan attempted to repatriate some 300 *binaalté* held by the Navahos. Riordan reported that "one old villain" objected, asking "who was to take care of him if his slaves were taken away from him?" The agent said that he had responded firmly that he himself would "take care of him and the whole band if they were *not* set free." His victory was short-lived, however, for he later reported that "most [freed slaves] beat a hasty path back to the hogans of their masters." Juanita, the New Mexican wife of the famous chief Manuelito, similarly refused liberation. The following year Riordan's successor argued that the only way to "free" these slaves "would be to take them away entirely, confine them, and subsist them at public expense."[75]

Chato Sánchez and the Hopi woman and child offer another, more painful example. In the 1860 census, Sánchez appeared as a common laborer in the household of Decidero Trujillo; in 1870, five years after the event at Fort Wingate, he headed a household in Cubero that included a woman named "Serafina" and her daughter. The woman carries no matronym, suggesting obscure origins. She is designated as "keeping house," and her daughter "at home." Sánchez seems to have made the system work quite well. In addition to acquiring a "wife" and child through capture, by 1870 he claimed $200 in real property and $100 in personal property.[76] His experience may be extrapolated for many of the ambitious poor in the region.

Chato Sánchez and his *compadres* may have made the most of their position on the margins of American control, but their days of such autonomy were numbered. As the "Santa Fe Ring" gained control of Territorial affairs in the 1870s, these villagers found their customary rights to grazing land undercut by American land tenure legalism, and by the turn of the century had lost 80 percent of their communal *mercedes*.[77] The Baltazar Baca grant (containing Encinal and Cubero) became the subject of litigation among his descendants, land speculators, and the people of Laguna

Pueblo in the U.S. Court of Land Claims that lasted from 1872 to 1931, when title was finally quieted and the land divided among the claimants.[78] Other lands, once the domain of the poor, were now enclosed by wealthy Hispano and Anglo sheep and cattle ranchers, and the villagers themselves became increasingly drawn into wage dependency. While some New Mexican *ricos* intermarried with Anglos and prospered under the new regime, most villagers, cut off from the economic and social ties with the Navahos, found no place for themselves in the modernizing economy. Following the lead of their *rico patrónes,* many spurned their rich and complex mixed-cultural past, recast themselves as "Spanish-Americans," and participated in new traditions that saw them as romantic and picturesque descendants of Peninsular *conquistadores.*[79]

Likewise, the Long Walk era (1864–68) proved a social and economic disaster for the Navahos. Stripped of their herds, removed from their canyon-sheltered cornfields, and hundreds of miles from their raiding zones along the Río Grande, they had no choice but to turn to paltry federal aid for subsistence. When General Sherman negotiated a return to their old homelands in 1868, he had both promised and threatened an end to local slavery, and urged the Navahos to abandon pastoralism and become "self-supporting farmers." Securing the allegiance of "progressive" mixed-blood *ricos* like Chee Dodge by appointing them dispensers of annuities, Indian agents brought pressure to bear on the more troublesome elements. By 1872, many of the young men who had once profited from *ladronismo* found themselves drafted into the "Navaho Cavalry," a police unit that punished renegades and assisted the U.S. Army in campaigns against the Chiricahua Apaches. In 1883 they were put to the task of protecting the new railroad right-of-way through the Río Puerco valley over the protests of Tohyelte, a descendant of the Diné Ana'aii. This two-pronged strategy of economic patronage to secure the loyalties of *ricos,* and military mobilization of marginal young men, had proved useful in earlier Indian wars and in the aftermath of the American Civil War. Hence the solution to the Navaho problem had its place in the larger liberal capitalist ordering of North America.[80]

The new reservation shifted the Navaho homelands westward away from their New Mexican neighbors, and seldom again would these men share "the pleasurable excitement of reprisal" with their distant cousins. With customary patterns of redistribution thus foreclosed, problems of economic inequality intensified, as a few Navaho bands controlled most of the bottomlands, sheep flocks, and government annuities.[81] The Diné Ana'aii, once center-people in the borderlands economy, became vilified and confined to a tiny reservation of their own at Cañoncito west of Albuquerque.[82]

Suppression of the borderlands economy may not have brought freedom to the Hopi woman, as it certainly did not to hundreds of others like her. Today, many New Mexican families recall an Indian *tía* or *tío*, who, it is whispered, was once the family "slave."[83] Among the Navaho, the family name Nakai (Mexican) has become commonplace, and made famous through the performances of N. Carlos Nakai, the Navaho-Ute flautist.

The imposition of state order in the pastoral borderlands of New Mexico produced contradictory effects. Severing customary webs of violence and exchange, it brought a measure of physical security to many women and children, the most vulnerable members of both societies, and a measure of "independence" to freed slaves. Economic dependency on federal annuities and poorly paid wage labor followed, with especially damaging results in the early years of the twentieth century. In subduing the pastoral borderlands, long-term connections of kinship and community were sundered and new, "state-sponsored" ethnic identities imposed on a complex ménage. As ethnicity became increasingly associated with claims against the state, and culture a means of constructing "exclusive" identities, the borderlands of New Mexico lost much of their terror, but also some of their possibilities.

NOTES

1. James S. Calhoun to Commissioner of Indian Affairs Orlando Brown, 15 November 1849, in *The Official Correspondence of James S. Calhoun While Indian Agent at Santa Fe and Superintendent of Indian Affairs in New Mexico*, ed. Annie Heloise Abel (Washington, D.C.: Government Printing Office, 1915), 50, 76–77.

2. For Navaho movements into the Río Puerco area, and their rejection of Franciscan missionizing efforts, see Frank D. Reeve, "The Navaho-Spanish Peace: 1720–1770," *New Mexico Historical Review* (hereafter cited as *NMHR*) 34, no. 9 (1959): 9–40. The exact causes and forces behind the Navaho migration out of Dinétah remain the subject of debate. The classic study is Dorothy Louise Keur, *Big Bead Mesa: An Archaeological Study of Navaho Acculturation, 1745–1812*, Memoirs of the Society for American Archaeology, no. 1 (Menasha, Wisc: S.A.A., 1941). For the most recent scholarship, see Ronald H. Towner, *The Archaeology of Navajo Origins* (Salt Lake City: University of Utah Press, 1996).

3. Antonio Baca v. Inhabitants of the Río Puerco, 20 July 1762, Spanish Archives of New Mexico (hereafter cited as SANM), vol. 1, no. 105; see Records of the Surveyor General, New Mexico (hereafter RSG), reel 31, frames 453–62. Baltazar Baca Grant, 1768: SANM, vol. 1, no. 114; RSG, reel 23, frames 191–221. For the Montaños settlement, see Partición de las tierras, Nuestra Señora de la Luz San Fernando y San Blas, 1772; SANM, vol. 1, no. 277; RSG, reel 2, frames 479–82. New Mexico State Records Center and Archives, Santa Fe. SANM is indexed and described in Ralph Emerson Twitchell, *Spanish Archives of New Mexico*, 2 vols. (1914; reprint, New York: Arno Press, 1976), vol. 1: Wills and Land Transfers, vol. 2: Judicial and Military Documents.

4. The mixed Navaho–New Mexican society of the eighteenth century is treated in detail in James F. Brooks, *Captives and Cousins: Slavery, Kinship, and Community in the Southwest Borderlands, 1680–1880*, forthcoming from the Omohundro Institute of Early American History and Culture (Chapel Hill: University of North Carolina Press).

5. For the Baca grant at Encinal, and evidence for Francisco Baca's mixed descent, see Myra Ellen Jenkins, "The Baltazar Baca 'Grant': History of an Encroachment," *El Palacio* 68, no. 1 (1961): 47–64; Frank McNitt, *Navajo Wars: Military Campaigns, Slave Raids, and Reprisals* (Albuquerque: University of New Mexico Press, 1972), 29. McNitt's text unfortunately contains a transposition of "1786" for the 1768 date of the Baca grant and union with the Navaho woman.

6. "Cordero's Description of the Apache—1796," ed. and trans. Daniel S. Matson and Albert H. Schroeder, *NMHR* 37, no. 4 (1957): 356. In 1791, Revilla Gigedo had expressed to Governor Concha his satisfaction with the growing trade in baskets, blankets, and peltries by the Navahos. See SANM, vol. 2, no. 1176; reel 12, frames 794–98.

7. Town of Cebolleta Grant, New Mexico Land Grants, Claim 46, RSG, reel 17, frames 935–1011, New Mexico State Records Center and Archives, Santa Fe.

8. Local memory of these events persists. See Marc Simmons, *The Fighting Settlers of Seboyeta* (Cerrillos, N.M.: San Marcos Press, 1971).

9. To Narbona's campaign is commonly attributed the origin of the place-names "Massacre Cave" and "Cañon de los Muertos." Archaeologist Earl H. Morris learned from Navaho informants in the 1920s that in 1805 the Navahos had hidden their elderly, women, and children in a high cave on the canyon wall, and from there a Navaho woman who had once been held captive by the Spanish taunted Narbona's men as those "who walked without eyes." In a fusillade that expended some 10,000 rounds, the cave ceiling rained ricocheted bullets on the victims, whose bones were still evident to Morris during his visit. See McNitt, *Navajo Wars*, 41–44.

10. Ibid., 37–46. Alencaster's agreement with Cristóbal and Vicente are contained in SANM, vol. 2, nos. 1810 and 1828; reel 15, frames 439–40, 591–93.

11. "Sumaria Información indagatoria sobre combocatoria, commoción, y escándolo cometido entre los vecinos de las Jurisdicciones Tenencia en Pecos y Alcaldia de la Cañada, 6–24 deciembre, 1805," SANM, vol. 2, no. 1930; reel 15, frames 1043–98. This incident, and its origins in the Plains village of San Miguel del Vado, is treated in Brooks, *Captives and Cousins,* serving as evidence for growing interdependency between the pastoral and plains borderlands, and the growing distance between borderland New Mexican villagers and their Spanish administrators.

12. McNitt, *Navajo Wars,* 72. "Carta à jefe politico sobre la venta de las tierras en Encinal y Cuvero para Francisco Baca, 1832," SANM, vol. 1, no. 1304; RSG, reel 6, frame 1832.

13. This view appears widely in the literature (beginning with Reeve's work in the 1950s through McNitt's 1972 monograph) and is reproduced in Daniel Tyler, "Mexican Indian Policy in New Mexico," *NMHR* 55, no. 2 (1980): 101–20, and in Thomas D. Hall's *Social Change in the Southwest, 1350–1880* (Lawrence: University of Kansas Press, 1989), 161.

14. Tyler, "Mexican Indian Policy" 115–16.

15. Long stagnant, New Mexico's *vecino* population increased dramatically after 1800, growing from 15,000 to 26,000 by 1821, and to 61,525 by 1850. In 1850, Valencia County on the Navaho border had the largest population of any territorial county (14,180). This coincides with a rapid expansion of settlement up the Río Puerco, first at Cebolleta (1800), then Cubero (1833). For an in-depth treatment of New Mexican economic expansion to 1820, see Ross H. Frank, "From Settler to Citizen: Economic Development and Cultural Change in Late Colonial New Mexico, 1750–1820" (Ph.D. diss., University of California, Berkeley, 1992). Martín González de la Vara notes a period of economic growth between 1821 and 1836 but finds the province struggling to maintain fiscal and political connections with a central government in turmoil; "La Política del Federalismo en Nuevo México, 1821–1836," *Historia Mexicana* 36, no. 1 (1986): 81–112. For a glowing (and probably exaggerated) report of New Mexico's economy in the period following independence, see "The Ojeada of Lic. Antonio Barreiro of 1832," in *Three New Mexico Chronicles: The Exposición of Don Pedro Bautista Pino, 1812; the Ojeada of Lic. Antonio Barreiro, 1832; and the Additions by Don José Agustín de Escudero, 1849,* ed. and trans. H. Bailey Carroll and J. Villasana Haggard (Albuquerque: Quivira Society, 1942), 109. Barreiro makes distinctions between the formal sheep trade, monopolized by a few families, and the informal "commerce in hides" conducted by the lowest and middle orders. Conservatively, the Navaho population appears to have more than doubled during the period 1800–1864, from 5,000 to 11,000 at the time of the Bosque Redondo census (most observers estimated some 2,000 Navahos never surrendered to U.S. authorities). Concurrently, Navaho sheep

flocks appear to have increased from approximately 100,000 in 1800 to a high point of 500,000 by 1850; Lynn R. Bailey, *If You Take My Sheep: The Evolution and Conflicts of Navajo Pastoralism, 1630–1868* (Pasadena: Westernlore Publications, 1980), 76–77.

16. Frank D. Reeve broke ground in the historical study of Navaho-Spanish relations, identifying cycles of peace and conflict; see "Navaho-Spanish Wars, 1680–1720," *NMHR* 33, no. 3 (1958): 205–31; "Navaho-Spanish Peace, 1720s–1770s," *NMHR* 34, no. 1 (1959): 9–40; "Navaho-Spanish Diplomacy, 1770–1790," *NMHR* 35, no. 3 (1960): 200–235. Lynn R. Bailey followed with an important but poorly referenced and conceptualized study of Spanish and Mexican slaving, *Indian Slave Trade in the Southwest* (Los Angeles: Westernlore Press, 1966). Frank McNitt explored the nexus of raid and reprisal in *Navajo Wars*, but paid little attention to Navaho seizure of Mexican captives, thus missing the reciprocal and redistributive aspects of the trade. Most recently, working as a tribal researcher for Navaho claims under the ICC, David M. Brugge has examined baptismal records for Navaho captives in New Mexico, as well as other tribes, and includes a chapter on Navaho slavery. As a documentary project, his work offers little in the way of a thesis or conceptual framework. See *Navajos in the Catholic Church Records of New Mexico, 1694–1875* (1968; Tsaile: Navajo Community College Press, 1985).

17. For a treatment of the reciprocal capture and assimilation of women and children in the New Mexico borderlands from a feminist perspective, see James F. Brooks, " 'This Evil Extends Especially . . . to the Feminine Sex': Negotiating Captivity in the New Mexico Borderlands," *Feminist Studies* 22, no. 2 (1996): 279–309.

18. The moral and economic webs established through *compadrazgo* relations in New Mexico remain understudied. The best local study to date is found in Frances Swadesh Quintana, *Pobladores: Hispanic Americans of the Ute Frontier* (1974; reprint, Aztec, 1990), 206–10. Quintana notes a carryover of the Old World endogamous functions of the institution among New Mexican elites, but she also sees a "New World" system that "helped to stabilize relations between native Indian populations and Spanish and mestizo groups" (207). Recently, Sandra Jaramillo Macias has begun tracing nineteenth-century *compadrazgo* webs in the Taos area; see her "Bound by Family: Women and Cultural Change in Territorial Taos," paper presented at the Carson Foundation, Taos, New Mexico, July 30, 1994.

19. See Sarah Garcia, "The Navahos," interview with Lester Raines, 31 August 1936, in WPA Writer's Project File 5, drawer 5, folio 50, no. 26, Museum of New Mexico, Santa Fe.

20. See Juan Pablo Apodaca vs. Manuela Chaves, District Court Records, Valencia County, Civil Case 329 (1861); Mariano Yrrisarri vs. Francisco Montoya et uxor, District Court Records, Bernalillo County, Civil Cases 259, 262 (1861, 1862);

Manuel Yrrisarri vs. Vicenta Arranda, District Court Cases, Bernalillo County, Civil Case 302 (1864).

21. For example, see the *testamento* of Maria de la Candelaria Gonzales, dated 1750, in which she "emancipated" her Indian *criada* with the condition that she "watch over and assist my daughter as if she were her mother" (SANM, vol. 1, no. 344; RSG, reel 2, frames 765–69); the *testamento* of Don Santiago Roibal, 1762, in which his *criada* is granted clear title to a parcel of land "in appreciation of years of service without salary" (fragment in the New Mexico State Records Center and Archives, Land Grant Records); and the case of José Riano's contestation of Gregoria Gongora's will in 1739, when he specifically excepted from the disputed property "a piece of land for the *india* who raised my youngest and other children" (SANM, vol. 2, no. 427; reel 7, frames 1023–25).

22. H. P. Mera, *The "Slave Blanket,"* General Series Bulletin 5, Laboratory of Anthropology (Santa Fe, 1938).

23. See Brooks, "This Evil Extends Especially . . . ," for the case of Juana Hurtado Galván, taken captive by Navahos in 1680, and redeemed in 1696. She settled on lands once held by her *encomendero* father near Zia Pueblo, and until her death in 1753 acted as a key intercultural trader between Pueblos, Spanish, and Navahos from her *rancho* near present-day San Ysidro. See SANM, vol. 2, no. 367; reel 6, frames 1010–23. Her case and others illustrating close trade links through kinship are discussed in Frances Swadesh, "The Structure of Hispanic-Indian Relations in New Mexico," in *The Survival of Spanish American Villages*, ed. Paul M. Kutsche (Colorado Springs: Colorado College Press, 1980), 53–61.

24. See C. C. Marino, "Los Selboyetanos y los Navahos," manuscript in New Mexico State Records Center and Archives, Santa Fe. Ruth Underhill claims that Navaho was used by both Zuni and Hopi as the language of diplomacy; *The Navajos* (Norman: University of Oklahoma Press, 1956), 65.

25. McNitt, *Navajo Wars,* 105–6, 169; another site named Moquino exists as the upper plaza of the village of Abiquiu, apparently due to the settlement of returning Tewa refugees in the 1740s. See Quintana, *Pobladores,* 22.

26. Frederick Webb Hodge, "The Early Navaho and Apache," *American Anthropologist* (o.s.) 8 (1895): 223–40; Washington Matthews, ed. and trans., *Navaho Legends* (Boston: American Folk-Lore Society, 1897), 29–32.

27. See Brooks, "The Political Economy of Captive Exchange," paper presented at the annual meeting of the Western History Association, Denver, Colorado, October 12, 1995.

28. W. W. Hill, "Navaho Warfare," *Yale University Publications in Anthropology* 5 (1936): 3–26; based on interviews with Curley of Chinlé, Roan Horse of Crystal, and Son of the Late Smith, of Fort Defiance (1933).

29. Gary Witherspoon, *Navajo Kinship and Marriage* (Chicago: University of Chicago Press, 1975), 23–28. David F. Aberle reports that in the late nineteenth century, 50 percent of Navaho men had "two or more wives," often sisters or classificatory sisters. Since by 1890 unequal sex-ratios consequent to the wars of the 1860s would have declined, polygyny probably reflected persistent differentials in men's wealth. See "Navaho," in *Matrilineal Kinship*, ed. David Schenider and Kathleen Gough (Berkeley: University of California Press, 1961), 122–25.

30. Hill, "Navaho Warfare," 14–15.

31. See McNitt, *Navajo Wars*, Appendix B, 434–35, for Ygnacio Maria Sanchez Vergara's report to Don Pedro Maria de Allande concerning the formation of the Diné Ana'aii; original in SANM, vol. 2, no. 2736; reel 19, frames 172–75. Quotation from "The *Ojeada* of Lic. Antonio Barreiro of 1832," in Carroll and Haggard, *Three New Mexico Chronicles*, 133.

32. According to the Franciscan Fathers, who evangelized among them in the nineteenth century, weaving remained the "sacred trust of Navaho women." See *An Ethnologic Dictionary of the Navaho Language* (New York: The Franciscan Fathers, 1910), 423–24. This probably helped to maintain the relatively egalitarian nature of Navaho gender relations, as compared to areas like the U.S. Southeast, where the deerskin trade among the Creek and Choctaw seems to have undercut the gender division of labor, and the Great Plains, where the hide trade produced similar erosion. See Kathryn E. Holland Braund, *Deerskins and Duffels: The Creek Indian Trade with Anglo-America, 1685–1815* (Lincoln: University of Nebraska Press, 1993); Richard White, *The Roots of Dependency: Subsistence, Environment, and Social Change Among the Choctaws, Pawnees, and Navahos* (Lincoln: University of Nebraska Press, 1983), 96–146; Alan M. Klein, "The Political-Economy of Gender: A 19th Century Plains Indian Case Study," in *The Hidden Half: Studies of Plains Indian Women*, ed. Patricia Albers and Beatrice Medicine (Lanham, Md.: University Press of America, 1983), 143–73.

33. An example of domestic slavery as a boundary-marking institution may be seen in James H. Vaughan's treatment of *mafakur* slavery among the Margi of northeastern Nigeria. Of this, Vaughan contends that "the outstanding general characteristic of *mafakur* is that all mafa, without regard to political position, private influence, or wealth, hold in common a status that in structural terms is fundamentally and irrevocably intermediate with regard to membership in Margi society." See "Mafajur: A Limbic Institution of the Margi," in *Slavery in Africa: Historical and Anthropological Perspectives*, ed. Suzanne Miers and Igor Kopytoff (Madison: University of Wisconsin Press, 1977), 85–102; quote, 100.

34. See Brugge, *Navajos in the Catholic Church Records*, 138.

35. For a description of the *milicias* in the late colonial period, see Don Pedro

Baptista Pino, *Exposición Sucinta y Sencilla de la Provincia del Nuevo Mexico* (Cadiz, 1812), in Carroll and Haggard, *Three New Mexico Chronicles*, 67 ff. In an intriguing reference to a widely held understanding of the vulnerability of women and children in borderland raiding, Pino states, "Llega, para decirlo de una vez, á tal extremo este mal que hasta la libertad de los hijos es sacrificada para cumplir con aquella obligacion como vecino" [Conditions have reached a point that it becomes necessary that the liberty of the children is sacrificed in order to fulfill the obligations of the citizen], 16, Cadiz edition.

36. Quintana, *Pobladores*, 55–56. An example is the 1839 campaign of militias from Cebolleta and Abiquiu, in which 9,253 sheep, 222 horses and mules, and seven Navaho captives were taken and one Mexican captive was redeemed between October 13 and December 13. See "Noticia al Público, por Disposición del Exelentísmo Sr. Gobernador y Commandante General deste Departmento de Nuevo Mexico, diciembre 16, 1839," Huntington Library, San Marino, California. For a circular condemning the "grave evil" suffered by the province due to the traffic in stolen stock that New Mexicans maintained with Apache and Navaho *ladrones* in the Socorro, Cebolleta, and Jemez regions, see "José María Oritz, Juez de Paz de San Ildefonso á Manuel Armijo, 22 febrero, 1843," Sender Collection, no. 282, reel 2, frames 533–35, New Mexico State Records Center and Archives, Santa Fe.

37. On October 5, 1846, Brigadier General Stephen Watts Kearny authorized Mexicans and Pueblos "to form War Parties, to march into the Country of their enemies, the Navajoes, to recover their Property, to make reprisals and obtain redress for the many insults received from them"; McNitt, *Navajo Wars*, 101. Later, on March 18, 1851, Governor Calhoun authorized civilians "to form Volunteer Corps to protect their families, property, and homes. . . . The property which may be captured from any hostile tribe of Indians, by any company raised under the foregoing provisions, shall be disposed of in accordance with the laws and customs heretofore existing in the territory"; in Abel, *Official Correspondence*, 300–302. As the politics of the territorial legislature turned from anti-slavery to pro-slavery, the Militia Act of 1851 was amended in 1860 to exclude the governor as ultimate dispenser of captured people and property, leaving this prerogative to "any man of experience and good character who shall raise and organize a force."

38. Marino, "Los Seboyetanos y los Navahos."

39. John O. Baxter, *Las Carneradas: Sheep Trade in New Mexico, 1700–1860* (Albuquerque: University of New Mexico Press, 1987), 61–110.

40. Ibid., 28–30.

41. These figures come from a report by Navaho agent Henry Dodge in 1853, published as "The Arrival of Captain Dodge," in the *Santa Fe Gazette*, December 31, 1853, microfilm in the New Mexico State Records Center and Archives, Santa Fe.

42. Lawrence David Weiss, *The Development of Capitalism in the Navajo Nation: A Political-Economic History* (Minneapolis: MEP Publications, 1984), 31; citing Klara Kelley, "Navajo Pastoralism Before Fort Sumner," manuscript (1976).

43. New Mexican sheep estimates may be found in William M. Denevan, "Livestock Numbers in Nineteenth-Century New Mexico, and the Problem of Gullying in the Southwest," *Annals of the Association of American Geographers*, December 1967, 691–703; estimates, 697–99. In the 1830s and 1840s, the six major sheep *ricos* exported some 200,000 sheep each year to Mexico; some families may have owned as many as 500,000 sheep themselves. See Baxter, *Las Carneradas*, 89–110.

44. For the New Mexico–California trade, see Joseph J. Hill, "Spanish and Mexican Exploration and Trade Northwest from New Mexico into the Great Basin, 1765–1853," *Utah Historical Quarterly* 3 (1930): 3–23; idem, "The Old Spanish Trail," *Hispanic American Historical Review* 6 (1921): 444–73; Baxter, *Las Carneradas*, 89 ff.; for the Yokuts horse-raiding network, see George Harwood Phillips, *Indians and Intruders in Central California, 1769–1849* (Norman: University of Oklahoma Press, 1993). For the lower-order and speculative composition of the caravans, see John Adams Hussey, "The New Mexico-California Caravan of 1847–1848," *NMHR* 18, no. 1 (1943): 1–16.

45. For detailed losses (including cattle, horses, mules, and captives) attributed to Navaho raiders, see Brooks, *Captives and Cousins*. On the term *ansh'í*, see Franciscan Fathers, *Ethnological Dictionary*, 503–4. On the raiders, see Hill, "Navaho Warfare," 3–19; Underhill, *The Navahos*, 68–72.

46. See José de Madriaga to Governor Pérez, 26 June 1836, in Mexican Archives, New Mexico State Records Center and Archives, Santa Fe, reel 21, frames 612–14. López had taken 3,500 sheep and goats from Madriaga's herders on the Río Salado.

47. See Enclosure of despatch from Luna to Vigil, in Sarracino to Calhoun, 20 January 1851, in Abel, ed., *Official Correspondence*, 283–86. William A. Keleher, *Turmoil in New Mexico, 1846–1868* (Santa Fe: Rydal Press, 1952), 138, note 93.

48. See Brooks, *Captives and Cousins*, Appendix B: New Mexican Livestock and Captive Raids, 1780–1864.

49. Brugge, *Navajos in the Catholic Church Records*, 22–23; Navaho baptisms for the period total 1,241. Although male *binaalté* could own both tangible and ceremonial property, marry, and attain prominence in tribal affairs, they remained subject to sale or transfer through inheritance, as Louisa Weatherill, wife of an American trader, discovered when she inherited thirty-two of Hoskannini's *binaalté* when the headman died in 1909. For a discussion of these and other cases, see Brugge (127–44).

50. McNitt, *Navajo Wars*, 26–51, 310, 364; Calhoun to Brown, 12 October

1850, in Abel, ed., *Official Correspondence*, 262–64; for firsthand accounts of Diné Ana'aii slaving against other Navahos, see Lansing Bloom, "The Reverend Hiram Walker Read, Baptist Missionary," *NMHR* 18 (1942): 113–47; for the Hopi view of these raids, see Katherine Bartlett, "Hopi History, II: The Navajo Wars," *Museum Notes* 8, no. 7 (1936): 35.

51. Tiana Bighorse, *Bighorse the Warrior*, ed. Noel Bennett (Tucson: University of Arizona Press, 1990), 18–21.

52. See Benedict's testimony, given in July 1865, in *Annual Report of the Commissioner of Indian Affairs, 1865* (Washington, D.C.: Government Printing Office, 1866), 325–27. For census figures, see *Compendium of the Ninth Census of the United States and Its Territories* (Washington, D.C.: Government Printing Office, 1870), 108, which lists figures for 1850, 1860, and 1870.

53. Calhoun to Brown, 12 February 1850, in Abel, ed., *Official Correspondence*, 141, 149–50.

54. Francis Paul Prucha, *The Great Father: The United States Government and the American Indian*, abridged ed. (Lincoln: University of Nebraska Press, 1984), 122–27.

55. Col. Sumner to Maj. General R. Jones, 20 November 1851, in Abel, ed., *Official Correspondence*, 445.

56. Lawrence R. Murphy, "Reconstruction in New Mexico," *NMHR* 43, no. 2 (1968): 99–115, esp. 100.

57. William Watts Hart Davis, *El Gringo, or New Mexico and Her People* (1857; Santa Fe: Rydal Press, 1938), 84, 303.

58. See Loomis Morton Ganaway, "New Mexico and the Sectional Controversy, 1846–61," *NMHR* 18, no. 3 (1943): 205–46, at 229. This phenomenon predated the American conquest, for Charles Bent had written U.S. envoy Manuel Alvarez in Santa Fe on March 30, 1845, that "*Cumancharus*" had brought in five "runaway negros" from the Plains that year, and he thought this might provoke conflict between the United States and Mexico. See Benjamin Read Papers, box 1, no. 71, March 30, 1845, New Mexico State Records Center and Archives. On Brown and Winters, see *Territory v. Harriet Brown* (1859) and *Territory v. John Winters* (1861), District Court, Santa Fe County Criminal Cases, in New Mexico State Records Center and Archives.

59. See "Slavery in the Territory of New Mexico," *Records of the 36th Congress, 1st Session, Report No. 508, House of Representatives* (Washington, D.C.: Government Printing Office, 1860), 1–39; Loomis Morton Ganaway, "New Mexico and the Sectional Controversy, 1846–1861," *NMHR* 17, no. 3 (1943): 205–46; 17, no. 4 (1943): 325–48; Lawrence R. Murphy, *Frontier Crusader: William F. M. Arny* (Tucson: University of Arizona Press, 1972), 115–34. For Connelly's Proclamation, see

"Condition of the Indian Tribes," *Report of the Joint Special Committee Appointed Under Joint Resolution of March 3, 1865* (Washington, D.C.: Government Printing Office, 1867), 333.

60. Darlis A. Miller, "Hispanos and the Civil War in New Mexico, A Reconsideration," *NMHR* 54, no. 2 (1979): 105–23.

61. For Carson's request that Ute scouts be allowed to retain, and resell to New Mexicans, captured Navaho women and children, see Carson to Carleton, 24 July 1863, and Carleton's response of August 18, in *Navajo Roundup: Selected Correspondence of Kit Carson's Expedition against the Navajo, 1863–1865*, ed. Lawrence C. Kelly (Boulder: Pruett Publishing Co., 1970), 29–32. For the Costilla and Conejos censuses, see Appendix D, "The Traffic in Slaves," in McNitt, *Navajo Wars*, 441–46.

62. William Haas Moore, *Chiefs, Agents, and Soldiers: Conflict on the Navajo Frontier, 1868–1882* (Albuquerque: University of New Mexico Press, 1994), chap. 4.

63. Testimony of Colonel Christopher Carson in "Condition of the Indian Tribes," 96–97.

64. See the running editorial debate between the *Sante Fe Weekly Gazette* (supporting internment) and the *New Mexican* (opposing the policy) in issues of 1864–68, microfilms in the New Mexico State Records Center and Archives.

65. Interview collection by Lou Sage Batchen, 19 June 1940, titled "*El Pelón: An Old Native Custom.*" Informants include José Librado Aron Gurulé, age 89, José Garcia y Trujillo, age 94, both of whom served under Carson. WPA Oral History Project, originals in New Mexico State Records Center and Archives.

66. Lt. Colonel Shaw to Major Benjamin Cutler, 12 August 1865; in the National Archives, New Mexico Superintendency microcopy T-21 (hereafter NA, NMS T-21); reel 6, film in the Center for the Study of the Southwest, Fort Lewis College, Durango, Colorado.

67. Copy, President Andrew Johnson to the Executive Departments, 9 June 1865, NA, NMS T-21.

68. Felipe Delgado, Superintendent of Indian Affairs in the Territory of New Mexico, to Commissioner of Indian Affairs William T. Dole, 16 July 1865, NA, NMS T-21.

69. Lt. George McDermott to Lt. Col. Shaw, 13 August 1865, NA, NMS T-21.

70. "Testimony of Chief Justice Kirby Benedict before the Doolittle Committee," in *Annual Report of the Commissioner of Indian Affairs, 1865*, 225–26.

71. Brugge, *Navajos in the Catholic Church Records*, 22–29; quote, 28. Navahos seem to have struck both the Hopi and Zuni pueblos at intervals of two or three years during the 1850s and 1860s, especially around harvest time, in order to steal corn and take captives. See J. Lee Correll, *Through White Men's Eyes: A Contribution to*

Navajo History (Window Rock: Navajo Community College Press, 1980), 1:311, 379; for alternating patterns of trade and warfare, see Underhill, *The Navajos*, 64–66.

72. The Territorial Legislature abolished peonage in New Mexico on March 2, 1867, but the practice still proved common in the late 1870s. See Lawrence R. Murphy, "Reconstruction in New Mexico," *NMHR* 43, no. 2 (1968): 99–115. For a treatment of Grant's Peace Policy (1869–82) and its roots in postbellum liberal reformers, see Robert H. Keller, Jr., *American Protestantism and United States Indian Policy, 1869–82* (Lincoln: University of Nebraska Press, 1983).

73. Murphy, "Reconstruction in New Mexico," 106–7.

74. Moore, *Chiefs, Agents, and Soldiers*, 98–100.

75. Reeve, "The Government and the Navaho," 22 (Riordan). Later report quoted in Brugge, *Navajos in the Catholic Church Records*, 142–43. Bowman [Riordan's successor] to Commissioner of Indian Affairs, 3 September 1884, *Annual Report of the Commissioner of Indian Affairs for the Year 1884* (Washington, D.C.: Government Printing Office, 1884), 401.

76. See household number 105, village of Cubero, Valencia County, Territory of New Mexico, *Ninth Census of the United States: 1870*, Schedule 1, p. 9. See Schedule 1 of the *Eighth Census of the United States: 1860*, household no. 1949, p. 218.

77. For overviews, see Robert J. Rosenbaum and Robert W. Larson, "Mexicano Resistance to the Expropriation of Grant Lands in New Mexico," in *Land, Water, and Culture: New Perspectives on Hispanic Land Grants*, ed. Charles L. Briggs and John R. Van Ness (Albuquerque: University of New Mexico Press, 1987), 269–312; Roxanne Dunbar Ortiz, *Roots of Resistance: Land Tenure in New Mexico, 1680–1980* (Los Angeles: UCLA Chicano Studies, 1980), 91–125.

78. Jenkins, "Baltazar Baca 'Grant,' " 87–105. Lands east of the village of Cebolleta now contain the world's largest open-pit uranium mine.

79. For the role of the Spanish Colonial Arts Society in inventing this tradition, see Charles L. Briggs, *The Woodcarvers of Córdova, New Mexico: Social Dimensions of an Artistic "Revival"* (Knoxville: University of Tennessee Press, 1980); and Charles Montgomery, "Glorifying the Spanish Folk: New Mexico's Arts and Crafts Revival, 1924–36," paper presented at the conference on Power of Ethnic Identities in the Southwest, Huntington Library, San Marino, California, September 23–24, 1994.

80. Moore, *Chiefs, Agents, and Soldiers*, 20–30; Sherman quote, 23; "Navaho Cavalry," 100. On the railroad protection, see Frank D. Reeve, "The Government and the Navaho, 1883–1888," *NMHR* 18, no. 1 (1943): 17–51, esp. 23–25.

81. Chee Dodge is the most obvious example. See Underhill, *The Navahos*, 230 ff.; see also White, *Roots of Dependency*, 250–89.

82. Myra Ellen Jenkins, "A History of the Cañoncito Navahos," manuscript in the Center for the Study of the Southwest, Fort Lewis College, Durango, Colorado.

83. For example, on July 20, 1990, the author interviewed Helen Gomez Silva in Bayfield, Colorado. Ms. Silva recalled a Gomez family *criado* named Juan José Pena, a Nambé [Pueblo] Indian who served the family until his death in 1931. Although called "Tío Juan" by the children, the family also referred to him, "affectionately," as their *esclavo*.

Making "Indians" in British Columbia

Power, Race, and the Importance of Place

JOHN LUTZ

Since race is one of the most enduring categories North Americans use to describe themselves, it is no wonder that historians and other social scientists use it, alongside class and gender, to explain uneven distributions of power, past and present. Indeed, the American Historical Association's membership form asks applicants to declare their "Race/ethnic origin" as African American, Native American, Asian American, Latino, White, or Other. With the exception of Latino, these choices differ little from Linnaeus's 1758 list of the varieties of mankind,[1] and this illustrates an important point. Despite all the attention to race, historians have generally accepted, rather than examined, racial categories inherited from the eighteenth and nineteenth centuries. Race has been seen as a neutral, natural category.

Building on research in related disciplines, my goal here is to historicize race—to argue that, for discernible reasons, race is a concept that has differed in meaning over time and in different places. Race and the racial category I focus on—Indian—have histories of their own, and they vary across continents, across borders, and even across town. In other words, the history of race is understandable only in relation to place.

Western scholars long ago rejected the once popular notion that people are genetically programmed to inherit the class status of their parents. Similarly, the nineteenth-century idea that the intellect, morality, emotional stability, and religiosity of men and women are biologically determined has been superseded. Class and gender differences once attributed to biology are now largely seen as products of culture and socialization. The discussion of race has begun to move in a similar direction. Since the 1930s, population geneticists have undermined the idea of a biological basis for racial categorization. They have found no gene that makes us "white," "black," "yellow," or "red." Although some geographically defined human populations have different skin pigments, hair textures, or facial features than others, there is no sharp break between these groupings. Those criteria all exist on a continuum. Indeed, scientists have found more genetic variability within the well-known divisions we call races than there is between them.[2]

These findings raise important questions for a historical understanding of race and racism. If there is no biological basis for the concept of race, there must be a sociological one. If skin, hair, and bone characteristics that we have been socialized to see as the important distinguishing features are no more "natural" boundaries between populations than blood group, or left- or right-handedness, why have the former characteristics divided the world's population? One way to answer this is to chart the construction of particular racial categories—in this case the relationship between race and power in the making of Indians—in a particular place over an extended period.[3] Starting in the late 1970s, scholars like Robert Berkhofer, Brian Dippie, and Daniel Francis began to focus attention on the images of Indians created by white society. I wish to argue that the idea of race itself, and not just one race's image of another, is socially constructed and linked to particular organizations of power. The distinction is an important one. The examination of how one race imagines the other assumes the existence of separate races. By contrast, the focus on racial definition charts the active creation of racial categories.[4]

The locale under my lens, British Columbia, is particularly instructive. Richard White has already noted that race in the West "has always been not so much of a biological fact as a cultural and historical creation."[5] After the 1846 boundary settlement, "Oregon Country" north of the 49th parallel became British Columbia, and the racial definitions in the American and Canadian far wests diverged. This article looks at the social construction and then reconstruction of "Indian" at different historical moments: during the first encounters; during the maritime fur trade, and then the land-based fur trade, when there was no United States or Canada on the West Coast; subsequently in the British colonial period; and finally in the aftermath of the 1871 confederation with Canada.

Words are the main tools for bringing the past into present visibility, but they are also the main handicap. It is hard to argue that race is socially constructed when our language assumes it is a biological reality. Phrases like *Indian blood, mixed-blood,* and *half-breed* are historic artifacts steeped in a worldview of inheritable racial traits. This is equally true of the shorthand labels like *red, white,* and *black,* which presume racial identities based on skin color. In English, "race" has become a neutral, biological phenomenon and "racism" a social one. But racism depends on a definition of race as part of a hierarchically ordered system that has been socially constructed to redistribute power. We urgently need a new vocabulary free of the language of biological determinism. In the interim I have adopted the uneasy compromise of challenging the existing terminology while at the same time using it.[6]

BEYOND THE PALE: NAMING "INDIANS"

When Captain George Vancouver, the first European to explore the inland waterways of British Columbia, called the indigenous people Indians in 1792, he placed them in a category already familiar to Europeans.[7] With this nomenclature, the indigenous people of the Pacific Northwest were classified with all the aboriginal people of North, South, and Central America—not to mention, thanks to the famous if disoriented navigator Christopher Columbus, the inhabitants of India. Biophysical (phenotypical) differences had something to do with this racial classification. The people he encountered on the Northwest Coast did have certain physical features different from those of Vancouver and his crew.

Yet, the phenotypical features of the people did not cry out for definition as Indians. Indigenous Americans, all called Indians, had a vast range of skin color, facial, and other features, spoke hundreds of different languages, and had cultures with a range of differences greater than that among the nations of Europe. The physically "repugnant" characteristics, like sloped foreheads and lip labrets, described by Vancouver, were quickly discovered to be cultural rather than natural, and many early observers remarked that, by their features, the people of the Northwest Coast more resembled Asians than other indigenous Americans. Others commented on how closely the coastal Indians resembled southern Europeans.[8] The first European expedition to the Northwest Coast described the indigenous people as "stocky and good looking, white in colour. . . . Many of them have blue eyes." If physical characteristics had been the main criteria for racial categorization, some of these northwest peoples belong in the Asian or European categories. But race does not depend on physical differences.[9] The category "Indian" had less to do with phenotypical features than with the relationship Europeans wished to have with the aboriginal people. Indian was a useful category for occupants of newly discovered lands.

For Columbus, the word *Indian* meant "inhabitant of India" and did not have the racial implications it had for Vancouver. In Columbus's time the word "race" did not exist in common parlance. As a concept it emerged in the sixteenth century—growing out of a folk category associated with inherited traits observed in animal breeding. By the eighteenth century the word had spread into all European languages and been expanded to include inheritable traits in humans. By the time of Vancouver's voyage, scientists had adopted these folk categories and divided human beings into "scientific" categories or races.[10]

The most influential among these scientists was Carolus Linnaeus, who worked out a system of classifying all living things according to certain visible criteria. When it came to classifying mankind, he combined his knowledge of heredity with descriptions of seafarers returning from distant regions of the world.[11] In his historic *System Naturae* of 1758, Linnaeus proposed that *Homo sapiens* fell into six varieties: monsters (dwarfs and giants), wild men, Africans, Americans (Indians), Asiatics, and Europeans. Like other classifiers of his time, Linnaeus associated phenotypical features with social characteristics. Thus he described the American (Indian) as copper colored, with hair black, straight, and thick, wide nostrils, scanty beard, and socially obstinate, content, and free. Asiatics were melancholy, rigid, severe, haughty, and covetous; Africans—phlegmatic, relaxed, crafty, indolent, and negligent. By contrast, Europeans were sanguine, gentle, acute, and inventive. Systems of governance were also linked to racial type. Asiatics were governed by opinions, Africans by caprice, and Americans (Indians) by custom. Europeans were defined as "governed by laws."[12]

Between 1770 and 1781, Johann Blumenbach, a German professor of medicine, promulgated a competing system of five varieties of humankind, which still enjoys wide usage today: Caucasian, Mongolian, Ethiopian, American, and Malayan. Blumenbach popularized the notion that all humans came from a single ancestor made in the image of God. That image was European. All other races had degenerated from this norm according to the environmental circumstances in which they lived. This "scientific system" ranked races according to a Eurocentric notion of physical beauty. The classificatory term "Caucasian" for European originated from his belief that the most beautiful women in the world came from the Caucasus region in Russia.[13]

Linnaeus had defined the American Indians as obstinate and carefree and the Africans as indolent, but the negative typing of non-Europeans blurred in the field. The early visitors to the Pacific Northwest were unanimous in their condemnation of Indians as indolent or lazy.[14] In the late eighteenth and early nineteenth centuries, "indolence" was generally applied as part of the definition of all non-Europeans. Wherever Europeans described indigenous populations, their conclusions were strikingly similar. Robert Brown, an early West Coast ethnographer, reflected this in his 1871 encyclopedic *Races of Mankind*, which reported: "The Central Africans, *like all barbarous or savage people*, are a lazy race."[15] "When you compare the nations of Asia or Africa with those of Europe," the difference, wrote Frenchman George Depping, is that "the former seemed to be plunged into a state of indolence as prevents them performing anything great." Depping proposed a moral science, "ethnography," that would study the indolent character of all non-Europeans, including "the savages of America [who] are so indolent that they chose rather to endure hunger than to cultivate the earth."[16] This last quotation hints at an ideological reason why non-Europeans might be defined in this way. So long as non-Europeans could be defined as "indolent" (or "vanishing," and preferably both), the imperial project of seizing the land, resources, and labor of the rest of the world was legitimate.

PARTNERS IN FURS

The characterizations of Indians that emerged in the eighteenth-century literature of exploration and the maritime fur trade sparked by Cook's 1778 voyage changed according to the needs and experience of the European classifiers, and these varied from place to place and time to time. The explorers and ship-based traders visited the West Coast only for a few months at a time, and often only once. Their homes, and their points of cultural reference, were in the coastal cities of Europe or the eastern American seaboard. These short-term visitors described aboriginal people in the most unflattering terms, rhetorically hesitant to find any point of connection with these "savages."[17]

Beginning in the early nineteenth century, small numbers of European men settled for long periods among the aboriginal people of the Northwest Coast. These fur traders depended on aboriginal people for food and security as well as furs. Their familiarity and dependence modified the racial definitions inherited from the maritime trade.[18] Many among this second wave of fur traders formed long-term relationships with aboriginal women or their so-called mixed-blood daughters. As Roderick Finlayson, the senior officer of the fur-trading Hudson's Bay Company (HBC) at Fort Victoria, observed, "Our French Canadian and Sandwich Islanders took wives from the native tribes," a practice which was encouraged because it "had a tendency to keep them in the service of the company."[19] Most of the senior officials of the company on the coast, including Finlayson and James Douglas, later governor of Vancouver Island and British Columbia, also married or formed long-term relationships with aboriginal or mixed-blood women. In addition to providing companionship, household labor, and families, these unions often had the political goal of cementing alliances with powerful aboriginal families.[20]

Since most traders had medium or long-term intimate relationships with aboriginal women, "Indian" was remade as something less strange and the language of race was redefined to suit the new circumstances. Several prominent fur traders published their thoughts on Indians, and most recorded something of their feelings in their correspondence.[21] Although they drew distinctions, these traders saw no firm dividing line between themselves and aboriginal people. They could see some of the virtues of their aboriginal trading partners and often could see, in their vices or vanities, parallels with European society. Alexander Ross compared the Indians' practice of flattening infants' foreheads to the European habit of compressing women's waists. He noted: "All nations, civilised as well as savage, have their peculiar prejudices." Peter Skene Ogden commented unfavorably on what he saw as the Indian love for gaming, but pointed out he was also "humiliated by the remembrance of similar scenes" back home. In his first encounters with the Kwakwaka'wakw people at Fort Rupert, J. S. Helmcken could even see their "boldness, bravery, war tendencies and aggressiveness being just what we admire in our own countrymen and ancestors." He was led to the conclusion:

> Their conduct to their friends and the peaceful condition of their villages, their faithfulness, must come in for a big share of praise. Untamed they were open and intelligent, not sneaks. They had plenty to eat, homes to live in, fire and clothing; in fact were provident, self-reliant, as so far well to do. Have civilized [men] much more?[22]

The land-based fur traders also considered Indians as indolent, but in fur-trade parlance the meaning of the term changed. George Simpson, governor of Hudson's Bay Company, declared the Indians of the Columbia "indolent and lazy to the extreme" in his 1825 tour of inspection, even though he noted that they were engaged in numerous productive activities.[23] They were indolent because they had little need for European goods, and so chose not to hunt extensively. In the fur-trade context, as Mary Black-Rogers points out, "indolence is an attribute of those who show independence of the fur trade."[24]

To fur traders, compared with explorers, the Indian became less exotic and more familiar.[25] The fur-trade journals show less frequent general characterizations of Indians and more discussion of the traits of individuals or, more commonly, local groups of Indians. The "scientific" racialization slipped away as a local culture developed in isolation, for most of the year, from outside influences. Indians, whites, and Kanakas (aboriginal Hawaiians) intermarried extensively, and what emerged was a "middle ground" similar in its multicultural nature to that described by Richard White in the *pays d'en haut* a century before: "Different peoples, to be sure, remained identifiable, but they shaded into each other."[26] Fur traders married into aboriginal families and aboriginal women married into the fur-trade hierarchy. Mixed-blood offspring of these relationships moved easily through fur-trade society. Male children were hired at the various trading posts, and female offspring married other traders. Indians, whites, and mixed-bloods were partners in the fur trade and often partners in the fur robes of the marriage bed.

"INDIANS" IN LAW

When the crown colony of Vancouver Island was established in 1849, the nonaboriginal population was made up entirely of HBC employees, and definitions of *Indian* that developed through the fur trade held sway. James Douglas, the chief local official of the HBC, was, after a brief interval, also appointed to the post of governor, ensuring a continuity of definition between the fur trade and colonial society.

This continuity is more evident when contrasted with the new patterns which developed in the part of Oregon Territory that became American. After the 1846 boundary settlement, most of the senior HBC traders moved to the new British colony, taking with them their Indian or mixed-blood wives and their children. To their way of thinking, there were no major divisions between races. Marriage or birth to a white man brought women and children into white society with full rights. In Washington and Oregon the new governments were dominated by recently arrived white male settlers, who brought more rigid biological definitions of race to the territory.[27] Although many men continued to forge relationships with Indian women, there was a new stigma attached. Such men were called "squaw men," a derogatory term that never gained wide currency in the British Territories. The condemnation of such unions was formalized in Washington Territory in 1854 when interracial marriages were prohibited by law.[28]

In British territory, the fur-trade definitions initially held sway. Indians and "half-breeds" were not legally distinguishable from nonaboriginal people. In law, at least, they had the same political and civic rights, including the right to purchase and later preempt land and to buy and sell alcohol.[29] However, newcomers attracted to the colony had different attitudes toward Indians. To the new wave of immigrants, Indians were a race lower on the "great chain of being" than whites. Indians and mixed-bloods, as well as white men living with them, were considered "purveyors of vice and immorality."[30] Indians were differentiated in law for the first time in 1850 by the first of fourteen treaties which "reserved" land for them at different places on Vancouver Island. In exchange for a lump-sum payment they would surrender the rest of their land. At least this was the understanding of the Euroamerican participants,[31] who believed themselves to belong to a "higher race"—one that would make proper use of the lands the Indians occupied and claimed. There seems to have been little initial ambiguity as to who was Indian and who was not. Since the treaties were made with adult male Indians, and since Europeans had settled on Vancouver Island for less than a decade, the mixed-blood population was still young. There was apparently no need of a definition in law for "Indian" or "white."[32]

The gold rush of 1858 brought a wave of immigrants who challenged the fur traders' control over colonial society. Many of the immigrants were from California, or fresh from the Indian Wars of Oregon and Washington. Some of them denied the humanity of Indians and were prepared to exterminate them.[33] Another large group of immigrants saw themselves as part of a distinct "British race" with a mission to rule the world. Joseph Chamberlain, British secretary of state for the colonies in the 1890s, revealed this sentiment when he declared: "I believe that the British race is the greatest of governing races the world has ever seen." Cecil Rhodes, an emissary of British imperialism across the globe, echoed this attitude: "As I walked, I looked up at the sky and down at the earth, and I said to myself this should be British. And it came to me in that fine, exhilarating air that the British were the best race to rule the world."[34] The British immigrants identified themselves as a "national race" at the pinnacle of human civilization, superior even to Americans and other Europeans. Part of British pride rested on their particular moral fitness, which demanded English "fair play" to colonized people as long as it was consistent with the English, racial hierarchy.[35]

The arrival on Vancouver Island of Britons with this attitude produced a power struggle with the landed fur-trade "aristocracy" involving competing definitions of race. The tone of the dispute is evident in the 1859 remarks of one of the English newcomers: "In my unsophisticated innocence, I foolishly imagined that I was entering a Colony governed by British Institutions, but I was quickly undeceived: it was far worse than a Venetian oligarchy,—a squatocracy of skin traders, ruled by men whose life had been spent in the wilderness in social communion with Indian savages."[36] These new immigrants, like the first explorers, had a definition of race that justified dispossessing the indigenous people. On February 19, 1861, the aptly named Victoria *Colonist* newspaper made the link between race and power clear to its readers: "As an inferior race . . . we believe they must give way in order to make room for a race more enlightened and by nature and habits better fitted to perform the task of converting what is now a wilderness into productive fields and happy homes."

This sentiment was pervasive and long-lasting among immigrants who wanted to make their living from the land and resources of British Columbia. It was still prominent in 1907 when a New Westminster paper reported Reverend R. W. Fraser's comment that God gave North America to the white race to develop and use. The Indians, he said, "had failed to utilize what was theirs."[37] And one of the province's premier industrialists, Henry Bell-Irving, president of a fish-canning corporation, told a federal commission, "It is the destiny of the white man to be worked for by the inferior races."[38]

Yet, until the retirement of Governor Douglas, the legal distinction between Indians and whites remained limited to two laws regarding alcohol and court testimony. In 1858, Douglas had become the governor of the new mainland crown colony of British Columbia, in addition to his earlier appointment on adjacent Vancouver Island. That same year, both colonies passed an Indian Liquor Act intended to stop the consumption of alcohol by Indians. These laws reflected the consensus of fur traders and more recent immigrants that Indians were incapable of handling alcohol and should be treated as legal minors in this one regard.[39]

The other legal element that distinguished Indians from whites under Douglas's governorship was drawn differently by the two colonies. British Columbia passed, in 1859, an act to allow "those unwilling from alleged conscientious motives to be sworn" in legal proceedings. These included Jews, Quakers, and Roman Catholics, as well as aboriginal people, who would not swear on the King James Bible, or were not considered competent to do so. Meanwhile, the colonial legislature on Vancouver Island stone-walled attempts to introduce a measure that would allow aboriginal people to take an oath and thus testify in court.[40] Until the two colonies were united in 1866, under the name British Columbia, aboriginal people on Vancouver Island could not seek protection through the courts. This differ-ence in how the races were created in law between the adjacent colonies stems from a very practical cause. Vancouver Island legislators were con-cerned that allowing Indians to testify would adversely affect the large part of the business community engaged in the illegal sale of liquor to Indians.[41]

Douglas's 1864 retirement signaled the end of the power of the fur traders to control the definition of *Indian*. The next amendments to the Land Act, in 1866, revoked the definition of Indians as real or potential equals. The act removed the right of Indians to buy or preempt (homestead) land, rights they had previously held and used. It declared the province open to preemp-tion for a nominal fee, by whites only.[42]

Laws allocating entitlements by race intensified after British Columbia joined the Canadian Confederation in 1871. In 1872 the provincial "Act to Amend the Qualification and Registration of Voters" removed the right of aboriginal people to vote in provincial and federal elections, enshrining in law the de facto exclusion of aboriginal people from the process of gover-nance. When disenfranchised, aboriginal people comprised over 70 percent of the provincial population. The act also disenfranchised the second largest ethnic group in the province—the Chinese. Legislators were elected by, represented, and drawn from the 25 percent of the population that was "of the white race."[43] In 1876, the right of Indians (and Chinese) to vote in municipal elections was also removed. Thereafter, legislators, responsible only to the minority white population, responded with legislation that re-inforced their racial attitudes and expanded the legal entitlements of whites at the expense of nonwhites.

The most important of the new racializing pieces of legislation was the federal Indian Act of 1876, which literally "re-created" Indians. It estab-lished a new "legal definition" of who was and was not Indian, and declared and defined federal control over a broad spectrum of aboriginal life, includ-ing schooling, health, morality, economy, and governance. The law, which remained fundamentally unchanged for seventy-five years, defined an In-dian as "any male person of Indian blood who is reputed to be a member of an Indian band," plus his wife and his children.[44] An "Indian band" was described as "any tribe, band or body of Indians who own or are interested in a reserve."[45] Any remnant of the fur-trade idea of a vast difference between groups of Indians was lost in the homogenizing force of the Indian Act.

The act clearly stated that "the term person means an individual other than an Indian." Indians were defined as unable to take care of themselves in many aspects of their economic and social lives. Permission in writing was required from the Indian agent before an Indian was allowed to sell hay or wood grown on the reserve. Moreover, "the proceeds arising from the sale or lease of any timber, hay, stone or minerals" did not belong to the Indian but "shall be paid to the Receiver General to the credit of the Indian fund." Indians were not permitted to borrow money based on collateral they owned on the reserve, including their own house. Nor could they sell or give away property they had acquired through money received from the federal government or an Indian band. Nor were they permitted to have alcohol in their possession or to be intoxicated.[46]

The legislation pathologized Indians by declaring them unable to take care of their own affairs. Placed in a category as subjects, but not citizens, they found themselves in a civic cell shared with felons and the insane.[47] Indeed, the state blurred the boundary between Indians and felons by criminalizing for Indians what was normal behavior for everyone else—the consumption of alcohol. Subsequent revisions to the Indian Act also criminalized traditional aboriginal practices. In each instance, the Indian Act legitimated popular associations of Indian as inferior.[48]

THE FLUID BOUNDARIES OF RACE

The social construction of race becomes apparent when it can be redefined, instantly, in law. It is even more obvious when individuals opt to change their race or others do it for them. In Canada, one's legal race was not necessarily permanent. So-called progressive Indians could apply to become citizens, a process known as "enfranchisement." The state could also change one's race. When so few applied for enfranchisement, the law was changed so the government could declare any educated Indian to be a person and not subject to the Indian Act. Indians who were admitted into university, holy orders, or the legal profession automatically became persons, and thus non-Indians. Following the conventions first established in fur-trade society, Indian women who married white men automatically became white. Axiomatically, non-Indian women who married Indians were classified as Indians.[49]

The fluid boundaries of race are most clearly visible in the debate over the status of mixed-bloods and control of access to liquor. In the earlier fur-trade society, mixed-bloods were accepted and their white parentage empha-sized. In settler society it was their Indian parentage that seemed important. It was strongly felt, particularly by the recent immigrants to the province, that in mixed-bloods the Indian "racial strain" outweighed the influence of the white elements. Many, like the Anglican bishop of British Columbia, believed: "Halfbreed children usually sink into a degraded state, combining the force of the white race with the viciousness and lowness of the savage." Indian Agent Lomas reflected the Department of Indian Affairs view: "The Half-Breed element is the source of trouble everywhere, as they combine the worst qualities of each people with few redeeming qualities." For his part, Indian Agent O'Daunt thought that "a breed invariably inclines to the Indian side of the house."[50]

Despite the prevailing popular view that mixed-bloods differed little from Indians, the Indian Act defined Indianness as following the male line. An Indian was a male of Indian blood, his wife, or his children. Since most of the mixed-blood population were offspring of non-Indian men and Indian women, most mixed-bloods were legally white.[51] Indians were not allowed to purchase liquor but mixed-bloods were, and this caused enormous frustra-tion to the Department of Indian Affairs. "It is well known," wrote the superintendent in 1892, "that half-breeds are to a great extent the medium through which the liquor is procured [by Indians], but there being no ac-knowledged law prohibiting the sale of liquor to them, it is impossible to stay the practice to any extent."[52]

As early as 1876, Indian Agent Lenihan suggested that race be redefined so that "half breeds residing upon, or in the vicinity of Indian Reserves should be placed upon the same footing as Indians, and held amenable to the law as if they were Indians."[53] Subsequently there were several attempts to legally redefine mixed-bloods as Indians to prevent alcohol from reaching Indians. In the 1890s the British Columbia attorney general suggested defin-ing mixed-bloods as nonstatus Indians. Since the Indian Act defined the latter as "any person of Indian blood who follows the Indian mode of life," the attorney general reasoned that mixed-bloods are "undoubtedly 'of Indian blood' which does not necessarily mean full blood."[54] This interpretation found favor with the Indian superintendent of British Columbia in 1892 and was finally incorporated into the 1894 amendments to the Indian Act. "Any person who follows the Indian mode of life, or any child of such person" was legally redefined as an Indian, but only with regard to liquor regulations.[55]

Although intended to clarify the ambiguous situation of mixed-bloods, the amendment only complicated matters. After 1894, mixed-blood people "who followed the Indian mode of life" had to be included as Indians so they could be restricted from the consumption of alcohol; but they had to be distinguished from Indians since they were ineligible for the small benefits, including the right to live on reserves, accorded to Indians. Then there were the ambiguous cases. Agent Graham wrote his colleague Agent Halliday inquiring about the race of a certain mixed-blood individual, since he "leads an Indian life one day, and a Whiteman's life the next."[56]

It becomes apparent that the agents themselves were confused by the multiple definitions of Indians and their authority regarding mixed-bloods. In the early 1900s, Agent Fougner asked his superiors: "Is there any distinction to be made between supplying a half breed with intoxicating liquor and supplying a registered Indian? I have [concluded] it would depend on the person's mode of life and if he considers himself to be an Indian and is assigned so by his fellows."[57] Although the legal extension of the Indian category to mixed-bloods applied only to liquor regulations, some Indian agents used their vast discretionary power to cut through this ambiguity: "In backtimes all . . . half-red who were habitual drunks were placed on the . . . Indian List." This made them "registered" Indians and liable to criminal prosecution for being intoxicated or having liquor in their possession.[58]

Some mixed-bloods were reclassified as Indians, predominantly those at the lower end of the social scale. There was also the possibility of being reclassified from mixed-blood to white. For example:

On the third of the present month Charles Mahoy was brought before me charged with supplying malt liquor to an Indian woman named Sarah Medcalf, wife of James Medcalf a white man living in this place. The charge was proven and I sentenced him to three months in jail with hard labor. . . . I was not aware at the time that an Indian woman marrying a white man ceased to be considered an Indian woman in the eyes of the law. I therefore consent to have the conviction quashed.[59]

Examples provided by women, married to prominent men in fur-trade and colonial society, also suggest the possibility of blanching mixed-bloods to whites as well as the racialized nature of historical sources. Amelia Connoly, daughter of William Connoly and his Cree wife Suzanne "Pas-de-Nom," wife of Governor James Douglas, appears in the 1881 census as Irish, not mixed-blood. Isabella Ross, daughter of an Ojibwa mother and French Canadian father, was listed as French Canadian. Josette Work, daughter of a Spokane Indian woman and Pierre Legacé, is listed as Scottish, as is her daughter Mary, wife of Roderick Finlayson.[60]

ABORIGINAL PARTICIPATION IN MAKING "INDIANS"

Dividing the world into categories that separate self from other seems to be an almost universal characteristic. What is unique to certain times, places, and peoples is the degree to which "selfs" can impose their categories on "others," how those categories get defined, and the rights accorded to each. The racial category "Indian" was one that was originally imposed on aboriginal people. There are numerous indications that the idea of races was foreign to aboriginal worldviews. For example, none of the aboriginal languages on the coast had a word like Indian that included all aboriginal people as a single group. Many groups had a term for themselves that meant simply "the people." Aboriginal people became familiar with the term Indian from Europeans. After prolonged contact with whites, many aboriginal people began to use the term Indian themselves, and now many see it as their primary identity.

The ideology of race was the unique product of European science, folk beliefs, and imperial aspirations. Through it, Europeans incorporated indigenous peoples into their conceptual world. Aboriginal people, on the other hand, incorporated Europeans into their worlds using different categories. The Haida initially placed Europeans in the realm of spirit beings, calling them "the ghost land people." Others, like the Nuu-chah-nulth, at first thought of Europeans as "moon-men," while some Clallam and Clatsop thought Vancouver's ship was a manifestation of Raven, the transformer. More familiarity demonstrated that whatever powers the whites may have, they did not have the power to transform themselves into spirits, so the conceptual category changed. Different aboriginal groups came up with different names for these strangers. The Sto:lo called them "the hungry people." The Nuu-chah-nulth called them the "people who lived on boats." The Puyallup-Nisqually called them "birds" because they seemed to have no fixed abode. The Clallam used "men who drift ashore," putting Europeans in the same class as the Asian mariners who drifted across the Pacific.

Unlike the Europeans, West Coast aboriginal people did not see themselves as a unified race with common interests in dealing with other peoples. In the early days of the seaborne trade, vulnerable European parties were robbed and enslaved by coastal people in the same way that they treated aboriginal groups with whom they had no familial ties.[61] The idea of "us" versus "them"—aboriginal people as a common front versus Europeans— was largely absent from aboriginal dealings with Europeans. Different aboriginal groups allied themselves with the Europeans to attack other aboriginal groups. Eventually, aboriginal groups accorded European strangers privileges they did not extend to other aboriginal people. One example of this, from the 1850s and 1860s, is that coastal tribes would automatically attack and enslave strangers from other aboriginal groups while they allowed unknown whites free passage.

The "middle ground," where Europeans and aboriginal peoples came together in the Pacific Northwest, developed its own language—the Chinook jargon. The jargon was based on a precontact trading language that used Chinookan grammatical structures and a mixture of Chinookan and Nootkan vocabulary. When Europeans arrived, new words from French and English were incorporated to refer to the exotic objects and concepts Europeans brought with them. Evidently there was no word for Indian in the precontact language, because the French word for Indian, *sauvage*, was incorporated into the language as *siwash*.[62]

Chinook jargon became the main medium of intercultural communication from the Columbia River to Alaska, and was spoken by an estimated 250,000 Indians and whites at its peak usage around 1880.[63] In using this language, aboriginal people may have begun to use the word *siwash* with a developing sense of common identity, but it seems unlikely. They did not attribute a common racial identity to the newcomers: no word for European or white existed in the pre- or postcontact jargon. Instead, aboriginal people introduced two terms to distinguish the newcomers from themselves and each other. Those who worked for the Hudson's Bay Company, whether they be British, Hawaiian, French Canadian, or Iroquois, were "King George Men" and American traders and their employees were "Boston Men." Later these terms came to distinguish Britons and British colonists from Americans.

White definitions of Indian became impossible for aboriginal people to ignore after the Indian Act of 1876 created them as a legally separate race. Yet there are many indications that aboriginal people continued to define themselves in their own way. First, it took the state some time to actually take control over the legal race of many of its charges. Not until 1882 were agents appointed to superintend Indians in the southern portions of the province, and it was another two decades before the full system of agents, superintendents, and inspectors was completely established. In the meantime, aboriginal people continued to define themselves insofar as they controlled the membership of their communities. Some accepted white men who had married women of the band. More commonly, bands accepted the mixed-race children of these liaisons. The population of one band, the Songhees, jumped by thirty-one in 1893 with the inclusion of mixed-blood children who had been deserted by their white fathers. Under the Indian Act these children were not Indians, but the Indian agent accepted the Songhees' definition.[64]

Second, there is little evidence that in the late nineteenth century Indians accepted the European idea that as a race they had common interests. All the political agitation by aboriginal groups, mostly on the question of land title, was conducted at a tribal level or, at its broadest level, by groups that shared a common language. Not until the formation of the Indian Rights Association in 1909 did an organization arise that represented Indians as a whole in British Columbia. Thereafter, an increasing number of organizations arose to represent Indian interests in the province, including the currently powerful BC Union of Indian Chiefs.[65]

Not surprisingly, individual Indians sought to escape the legal restrictions placed on them, and after the Indian Act of 1876 some adopted the strategy of becoming legally white. They gave several reasons for their applications for enfranchisement. Some wanted to pursue business opportunities denied them as Indians. Many wished to be able to send their children to the nearby provincial schools instead of the distant, inferior, and oppressive residential boarding schools. Some wished to escape the demeaning status of legal minor. And others, including some mixed-bloods who had been declared Indians so they could not buy alcohol, just wanted to be able to consume liquor legally. Yet, on the whole, the numbers who applied for enfranchisement were small, less than a hundred a year when applications peaked in the 1950s out of a registered Indian population of about 28,500 at that time.[66]

Although some Indians changed their racial status to white, by the 1960s it was more common to find Indians celebrating their race. It is one of the ironies of the interplay of power, race, and naming that in the last several decades, race has become a tool in the struggle against racism. Across the province, beginning in the late 1950s, Indians formed new political and cultural links with other Indians. When, in the late 1960s, the federal government reversed its strategy of isolating Indians and initiated efforts to "integrate" them into white society by dismantling the Indian Act, aboriginal people strongly resisted these moves. Indian identity is now a tool to resist assimilation and preserve some benefits the status accords them. The category "Indian," invented by Europeans and subsequent immigrants, is in the process of being reinvented by Indians themselves.[67]

REINTERPRETING "RACE"

Acknowledging the constructed nature of race opens a new range of research questions linking power, place, and time. The making of Indians in British Columbia reveals the construction of specific racisms, different from those across the 49th parallel. It is clear that ideas of race, as well as the imposition of those ideas on others that is racism, change from place to place and also over time. It is no coincidence that the term "race" and the ideology of racial hierarchies developed during the era of European colonial expansion, or that this ideology softened in the era when whites depended on Indians in the Pacific Northwest. The legal enforcement of rigidly defined racial differences in the colonial and federal period by whites can be contrasted with the pressure by whites since the 1960s to dissolve those distinctions, which Indians now wish to maintain. Treating race as a social construct helps us find answers to the questions: Where does racism come from? Who benefits?

NOTES

My thanks to Cheryl Coull, John Findlay, Chad Gaffield, Sasha Harmon, and Richard White, all of whom commented on earlier drafts of this paper. Thanks also to the Canada–United States Fulbright Program, the Social Sciences and Humanities Research Council of Canada, and the Multiculturalism Secretariat of the Secretary of State of Canada for financial support while this research was being conducted.

1. The AHA does say that "more than one may apply," something that Linnaeus would have objected to. Linnaean categories are discussed below.

2. Martin N. Marger, *Race and Ethnic Relations* (Belmont, Calif.: Wadsworth, 1985), 12; R. C. Lewontin, Steven Rose, and Leon J. Kamin, *Not in Our Genes: Biology, Ideology, and Human Nature* (New York: Pantheon, 1984), 127; A. Appiah, "The Uncompleted Argument: Du Bois and the Illusion of Race," *Critical Inquiry* 12, no. 1 (1985): 21–37; Kay J. Anderson, *Vancouver's Chinatown: Racial Discourse in Canada, 1875–1980* (Montreal: McGill-Queen's University Press, 1991).

3. This attention to place, without losing sight of the global forces that bear on

it, is what Giovanni Levi calls microhistory in "On Microhistory," in *New Perspectives on Historical Writing,* ed. Peter Burke (Cambridge: Polity Press, 1991).

4. Robert F. Berkhofer, Jr., *The White Man's Indian* (New York: Knopf, 1978); Brian W. Dippie, *The Vanishing American: White Attitudes and U.S. Indian Policy* (Middletown, Conn.: Wesleyan University Press, 1982); Daniel Francis, *The Imaginary Indian: The Image of the Indian in Canadian Culture* (Vancouver: Arsenal Pulp Press, 1992).

5. Richard White, "Race Relations in the American West," *American Quarterly* 38, no. 3 (1986): 396–416. For a detailed analysis of the creation of *Indian* in the Puget Sound region with broad implications, see Alexandra Harmon, *Indians in the Making: Ethnic Relations and Indian Identities around Puget Sound* (Berkeley and Los Angeles: University of California Press, 1998). For a study that focuses on the different seventeenth-century creations of Indian on the east coast of North America, see Ronald Takaki, "The Tempest in the Wilderness: The Racialization of Savagery," *Journal of American History* 79, no. 3 (December 1992): 892–912.

6. Manuel Castells has noted that without a critical vocabulary we have become "prisoners of notions which correspond to the terms of everyday language," which is usually dominated by ideology, and "as soon as we try to set out from other theoretical foundations, we are forced to employ a different language." Castells, *The Urban Question: A Marxist Approach* (Cambridge: MIT Press, 1979), 440–41.

7. Vancouver's journals were published in 1798. Interestingly, his predecessor Captain James Cook did not use the word *Indian* here; instead he used the term "natives," meaning "natives of this place," when he spoke about the indigenous people. James Cook, *Captain Cook's Voyages of Discovery* (London: J. M. Dent, 1906), 339–84; George Vancouver, *A Voyage of Discovery to the North Pacific Ocean and Round the World* (1798; reprint, W. Kaye Lamb, ed., London: Hakluyt Society, 1984), 236.

8. See, for example, Alexander Walker, *An Account of a Voyage to the North West Coast of America in 1785 and 1786* (Vancouver: Douglas and McIntyre; Seattle: University of Washington Press, 1982), 74; Walker noted persons "as fair as many Portuguese and Spaniards." At Nootka, James Cook thought that the "whiteness of the skin appeared almost equal to that of Europeans"; *Captain Cook's Voyages of Discovery,* 347.

9. Quote from Herbert K. Beals, trans., *Juan Perez on the Northwest Coast: Six Documents of His Expedition in 1774* (Portland: Oregon Historical Society Press, 1989), 78. Phenotypical differences are not prerequisites for racial differentiation. One only has to look at the English-versus-Irish conflict during Vancouver's own lifetime, or more recently the Nazi persecution of Jews.

10. Audrey Smedley, *Race in North America: Origin and Evolution of a Worldview*

(Boulder: Westview, 1993), 36–72; Berkhofer, *White Man's Indian*, 3–22; Nancy Stepan, *The Idea of Race in Science: Great Britain, 1800–1960* (London: Macmillan, 1982).

11. For a provocative discussion of the role of explorers and travelers in "creating" the rest of the world for Europeans, see Mary Louise Pratt, *Imperial Eyes: Studies in Travel Writing and Transculturation* (London: Routledge, 1992), 32.

12. Carl Linnaeus, *Systema Naturae*, quoted in Pratt, *Imperial Eyes*, 32.

13. Smedley, *Race in North America*, 166–67.

14. For examples see Cook, *Captain Cook's Voyages of Discovery*, 350; Walker, *Account of a Voyage*, 84.

15. Brown was one of the earliest ethnographers to work in British Columbia; Robert Brown, *The Races of Mankind: Being a Popular Description of the Characteristics, Manners and Customs of the Principal Varieties of the Human Family*, 4 vols. (London: Cassell, Peter and Galpin, 1873–76), 3:31, emphasis mine.

16. George Bernhard Depping, quoted in Timothy Mitchell, *Colonising Egypt* (Cambridge: Cambridge University Press, 1988), 106, and for a description of Egyptians as indolent, see page 107; see also Gaspar Mollien, *Travels in the Republic of Colombia in the Years 1822–23* (London: C. Knight, 1824), 57, quoted in Pratt, *Imperial Eyes*, 151.

17. Though, in practice, they had no qualms about forming sexual relations with indigenous women.

18. Robin Fisher, *Contact and Conflict: Indian-European Relations in British Columbia, 1774–1890* (Vancouver: University of British Columbia Press, 1977), 73–85, develops this contrast more fully.

19. Roderick Finlayson, "Biography," British Columbia Archives (Victoria; hereafter cited as BCA), A/B/30/F49A; Charles A. Bayley, "Early Life on Vancouver Island," BCA, E/B/B34.2. The missionary Bolduc reported that all the current and former French Canadian employees of the Hudson's Bay Company had Indian wives at Willamette in Oregon Territory in 1843; Jean B. Z. Bolduc, *Mission of the Columbia*, trans. Edward J. Kowrach (1843; reprint, Fairfield, Wash.: Ye Galleon Press, 1979), 90.

20. For a general discussion of these relationships, see Jennifer S. H. Brown, *Strangers in Blood: Fur Trade Company Families in Indian Country* (Vancouver: University of British Columbia Press, 1980); and Sylvia Van Kirk, *"Many Tender Ties": Women in Fur-Trade Society in Western Canada, 1670–1870* (Winnipeg: Watson and Dwyer, 1980).

21. Among the published versions: Alexander C. Anderson, "Notes on the Indian Tribes of British North America and the Northwest Coast," *Historical Magazine* 7 (1863): 80; [Peter Skene Ogden], *Traits of American-Indian Life and Character*

(London: Smith, Elder, 1853); F. W. Howay, who argues convincingly that Ogden was the author of this text in "Authorship of the Traits of Indian Life," *Oregon Historical Quarterly* 35 (1934): 42–49; William Fraser Tolmie, "Utilization of the Indians," *The Resources of British Columbia* 1, no. 12 (February 1, 1884): 7; and J. W. McKay, "The Indians of British Columbia," *BC Mining Journal* (1899), reprinted in the Canadian Institute for Historical Microreproductions, no. 15555.

22. [Ogden], *Traits of American Indian Life*, 79; Alexander Ross, *Adventures of the First Settlers on the Oregon or Columbia River* . . . (London: Smith, Elder, 1849), 99–100; and J. S. Helmcken, *The Reminiscences of Doctor John Sebastian Helmcken*, ed. Dorothy B. Smith (Vancouver: University of British Columbia Press, 1975), 328.

23. Mary Black-Rogers, "Varieties of 'Starving': Semantics and Survival in the Subarctic Fur Trade, 1750–1850," *Ethnohistory* 33, no. 4 (Fall 1986): 353–83; Elizabeth Vibert, *Traders' Tales: Narratives of Cultural Encounters in the Columbia Plateau, 1807–1846* (Norman: University of Oklahoma Press, 1997), 120–33.

24. Black-Rogers, "Varieties of 'Starving,' " 364; this use of *indolent* to mean not interested in participating in a particular European-ordered form of labor subordination, to refuse to exchange leisure and subsistence activities for accumulation, coincided with Linnaeus's racial categorization of Indians as "content and free." There is evidence that this meaning of indolent also became widespread in other colonies. See, for example, Michael Taussig, *Shamanism, Colonialism, and the Wild Man: A Study in Terror and Healing* (Chicago: University of Chicago Press, 1987), 56.

25. Sherry Smith emphasizes the effect of local conditions on racial definitions in "Beyond Princess and Squaw: Army Officers' Perceptions of Indian Women," in Susan Armitage and Elizabeth Jameson, eds., *The Women's West* (Norman: University of Oklahoma Press, 1987), 63–76.

26. Richard White, *The Middle Ground: Indians, Empires, and Republics in the Great Lakes Region, 1650–1815* (Cambridge: Cambridge University Press, 1991), xi.

27. The more positive definition of "half-breeds" in Britain than in America is also evident in the popular literature. See William J. Scheick, *The Half-Blood: A Cultural Symbol in 19th Century American Fiction* (Lexington: University Press of Kentucky, 1979), 95.

28. Phoebe Goodell Judson, a settler in Washington just south of the international border, describes the opprobrium against these liaisons and gives an account of a father who "never ceased to regret the part he bore in bringing upon [his daughters'] innocent lives the sorrow which is the sure result of mixed marriages." Judson, *A Pioneer's Search for an Ideal Home* (Lincoln: University of Nebraska Press, 1984), 196. For a discussion of how racial ideas developed in Washington Territory/State, see Harmon, *Indians in the Making*.

29. In practice, aboriginal people did buy and preempt land, but I have found no

record of them voting, running for office, or attending schools not explicitly established for Indians by missionaries.

30. Fisher, *Contact and Conflict,* 93; Rev. Herbert Beaver quoted in Hollis Slater, "New Light on Herbert Beaver," *British Columbia Historical Quarterly* 6 (1942): 24.

31. For the text of the treaties and the debate over reserves, see British Columbia, *Papers Relating to the Indian Land Question* (1876; reprint, Victoria, 1987); and Wilson Duff, "The Fort Victoria Treaties," *BC Studies* 3 (Fall 1969): 3–57.

32. Questions about the status of Indian women living with nonaboriginal men did not arise, apparently reflecting the fur traders' assumption that they had the status of their spouses.

33. See, for example, Herman Reinhart, *The Golden Frontier: The Recollections of Herman Francis Reinhart, 1851–1869,* ed. Doyce B. Nunis, Jr. (Austin: University of Texas Press, 1962); and Daniel Marshall, "The Fraser River War," *Native Studies Review* 11, no. 1 (1996): 139–45.

34. Rhodes and Chamberlain quoted in Robert A. Huttenback, *Racism and Empire: White Settlers and Colored Immigrants in the British Self-Governing Colonies, 1830–1910* (Ithaca: Cornell University Press, 1976), 15–16.

35. Ibid., 15; these immigrants were also influenced by contemporary anthropology and popular literature that reinforced their Anglo-Saxon pride. See Brian V. Street, *The Savage in Literature: Representation of "Primitive" Society in English Fiction, 1858–1920* (London: Routledge and Kegan Paul, 1975), 49–78.

36. C. Aubrey Angelo, *Idaho: A Descriptive Tour and Review of Its Resources and Route, Prefaced by a Sketch of British Misrule in Victoria, V.I.* (San Francisco: H. H. Bancroft and Co., 1865), 8.

37. *New Westminster Daily News,* November 4, 1907, quoted in Patricia E. Roy, *A White Man's Province* (Vancouver: University of British Columbia Press, 1989), 311, note 4.

38. Henry Bell-Irving, of Anglo CB Packing Co., quoted in Anderson, *Vancouver's Chinatown,* 36, note 9.

39. In fact, the acts penalized non-Indians who sold alcohol to Indians and were largely ineffective; Colony of Vancouver Island, "Proclamation," 1858; Colony of British Columbia, "Penalty for Selling Liquor to the Natives," 1858; and "An Act for Better Prohibiting the Sale or Gift of Intoxicating Liquors to the Indians," 1860. The treatment of Indians as legal minors mirrored a long-standing element in their racialization as "grown-up children."

40. Vancouver Island, "Proclamation," 1859; British Columbia, "The Oaths Act," 1859; "An Ordinance to Amend the Law of Evidence," 1865; and "An Ordinance to Provide for the Taking of Oaths and Admission of Evidence in Certain Cases," 1867.

41. Douglas and subsequent governors tried to have the law allow Indians to testify in court, but the legislative councils and assembly blocked any changes. See Colonial Office, 305/29, A. E. Kennedy to Colonial Office, 10226, 3 September 1866.

42. Whites could claim land by right; Indians were only able to obtain land with special permission from the governor. This provision was extended in subsequent revisions of the legislation in the colony and the province. See Colony of British Columbia, "An Act to Amend the Land Ordinance," and Province of British Columbia, "An Act to Amend and Consolidate the Laws Affecting Crown Lands in British Columbia," March 1874; "Lands Act" Statutes of British Columbia (SBC), 1888, sec. 5. There is no good study of aboriginal preemption applications to the governor; the most detailed account is in Paul Tennant, *Aboriginal Peoples and Politics: The Indian Land Question in British Columbia, 1849–1989* (Vancouver: University of British Columbia Press, 1990), 35–42.

43. The percentages are approximate since they are based on the Blue Books of the Colony of British Columbia and the federal census, which estimated the 1870 population at 36,247, of which 25,661 were Indians and another 1,548 were Chinese. Canada, *Census*, 1871, 4:376–77; "An Act to Amend the Qualification and Registration of Voter's Act," SBC 1872, 35 Vict., chap. 37, s. 13 (this act was reserved by the lieutenant governor and proclaimed in 1875); "An Act to Make Better Provision for the Qualification and Registration of Voters," SBC 1875, 35 Vict., chap. 26, s. 22; and "An Act to Amend the Municipal Act," SBC 1876, chap. 3, and 1883, 51 Vict., chap. 15. For a discussion of the creation of Chinese as a racial category, see Anderson, *Vancouver's Chinatown*.

44. This reversed the whole basis of membership for many aboriginal groups that were matrilineal and matrilocal; "The Indian Act," Statutes of Canada (SC) 1876, chap. 18, s. 3(a). The definition of an Indian as someone "reputed to belong to an Indian band" remained in effect until the 1951 "Act Respecting Indians," SC 1951, chap. 59, s. 2, redefined Indian as "a person who is registered as an Indian" on a band or general list. A member of a band "means a person whose name appears on a Band List"; band lists had apparently been in existence for most bands since the late 1890s.

45. "The Indian Act," 1876, SC 1876, chap. 18, s. 3(1).

46. "Indian Act," SC 1876, chaps. 17, 18, 60, 79, 83; "Indian Act," SC 1880, chap. 80.

47. Prisoners came under closer scrutiny but only for a specified term.

48. Douglas Cole and Ira Chaikin, *An Iron Hand Upon the People: The Law Against the Potlatch on the Northwest Coast* (Vancouver: Douglas and McIntyre; Seattle: University of Washington Press, 1990).

49. "Indian Act," SC 1876, chap. 18, s. 86; the sections of the act relating to

enfranchisement did not initially apply to the Indians of British Columbia or the North-West Territories because they were thought to be too backward. Amendments to the Indian Act in 1920 gave the minister of Indian affairs the power to declare any Indian enfranchised without his consent; this was repealed in 1922 but reenacted in a milder form in 1933. The definition of race was bound up as well with contemporary definitions of gender roles: upon enfranchisement an Indian man's wife and minor children automatically became enfranchised as well.

50. Ecclesiastical Province of British Columbia Archives, Bishop Hill's Diary, March 30, 1862; thanks to Jean Barman for providing me with a typescript of this diary. W. H. Lomas, *Canada Sessional Papers* (Cda. SP) 1894, vol. 10, no. 14, pp. 116–18. National Archives of Canada (NAC), Record Group (RG) 10, vol. 10896, file: 987/1-1-10, pt. 1, A. O'Daunt to Assistant Deputy Director, Department of Indian Affairs, 5 March 1923.

51 However, in aboriginal society, descent was traced either through the maternal line (in north-coast societies) or through both lines (in south-coast societies), so children of mixed marriages were often more welcomed by their aboriginal extended families than by their nonaboriginal relations. Moreover, large numbers of aboriginal women were deserted or widowed by their non-Indian husbands and returned to their own families with their children.

52. A. W. Vowell, Visiting Indian Superintendent for British Columbia, in Cda. SP 1892, no. 14, pp. 181–88.

53. James Lenihan, Cda. SP 1876, pp. 53–56.

54. NAC, RG 10, vol. 1350, reel C13917, file: Cowichan Agency Departmental Circulars 1892–1910, Arthur G. Smith, Deputy Attorney General of BC, 30 August 1892.

55. Ibid.; "An Act to Further Amend the Indian Act," S.C. 1894, chap. 32, s. 6; Cda. S.P. 1892, no. 14, pp. 181–88.

56. NAC, RG 10, vol. 11142, file: Alert Bay-Kwawkewlth–Campbell River Agency, 1916–1949, II. Graham, Indian Agent at Duncan to W. M. Halliday at Alert Bay, October 30, 1931. The response, dated 5 November 1931, states that his mother is an Indian who married a white and was struck off the roles. "He is not an Indian under the strict letter of the Indian Act, through he has lived more or less with the Indians. . . ."

57. NAC, RG 10, vol. 10888, file: 1912–13, Bella Coola Agency, Letter Book, Iver Fougner, 7 June 1912.

58. NAC, RG 10, vol. 10922, file: Stikine-George Campbell, Harper Reed, 1 January 1940.

59. BCA, Attorney General Department, GR 429; box 1, file 5, I. R. M. Innis to A. C. Elliot, Attorney General, 31 October 1876.

60. The 1881 census was the first to cover British Columbia. Canada Census, manuscript for Victoria 1881 (microcopy available through National Archives); Van Kirk, *Many Tender Ties*, 133; Sylvia Van Kirk, "Josette Legacé," in *Dictionary of Canadian Biography*, vol. 12 (Toronto: University of Toronto Press, 1990), 550–51; Peter Baskerville and Eric Sager, *The 1881 Canadian Census: Vancouver Island* (Victoria: Public History Group, 1990); and Eric Sager et al., *The 1891 Canadian Census: Victoria, British Columbia* (Victoria: Public History Group, 1991).

61. See, for example, John Jewitt, *The Adventures and Sufferings of John R. Jewitt, Captive Among the Nootka, 1803–1805*, ed. Derek G. Smith (Toronto: McClelland and Stewart, 1974).

62. Edward H. Thomas, *Chinook: A History and Dictionary of the Northwest Coast Trade Jargon* (Portland: Metropolitan Press, 1935).

63. Ibid., 4.

64. The Songhees are now called the Lekwammen (W. H. Lomas, Cda. S.P. 1894, no. 14, p. 117).

65. Tennant, *Aboriginal Peoples and Politics*, 87.

66. Canada, *Annual Report of the Department of Indian Affairs*, 1921–70.

67. For an excellent discussion of this process in the Puget Sound area of present-day Washington State, see Harmon, *Indians in the Making*.

PART II

RACE IN THE URBAN WEST

Federal Power and Racial Politics
in Los Angeles during World War II

KEVIN ALLEN LEONARD

The crude, fertilizer-and-fuel-oil bomb that killed 169 people and destroyed a federal office building in Oklahoma City on April 19, 1995, drew media attention to the violent potential of an antifederal populist movement. During that spring and summer, countless reports appeared in newspapers and magazines and on television about the growing "militia movement."[1] Although right-wing militias have emerged throughout the United States, antifederal activists seem to be concentrated primarily in the South and the West.[2] Scholars and journalists have depicted antifederal sentiment in the South as understandable, if regrettable, and have frequently characterized white southerners—especially men—as racists who resent the Union's victory in the Civil War and the federal government's support of the African American civil rights movement in the 1950s and 1960s.

Antifederal sentiment in the West, however, has proved more difficult to comprehend. The points of contention seem less concrete. Why should residents of a region that has benefited consistently from federal spending resent the government that has subsidized western business and agriculture by building roads, dams, and military bases? Why should people who live in an increasingly urban and suburban region respond violently to federal policies and actions having little direct impact on urban areas, such as Bureau of Land Management policies and increases in grazing fees on federally owned land? In his presidential address at the thirty-sixth annual meeting of the Western History Association, Richard White described this phenomenon as "the current weirdness in the West." Although he acknowledges the complex origins of the "current weirdness," he emphasizes the impact of wrenching economic

87

changes in rural areas. Some of the farmers, miners, and loggers displaced by consolidation, contraction, and mechanization, White argues, have embraced the Wise Use movement. At the extreme, some have joined militias or groups such as the Freemen. All have lashed out at the largest and strongest institution in the region—the federal government. White's comments insightfully explain the growth of antifederal organizations in the rural West but do not offer a satisfying interpretation of antifederal sentiment in urban and suburban areas.[3]

More people live in the suburbs of the West's large cities than in the cities themselves or in the region's rural hinterlands. Although some suburbanites have embraced the Wise Use movement and a few have joined militias, in the past thirty years they more frequently have organized to oppose busing and affirmative action and support restrictions on what they perceive as the rights of "illegal immigrants." In each case, they have portrayed themselves as taxpayers—devoted to the welfare of their children and communities—whose rights have been trampled by arrogant and insensitive federal judges and bureaucrats. These suburban voters have emerged as the core constituency for many of the most outspoken conservative politicians in the region. At the extreme, some suburbanites have joined avowedly racist groups such as the Ku Klux Klan and the Aryan Nations.

There seems to be, then, an important link between ideas about race and antifederal sentiment in the West. This essay will explore that connection and argue that there has always been the potential for disagreement between European American residents of the West and federal officials over the rights of racial minority groups. Until World War II, however, federal officials usually supported the efforts of western white supremacists. During the war, the federal government began to take seriously the complaints of some minority group members. Two agencies—the President's Committee on Fair Employment Practice (or Fair Employment Practice Committee, FEPC) and the War Relocation Authority (WRA)—actively opposed racial discrimination during World War II, and their actions sparked a backlash by many western white supremacists. Although this essay cannot prove that the current antifederal sentiment in the West emerged from the anti-FEPC and anti-WRA backlash, it will suggest that the "current weirdness" is related to the postwar reaction to federal antidiscrimination efforts. Since World War II, many western residents have continued to perceive the federal government as an entity obsessed with the rights of minority groups.

White supremacy influenced the history of the West even before European Americans began to move west of the Mississippi in the mid-nineteenth century.[4] Democratic institutions evolved in North America in the seventeenth and eighteenth centuries in part because divisions among European men, such as class or ethnic differences, were less salient than the differences that separated "white" men from Africans, African Americans, and American Indians.[5] Since the European and Creole population of the English colonies and the United States grew continuously, the supply of resources—especially land—had to expand in order to prevent class resentments from undermining the North American form of democracy.

"White" Americans looked westward to sate their hunger for land. West of the new republic, however, lay territories occupied by American Indians and Mexicans. Drawing upon their developing ideas about "race," which dehumanized Indians and racially mixed Mexicans, many European Americans imagined the West as an uninhabited "virgin land" waiting to be cultivated and civilized by industrious "white" people. Succeeding myths continued to place little value on the lives of American Indians, Latin Americans, African Americans, and Asian immigrants.[6]

Many whites who moved onto western lands inhabited by American Indians and Mexican *mestizos* continued to perceive the West as a region where they could avoid the racial "problems" that had engulfed the eastern United States.[7] In Oregon in 1844, the provisional government's legislative committee passed laws designed to exclude African Americans, whether enslaved or free, from the territory.[8] Five years later, delegates to the California constitutional convention debated a clause to make it illegal for African Americans to reside in the state. At this point, federal power—or, more accurately, perceived federal power—for the first time limited the actions of western white supremacists. Convention delegates omitted the clause, for they feared it would have offended some members of Congress and thereby delayed their state's admission to the Union.

The fear of federal power as well as the presence of American Indians and Mexican Americans in California prevented the framers of the California constitution from realizing their dream of creating a "white man's state." The fear of federal power, however, did not prevent them from taking action to ensure that American Indians, African Americans, and Asian Americans in California would remain inferior to white men. The constitution included a clause restricting the franchise to "white male" citizens.[9]

Legislators in California and other western states and territories soon discovered that establishing and maintaining white supremacy in the West was more difficult than they had anticipated. Restricting the franchise to white men did not prevent American Indians, Mexican Americans, African

Americans, and Asian Americans from competing with white men for economic opportunities. Western legislators passed a number of bills to restrict the rights and regulate the behavior of those groups, but the power of the federal government complicated their efforts. After the Civil War, for example, federal officials could have invoked the fourteenth and fifteenth amendments to the U.S. Constitution to prevent state legislators from taking all of the actions they felt necessary to protect white people from the potential political power of African Americans. Legislators also confronted the fact that the treatment of American Indians, Mexican Americans, and Asian Americans involved the federal government. Treaties between the United States and the various Indian nations and Mexico, China, and Japan restricted the actions of state and territorial legislatures. As Richard White has written: "Only in the West were the conditions of foreign nationality and race so intimately intertwined. This linkage placed the status of racial minorities in the American West partially beyond the control of the various state and territorial governments. Race relations became to a significant degree foreign relations, regulated by treaties between independent foreign nations and the United States. Minority communities not only differed internally from surrounding white communities, but they differed in their relationship to the federal government."[10]

The president (with the Senate's approval) had the power to negotiate treaties that could supersede state laws, and federal courts had the power to nullify state laws if they violated terms of U.S. treaties. Federal officials, however, rarely exercised their power to restrict the actions of western white supremacists. Throughout the late nineteenth and early twentieth centuries, federal officials often worked with state and local leaders to create a system of white supremacy that resembled segregation in the South. Local and state leaders established segregated educational and recreational facilities and worked to keep people of color in Chinatowns, Little Tokyos, and Sonoratowns. State legislators passed "alien land laws" to prevent Asian immigrants from buying land in their states. Federal troops engaged in a campaign to concentrate American Indians on reservations, whose size decreased as the demands of white "settlers" increased.[11] Congress passed the Chinese Exclusion Act in 1882.[12] After the San Francisco School Board provoked an international incident by attempting to force children of Japanese immigrants to attend the Chinese school in 1906, President Theodore Roosevelt concluded the "Gentlemen's Agreement" with Japan. The intent of this diplomatic agreement was to restrict further immigration from Japan.[13] In 1924, Congress enacted exclusionary laws that prohibited most Asians from migrating to the United States.[14] In the early 1930s, federal officials cooperated with state and local officials to deport hundreds of thousands of residents of Mexican ancestry. Some people who were forced to leave the United States were U.S. citizens.[15]

By listing these federal and state actions, I am not suggesting that the development of white supremacy in the West was even and linear or that all European Americans in the region were white supremacists. The process, like most historical processes, was halting, uneven, and frequently contested. Throughout the late nineteenth and early twentieth centuries, however, the majority of white westerners and federal officials agreed that white men should rule the West, and they collaborated to deny economic and political power to American Indians, Mexican Americans, African Americans, and Asian Americans.

Ironically, the establishment of a system of racial inequality undermined efforts to prevent the growth of minority groups in the West. White Americans and some European immigrants often refused to work for the wages that railroad owners, mining companies, and large farmers were willing to pay. The inequalities established in the 1840s and 1850s encouraged employers to recruit laborers from China, Japan, Mexico, and the southern United States, where capitalist transformation had left millions of people impoverished and desperate.[16] White workers objected strenuously and sometimes violently to the importation of Asian, Mexican, and African American labor, but the region's minority population nonetheless increased significantly.[17]

A series of cataclysmic events in the early twentieth century dramatically increased the size of minority communities throughout the region. The revolution in Mexico and the resulting economic problems led nearly one-tenth of that country's citizens—1.5 million people—to come to the United States. African Americans moved west in large numbers during World War I. In the first three decades of the century, parts of the West became more ethnically diverse than other parts of the country. No western city could match the diversity of Los Angeles. By 1940, around 300,000 Mexican Americans, 70,000 African Americans, and 40,000 Japanese Americans lived in the Los Angeles area. More people of Mexican ancestry lived in Los Angeles than in any other place except Mexico City. More Japanese Americans lived in Los Angeles than in any other U.S. city. And the city's African American community was the largest in the West and the sixth largest in the nation. Los Angeles's diversity makes it an excellent venue in which to study the connections between racial ideologies and antifederal sentiment. In the West's largest city (White refers to it as the "capital of the West"), many of the most powerful people lived in fairly close proximity to some of the most powerless people in the region.

Most American Indians, African Americans, Mexican Americans, and Asian Americans rejected white supremacist visions of the West. Many people of color perceived the West as a land of opportunity for all residents, not just white men. As early as the 1850s, African Americans in the region had organized to gain and protect their civil rights;[18] and in the 1910s and 1920s, civil rights activists established local branches of the National Association for the Advancement of Colored People and the National Urban League. Mexican American leaders formed the League of United Latin American Citizens in the 1920s and El Congreso de Pueblos de Habla Española in the 1930s. These organizations frequently lodged protests with local, state, and federal agencies. Officials ignored most of their protests, however, until the United States entered World War II.[19]

When A. Philip Randolph first announced plans for a July 1, 1941, March on Washington to protest discrimination in defense employment, the labor leader estimated that 10,000 people would participate. As the day approached, tens of thousands—possibly 100,000—African Americans made plans to journey to the capital. The march threatened to embarrass Franklin D. Roosevelt's administration in both international affairs and domestic politics. Randolph's march would have given foreign observers proof that the United States was a society not clearly united behind its government. It would also have publicized the rupture within the Democratic Party caused by the fact that it had become both the party of white supremacists and the party of African Americans. To prevent African Americans from marching in the streets of the capital, in June 1941 President Roosevelt reluctantly issued Executive Order 8802, which prohibited employment discrimination in defense industries. The executive order itself did not dramatically affect discrimination in the West or anywhere else in the country. The Fair Employment Practice Committee (FEPC), created to enforce the order, consisted of six members, each of whom served part-time. A small staff in Washington served the committee, which had almost no power and had to rely on negative publicity to try to end widespread racial and religious discrimination.[20]

Despite its weakness, the FEPC did have a small but noticeable impact on discrimination in Los Angeles. The committee arrived in that city in October 1941 to investigate discrimination in aircraft plants and shipyards. The threat of negative publicity led one major employer—Lockheed-Vega—to implement an antidiscrimination program less than a month before the hearings. The aircraft manufacturer hired some African American applicants, and it changed its application forms and interview procedures in an effort to eliminate discrimination.[21] As a result, the number of black employees at Lockheed-Vega increased significantly. Still, at the time of the FEPC hearings, only 54 of the company's 48,000 employees were African Americans.[22] Although the hearings proved beneficial to those 54 employees, the weakness of the agency allowed many employers to continue to discriminate throughout 1942. Black employment in the aircraft and shipbuilding industries did not increase substantially until 1943, when employers could not find enough white workers, men or women, to keep the plants operating at full capacity.[23]

African American workers around the nation were not satisfied with the FEPC's inability to eliminate widespread discrimination. Continued pressure from African American leaders prompted President Roosevelt to reorganize the FEPC in 1943, expanding its base in Washington and opening fifteen field offices. The agency's offices in San Francisco and Los Angeles, staffed by a regional director and four examiners, fielded complaints from the Pacific Coast and Rocky Mountain states.[24]

Reorganization of the FEPC was a sign that some federal officials were seeking to dismantle the discriminatory institutions white westerners had constructed. When the agency was reorganized, Harry Kingman was appointed western regional director. Kingman was known throughout California if not the entire region as a committed proponent of racial equality. He had served as the director of the University YMCA in Berkeley for many years and had used his position to criticize racial intolerance. As a regional director, he argued for changes in FEPC procedures so that the committee would "make a lasting rather than a fleeting and insignificant dent on employment discrimination."[25]

African American workers in Los Angeles, like black workers across the country, tried to take advantage of the FEPC's reorganization. Black shipyard workers filed a complaint against their employers and the Boilermakers Union, which relegated African American workers to a powerless auxiliary. Although these shipyard workers hoped that the stronger FEPC would help them gain equality in the union, they decided not to let their hopes rest on the actions of a single federal agency. In addition to filing a complaint with the FEPC, the Shipyard Workers Committee for Equal Participation sent telegrams to the War Labor Board and the War Manpower Commission. The telegrams said that discrimination by the Boilermakers threatened the morale of black workers and violated Executive Order 8802.[26] Shipyard

Workers Committee members and supporters also pledged to refuse to pay their union dues until the union dissolved the auxiliary. The committee found nearly 300 African American workers and more than 700 white workers who were willing to sign a petition addressed to the union's leadership.[27] The petition demanded the abolition of the auxiliary and the admission of black shipyard workers into the previously all-white local.[28]

The FEPC responded by conducting hearings in Los Angeles in November 1943. It heard testimony from African American workers who had been denied promotion, threatened, and fired, and from shipyard managers. Representatives from the Boilermakers Union refused to attend the hearings. The FEPC concluded that shipyard managers and unions had violated Executive Order 8802 by discriminating against African American employees, and ordered employers and the union to cease their discrimination.[29] Union officials and shipyard managers, however, refused to obey the committee, and when the FEPC returned to Los Angeles in August 1944, it found that, "to date, the companies and unions involved have not complied with the directives issued by the committee."[30]

The FEPC failed to curtail discrimination in the shipyards because it received no support from other federal agencies, and without assistance from more powerful agencies it could not force employers to obey its orders. Two such agencies, the War Manpower Commission and the War Labor Board, decided that the production of ships was more important than shipbuilders' civil rights.[31] If the FEPC's failure to end discrimination against African American shipyard workers suggested to western white supremacists, especially those in the Boilermakers Union, that they had no cause to fear the federal government's support of racial equality, a second case from Los Angeles offered reason for concern. WMC and WLB officials did not categorically oppose the FEPC, but in some industries they joined the FEPC in attacking racial discrimination. The Los Angeles Railway (LARY), the city's mass transit system, confronted the power of a united federal bureaucracy.

Although a large number of the Los Angeles Railway's patrons were poor African Americans who could not afford cars, the railroad refused to hire black applicants for positions as rail car and bus operators. As early as December 1942, representatives of several federal agencies, including the FEPC, met with LARY's managers and encouraged them to comply with Executive Order 8802. Two months later, the president of the railway, P. B. Harris, told the FEPC that he had attempted to hire and promote African Americans, but white workers refused to work beside them. As a result, Harris said, he had halted his company's efforts to comply with the president's order.[32] Throughout 1943, FEPC officials continued to urge Harris to hire and upgrade black employees. He refused, saying that since the transit workers' union could not guarantee that its members would not walk out or strike in response to the upgrading of black employees, "we have not deemed it advisable to proceed further."[33]

Internal FEPC reports from the LARY case indicate that the agency was not simply trying to enforce the executive order against discrimination in war industries. Many FEPC employees believed deeply that racial discrimination was hindering the war effort and earnestly sought to end employment discrimination. They refused to accept Harris's explanations for his behavior and questioned the sincerity of LARY executives. One internal memo said that Harris had "in the past shown anti-Negro sentiments."[34] The FEPC also expressed concern about the social effects of employment discrimination. Two of its investigators reported that by May 1944, "hostile feelings in the Negro community have become so violent that there are almost daily attacks upon operators working lines which run through colored neighborhoods." The tension had fueled wild rumors, they said. "A riot was supposedly scheduled for January 1, 1944. Negroes were reputedly organizing a group known as the Obnoxious Society, with a subgroup of Bumpers, who were to go about bumping shoppers—and so forth."[35]

As the FEPC worked behind the scenes to convince LARY's managers to hire and promote African American workers, it received assistance from the War Manpower Commission, which at the end of March 1944 suspended the railway's manpower priority rating, preventing it from recruiting workers through the U.S. Employment Service.[36] Although this action did not immediately prompt LARY's managers to abandon their discriminatory practices, the move did earn the praise of leaders in the African American community. The *California Eagle*, Los Angeles's oldest black newspaper, noted that the WMC's action "proves truly that we have a government that is really for the people."[37]

The War Manpower Commission's action and the exultation of the *California Eagle* may have led some white supremacists in Los Angeles to doubt that the federal government was still supporting white supremacy in the West. The FEPC hearings in the LARY case would have confirmed those suspicions. At the August 1944 hearings, the FEPC offered community activists in Los Angeles an opportunity to appeal to the federal government and to the public. Everett Wile, the executive secretary of the Los Angeles Council for Civic Unity, suggested a plan by which black employees could be integrated into all job classifications within the railway. The Council for

Civic Unity, comprising 44 churches and church groups, 32 labor unions, 20 youth organizations, and 39 clubs and societies, was "concerned with the promotion of unity between all sections of the community" and "dedicated to the proposition that the problems of any minority are not the concern of that minority alone, but of the entire community," Wile said. The Council for Civic Unity's concrete proposal for eliminating discrimination at LARY called for timetables and publicity campaigns to reduce the tensions involved in the hiring and upgrading of black workers.[38] By allowing antiracist westerners the chance to express themselves, the FEPC tacitly acknowledged that it had abandoned the traditional position of the federal government in the West.

When the hearings concluded, the FEPC announced that the Los Angeles Railway was guilty of discrimination for refusing to hire any of the more than seventy black workers who had applied for jobs as operators or conductors in 1943 and 1944.[39] Under the combined weight of the evidence presented at the public hearing, the suspension of its manpower priority rating, and the glare of negative publicity, LARY's management finally buckled. Less than a week after the hearings, the railway's managers hired African American conductors and promoted black employees.[40] The company's action prompted the War Manpower Commission to restore its manpower priority rating on August 19, 1944. Harry Kingman noted that the employment and promotion of African Americans at LARY proceeded smoothly. The company posted bulletins and had briefings for supervisors, and the union sponsored discussions among workers. The hiring of black operators and mechanics did not result in white workers' quitting their jobs.[41]

These two cases illuminate the complexities of the changes in the use of federal power to support white supremacy in the West. Over the course of the war, FEPC employees increasingly argued that the West should be a region defined by "color blindness" rather than by its tradition of white supremacy.[42] At the same time, the FEPC's ability to promote its vision of the West depended on support from larger and stronger federal agencies. Although employees of those agencies were willing to endorse some FEPC actions, most of the WMC and WLB officials were more interested in conducting the war efficiently than in reshaping the West. But even though the FEPC did not always succeed, its efforts made it clear that at least one federal agency wanted to dismantle white supremacy in the West.

Many western politicians objected strenuously to this change in federal policy. Both senators from Colorado and South Dakota and one each from

Texas and Wyoming voted to kill the FEPC in 1944. This number may seem insignificant—after all, six senators represented less than one-fifth of the thirty-two western senators, and only two other senators from outside the South (both of them from Maine) voted to eliminate funds for the FEPC.[43] But in later votes, western senators, many of them Republicans, lined up more closely with southern Democrats. Eleven western senators voted against cloture in a key vote on fair employment practices in 1946. This time four senators from the Northeast voted against cloture. By refusing to end Louisiana Senator Allen Ellender's filibuster, western senators effectively killed the legislation that would have created a permanent FEPC.[44]

Although the actions of legislators do not necessarily reflect the attitudes of their constituents, many white western voters agreed with their elected representatives. In 1946, the voters of California overwhelmingly rejected an initiative that would have outlawed employment discrimination and created a state version of the FEPC.[45] Many western state legislatures made no effort to outlaw employment discrimination, although Oregon, Washington, and New Mexico did pass fair employment practices legislation in 1949.[46]

At the same time as one small and relatively powerless federal agency began to attack white supremacy in the West, another promised to fulfill the fondest dreams of western white supremacists. Since the late nineteenth century, political leaders in California, Oregon, and Washington had hoped that Japanese Americans could be removed from their states. After the Army incarcerated those who lived near the coast in 1942, many West Coast politicians attempted to maintain pressure on the federal government in the hope that Japanese Americans would never be allowed to return to their homes.[47] Newspapers railed against Japanese Americans for sabotaging the war effort by refusing to relinquish their farm equipment. The sheriff of Los Angeles County and several members of the state legislature endorsed an effort to strengthen the Alien Land Law, which prevented Japanese immigrants from owning land in California.[48] By the end of the war, however, the federal government had begun a campaign of its own to thwart the efforts of western white supremacists.

The key agency in this campaign was the War Relocation Authority (WRA), established by President Roosevelt in 1942 to operate the concentration camps where Japanese Americans were taken. In the early days of the WRA's existence, many of its employees believed and repeated the rumors that the Army had used to justify imprisonment of Japanese Americans. In an August 1942 speech, for example, the chief of the WRA Reports Division told a Denver audience that "strange radio calls from secret stations hidden in the hills along the coast" and "a searchlight cunningly concealed in a chimney" in a Japanese American's home had convinced military authorities that the removal of all Japanese Americans was "necessary to the security of the area along the Pacific coast."[49]

Not all WRA employees harbored suspicions about the loyalty of Japanese Americans, for a significant number who worked in the camps had volunteered for their positions out of a sense that they could help to serve Japanese Americans.[50] Many of the teachers in the camps were Quakers, and some WRA employees, especially those in the "community analysis" section, were liberal or left-leaning academics who had some influence over their coworkers. They prepared reports that debunked myths about Japanese Americans, and the WRA distributed them to all of the agency's employees. John Embree, an anthropologist who worked as a community analysis officer, advised other WRA employees: "Each staff member should make every effort to know personally and well as many evacuees of as many social types as he can. Only in this way can some of the fears and rumors prevalent among the evacuees be brought to light and so killed off just as darkness-loving bacteria die when exposed to sunshine."[51] As WRA employees worked with Japanese Americans (throughout the agency many clerical workers were Japanese American women), they frequently came to view them as being much like other groups of Americans. This contact across racial boundaries led some WRA employees to defend the loyalty of their coworkers.

Some of the WRA officials' attitudes changed, too, because many other federal employees treated them as if they were Japanese Americans. The U.S. Civil Service Commission, for example, did not accept a WRA clearance as proof of loyalty but conducted its own special investigation of every Japanese American who applied to work for the federal government. People "with little or no background in dealing with" Japanese Americans usually conducted the special investigations, according to WRA Director Dillon S. Myer. "On several known occasions," Myer complained to Interior Secretary Harold L. Ickes, "adverse decisions have been based on the flimsiest of evidence or on totally wrong information." These special investigations unduly delayed the appointment of qualified Japanese American employees.[52] In an effort to resolve the problem, Myer met with Civil Service Commissioner Arthur Flemming in July 1943. In a heated discussion, Myer told Flemming: "I'm having a hard time in getting our folks to keep their faith in our government with so many people in the government running out on us after we made a commitment, and particularly the Civil Service, whom they'd had a good deal of feeling about."[53] It is not clear if Myer was referring to Japanese Americans or WRA employees as "our folks," but the Civil Service Commission, like many other Americans, viewed both groups as potential traitors. In defending Japanese Americans and their civil rights, War Relocation Authority officials were also defending their own loyalty.[54]

The WRA's history as an advocate of racial equality began in 1943. Some WRA employees recognized that the anti–Japanese American campaign raging on the Pacific Coast could have tragic consequences. WRA attorney Edgar Bernhard, for example, realized that the effort to strip Japanese American citizens of their constitutional rights would fail. They would eventually be free to return to the coast, and Bernhard believed that if the WRA did not try to influence public opinion, gunshots and arson would greet them when they came home. "What is needed," he told the agency's director, "is the best publicity brains that can be hired and a large budget devoted to favorable propaganda."[55] Although it moved haltingly, the WRA acted upon some of Bernhard's recommendations.

The War Relocation Authority's propaganda campaign began in 1944 and expanded in 1945, when Japanese Americans began returning to the coast. In Los Angeles, WRA public relations officers spoke frequently to clubs and organizations. According to WRA records, members spoke to nearly 15,000 people at meetings of church organizations, service clubs, and women's groups between May 1945 and March 1946.[56] In their speeches, they emphasized the loyalty of Japanese Americans and the valor of Japanese American soldiers. They tried to convince their audiences that Japanese Americans were Americans who belonged in the West.

As WRA employees worked to defuse hostility, they began to recognize the similarities between discrimination against Japanese Americans and discrimination against other groups, especially African Americans and Mexican Americans. Some agency officials cooperated with other civil rights activists. The WRA's Human Relations Committee, for example, "dealt with practically all minorities, with the Japanese element sandwiched in between."[57] WRA propaganda reflected a growing concern for African Americans and Mexican Americans. In December 1945, the WRA released an editorial that claimed that racism had prevented the United Nations from locating their headquarters in San Francisco. The home of the United Nations, the release said, must be a city free from racial prejudice. "Here in California the Negroes and the Nisei have been the brunt of attacks by homefront Nazis. Fortunately most Californians are democratically minded—but enough of them indulged in witch-burning, if you please, to turn the United Nations away from this state, despite San Francisco's splendid reception."[58]

In an October 1945 speech before a California peace officers' convention, the WRA's assistant director explained the agency's outlook. Robert Cozzens insisted that the WRA's struggle against racial discrimination rested on its interpretation of the Constitution. "Those of us who recognize the constitutional demands for political and economic equality of all men must also recognize that there are elements among us who adhere to a long-rejected doctrine that this is a white man's country," Cozzens said. "Our two-front war was fought to defeat the conflicting theories that this was a white man's world on the one hand or that it was a Japanese world on the other. Both theories having been blasted out of existence, it is assumed that we are now in a world that makes no color distinction."[59] Although it seems doubtful that Cozzens naively believed that the Constitution and the war had created a "color-blind" society, his words did carry the weight of federal authority. Later in the speech, he emphasized the importance of obedience to federal and state laws: "I don't happen to believe that breaking the state laws and violating the Federal constitution can or should be condoned by anyone claiming to support a government of law and order," he said. "If anyone in any state acts in a way that abrogates the Bill of Rights, he attempts to secede by that much from the Union."[60]

Western white supremacists lashed out at the WRA more fiercely than they attacked the FEPC, most likely because the WRA had a much larger staff and budget.[61] The WRA, an independent agency for the first two years of its existence, gained even greater stature in early 1944 when it became an agency of the Department of the Interior. Almost from its inception, the War Relocation Authority was a target of anti–Japanese American "patriots." In July 1942, U.S. Representative Leland Ford of California said that the "WRA program now is going to be run as one of the 'social gain' ideas, rather than the original principle of placing these people in camps for the protection and safety of this country." Ford also said, "We thought that the Japanese should not be given consideration above our own American people."[62] In 1943, newspapers reported that the WRA was "coddling" Japanese Americans. Articles first printed in the *Denver Post* claimed that the evacuees had more and better food to eat than Americans outside the camps. The publicity resulted in two congressional investigations.[63]

Congressional antagonism toward the War Relocation Authority resembled the hostility to the FEPC. In both cases a minority of representatives and senators objected to these agencies and their policies. The minority of members who did object, however, worked diligently to maintain white supremacy. Southern representatives and senators spearheaded the attacks on the FEPC. They relied for support on western members of Congress and on a few members from the Midwest and Northeast. Westerners led the campaign against the WRA, and southerners provided support. As soon as rumors about the WRA's "coddling" of Japanese Americans began to circulate in early 1943, Representative John E. Rankin of Mississippi rose on the floor of the House to "protest against coddling the Japs." He said: "The American people are sick and tired of this policy of pampering the Japs in these concentration camps. Those camps should be turned over to the Army, and every one of them should be put under strict military control."[64]

Politicians' hostility toward the WRA increased as the public became more aware of agency officials' ideas about racial equality. When the WRA initiated its propaganda campaign, California's congressional delegation and newspaper editors complained. "Fat envelopes, sent under government frank, are pouring from the WRA offices, stuffed with out and out propaganda in behalf of the Japanese," the *Fresno Bee* of August 19, 1944, insisted. Three members of Congress asked the House Appropriations Committee to prohibit the WRA from using funds to print and disseminate "propaganda favoring the Japanese people." These members of Congress—Clair Engle, J. Leroy Johnson, and Jack Anderson—showed members of the committee copies of WRA publications, including "Nisei in Uniform," which described the heroic fighting of the Japanese American 442nd Infantry Regiment in Italy. "There were hundreds, or perhaps thousands, of units in our army which made as good or a better record than that of the Japanese unit," Johnson erroneously reported, "but there is no bureau sending out expensive articles telling of their glorious exploits." Engle insisted that "tax funds should not be used to propagandize for any racial group. . . . The free American press can and is taking care of the controversy in regard to the merit or lack of merit of the Japanese as a racial group, and that is where the matter should be left. . . . The WRA was never set up for the purpose of convincing the American people the Japanese are a superior or better race, but that seems to be their concept of their mission."[65]

State and local officials as well as members of Congress criticized the WRA. Like the white southerners who attacked the FEPC and other federal agencies, some of these politicians insisted that the WRA's actions infringed on states' rights. According to one California state senator, the WRA had decided that Japanese Americans did not need to obey California state laws. Hugh Donnelly of Fresno told a newspaper editor in 1945 that WRA attorneys were giving Japanese Americans advice on how to circumvent the Alien Land Law.[66]

Some newspaper reporters, editors, and publishers broadened their attacks on "federal agencies," claiming that officials other than those working for the WRA had begun to favor Japanese Americans over European Americans. In November 1945, one Los Angeles daily reported that "federal agencies acted with frenzied speed here yesterday to provide emergency housing—but for Japs, exclusively! Forgotten were thousands of returned war veterans and their families, and other solid citizens" who were forced to roam "the streets in vain, searching for domestic shelter—a hovel, a room—anything. It was everything for the Japs. Nothing for others."[67] The same newspaper later published an article that contradicted this article, although the conflicting information did not surface in the lead paragraphs. A public housing official cited in the later article said that Japanese Americans had not been given priority over other people on waiting lists. "In fact, we still have approximately 75 vacancies," John E. Peterson, Federal Public Housing Administration manager for the area, told a reporter for the *Los Angeles Examiner*.[68] Despite this contradiction, these articles clearly suggested that white people should be concerned by the federal government's waning commitment to white supremacy.

Not all of the WRA's opponents expressed their dislike for the agency or for Japanese Americans in words. Japanese Americans who returned to California in 1945 endured more than 275 reported attacks by "night riders" (terrorists who shot into homes), cases of arson, threats, and other acts of intimidation.[69] WRA employees and other federal officials also received threats. When Interior Secretary Ickes denounced West Coast terrorism, some people threatened his life. One man who identified himself as a Beverly Hills businessman sent Ickes a telegram that said, "Perhaps when some of the boys come back from the Pacific . . . and know of your sentiments in regards to the beasts that go by the name of Japs, you will turn up missing some morning." The telegram's author also applauded the actions of "the hoodlums as you call them. They are at least trying to do more for the future generations of this country than you can ever do."[70]

WRA officials responded forcefully to attacks from politicians and other critics. In 1945, for example, U.S. Representative Harry R. Sheppard of San Bernardino County accused the WRA of being party to an "official conspiracy to release Japanese Americans from internment camps."[71] When Sheppard questioned the WRA's loyalty, the agency's Los Angeles area supervisor, Paul G. Robertson, argued that the WRA's fellow conspirators must have been the War Department and the U.S. Supreme Court, both of which had decided that Japanese Americans should be released from the camps. In a skillful reversal of the charges, Robertson insisted that "Sheppard's assertion that persons likely to engage in sabotage are returning to the West Coast" was "a very satisfactory method for shaking public confidence in government agencies vital to the war."[72]

The WRA's response to Sheppard's charge did not relieve the suspicions that Sheppard and other white westerners harbored about a federal conspiracy to destroy white supremacy in the West.[73] Sheppard's perceptions both reflected and shaped the beliefs of many of his white constituents. Throughout the war years, some constituents complained to their elected officials about actions that they perceived as government favoritism toward racial minorities. In November 1943 an attorney wrote to Los Angeles County Supervisor John Anson Ford to warn him that "the danger now is not that minorities will not be afforded equal opportunity but that we may be ruled by minorities. It will mean viciously bad government for us if we get into the frame of mind to which minorities are endeavoring to persuade us that all races are the same, that there are no differences, in the hope that we will ignore their deficiencies and differences and permit them to attain positions of power and oppression over the majority."[74]

Although historians may be tempted to dismiss this letter and others like it as the rantings of irrational people, it makes sense to take these letters seriously. The writers knew that government policies were changing, if only slightly, in ways that foretold the end of white supremacy in the West and throughout the nation. These changes in federal policies conflicted with their fundamental belief that God had made white people superior to all other groups. Many of these people tried to convince elected officials that American Indians, African Americans, Mexican Americans, and Asian Americans were inferior to whites. When elected officials dismissed white supremacists' fears, as some did, these people were more inclined to believe that their elected officials and government bureaucrats had conspired to deprive them of their rights.

Nearly one hundred years after U.S. conquest of the West, then, two federal agencies began to embrace the vision of the West advanced by many African Americans, Mexican Americans, Asian Americans, American Indians, and white racial liberals. White supremacists throughout the country recognized the actions of the FEPC and WRA as indications that the federal government's racial policies had begun to change. By the end of the war, many white residents of Los Angeles had come to mistrust the federal government. Each year brought them news of federal actions that threatened to destroy white supremacy. In 1946, a federal district court ordered school districts in Orange County to cease segregating Mexican American students from white students. In 1948, the U.S. Supreme Court decided that courts could no longer enforce racially restrictive covenants that governed the buying and selling of property. In southern California this decision moved many white people to action. The Los Angeles Realty Board, for example, urged the National Association of Real Estate Boards to begin a campaign to amend the U.S. Constitution in order to "confer upon the courts of the states and the United States power to enforce conditions, covenants or provisions in deeds, contracts or other instruments restricting the ownership or occupancy of real property to Caucasians or to Negroes, respectively."[75] In many districts people formed homeowners' associations in an effort to keep African Americans from purchasing homes in their neighborhoods. These organizations and some individuals often tried to intimidate people of color who sought to purchase homes in previously all-white neighborhoods. In the Eagle Rock district of Los Angeles, a police officer and more than fifty neighbors burned a cross in a vacant lot across from a house that a white homeowner had listed with an African American realtor. At a meeting of the local Kiwanis club the next day, a white realtor asked club members to help him keep African Americans from moving into Eagle Rock, and the publisher of the local newspaper said that "it sometimes becomes necessary to go outside the law in order to protect the community."[76]

In this atmosphere, in which seemingly "respectable" and "upstanding" citizens could endorse terrorism, a more extreme white supremacist and antifederal movement soon emerged. By the early 1950s, the Los Angeles County Human Relations Committee reported that several white supremacist groups had established themselves in Los Angeles. They included Wesley Swift's Anglo-Saxon Christian Congregation, the Great Pyramid Club, the Peoples Lobby, and the Cinema Educational Guild. According to the Human Relations Committee, the Anglo-Saxon Christian Congregation opposed the United Nations, "the national administration, bipartisan foreign policy, the Roosevelt family, Jews, Negroes and labor unions." The Great Pyramid Club served as an "avenue for the anti-Semitic, anti-Negro, racist expressions of professional hatemongers." In addition to holding weekly or monthly meetings, these organizations distributed white supremacist literature throughout the Los Angeles area.[77] Gerald L. K. Smith first spoke in Los Angeles in 1943, and he returned to southern California every year in the 1940s. Although Smith's mass rallies did not attract the number of people that counterdemonstrations did, he attracted significant audiences with his diatribes against an international conspiracy of Jewish bankers.[78] In 1953,

Smith moved the headquarters of his "Christian Nationalist Crusade" from St. Louis to Los Angeles.[79]

In the 1950s and 1960s, the federal government continued to move in the opposite direction from many white westerners. As the Warren Court embraced racial equality and Congress enacted civil rights legislation, both the widespread antifederal sentiment and the more radical and militant white supremacist organizations persisted. Numerous western politicians have since tapped the reservoirs of antifederal sentiment and white supremacist attitudes. The antifederal, anti-immigrant, anti-affirmative-action rhetoric of a growing number of western politicians has granted greater legitimacy to the increasingly violent radical white supremacist organizations. A few politicians have actively supported these organizations.[80] The radical groups in the West that gained the attention of the media in 1995 are, to a considerable extent, the progeny of the hostility toward the federal government that surfaced during and after World War II.

NOTES

1. My understanding of media coverage of the Oklahoma City bombing and of the militia movement draws primarily upon articles published in the *New York Times* and upon Cable News Network and CBS Evening News broadcasts. The first articles about the militia appeared a few days after the explosion. See "Links in Blast: Armed 'Militia' and a Key Date," *New York Times*, April 22, 1995, 1; and "Authorities Hold a Man of 'Extreme Right-Wing Views,' " *New York Times*, April 22, 1995, 9.

2. According to the Southern Poverty Law Center's Klanwatch Project, which maintains the largest database on violent extremist groups in the United States, the Christian Identity sect's "hatred of the federal government is unmatched." Although most of the major Christian Identity congregations are located in the South and West, there are significant congregations in the Midwest—two each in Illinois, Indiana, and Michigan, and one each in Minnesota and Wisconsin. There are armed Identity compounds in Arizona (two), Idaho, Missouri (three), Oklahoma (three), and Texas. The Klanwatch Project reports two Identity compounds in Pennsylvania, although there is no major congregation north of Virginia or east of Indiana. See *Klanwatch Intelligence Report*, no. 79 (August 1995), 1–4.

3. Richard White, "The Current Weirdness in the West," *Western Historical Quarterly* 28 (Spring 1997): 5–16.

4. A number of scholars have examined the history of white racial attitudes and

their influence on westward expansion, especially in the nineteenth century. For a good bibliography of sources published before 1986, see Richard White, "Race Relations in the American West," *American Quarterly* 38 (1986): 396–416. Authors whose work has influenced my interpretation of racial attitudes and race relations in the West include Leonard Pitt, *The Decline of the Californios: A Social History of the Spanish-Speaking Californians, 1846–1890* (Berkeley: University of California Press, 1966); Eugene H. Berwanger, *The Frontier Against Slavery: Western Anti-Negro Prejudice and the Slavery Extension Controversy* (Urbana: University of Illinois Press, 1967); Alexander Saxton, *The Indispensable Enemy: Labor and the Anti-Chinese Movement in California* (Berkeley: University of California Press, 1971); Robert F. Berkhofer, Jr., *The White Man's Indian: Images of the American Indian from Columbus to the Present* (New York: Knopf, 1978); Ronald T. Takaki, *Iron Cages: Race and Culture in Nineteenth-Century America* (New York: Knopf, 1979); Richard Drinnon, *Facing West: The Metaphysics of Indian-Hating and Empire-Building* (Minneapolis: University of Minnesota Press, 1980); Eugene H. Berwanger, *The West and Reconstruction* (Urbana: University of Illinois Press, 1981); Reginald Horsman, *Race and Manifest Destiny: The Origins of American Racial Anglo-Saxonism* (Cambridge: Harvard University Press, 1981); Arnoldo de León, *They Called Them Greasers: Anglo Attitudes Toward Mexicans in Texas, 1821–1900* (Austin: University of Texas Press, 1983); Patricia Nelson Limerick, *The Legacy of Conquest: The Unbroken Past of the American West* (New York: Norton, 1987); David Montejano, *Anglos and Mexicans in the Making of Texas, 1836–1986* (Austin: University of Texas Press, 1987); Alexander Saxton, *The Rise and Fall of the White Republic: Class Politics and Mass Culture in Nineteenth-Century America* (London: Verso, 1990); and Tomás Almaguer, *Racial Fault Lines: The Historical Origins of White Supremacy in California* (Berkeley: University of California Press, 1994).

5. The classic statement of this argument is Edmund S. Morgan, *American Slavery, American Freedom: The Ordeal of Colonial Virginia* (New York: Norton, 1975), esp. 338–46 and 363–87.

6. For an early discussion of some of these myths, see Henry Nash Smith, *Virgin Land: The American West as Symbol and Myth* (Cambridge: Harvard University Press, 1950). Smith does not always unravel the racial content of the myths about the West, but a careful reading of his analysis allows for some appreciation of the importance of "whiteness" to the people who shaped and embraced these myths. More recent discussions include Richard Slotkin's trilogy, *Regeneration Through Violence: The Mythology of the American Frontier, 1600–1860* (Middletown, Conn.: Wesleyan University Press, 1973), *The Fatal Environment: The Myth of the Frontier in the Age of Industrialization, 1800–1890* (New York: Atheneum, 1985), and *Gunfighter*

Nation: The Myth of the Frontier in Twentieth-Century America (New York: Atheneum, 1992). See also the relevant chapters in Saxton, *The Rise and Fall of the White Republic*, 165–203, 321–47.

7. See Berwanger, *The Frontier Against Slavery*, 79; Quintard Taylor, "Freedmen and Slaves in Oregon Territory, 1840–1860," in *Peoples of Color in the American West*, ed. Sucheng Chan, Douglas Henry Daniels, Mario T. García, and Terry P. Wilson (Lexington, Mass.: Heath, 1994), 77; John Mack Faragher, *Women and Men on the Overland Trail* (New Haven: Yale University Press, 1979), 16; and John D. Unruh, Jr., *The Plains Across: The Overland Emigrants and the Trans-Mississippi West, 1840–1860* (Urbana: University of Illinois Press, 1979), 91. Reginald Horsman has argued persuasively that the westward movement of the 1840s and 1850s coincided with the growth of "scientific" racialism. As physicians and other "scientists" gathered evidence to prove that Indians, Asians, Latin Americans, and African Americans were inferior to white people, politicians and promoters used this evidence to justify U.S. expansion and the subjection of native peoples. See Horsman, *Race and Manifest Destiny*.

8. Taylor, "Freedmen and Slaves," 75–81; Burnett quote, 78. In 1849, Burnett, who had moved from Oregon to California, became California's first elected governor. In his initial speech to the legislature, he asked for passage of a law to exclude free African Americans from moving to California. See Berwanger, *The Frontier Against Slavery*, 70–71.

9. Virginia native Charles T. Betts proposed the amendment. When another delegate pointed out that "many citizens of California have received from nature a very dark skin" but have been allowed to vote, Betts said that he "had no objection to color, except so far as it indicated the inferior races of mankind." Betts said that he "would be perfectly willing to use any words which would exclude the African and Indian races. It was in this sense the word white had been understood and used. His only object was to exclude those objectionable races—not objectionable for their color, but for what that color indicates." J. Ross Browne, *Report of the Debates in the Convention of California* (Washington, D.C.: J. T. Towers, 1850), 48. See also Walton Bean, *California: An Interpretive History* (New York: McGraw-Hill, 1968), 130.

10. Richard White, *"It's Your Misfortune and None of My Own": A History of the American West* (Norman: University of Oklahoma Press, 1991), 322. White first developed this interpretation in "Race Relations in the American West."

11. In western towns and cities, residential and occupational segregation became more complete in the late nineteenth and early twentieth centuries. See Victor G. Nee and Brett de Bary Nee, *Longtime Californ': A Documentary Study of an American Chinatown* (New York: Pantheon, 1972), 52–55; Albert Camarillo, *Chicanos in a*

Changing Society: From Mexican Pueblos to American Barrios in Santa Barbara and Southern California, 1848–1930 (Cambridge: Harvard University Press, 1979); and Montejano, *Anglos and Mexicans*, 157–254.

12. The classic study of the politics of Chinese exclusion is Elmer Clarence Sandmeyer, *The Anti-Chinese Movement in California* (Urbana: University of Illinois Press, 1939).

13. For a thorough discussion of the events leading to the Gentlemen's Agreement, see Roger Daniels, *The Politics of Prejudice: The Anti-Japanese Movement in California and the Struggle for Japanese Exclusion* (Berkeley: University of California Press, 1962), 34–45.

14. Ibid., 65–107.

15. See Francisco E. Balderrama and Raymond Rodríguez, *Decade of Betrayal: Mexican Repatriation in the 1930s* (Albuquerque: University of New Mexico Press, 1995).

16. For discussions of reasons why people from Asia, Latin America, and the South moved to the West, see Nell Irvin Painter, *Exodusters: Black Migration to Kansas After Reconstruction* (New York: Knopf, 1977); Quintard Taylor, *The Forging of a Black Community: Seattle's Central District from 1870 through the Civil Rights Era* (Seattle: University of Washington Press, 1994); Mario T. García, *Desert Immigrants: The Mexicans of El Paso, 1880–1920* (New Haven: Yale University Press, 1981); and Henry Shih-Shan Tsai, *The Chinese Experience in America* (Bloomington: Indiana University Press, 1986).

17. Most of the discussions of working-class white supremacy in the West have focused on the anti-Chinese movement. See Isabella Black, "American Labour and Chinese Immigration," *Past and Present* 25 (1963): 59–76; Stuart Creighton Miller, *The Unwelcome Immigrant: The American Image of the Chinese, 1785–1882* (Berkeley: University of California Press, 1969), 145–204; Saxton, *The Indispensable Enemy*; Herbert Hill, "Anti-Oriental Agitation and the Rise of Working-Class Racism," *Society* 10 (January/February 1973): 43–54; and David R. Roediger, *The Wages of Whiteness: Race and the Making of the American Working Class* (London: Verso, 1991), 179–80.

18. See W. Sherman Savage, *Blacks in the West* (Westport, Conn.: Greenwood, 1976), 139–56; and Douglas Henry Daniels, *Pioneer Urbanites: A Social and Cultural History of Black San Francisco* (Philadelphia: Temple University Press, 1980), 106–22.

19. For discussions of the activities of these organizations in various locations, see Albert S. Broussard, *Black San Francisco: The Struggle for Racial Equality in the West, 1900–1954* (Lawrence: University Press of Kansas, 1993); Taylor, *Forging of a Black Community*; and Mario T. García, *Mexican Americans: Leadership, Ideology, and Identity, 1930–1960* (New Haven: Yale University Press, 1989).

20. U.S. Fair Employment Practice Committee, *Final Report* (Washington, D.C.,

1946), 2. Scholars have been debating the FEPC almost since its demise. See Louis C. Kesselman, *The Social Politics of FEPC: A Study in Reform Pressure Movements* (Chapel Hill: University of North Carolina Press, 1948); Louis Ruchames, *Race, Jobs, and Politics: The Story of FEPC* (New York: Columbia University Press, 1953); Richard M. Dalfiume, "The 'Forgotten Years' of the Negro Revolution," *Journal of American History* 55 (1968): 90–106; Harvard Sitkoff, "Racial Militancy and Interracial Violence in the Second World War," *Journal of American History* 58 (1971): 661–81; Merl E. Reed, "FEPC, the Black Worker and the Southern Shipyards," *South Atlantic Quarterly* 74 (1975): 446–67; Reed, "FEPC and the Federal Agencies in the South," *Journal of Negro History* 55 (1980): 43–56; William H. Harris, "Federal Intervention in Union Discrimination: FEPC and West Coast Shipyards During World War II," *Labor History* 22 (1981): 325–47; Reed, "Black Workers, Defense Industries, and Federal Agencies in Pennsylvania, 1941–1945," *Labor History* 27 (1986): 356–84; Clete Daniel, *Chicano Workers and the Politics of Fairness: The FEPC in the Southwest, 1941–1945* (Austin: University of Texas Press, 1991); Reed, *Seedtime for the Modern Civil Rights Movement: The President's Committee on Fair Employment Practice, 1941–1946* (Baton Rouge: Louisiana State University Press, 1991); and Emilio Zamora, "The Failed Promise of Wartime Opportunity for Mexicans in the Texas Oil Industry," *Southwestern Historical Quarterly* 95 (1991–92): 323–50.

21. "A Summary of the Hearings of the President's Committee on Fair Employment Practice Held in Los Angeles, California, October 20 and 21, 1941, with Findings and Recommendations" (pp. 3–4), in "Los Angeles Summaries" folder, box 464, Division of Field Operations, Office Files of Eugene Davidson, 1941–46, Records of the FEPC, Record Group 228, National Archives, Washington, D.C. (hereafter cited as FEPC Records). There is a discrepancy between this report and the final report of the FEPC. See the *Final Report*, 11.

22. "A Summary of the Hearings of the President's Committee," 3.

23. The most complete discussion of employment among African Americans in Los Angeles is Alonzo N. Smith, "Black Employment in the Los Angeles Area, 1938–1948" (Ph.D. diss., University of California, Los Angeles, 1978).

24. FEPC, *Final Report*, 2, 37.

25. Harry L. Kingman to Will Maslow [FEPC director of operations] and Theodore Jones [FEPC budget director and chief administrative officer], 18 January 1945, reel 41, Headquarters Files, FEPC Records, quoted in Daniel, *Chicano Workers and the Politics of Fairness*, 218. Kingman was not the only civil rights activist serving as a regional director for the FEPC in the West. The regional director for the FEPC's Region X, headquartered in Dallas, was Dr. Carlos Castañeda, a University of Texas history professor and a Mexican American civil rights leader. See Zamora, "Failed Promise," 330–31.

Kingman's wife was also a proponent of racial equality. During the war, Ruth Kingman served as the secretary of the Pacific Coast Committee on American Principles and Fair Play, which worked to convince the public and federal officials that Japanese Americans should be treated fairly. After the war, she worked for the American Council on Race Relations. For an organizational history of the Fair Play Committee, see Atlee E. Shidler, "The Fair Play Committee: A Study in the Protection of the Rights of Minority Groups" (M.A. thesis, Claremont Graduate School, 1951).

26. Memorandum, Frank B. Reeves to FEPC Special Counsel and Staff Working on West Coast Hearings, 15 October 1943, box 330, Legal Division, FEPC Records. My understanding of the shipyard workers' case has been influenced by Josh Sides, "Battle on the Home Front: African American Shipyard Workers in World War II Los Angeles," *California History* 75 (Fall 1996): 251–63.

27. "Appendix A: Documentary Evidence submitted in connection with complaints against Boilermakers Local #92," box 330, Legal Division, FEPC Records.

28. The petition said that the taking of dues from black auxiliary members "constitutes taxation without representation and violates the basic democratic principles of our nation." Like other black people trying to gain guarantees of their civil rights, the committee relied on the rhetoric of wartime. "We are engaged in a desperate life and death struggle with the Axis all over the world in an effort to preserve our democratic principles of justice, freedom and equality," the petitions continued. "Certainly we do not intend to lose the war on the home front." Transcript of hearing, "In the Matter of Western Pipe and Steel Company, Consolidated Steel Corporation, California Shipbuilding Corporation, and Auxiliary Lodge A-35 and Subordinate Lodge No. 92, International Brotherhood of Boilermakers, Iron Ship Builders, and Helpers of America" (p. 50), Los Angeles, 19 November 1943, box 330, Legal Division, FEPC Records.

29. "In the Matter of Western Pipe and Steel Company," 10.

30. "Transcript of Proceedings Before the President's Committee on Fair Employment Practices" (p. 7), Los Angeles, 7 August 1944, box 330, Legal Division, FEPC Records. For more complete discussions of the shipyard discrimination cases, see Harris, "Federal Intervention in Union Discrimination."

31. A parallel case in the San Francisco area resulted in the California Supreme Court's ruling that the discrimination by the Boilermakers violated state laws. Still, the union resisted integration. The FEPC pursued the case more zealously than it did the case of shipbuilders in Los Angeles. See Harris, "Federal Intervention in Union Discrimination," and Charles Wollenberg, "*James v. Marinship:* Trouble on the New Black Frontier," *California History* 60 (Fall 1981): 262–79. Similar cases occurred throughout the nation. The FEPC often failed to convince employers and unions in

"vital" war industries to cease their discrimination. Malcolm Ross wrote about the case of the Western Cartridge Company, a subsidiary of Olin Industries, Inc.: "It was a clear issue. Tucked away in a rural area of southern Illinois was a munitions plant of first importance to the war. Here 13,000 white workers were turning out bullets and cartridge brass. No Negroes were allowed to work in the plant or live in the community. Yet the company's contract with the government provided that it would 'not discriminate against any worker because of race, creed, color or national origin.' In theory the company's refusal to hire qualified Negro workers should have canceled its entire contract. But suppose American lives are dependent on the production of Olin cartridges? Who is to judge the present value of lives against the long-term value of democracy?" Malcolm Ross, *All Manner of Men* (New York: Reynal and Hitchcock, 1948), 49–66; quote, 50.

32. P. B. Harris to Thomas F. Neblett of the War Labor Board, 26 February 1943, box 345, Legal Division, FEPC Records.

33. Telegram from FEPC executive secretary Lawrence W. Cramer to P. B. Harris, 23 February 1943; telegram from Francis J. Haas, FEPC chairman, to Harris, 9 July 1943; Harris to Haas, 13 July 1943; box 345, Legal Division, FEPC Records.

34. "Los Angeles and the LARY Case," memo from Carol Coan and C. L. Golightly to John A. Davis, 27 May 1944 (p. 3), box 346, Legal Division, FEPC Records.

35. Ibid.

36. "LARY Losing Ground in Its Discrimination Stand," *California Eagle*, March 30, 1944, 11.

37. "WMC Rule Out LARY," *California Eagle*, March 30, 1944, 10.

38. "Presentation by Dr. E. C. Farnham before President's Committee on Fair Employment Practice, Los Angeles, California, August 8, 1944" (pp. 1–2), box 345, Legal Division, FEPC Records. Farnham was unable to present his speech, so Wile read the presentation. See "Transcript of Proceedings," Case 66 [Los Angeles Railway], 8 August 1944, box 345, Legal Division, FEPC Records.

39. "Transcript of Proceedings," 187–88.

40. Harris to FEPC, 9 August 1944, box 345, Legal Division, FEPC Records.

41. Undated teletype from Harry L. Kingman, regional director of the FEPC, to Malcolm Ross, box 346, Legal Division, FEPC Records. Historians who have previously interpreted the LARY case have not noted that the railway's manpower priority rating was suspended. See the discussion of the case in Smith, "Black Employment in the Los Angeles Area," 262–70; and Alonzo N. Smith, "Blacks and the Los Angeles Municipal Transit System, 1941–1945," *Urbanism Past and Present* 6 (1980–81): 25–31.

42. The radicalism of the FEPC was apparent in the agency's final report, which argued that "nothing short of congressional action to end employment discrimina-

tion can prevent the freezing of American workers into fixed groups, with ability and hard work of no account to those of the 'wrong' race or religion." See the FEPC *Final Report*, esp. viii–xii and 41–97; quote, viii.

43. For a record of the U.S. Senate's vote on the elimination of funds for the FEPC, see *Congressional Quarterly Almanac* 1 (1945): 167–70. The House managed to avoid voting on any legislation or amendment related either to the wartime FEPC or to a permanent FEPC. For a discussion of congressional hostility toward the FEPC, see Ruchames, *Race, Jobs, and Politics*, 73–99 and 121–36; and Ross, *All Manner of Men*. Both authors emphasize that most of the overt hostility toward the FEPC came from the South, but congressional actions against the FEPC had support from a number of members from all over the country. Ross said that many members of Congress disliked the FEPC because its members and staff were not "respectable by congressional standards. There were Jews and many Negroes in this agency. Let's face it. That fact was the subject not only of whispering campaigns but of derisive shouts on the floor of Congress." Ross, *All Manner of Men*, 83.

44. *Congressional Record*, 79th Cong., 2d sess., 92 (9 February 1946): 1219. Not all western politicians, however, were hostile toward fair employment practices. Malcolm Ross, who served as the chairman of the FEPC for three years, observed that U.S. Senator Wayne Morse of Oregon "alone took a stand diametrically opposed to his own political fortunes" in 1945. "The 20,000 Negro war workers newly settled in Portland would affect no Oregon elections. Portland looked forward to getting rid of them. But Morse knew that they would remain and that Portland would someday have to decide whether to let them be wage-earning citizens or pariah objects of city relief. He extended the dilemma to the national scene, and staged—at the night session of the last day of debate—a one-man revolt in support of no compromise on FEPC's appropriation." Ross, *All Manner of Men*, 260.

45. For a brief treatment of the debates surrounding the fair employment practices initiative in California, see Kevin Allen Leonard, "Years of Hope, Days of Fear: The Impact of World War II on Race Relations in Los Angeles" (Ph.D. diss., University of California, Davis, 1992), 327–31. California did not outlaw employment discrimination until 1959, just five years before Congress passed the landmark Civil Rights Act of 1964.

46. Ruchames, *Race, Jobs, and Politics*, 165. The question of why these states enacted fair employment practices legislation has yet to be addressed by scholars.

47. For a discussion of opposition to Japanese Americans in the West and its relation to their removal by the Army from the Pacific Coast, see Roger Daniels, *Concentration Camps USA: Japanese Americans and World War II* (Hinsdale, Ill.: Dryden Press, 1971), 1–41. Although many coastal politicians were pleased to see Japanese Americans removed during the war from most of California, Oregon, and

Washington, politicians in the western interior expressed fears that Japanese Americans would overrun their states. One of the most vocal of these politicians was Wyoming Governor Nels Smith (ibid., 94).

48. For a thorough discussion of the anti–Japanese American campaign, see Carey McWilliams, *Prejudice: Japanese-Americans, Symbol of Racial Intolerance* (Boston: Little, Brown, 1944).

49. Frank C. Cross, address before the Women's Council on International Affairs, Denver, 25 August 1942, "Speeches 1942" folder, box 12, Washington Office Records, Records of the War Relocation Authority, Record Group 210, National Archives, Washington, D.C. (hereafter cited as WRA Records).

50. Erica Harth's mother worked for the WRA at Manzanar for a year. Both of Harth's parents, "as Communists, . . . could not have been completely happy with the party line from our wartime allies in Moscow to support Roosevelt's policies. They embraced the party's now paradoxical stand against racism and were profoundly opposed to the internment." Harth's mother "coached me in the WRA line, urging me to avoid 'prejudice,' to practice 'tolerance,' and never to say 'Jap.' " Erica Harth, "Children of Manzanar," *Massachusetts Review*, Autumn 1993, 373–74.

51. John F. Embree, "Dealing with Japanese-Americans" (mimeographed report for internal use by WRA staff members), October 1942, 6. See also "Myths and Facts About the Japanese Americans: Source Information and References for Use of WRA Staff Members" (no date). Copies of both reports can be found in box 1, folder 3, Carey McWilliams Japanese War Relocation Collection, Department of Special Collections, Honnold Library of the Claremont Colleges, Claremont, California.

52. Memo from Myer to Ickes, 27 June 1944, box 472, folder 71.601 #2, Headquarters Subject-Classified General Files, WRA Records. According to this memo, the Civil Service Commission had not discriminated against Japanese Americans before June 1943. In that month, however, the House Committee on Un-American Activities began an investigation of the WRA, and the Civil Service Commission began "pussyfooting." At first the Commission simply held up the cases of some individuals, but in August it issued a circular letter prescribing "a special pre-clearance procedure for *all* persons of Japanese ancestry."

53. Transcript of recorded conversation between Dillon S. Myer and Arthur Flemming, 16 July 1943, box 472, folder 71.601 #1, Headquarters Subject-Classified General Files, WRA Records.

54. This essay places a great deal of emphasis on the WRA's struggle against racial discrimination, but I recognize that the WRA was a fairly large and complex organization. Although some of its employees promoted racial equality, the WRA enforced policies that perpetuated a racial caste system within the concentration camps.

55. "Excerpt from Memorandum to John Provinse," 10 June 1943, in "Miscella-

neous Material" folder, box 7, Headquarters Records, Basic Documentation and Informational Files, WRA Records.

56. For reports of when and where WRA officers spoke, see box 72, Records of Relocation Offices, WRA Records. For copies of some of their speeches, see "Speeches 1945 and 1946" folder, box 12, Washington Office Records, WRA Records.

57. War Relocation Authority, "Final Report, Southern California Area" (p. 118), 1 March 1946, box 11, Field Basic Documentation, WRA Records.

58. WRA press release, 28 December 1945, in "California, Los Angeles Press Releases" folder, box 15, Field Basic Documentation, WRA Records. Members of organizations that maintained close ties to the WRA and that distributed WRA propaganda, such as the Pacific Coast Committee on American Principles and Fair Play, also realized that the problems of Japanese Americans were similar to those confronting other minority groups. In one report, the WRA said that a number of committees "were set up primarily for American Japanese problems but have now extended their interests and activities to all minority groups." Gracia Booth of the Fair Play Committee said that "more and more the organizational work of the Fair Play Committee tends to broaden out to include the problems of all minority groups." Booth had begun to understand the relationship between Japanese Americans and other minority groups. "We must consider the problems and reactions of all minority groups in every community before we can hope to solve, even in the slightest degree, the problems of any one group." Gracia Booth, Report to Homer Crotty, August 1945, box 64, John Anson Ford Papers, Huntington Library, San Marino, California.

59. Text of speech (p. 2) delivered by Robert B. Cozzens, Assistant Director of the War Relocation Authority, before the Peace Officers of California, Salinas, 9 October 1945, in "Speeches 1945 and 1946" folder, box 12, Washington Office Records, WRA Records.

60. Ibid., p. 14.

61. Congress appropriated $250,000 to fund the FEPC on June 30, 1945, the last day of the fiscal year. In March 1943, the FEPC had 110 full-time employees, more than half of whom worked in the agency's headquarters in Washington, D.C. See *Congressional Quarterly Almanac* 1 (1945): 287–88, and the appendix to the *Congressional Record*, 79th Cong., 1st sess., 91 (13 March 1945): A1159–A1162. For the fiscal year that began July 1, 1945, the WRA had a budget of $25 million. For the previous fiscal year, its budget was $39 million. At the end of December 1944, the WRA had 2,422 employees. See the *Congressional Record*, 79th Cong., 1st sess., 91 (17 July 1945): 7642–43 and 91 (18 January 1945): 357–59.

62. See Tad Uyeno, "The Lancer: California's Leland Ford Plays Politics," *Pacific Citizen*, July 30, 1942, 5.

63. See McWilliams, *Prejudice*, 248–56. Senator Edward V. Robertson of Wyo-

ming had the articles from the *Denver Post* reprinted in the *Congressional Record*, 78th Cong., 1st sess., 89 (6 May 1943): 4041–44.

64. "Quit Coddling the Japs," Remarks of U.S. Representative John E. Rankin of Mississippi, *Congressional Record*, 78th Cong., 1st sess., 89 (3 February 1943): A408.

65. "Californians Would Ban WRA 'Propaganda' Favoring Nisei," *Sacramento Bee*, May 23, 1945, 1.

66. Transcript of conversation between Robert Cozzens and State Senator Hugh Donnelly, no date, box 278, folder 39.020A #1, Headquarters Subject-Classified General Files, WRA Records.

67. *Los Angeles Examiner*, November 9, 1945, 1.

68. "Japs Given U.S. Housing," *Los Angeles Examiner*, November 12, 1945, 1.

69. U.S. Department of the Interior, War Relocation Authority, "Final Report, Northern California Area, May 15, 1946" (p. 8), and War Relocation Authority, "Final Report, Southern California Area" (p. 54). Copies of both reports can be found in box 11, Field Basic Documentation, WRA Records.

70. Telegram from Malcolm McClean to Harold L. Ickes, 15 May 1945, in "War Relocation Authority" folder, Robert Walker Kenny Papers, Bancroft Library, University of California, Berkeley.

71. WRA press release, 18 July 1945, in "California, Los Angeles Press Releases" folder, box 15, Field Basic Documentation, WRA Records.

72. Ibid.

73. The WRA's responses to congressional hostility won it few friends in either the House or the Senate. The votes of only twenty representatives saved the WRA from liquidation in 1945. Dillon Myer to Paul Robertson, 15 June 1945, in "Relocation Office (Los Angeles, CA) May–June 1945" folder, box 2, Washington Office Records, Chronological File, WRA Records.

74. Kemper Campbell to John Anson Ford, 2 November 1943, box 64, John Anson Ford Papers, Huntington Library, San Marino.

75. Anti-Defamation League of B'nai B'rith, "Report on Efforts in the Los Angeles Area to Circumvent the United States Supreme Court Decisions on Restrictive Covenants" (p. 1A), 31 December 1948, in "A. D. L." folder, box 45, American Civil Liberties Union of Southern California Collection, Department of Special Collections, University Research Library, UCLA.

76. Ibid., 9.

77. Los Angeles County Committee on Human Relations, "These Would Divide America" (p. 2), [no date], box 62, Ford Papers, Huntington Library.

78. According to one historian, "Smith claimed that his followers constituted a balance of power . . . in Southern California in the 1950s and 1960s. Though certainly an exaggeration, the claim is not entirely without foundation." Glen

Jeansonne, *Gerald L. K. Smith: Minister of Hate* (New Haven: Yale University Press, 1988), 8.

79. Ibid., 100.

80. For material on the radical right, see Sidney Blumenthal, "Her Own Private Idaho," *New Yorker*, July 10, 1995, 27–33; Ralph Lord Roy, *Apostles of Discord: A Study of Organized Bigotry and Disruption on the Fringes of Protestantism* (Boston: Beacon Press, 1953); David H. Bennett, *The Party of Fear: From Nativist Movements to the New Right in American History* (New York: Vintage, 1990); James Ridgeway, *Blood in the Face: The Ku Klux Klan, Aryan Nations, Nazi Skinheads, and the Rise of a New White Culture* (New York: Thunder's Mouth Press, 1990); and Michael Barkun, *Religion and the Racist Right: The Origins of the Christian Identity Movement* (Chapel Hill: University of North Carolina Press, 1994).

Race, Rhetoric, and Regional Identity

Boosting Los Angeles, 1880–1930

WILLIAM DEVERELL AND DOUGLAS FLAMMING

The relationship between region and race in the modern American West is at the heart of much recent historical scholarship. This work is often at its best and most dynamic when it reexamines traditional subjects from new vantage points. Consider, for example, urban boosters and the ways that western promotionalism intersected with racial attitudes. Taking boosters and their hyperventilated rhetoric seriously may be difficult at times, but making sense of their role in the creation of regional identity is essential if we are to understand the complicated racialization of modern western society.

Western boosters spoke in terms of race as much as real estate. That is, they inevitably mediated regional racial attitudes, stereotypes, and commitment to hierarchies, and they did so through influential and powerful media. "Boosterspeak" often meant "racespeak," albeit in encoded or symbolic language. Scholars have been generally slow to analyze the relationship between racial attitudes and urban promotion, even though the two have often existed symbiotically.[1]

What is more, boosterism was not a game played by whites alone. There were black boosters in the West, community leaders whose language echoed that of white promoters but whose message was decidedly different. Although their language and symbols might have looked and sounded alike, their purposes were not necessarily the same.

To investigate these complexities of race and regional vision (and to underscore the racial dynamics inherent to western boosterism), this essay surveys the booster scene in Los Angeles from the end of the nineteenth century through the 1920s. Los Angeles grew in those years from a small town into one of the nation's largest cities, a sprawling metropolis seemingly shouted into existence by booster willpower and bluster. Like scriptwriters, leading boosters created narratives about their city. In countless newspaper articles, reams of promotional literature, and cultural productions, these scripts often shared a language common to all western boosterism. But, given the stark racial and class realities of the region and the city, black and white boosters offered markedly different interpretations of Los Angeles and the American West.

In shaping these narratives, black and white promoters wrote in confident opposition to "the East." Notions of life "back East" were critical to booster enunciations of "the West." Yet western historians have seldom explored how ideas about the East shaped western identities. As historian John Findlay has noted, "For all the scholarship on the mythic American West, there ought to be at least some work on the mythic East in western minds." Findlay suggests that "flawed and largely negative perceptions of the East contributed strongly to the identity of twentieth-century westerners, who frequently explained their chosen place of residence as an effort to escape from an older, less promising, more troubled region."[2]

Findlay's concerns about regional identity and city building provide a useful means of reading booster rhetoric in fresh and revealing ways. Without question, visions of the East shaped the promotion of Los Angeles in the early twentieth century. For whites, the ultimate booster project seemed designed to accelerate northern-style urban growth softened by the graceful reminders and romance of a manufactured Spanish past. Although black Angelenos sometimes made reference to "the East," they usually specified "the South," and often spoke of it from firsthand experience, with a painfully accurate vision of racial oppression in Dixie. Consequently, they sought not only to advertise their West Coast city but to make it into a place very different from Atlanta or New Orleans or Houston. Their "East" was all too well understood; their West was yet to be.

Turn-of-the-century Los Angeles was a booster's paradise, and its promoters took pride in their city-building innovations and successes.[3] From orange-laden exhibition trains that lured pale easterners to Southern California, to the town-lot excursions that sealed their investment in Los Angeles, the city's publicists and real estate developers concocted new methods for creating a big city out of a small village. Possessing no natural harbor, no navigable river, and not enough fresh water to support unbridled growth, Los Angeles nonetheless grew with astonishing speed; it had been built, as one journalist remarked, "out of nothing but sunshine and earth."[4] Population skyrocketed from barely 11,000 in 1880 to more than 100,000 by the turn of the century, more than half a million in 1920, and an eye-popping 1.2 million by 1930. There were many reasons for such growth—a magnificent climate, critical railroad connections, a hugely successful citrus industry— but at times it seemed that the boosters had simply willed, and written, the metropolis into being.

"The prosperity of Los Angeles," noted the secretary of the chamber of commerce in a typical turn-of-the-century pronouncement, "is founded on the immutable forces of nature." Such prosperity, as immutable as the natural forces upon which it relied, would assuredly increase "as the nation and the race increases." No one had to guess the racial reference. For it was in Los Angeles, as one booster publication declared, where "Anglo-Saxon civilization must climax in the generations to come."[5] But the racial "other" for whites in the urban West was less obvious. It might have been Asian, African American, Mexican, or all three. As it turned out, Los Angeles's Anglo boosters largely ignored blacks and Asians in their promotional schemes. At the same time, they expressed a deliberate, obsessive fascination with appropriating or manipulating a Spanish cultural and historical presence. Fascination with "things Spanish" helped white boosters create a self-congratulatory regional ideal replete with promises of commercial windfall, explanations of ethnic hierarchy, and lessons of civilization's "progress."

As far as sheer picturesqueness is concerned, booster language aimed at comfortable tourists reached peaks during the boom/bust cycles of the 1880s and 1890s. This would come primarily from the "Mediterranean school"— writers and publicists who would continue to have difficulties controlling their metaphors well into the twentieth century.[6] "Here is the climate of the tropics without its perils," noted one representative writer, "here is the fertility of Egypt without its fellaheen; here are the fruits and flowers of Sicily without its lazzaroni; here are the beauties of Italy without its limited market; the sunshine of Persia without its oppressions. For this is America, with its unfettered freedom and unfettered energy."[7] Typified by such well-known publicists as Charles Nordhoff and George Wharton James, but amply backed by municipal and county-level organizations, boosters breathlessly extolled the region to the outside world.

Such external boosterism ("Los Angeles is great: come on out") eventually gave way to internal boosterism ("Los Angeles is great: behave yourself, be orderly and disciplined") once demographic and urban expansion appeared inevitable, sometime around the turn of the century. To borrow phrases from labor relations, boosters had effectively recruited and now turned their attention to training and retaining. People "here" as opposed to people "there" increasingly became the focus of booster campaigns.[8] And in this rhetorical and metaphorical arena boosterism explored new themes, many of them inherently racialized in expressions of Anglo supremacy.

Such a disciplinary stance required power to begin with, power already accrued through the successful implementation of earlier booster schemes. The conventional rendering of Los Angeles as a promoters' extravaganza portrays a city in which every scrambling citizen became a booster. As journalist Paul Augsberg quipped in 1922, "These square miles are peopled with nothing but boosters."[9] But failing to discriminate between "boosters on the make" and "boosters made" encourages a misperception about the distribution of power. And, more to the point, it also obscures differences between booster objectives.

The white boosters who concern us here included a small group of extraordinarily powerful men working to consolidate and add to their power. Newspaper editors and owners such as Harrison Gray Otis and Harry Chandler of the *Los Angeles Times* and T. E. Gibbon of the *Los Angeles Herald* fit the profile, as do stalwarts from the chamber of commerce (Frank Wiggins, Charles Dwight Willard, Daniel Freeman, and William Lacy) and local real estate or industrial magnates (Fred Baker, F. J. Zeehandelaar, Joseph Mesmer, Henry O'Melveney, and Joseph Widney). Linked by family ties, cooperative business ventures, and carefully exclusive social and neighborhood networks, these men sat atop the booster food chain, and they knew it. Their booster project was about the consolidation of power and the expansion of what were for many already substantial fortunes. In the 1890s, elites such as these figured out new ways of taking boosterism to the streets and to the people of Los Angeles. They had the media and the money to create cultural scripts that enhanced their influence on every front: cultural, financial, political, even racial.[10] But this booster crowd must also include those Los Angeles residents, men and women alike, who so very much wanted to be a magnate, an industrialist, a society maven, a well-to-do merchant. These largely anonymous and lesser-known individuals were the troops led into booster battle by their recognizable generals.[11]

One manifestation of such effort was La Fiesta de Los Angeles, a strain of boosterism akin to carnivalized Manifest Destiny, complete with pageantry and tableau performances that taught as well as congratulated and entertained. The first Fiesta, held in the spring of 1894, witnessed three full days of parades and processionals, replete with ten miles of rope decorations and

10,000 flags. The infant Merchants' Association, just five months old, pinned high hopes on the Fiesta's abilities to entertain, to teach, and to uplift. In a salutary introduction to the week's festivities, the association assured the city that events would be only of "the highest character" (a phrase repeated three times in the space of a few sentences). The pageant would be an inspiration and would demonstrate that Los Angeles had become the first city of the Pacific Coast. Indeed, Fiesta promoters expected the festival to anoint Los Angeles as nothing less than "The Chicago of the West."[12]

But this vision of metropolitan grandeur was more than generic urban enthusiasm adopted by Los Angeles. The Fiesta's expression of civic pride could also be instructional, a carefully orchestrated interpretation of the region's distinct culture and history. Aside from the "thousands of strangers" who would be welcomed into the city to witness the grand processionals, the Fiesta would be watched by 6,500 schoolchildren. For these children the Fiesta would be "impressed upon their mind . . . for years to come," a kind of outdoor classroom. Organizers were no doubt thrilled by the remarks of one admiring journalist in 1895, who wrote that the Fiesta "was such an object lesson as never before seen in the country . . . second to none in gorgeousness and historically correct."[13]

The biggest object lesson of all was the Fiesta's grandest production, the parade attached to Historical Day. Discrete historical periods, broken into "divisions," worked their way through time, space, and downtown streets. It all began with a float of "angels" accompanied by "Spanish cavaliers," and moved through "Aztec Indians" (actually Pueblo Indians shipped in via boxcar from Yuma), the mission period, mining days, and, eventually, the "solid prosperity" float of Anglo-American mercantilism. The day closed, significantly, with a platoon of police, an unmistakable representation of the orderliness of it all.

The whiggish racial determinism inherent in such cultural productions should not be overlooked. As historian David G. Gutiérrez has recently noted, affairs such as La Fiesta were "much more complex and had much deeper implications than mere hucksterism and regional promotion." The sheer linearity of it suggests that these productions were lessons in understood patterns of civilization's progress. Viewed from this angle, we can see the city's leading white boosters for what they were: already powerful individuals organized and engaged in displaying, interpreting, and consolidating that power.[14]

The Fiesta was Spanish in name only, save for a few fictional Franciscans and the occasional land grant descendant riding bedecked in silver. The Fiesta was Mexican not at all and never would be.[15] As a nod toward the ethnic Los Angeles "that once was," Fiesta organizers trotted out the quaintly ancient survivors—maybe Indian, maybe Spanish (probably Mexican), said to be 100, 115, perhaps 130 years old—who could still recall the sentimental days of the missions.[16]

Culture could also be the handmaiden of commerce, as the energetic backing of the Merchants' Association showed. The Fiesta was aimed not only at tourists but also at local Anglo residents, who, organizers doubtless hoped, would absorb the cultural messages and then spend their holiday dollars on more prosaic goods at downtown stores.[17] La Fiesta de Los Angeles continued to be the region's most magnificent and successful urban production until overshadowed in later years by the Tournament of Roses Parade. And for their work on the first Fiesta, the Merchants' Association (which would grow into the immensely powerful Merchants and Manufacturers Association shortly) received the equivalent of a booster pat-on-the-back from the *Times*: "Don't you think the Merchants' Association is a hummer from Hummersville?"[18]

Except for the Uncle Tom's Cabin float—which explicitly froze African Americans in time (and seems to have been peopled by white actors in blackface)—the Fiesta appears not to have paid much attention to blacks beyond stereotypical rendering.[19] Anglo boosters apparently thought little of including African Americans in the manufactured presentations of regional history, culture, and self-congratulation, despite the predominance of Afro-Spaniards in the city's eighteenth-century founding. The official program of the first Fiesta whitewashed blacks out of the city's origins. "Twelve heads of families, numbering in all about forty four persons were the founders of the town," the program asserted. "Of the twelve men one is said to have been from China, two from Spain and the others from Lower California." The "others" were thus rendered a vague and inconsequential mass. For the next half century, black Angelenos would proudly assert that most of the town's first settlers were of African descent, but their demands for official recognition of this fact—in textbooks and public ceremonies—met resistance from white leaders.[20]

When boosters and community leaders mentioned blacks at all, the constructions were invariably present-minded, paternal encouragements of vocational progress and peaceableness. All was cast in a "credit to the race" light.[21] White booster momentum was reserved for hammering home a cultural setpiece that taught Angelenos about the inexorable (and comforting) progression from missions to merchants, from a Spanish village to an Anglo metropolis.[22]

Perhaps the clearest public expression of this cultural logic was *The Mission Play*. A Los Angeles Fiesta come indoors complete with admission fee, *The Mission Play*, which opened in 1912, was an operatic morality play of California history. The pageant's three hundred actors marched across the stage reenacting the state's glorious past. No one seemed to mind that playwright John Steven McGroarty lifted the Fiesta from the city streets and dropped it within the grounds of the Mission San Gabriel. Here again was a past of stereotypical, one-dimensional simplicity, expressed precisely the same way as in the Fiesta. The emphasis was on the nostalgic, fleeting purity of the mission era and the ways the audience could learn history while watching it parade before them. McGroarty, wrote one early reviewer, "has rendered a great service to California by this visualization of the Franciscan missions and the interpretation of their ideals. For the first time in drama their romance has been adequately caught and transmitted to the present-day people of El Camino Real."[23]

This historical pageantry took Los Angeles by storm at a time when tens of thousands of Mexican nationals were pouring into the city as a result of economic hardships and revolutionary turmoil. Between 1910 and 1930, the generation of the drama's immense popularity, the ethnic Mexican population of Los Angeles increased by perhaps 120,000.[24] In the midst of this dramatic demographic change, Angelenos who flocked to the production (as many as three million over these two decades) may have found solace in the not-so-subtle ways *The Mission Play* reinforced familiar ideas about appropriate ethnic hierarchies. A pastoral past—quaint, romantic, and fleeting—was both where and when Mexicans existed in California. They belonged to that past, and they had played their part. Now, as McGroarty's play suggested, their destiny was to fade away, in the words of one contemporary Anglo writer, "as if a blight had fallen upon them."[25]

"No one ever tires of it," ran one piece of promotional literature about *The Mission Play*. "Those who have come to it as children have grown up to womanhood and manhood in its service."[26] It was as if the "object lesson" that had marked the first Fiesta's importance had been bottled and sold to the millions of *Mission Play* ticketholders. Contemporary scholars congratulated McGroarty on telling the story of California history in one afternoon's linear tableau. The tale's inevitable cultural transitions offered simplicity: the Spanish past had gone sadly, if romantically, away, but it could be beautifully commemorated on stage (as well as over a "Genuine Spanish Dinner" served just across the street at El Cafe Los Tres Hermanos).

The play was backed first by McGroarty's Mission Play Association and then by the Mission Playhouse Corporation made up of stalwarts from the chamber of commerce. In the 1920s, the corporation issued several hundred thousand dollars of stock, built a new playhouse, and continued to count gate receipts, making history pay.[27] The Great Depression thinned *Mission Play* crowds, but by then the theatrical script was an important part of an established regional narrative.

Like their white counterparts, Los Angeles's black leaders loved McGroarty's *Mission Play* and sent him letters praising the pageant. Even out-of-town dignitary W. E. B. Du Bois, the nation's leading African American intellectual, thanked McGroarty "for the beautiful experience of witnessing your Mission Play. I shall not soon forget it."[28] But black boosters wrote alternative scripts because they needed Los Angeles to be something different. They were not the city's power brokers. The black leaders and journalists who boosted Los Angeles ranked at or near the top of wealth and influence within the African American community. Their words figured prominently in local black newspapers and national black journals. But because even the most brilliant and aspiring blacks in Los Angeles faced restrictions that white boosters never did, they wielded virtually no clout within the larger structures of power. Within their own community, however, their importance and influence were unquestioned.

The urban West offered ambitious blacks a curious mix of exciting opportunities and frustrating restrictions.[29] On the positive side, homeownership rates for African Americans were far higher in western states than in the North or the South.[30] Segregation in the West was not as severe as it was in the South, and ghettoization was not as evident as it was in northern cities. Turn-of-the-century black communities in the West were relatively new and unstratified, and young blacks with economic savvy and an eye for the main chance could rise rapidly within the circumscribed arena of African American power and status.

The critical problem, of course, lay in the limitations imposed by the dominant white mainstream. Outside of the menial service sector, few jobs were open to blacks. Few residential areas were open to African Americans, and racial housing restrictions grew increasingly strict over time. To be sure, a black migrant might arrive in town with nothing more than ambition and become a person of status in the African American community, usually due to successful real estate speculation. And there were impressive success stories—black professionals and entrepreneurs who beat the odds—stories that formed an important part of Los Angeles's African American history. But the black ladder of success led to a rock hard, low ceiling beyond which

African Americans could rise no further, and Anglo Americans made sure that ceiling stayed in place.

In this context of opportunity and discrimination, black Los Angeles grew steadily, from about 2,000 in 1900 to nearly 40,000 ten years later. In the process, the economic and political institutions of the black community expanded and the core of local leaders grew more powerful and entrenched. Given the restrictions on black job opportunities, the buying and selling of land was critical to the success of the city's African American leadership. And successful real estate speculators tended to make good boosters.

If boosterism was a way of life in Los Angeles, the city's African American leaders were fully alive. From the 1890s to the 1930s, black editors and civic leaders trumpeted a western ideal: they expressed the notion that the West, and especially Los Angeles, was a special place in which African Americans of talent and drive could find a good life, free from the restraints that confronted them back East. Some scattered examples can convey something of the tone and message of this black booster ethos.

Robert C. Owen, described as "the richest Negro west of Chicago" in a 1905 article in *The Colored American Magazine*, exemplified the power of real estate in the black West. A native Angeleno, Owen inherited several parcels of centrally located downtown lots and shepherded his holdings well. He easily adopted traditional booster rhetoric when discussing black Los Angeles. Like so many black and white boosters before and after him, Owen urged sluggards to stay away: "It is truly hoped that no colored man who does not want to pursue an industrious life will come to California, for they are as undesired here as they are anywhere in this great nation." But the migrants that Owen had in mind were more than a sturdy work force; they were to be beneficiaries of a western political system far removed from the realities of the Jim Crow South, where African Americans had been violently disfranchised. He urged all "colored men . . . who want to better their condition and enjoy every political right as American citizens [to] come to the golden West."[31]

E. H. Rydall had a slightly different slant in his article, "California for Colored Folks," published in the same national black journal two years later. "Southern California is more adapted for the colored man than any other part of the United States," he wrote. His reasoning: "The climate of Southern California is distinctively African, . . . this is the sunny southland in which the African thrives." Rydall's geographical determinism was most likely an intentionally ironic twist on the classic white southern justifications of slavery. But his emphasis on climate—the "sunny southland" of the

West—did operate as a rhetorical setpiece for the city's black boosters, just as it did for white boosters.[32]

Frederick M. Roberts, owner of the Los Angeles *New Age* and a political activist (who in 1918 would become California's first African American legislator), was fully into the spirit in 1915, when both San Francisco and San Diego held international expositions. He was sure Los Angeles would lure its share of tourists, and urged his *New Age* readers to be ready. In an editorial titled "For the West" he insisted that "a real Westerner, whether by birth or residence, is loyal above all other things, and the expression of Western loyalty has been the making of our fine Western country. This spirit has been so typical of Los Angeles and her people that 'Boosting' has come to be our characteristic." He thought the "Exposition year" a

> proper time to renew our Western covenant, to get our Western and civic pride aglow. We are going to be hospitable to the visitors, . . . but we are also going to impress them with our absolute satisfaction with our Western home, our Western people and our Western ways. There will be nothing apologetic about us. There isn't anything South or North or East which we can't duplicate or excel here. . . . Individually and collectively we are doing better than any other equal number of a class of people in the country and there is nothing boastful in saying so, often and loud.[33]

Roberts's incantations were not simply echoes of white boosterism, for he explicitly racialized his message for readers who were, after all, virtually all African Americans (whom Roberts usually referred to as "the Race" or "our group"). "Whenever we find a lukewarm Angeleno," he instructed, "[we should] inject a little stiffening. Don't leave him until he realizes that he is living in the best part of the world and that his Race in this section is behind no one else." His concluding proclamation: "California for ours, Los Angeles and Southern California always, and our people here, the best forevermore."[34]

The black booster ethos sometimes surfaced in unexpected ways. In a 1915 obituary for Dr. Melvin E. Sykes, the city's first African American physician, black attorney G. W. Wickliffe wrote: "Dr. Sykes took to himself the advice of a sage who told young men to 'go west and grow up with the country.' He came west and grew up with Los Angeles, and as Los Angeles grew, he grew; as it acquired, he acquired, until he had accumulated real estate of some proportions and had gained eminence as a physician. When a history is written of the part that colored men took in building up this western country, Dr. Sykes's struggles will stand out to encourage young men of the Race to go as pioneers into a country where they can by their own efforts build a foundation upon which will arise a condition that will be a hope and fulfillment to us all."[35]

Writing in a different context but to the same effect was Senola Maxwell Reeves, who wrote the "Schools" column for *The Western Dispatch,* one of the city's black weeklies. Outlining a plan for "progressive" education in the state, she felt compelled to add that "as Californians, we indulge ourselves in the thought that California, a state with a splendid history, a great people, magnificent resources; our California, will set the American standard; and therefore that of the world."[36]

And, indeed, the African American world had its eye on California, just as the Anglo American world did. Not surprisingly, black dignitaries who visited the city—especially those who were editors—were adeptly courted by black civic leaders in hopes that their fair western city would win some good press back East. The plan usually worked. Every time W. E. B. Du Bois came to Los Angeles to speak or support a cause, he went back to New York and splashed sunshine all over the pages of *The Crisis,* the official organ of the National Association for the Advancement of Colored People (NAACP). "One never forgets Los Angeles and Pasadena," he wrote in 1913. "The sensuous beauty of roses and orange blossoms, the air and the sunlight and the hospitality of all its race lingers long." Fifteen years later, reporting on the nineteenth annual convention of the NAACP that was held in Los Angeles, he confessed that "the boulevards of Los Angeles . . . grip me with nameless ecstasy. To sing with the sun of a golden morning and dip, soar and roll over Wilshire or out to Pasadena where one of the Seven Streets of the World blooms; or out Washington to the sigh of the sound of the sea—this is Glory and Triumph and Life." This was the West, where upon arrival in Los Angeles he found "the depot swarmed with flags and autos and welcoming faces so that we seemed few and lost—we wise men of the East."[37]

Chandler Owen, New York socialist and editor of the sometimes radical *Messenger,* was equally enchanted by Los Angeles. "Verily she is a queen!" he wrote in 1922, calling the predominantly black Central Avenue district "a veritable little Harlem." Lauding the spirit of the black community, which attended his lectures in throngs, he added: "There was a remarkable laying aside of petty prejudices, such as we *seldom* find in the East."[38] Owen did more than praise Los Angeles; he invested in it. In 1923, he helped organize the California Development Company, which owned and operated an apartment building in the heart of the black community.[39]

One of Owen's close associates in Los Angeles was Noah D. Thompson, a western journalist who raised black boosterism to new heights in his article "California: The Horn of Plenty," published in the *Messenger* in 1924. Thompson neatly fused the history of freedom with the history of his home state. In his view, California's admission as a free state in 1850 "was the morning star appearing at the dawn of a new day in the Western Empire, marking the beginning of the end of slavery on this troubled continent." California statehood "precipitated the great Civil War." Then, "with the flow of gold and silver from her rich mines, she gave the Union its financial strength to carry on the battle of freedom to a glorious and successful conclusion." In Thompson's view, the relationship between black freedom and California glory was a lasting one. In Los Angeles and other California cities, he said, "the very stars of heaven spell Opportunity! Opportunity!! for all who care to come and work and work and then work some more to achieve the success that is the reward for efficient work."[40]

One way to succeed in the urban West, Thompson and others suggested, was to establish businesses that catered to the growing black community in Los Angeles. This was the implicit message of *Western Progress: A Pictorial Story of Economic and Social Advancement in Los Angeles, California*, published in 1928 by Louis S. Tenette and B. B. Bratton, young African American entrepreneurs who had started their own local publishing company. They hired black photographer G. C. Ecton, who owned and operated the California Studio on Central Avenue, to take pictures of the black-owned businesses in town. In all, *Western Progress* advertised some sixty black businesses and sprinkled in some pictures of Southern California homes owned by African Americans.[41]

"The phenomenal growth of Los Angeles and its environs during the last decade has attracted world-wide attention," Tenette and Bratton wrote in their preface to *Western Progress*. To picture all of the city's growth would have been too large a task, they explained. "Therefore, the publishers selected the progress of a group whose achievements economically and socially would furnish the most potent basis of reflection and the greatest inspiration." It was a publication by blacks, about blacks, and intended primarily for blacks—to inspire entrepreneurship within the local community, and to capture the attention of those back East who were contemplating the business opportunities for blacks in the West.[42]

The "Western" emphasis resurfaced continually in the book, which offered photos or sketches of black businesses described by short blurbs. The Golden State Life Insurance Company, destined to become the largest black business west of the Mississippi, was described as the "growing giant of the west." The local newspaper, the *California Eagle,* was "the oldest and most widely known publication in the West." Nickerson's Drug Store was heralded as "an excellent example of the new idea in western business." Western Cosmetic Company sold its special brand of hair straighteners "throughout the west," and the Conner-Johnson funeral home "typifies so well the progressive west." Naturally, too, there were businesses that found a ready association with the Southern California climate, such as Blodgett Motor Company, which sold Hudsons and Essex automobiles and stood "ready to satisfy your longing for California's open spaces and her matchless scenic beauties." The Pansy Flower Shoppe entry noted that "flowers, beautiful blossoms kissed by the morning dew, caressed by magical sunshine, are always in season in Los Angeles"—"California's natural beauty on sale here!"[43]

It was clear that promotionalism and commercial success went hand in hand. After all, the publishers of *Western Progress* promoted their city—black Los Angeles—partly for their own profit. Every book sold in the black community represented both advertising and income for their fledgling company. As printers and publishers they stood to gain from black commercial expansion and population growth. They doubtless embraced the universal booster creed that their prosperity was inseparable from the community's well-being. And in the pages and pictures of *Western Progress* it is not difficult to see the lingering influence of Booker T. Washington's ideals of race uplift through economic self-help.

But it would be misleading to divide western black boosterism into camps marked by calls for economic progress versus political and social freedom. That dichotomy had been made manifest by Washington's leadership in the South and by Du Bois's opposition to accommodationism in the North. But the West was different, and western black boosters could champion both civic liberty and economic prosperity without having to choose one over the other. The promise of black boosters in Los Angeles was that life in the West was simply better in all respects, and that one need not sacrifice political representation for financial security. The two, black boosters suggested, were indivisible.

Some aspects of black boosterism in Los Angeles reflected emerging trends in the nationalization of African American thought and culture. Efforts by black journalists in the North and West to persuade Afro-southerners to leave Dixie for "the promised land" come to mind. African American leaders and developers who established all-black towns and farming communities in the late nineteenth and early twentieth centuries (from the South to the Far West) depended heavily on promotional rhetoric and booster advertising strategies. Race pride, Washingtonian self-help ideas, and black nationalism all adopted a language similar—in tone at least—to black urban boosterism. There were many promised lands.[44]

But that said, black boosters in Los Angeles were identifiably western. They viewed their civic activism and the fate of their community through a regional prism, just as local white boosters did, but without the compulsive fascination with the Spanish past. Over and over again, the city's black promoters and journalists identified themselves with the West. From Robert Owen's "golden West" to Noah Thompson's "new day in the Western Empire," black boosters explicitly tied region to racial promise. There was more to their boosterism than simple materialism or even a vision of community prosperity.

Viewed as self-conscious westerners, the city's black boosters had two fundamental goals. First, they were trying to write blacks into the western narrative. They were claiming a role in the conquest, Americanization, and economic development of the Great West. As white boosters scripted their version of a grand and romantic conquest, they deliberately left blacks out of the story. Such exclusion helps explain why African American boosters constantly referred to the black presence in the gold rush, in the Indian Wars, in the development and settlement of the West and Los Angeles.[45] Delilah L. Beasley's sprawling compilation, *The Negro Trail Blazers of California* (1919), was primarily an attempt to give blacks their rightful place in the history of the western American advance. The Anglo historian Charles E. Chapman of Berkeley gave the work a glowing review. He insisted: "Beasley has rendered a great service to the Negro race, not only in California, but also in the country at large. She has given them a tradition that few realized they had a right to possess." If Chapman's enthusiasm carried an awkward tone, it was nonetheless true that African American leaders generally shared his explanation of Beasley's contribution. Not surprisingly, black boosters loved the book.[46]

By highlighting black success stories in the West, and offering a tradition, California's black boosters sought to ensure that African Americans were seen as part of the national developmental force. Although they lived in a multiracial, multinational urban environment, black boosters of the day saw little to gain from an alliance with other ethnic minorities. In their struggle to avoid the designation of "other," African Americans emphasized their Americanism above that of other ethnic groups. Boosters hoped to give newly arrived blacks a regional identity—and perhaps a higher standing in the West's ethnic hierarchy—based on historical legitimacy. What is more, if whites could be convinced that African Americans played vital roles in the western past, blacks might enjoy greater economic and social freedom in the present and future West.

From this vantage point the second overarching goal of black boosterism is easily seen: the western ideal could be wielded as a weapon in the cause of black civil rights. Black leaders trumpeted the notion that the West was a land of rare opportunities, open to talent and verve. Simultaneously, however, they noted that white racism was undermining black advancement in the West. In tandem with glowing promotions, black boosters always added a note of caution (as if to say, "It's great here, but you will find no easy escape from racism"), a note never heard in white boosterism, whatever the region. This repeated juxtaposition of the idealized West and the racist West created a distinctly African American vision of the urban West, somewhere between an endorsement and an indictment.

Far from offering African Americans equality of opportunity, western urban society operated in a racially charged, deeply discriminatory environment.[47] The most enthusiastic black boosters acknowledged the point—and did so consciously—as a rallying cry for the black community and a campaign of moral suasion aimed at white leaders. Even the exuberant Du Bois paused long enough in 1913 to warn his readers: "To be sure Los Angeles is not Paradise. . . . The color line is there and sharply drawn."[48]

Throughout the early twentieth century, black newspaper editors in Los Angeles masterfully contrasted the idealized West with the racial discrimination blacks experienced there. Jefferson Lewis Edmond, editor of *The Liberator*, one of the city's first black papers, was an early African American booster. He repeatedly stated that California offered the best opportunities for blacks in all of America, and in 1902 wrote that "the law-abiding Christian people of this state, by their humane treatment of their colored citizens, are doing great work not only for them, but for humanity." He even approvingly reprinted the message of the white *Los Angeles Herald*, which told southern blacks that they would find "no race problem in Los Angeles, only prosperity." But at the same time, Edmond was one of the most vocal critics of the city's racism, and he helped found the local Forum, a black organization that soon became a center for civil rights activism.[49]

Frederick Roberts followed the pattern. In his beaming "For the West" editorial, he excoriated local critics as a contemptible lot: "Away with the person who remains in a place only to knock it." And yet in the mid-1910s the city probably had no harsher critic of local racism and prejudice than Roberts himself, as even a cursory look at the *New Age* will show.[50] And in

G. W. Wickliffe's glowing eulogy of Dr. Sykes, in which Los Angeles shines as the best place for blacks to live, the author nonetheless emphasized that while Sykes "blazed the trail in Southern California for the professional men of his Race," that trail would need "be trod so often and by such numbers" that it would not be blocked or grown over. If many others follow Sykes's narrow path, then "in this western country [we will] share in a power that will bring to every man, regardless of his race or color, all the rights and privileges due an American citizen." Even in the West, the essential rights and privileges were still due, as all of Wickliffe's readers well knew.[51]

The leading black newspaper in the city, the *California Eagle,* boosted and condemned Los Angeles in each and every issue. Edited by Charlotta Bass (who came to the city in 1910 to regain her health) and her husband, Joseph B. Bass (who, as Charlotta put it, "had been bitten by the 'Go West' bug"), the *California Eagle* often compared the opportunity-filled West with the discrimination-riddled East. But no sooner than they wrote about "the mighty march of progress on these Western shores," the Basses would lambaste the racism and hypocrisy of white Los Angeles.[52] In the inaugural issue of the Los Angeles *Western Dispatch,* a black weekly launched in 1921, editors boasted that Los Angeles is the "logical mart for the world's commerce. It is the logical industrial center of the North American continent." Just below this unfettered boosterism, the editors ran a story about the local NAACP fight against the city's swimming-pool segregation policies.[53]

By simultaneously holding up the ideal of western opportunity and the realities of western discrimination, black boosters fostered a regionally distinct language of civil rights activism and aimed their exuberant prose at race uplift. They wrote with the West in mind. They wanted to be a part of the West—to be remembered and recognized as part of its history, to be included as part of its future. They embraced the western ideal in part because they were Americans come West and found an identity and purpose in the regional myths. They embraced it as well because the ideal could be used to highlight the racial discrimination that was not mythical in the least.

With the rise of the New Deal and the federal welfare state, black boosterism and western civil rights activism took a different track, but even so the older strategies sometimes resurfaced. As late as 1960, when Charlotta Bass published her memoir of African American life in Los Angeles, she sought once again to write blacks into the western narrative and to highlight western racial discrimination by holding up the regional ideal. She wrote that "from the very beginning, the Negro people played an important part in the building of the pueblo of Los Angeles into one of America's greatest cities." Even before the railroads spanned the West, she noted, black guides helped bring many a family to southern California. "Blazing a trail through forests and mountains," she wrote, ". . . these early guides did a great work of pioneering. But at the same time, they were obliged to battle against the ever-growing tendency toward racial prejudice brought into California mainly by white southerners. By right of birth and by right of a common struggle for survival shared together on the long journey across the plains and the Rocky Mountains, the Negro should have had the opportunity to live in the fellowship of brotherhood with his white compatriots." "But," she added, "this was not to be."[54]

By asserting historical legitimacy in the region, black boosters asked white westerners to live up to the promise of their own sunny rhetoric, lest the West become like the South. But for white boosters, the regional ideal did not include the expectation of racial egalitarianism. On the contrary, the white ideal promised opportunity based on fundamental assumptions of racial hierarchy and the furtherance of Anglo power. Instances of common discourse notwithstanding, black and white boosters of Los Angeles spoke with different voices. Both groups believed in the power of the past to shape the future. But competing visions of the future prompted competing interpretations and scripts.

The extent to which boosters actually influenced development is open to debate. Without doubt, they permanently altered the vocabulary of local and regional growth—and of racial identity. In so doing, they fashioned new expectations and understandings of what life in the urban West could be— indeed, *should* be—as distinct from life "back East." But as to what alternatives Los Angeles might offer, black and white promoters differed sharply. As a result, the racial messages embedded in their booster rhetoric helped create two distinctive, perhaps incompatible, notions of identity, opportunity, and promise. Black and white boosters lived in the same city, but they lived words and worlds apart.

NOTES

The authors wish to thank Richard White, John Findlay, Marilynn Johnson, Elliott West, Clark Davis, Andrew Robertson, Howard Shorr, and Quintard Taylor for their helpful comments and criticisms of this essay.

1. Charles N. Glaab jump-started modern scholarship on nineteenth-century boosters in the Midwest in his "Visions of Metropolis: William Gilpin and Theories of City Growth in the American West," *Wisconsin Magazine of History* 45 (1961): 21–31; and idem, "Jesup W. Scott and a West of Cities," *Ohio History* 73 (1964): 3–12, 56. Glaab's larger argument was cultural; he was taking issue with his peers' fixation with the agrarian ideal and their blindness to the urban ethos in American culture. His concerns did not include matters of race, however.

But the boosterism of Gilpin and Scott was fundamentally racialized. They found an ally in German geographer Alexander von Humboldt, who argued that all great civilizations had risen (and would continue to rise like some race-specific yeast) in an "Isothermal Zodiac" region, in which cyclical extremes of temperature had created a stronger, more intelligent breed of the human race. According to von Humboldt, seconded by Gilpin and Scott, the zone's "Axis of Intensity" snaked directly through the north-central region of the United States and included such cities as Toledo and Kansas City. Midwestern promoters thus heralded white urban supremacy, which presumably would rest upon services performed by darker peoples.

Moreover, David Hamer has shown that white boosters everywhere in the early nineteenth century relied on representations of racial superiority. In both rhetoric and images, whites portrayed Anglo urban civilization in triumphal displacement over "savage" or "barbaric" indigenous "primitives" (be they Native Americans, Australian aborigines, or the native Maoris of New Zealand). See David Hamer, *New Towns in the New World: Images and Perceptions of the Nineteenth-Century Urban Frontier* (New York: Columbia University Press, 1990), 213–23, and select photos following page 148.

Postbellum boosters in cities such as Chicago (an important model for Los Angeles boosters) simply continued coloring in the pattern. As late as 1887, for example, Chicago boosters issued a depiction of urban (and white) superiority in a cartoon intended to confirm Chicago's role in the Midwest's "Great Contest for Supremacy." The scene depicts a classical chariot race in which the Chicago chariot easily outdistances those representing St. Louis and Cincinnati. Chicago's chariot boasts an all-white team and a proud white rider. St. Louis, closer to the taint of the South, has a black rider and black team. Cincinnati has to make do with an absurd-looking white rider and black horses. See William Cronon, *Nature's Metropolis: Chicago and the Great West* (New York: Norton, 1991), 42; Cronon explicitly notes the racism of antebellum boosters, but his point here is not about race but about booster allusions to classical imperial greatness. On nineteenth-century Midwestern boosterism generally, see Carl Abbott, *Boosters and Businessmen: Popular Economic Thought and Urban Growth in the Antebellum Middle West* (Westport, Conn.: Greenwood Press, 1981); Cronon, *Nature's Metropolis*; Don Harrison Doyle, *The Social Order of a Frontier*

Community: Jacksonville, Illinois, 1825–1870 (Urbana: University of Illinois Press, 1978); Hamer, *New Towns*.

More obvious were the racial cornerstones of southern boosterism that emerged after the Civil War in the frenzy of New South city-building and identity-making. See, for example, Don H. Doyle, *New Men, New Cities, New South: Atlanta, Nashville, Charleston, Mobile, 1860–1910* (Chapel Hill: University of North Carolina Press, 1990); Paul M. Gaston, *The New South Creed: A Study in Southern Mythmaking* (New York: Vintage Books, 1973); David Carlton, *Mill and Town in South Carolina, 1880–1920* (Baton Rouge: Louisiana State University Press, 1982); Douglas Flamming, *Creating the New South: Millhands and Managers in Dalton, Georgia, 1884–1984* (Chapel Hill: University of North Carolina Press, 1992); C. Vann Woodward, *Origins of the New South* (Baton Rouge: Louisiana State University Press, 1951).

2. John M. Findlay, "Far Western Cityscapes and American Culture Since 1940," *Western Historical Quarterly* 22 (February 1991): 19–43; quote, 24.

3. On western boosterism, specifically that practiced in Los Angeles, see, for instance, Norman Klein, "The Sunshine Strategy: Buying and Selling the Fantasy of Los Angeles," in *20th Century Los Angeles: Power, Promotion, and Social Conflict*, ed. Norman M. Klein and Martin J. Schiesl (Claremont, Calif.: Regina Books, 1990), 1–38; Clark Davis, "From Oasis to Metropolis: Southern California and the Changing Context of American Leisure," *Pacific Historical Review* 61 (August 1992): 357–86; Donald Ray Culton, "Charles Dwight Willard: Los Angeles City Booster and Professional Reformer, 1888–1914" (Ph.D. diss., University of Southern California, 1971); Kevin Starr, *Americans and the California Dream* (New York: Oxford University Press, 1973), 365–414; Starr, *Inventing the Dream: California Through the Progressive Era* (New York: Oxford University Press, 1985); Starr, *Material Dreams: Southern California Through the 1920's* (New York: Oxford University Press, 1990), chap. 5; Robert Fogelson, *The Fragmented Metropolis: Los Angeles, 1850–1930* (Berkeley: University of California Press, 1993), chap. 4; Richard White, *"It's Your Misfortune and None of My Own": A History of the American West* (Norman: University of Oklahoma Press, 1991), chap. 15; and Mike Davis, *City of Quartz: Excavating the Future in Los Angeles* (London: Verso Press, 1990), chaps. 1 and 2.

4. Joseph Lilly, "Metropolis of the West," *North American Review* 232 (September 1931): 239–45; quote, 240.

5. Chamber secretary Charles Dwight Willard quoted in Klein, "The Sunshine Strategy," 1. "Anglo-Saxon" quote from Clarence Matson, "The Los Angeles of Tomorrow," *Southern California Business*, November 1924.

6. For more on the Mediterranean metaphor, see Starr, *Americans and the California Dream*, esp. 365–414.

7. Unidentified writer quoted in Dana Bartlett, *The Better City* (Los Angeles:

Neuner Company, 1907), 19. Bartlett noted that the writer was "enthusiastic, yet keeping well within bounds."

8. After 1900, the region was less vulnerable to single-economy (real estate or citrus) bubble bursts as well. We also suspect that the inevitability of urban growth, made plain by the completion of the harbor and aqueduct (ca. 1900, 1913), accompanied by self-confident predictions of demographic expansion ("A Million by 1920"), helped focus booster attention on residents as opposed to tourists.

9. Augsberg quoted in Jules Tygiel, *The Great Los Angeles Swindle: Oil, Stocks, and Scandal During the Roaring Twenties* (New York: Oxford University Press, 1994), 11.

10. Contemporary commentator Louis Adamic wrote that these men were "possessed by a mad and powerful drive" and were "grim, rather inhuman individuals with a terrifying singleness of intention: they see a tremendous opportunity to enrich themselves beyond anything they could have hoped for . . . and they mean to make the most of it." Tygiel, *Great Los Angeles Swindle*, 11. For an in-depth discussion of the elite in Los Angeles during this period, see Frederic Jaher, *The Urban Establishment* (Urbana: University of Illinois Press, 1982).

11. A representative of this larger group appears in the 1923 novel *The Boosters*. In rollicking prose, he sings the praises of pre-Depression Los Angeles: "I don't care where you go, you can't beat Southern California. It's the garden spot of the globe and Los Angeles is the pick of the garden. She's a living proof that truth is stranger than fiction. The sober facts sound like a pipe dream. In 1880 we had only eleven thousand inhabitants. To-day we've over six hundred thousand. There she sits on her rolling hills—Our Lady, Queen of the Angels—the Sierra Madre at her back, the blue Pacific at her feet, the wonder city of the world. Our people are the salt of the earth. You betcha. You'll find no starch in their manners. They're first of all Americans; second, Californians; third, Angelenos; and, fourth, boosters every minute they're awake." Mark Lee Luther, *The Boosters* (Indianapolis: Bobbs-Merrill, 1923), 9–10.

12. *Los Angeles Times*, April 8, 1894; see also, Marco R. Newmark, "La Fiesta de Los Angeles," *Southern California Historical Quarterly* 29 (March 1947): 101–11; Christina W. Mead, "Las Fiestas de Los Angeles: A Survey of the Yearly Celebrations, 1894–1898," *Southern California Historical Quarterly* 31 (March and June 1949): 63–113.

13. *Los Angeles Times*, April 8, 1994; Frank Van Vleck, "La Fiesta de Los Angeles, 1895," *Land of Sunshine*, April 1895, 83–84.

14. David G. Gutiérrez, "Myth and Myopia: Ethnic Mexicans and the Politics of Representation in the History of the West," paper presented at "The Frontier in American Culture," a symposium held at the Newberry Library, Chicago, October 1994. See also David H. Thomas, "Harvesting Ramona's Garden: Life in California's

Mythical Mission Past," in *Columbian Consequences*, vol. 3: *The Spanish Borderlands in Pan-American Perspective*, ed. David H. Thomas (Washington, D.C.: Smithsonian Institution Press, 1991), 119–57.

15. A blurb in the *Los Angeles Times* in the spring of 1896 notes: "It is particularly desirable that the Spanish features of La Fiesta—itself Spanish in name—should be made as prominent as possible. California abounds in reminders of the Spanish occupation, the nomenclature of the towns and all the points of consequence being of Spanish origin. With such a romantic glamour over the land, visitors to the great festival of Los Angeles will look for a distinctive exhibition reminiscent of the early days. Let them not be disappointed." *Los Angeles Times*, April 11, 1896.

16. *Los Angeles Times*, April 8–11, 1894.

17. A representative advertisement along this line appeared in the *Los Angeles Times* on April 8, 1894, celebrating "Two Great Attractions: La Fiesta de Los Angeles, and J.M. Hale & Co.'s Grand Annual Muslin Underwear Sale."

18. *Los Angeles Times*, April 8, 1894. Harris Newmark wrote in his classic memoir *Sixty Years in Southern California*: "This first Fiesta and the resulting strengthening of the [Merchants'] Association have been among the earliest, and in some respects, the most important elements contributing to the growth and development of our city." Maurice Newmark and Marco Newmark, eds., *Sixty Years in Southern California* (New York: Knickerbocker Press, 1916), 608.

19. The 1894 African American entry sparked this comment from the *Times*: "The colored brother was also very prominent and many were the jokes at his expense. The gay carnival colors became his brunette style of beauty in marked degree." *Los Angeles Times*, April 11, 1894.

20. "The 'La Fiesta de Los Angeles' celebration, held in 1894, commemorating the city's history and progress," p. 23 (La Fiesta de Los Angeles program), 1894, Henry E. Huntington Library, Santa Marino, California. See also Charlotta A. Bass's 1960 autobiographical memoir, *Forty Years: Memoirs from the Pages of a Newspaper* (Los Angeles: by the author, 1960). Bass begins *Forty Years* not with her arrival in Los Angeles but with the founding of the pueblo in 1781. "The most interesting thing about the founding of Los Angeles is the racial composition of the founders. There were only two white founders, while there were sixteen Indian and twenty-six Negro founders" (p. 2). She condemned the white community for writing these black people out of the historical record. As she points out, there was a virtual whitewashing in the public schools. In 1947, the L.A. school district published a pamphlet on the founding of the city, which presented the racial composition of the founders. But in 1951, the school district issued new texts that eliminated all racial designations and added illustrations of the founders—looking very unlike people of color and very much like Anglo-Saxons (ibid., 2–3).

21. One interesting exception in which African Americans did receive attention in white booster literature was the *Los Angeles Times* special edition marking, on February 12, 1909, the one-hundredth anniversary of Lincoln's birth. Leading off the special centennial section, journalist and inveterate booster John Steven McGroarty praised the city's African Americans in an article titled "The Emancipated." There was no "Negro Problem" in Los Angeles, McGroarty declared. Despite the fact that "they are living among us in comparatively large numbers . . . we hear little of them in the police courts." So where were the black citizens? In their homes, McGroarty assured his readers, reclining in respectable middle-class repose, more than ready to "assume a place in modern civilization." If these congratulatory words had a some-what patronizing tone, black leaders nonetheless recognized such concessions as extraordinary for the period. For that (and for occasional articles thereafter), they became admirers of McGroarty. Indeed, black assemblyman Frederick M. Roberts was responsible for McGroarty being named California's poet laureate in 1933.

22. Some scholars have suggested that Anglos enjoyed and exploited pastoral images and pastoral enthusiasms out of dissatisfaction with wearying capitalism. This explanation lessens the role played by race in favor of one in which emotional voids created by the marketplace are assuaged by sentimental nostalgia. Douglas Monroy suggests as much, if only briefly, in *Thrown Among Strangers: The Making of Mexican Culture in Frontier California* (Berkeley: University of California Press, 1992), 260. Borrowing from Carey McWilliams, Monroy posits that elite Anglos "gave birth to the study of California Pastoral to fulfill something of what was lost to them in the inhuman marketplace." But McWilliams's idea was more complicated. He wrote that Anglo reenactment of such affairs as the *rancheros visitadores* was "a rather grim and desperate effort to escape from the bonds of a culture that neither satisfies nor pleases." It is within these "bonds of culture" (which are not limited to the features of the marketplace) that we must look to find answers to our questions about Anglo obsession with "Spanish" traditions. Carey McWilliams, *Southern California Country: An Island on the Land* (New York: Duell, Sloan, and Pearce, 1946), 82.

23. Willard Huntington Wright, "The Mission Play: A Pageant-Drama of the History of the Franciscan Missions in California," *Sunset* 29 (July 1912): 100.

24. Albert Camarillo, *Chicanos in a Changing Society: From Mexican Pueblos to American Barrios in Santa Barbara and Southern California, 1848–1930* (Cambridge: Harvard University Press, 1979), table 21, pp. 200–201, offers broad estimates of ethnic Mexican population in Los Angeles County; the figure we use here—a 120,000 increase from 1910 to 1930—splits the middle of Camarillo's high and low estimates.

25. C. A. Higgins, *To California over the Santa Fe Trail* (Chicago: Passenger Dept., Santa Fe Railroad, 1907), 124.

26. "It is believed that no other drama of either ancient or modern times has anywhere equaled [its] record." See the souvenir book *The Mission Play by John Steven McGroarty* (n.p., ca. 1930), Huntington Library.

27. As always for boosters, cultural loyalties mixed with economic calculations in complicated ways, as reflected in a letter from playwright McGroarty to financial backer Henry Huntington: "We can't truly say we love California unless we take care of the Mission Play. . . . The beauty of it is that we are making a good 7% investment at the same time that we are performing a patriotic duty. Please do this, dear Mr. Huntington. Do it for me, for the Mission Play, for California." Mission Playhouse Corporation to Henry E. Huntington, June 15, 1926, Henry E. Huntington Library Manuscripts.

28. Du Bois to McGroarty, April 12, 1923; McGroarty "Happy Book," vol. 1, Archival Center, Archdiocese of Los Angeles, Mission San Fernando. For local responses from the African American community regarding the *Mission Play* and McGroarty's popularity among black Angelenos, see, for instance, J. A. Somerville to McGroarty, June 5, 1922; Crystal Albright Marshall to McGroarty, December 26, 1922; James Vena to McGroarty, December 24, 1922; Rev. John D. Gordon to McGroarty, February 26, 1925; all in "Happy Book," vol. 1.

29. No work to date deals synthetically with black boosters, but in recent years scholars have paid increasing attention to African Americans in the Far West. Works dealing with the late nineteenth and early twentieth centuries include Albert S. Broussard, *Black San Francisco: The Struggle for Racial Equality in the West, 1900–1954* (Lawrence: University Press of Kansas, 1993); Douglas Henry Daniels, *Pioneer Urbanites: A Social and Cultural History of Black San Francisco* (Berkeley: University of California Press, 1990); Rudolph M. Lapp, *Blacks in Gold Rush California* (New Haven: Yale University Press, 1977); W. Sherman Savage, *Blacks in the West* (Westport, Conn.: Greenwood Press, 1976); James Adolphus Fisher, "A History of the Political and Social Development of the Black Community in California, 1850–1950" (Ph.D. diss., State University of New York at Stony Brook, 1971); and several works by Quintard Taylor: *The Forging of a Black Community: Seattle's Central District from 1870 Through the Civil Rights Era* (Seattle: University of Washington Press, 1994); "The Emergence of Black Communities in the Pacific Northwest, 1865–1910," *Journal of Negro History* 64 (Fall 1979): 342–54; "Black Urban Development—Another View: Seattle's Central District, 1910–1940," *Pacific Historical Review* 58 (November 1989): 429–48; "Blacks and Asians in a White City: Japanese Americans and African Americans in Seattle, 1890–1940," *Western Historical Quarterly* 22 (November 1991): 401–29. Principal works on African Americans in Los Angeles include J. Max Bond, "The Negro in Los Angeles" (Ph.D. diss., University of Southern California, 1936); Douglas Flamming, "African Americans and the Politics of Race in Progressive-Era Los An-

geles," in *California Progressivism Revisited*, ed. William Deverell and Tom Sitton (Berkeley: University of California Press, 1994), 203–28; Lawrence B. de Graff, "The City of Black Angels: The Emergence of the Los Angeles Ghetto, 1890–1930," *Pacific Historical Review* 39 (August 1970): 323–52; and Emory J. Tolbert, *The UNIA and Black Los Angeles* (Los Angeles: Center for Afro-American Studies, University of California, 1980).

30. Black Home Ownership by Region, 1890–1910.

(Percentage of Black Homes, Rural and Urban, Owned)

	1890	*1900*	*1910*
Northeast	19.7	17.1	16.7
Midwest	29.3	28.6	28.8
South	17.1	19.4	22.0
West	43.9	43.4	37.8
U.S.	18.7	20.4	22.5
California	29.9	32.4	37.8

Source: Figures calculated from U.S. Bureau of the Census, *Negro Population, 1790–1915* (Washington, D.C., 1918), 465–70.

31. F. H. Crumbly, "A Los Angeles Citizen," *The Colored American Magazine* 9 (September 1905): 482–85. On southern disfranchisement, see J. Morgan Kousser, *The Shaping of Southern Politics: Suffrage Restriction and the Establishment of the One-Party South, 1880–1910* (New Haven: Yale University Press, 1974).

32. Whether or not Rydall knew it, his views marked an exotic reversal of the mid-nineteenth-century "Axis of Intensity" theory, whereby Anglo-Saxon boosters linked urban greatness to northern climates (see note 2 above). E. H. Rydall, "California for Colored Folk," *The Colored American Magazine* 12 (May 1907): 386.

33. *New Age*, March 26, 1915.

34. Ibid.; another example of Roberts's boosterism is in *New Age*, October 9, 1914.

35. *New Age*, July 23, 1915. Sykes passed the California State Medical Board examination in 1893 and from that point until his death practiced in Los Angeles.

36. *The Western Dispatch*, October 6, 1921.

37. W. E. B. Du Bois, "Colored California," *The Crisis*, August 1913, 192–93; and "The California Conference," *The Crisis*, September 1928, 311–12.

38. Chandler Owen, "From Coast to Coast," *The Messenger*, May 1922, 409; emphasis in original.

39. Noah D. Thompson, "California: The Horn of Plenty," *The Messenger*, July 1924, 221.

40. Ibid., 215, 220.

41. Louis S. Tenette and B. B. Bratton, *Western Progress: A Pictorial Story of Economic and Social Advancement in Los Angeles, California* (Los Angeles: Tenette and Bratton, 1928).

42. Ibid., "Publishers' Preface."

43. Ibid., 2, 9, 10, 13, 60, 63.

44. See James R. Grossman, *Land of Hope: Chicago, Black Southerners and the Great Migration* (Chicago: University of Chicago Press, 1989); Allan H. Spear, *Black Chicago: The Making of a Negro Ghetto, 1890–1920* (Chicago: University of Chicago Press, 1967); Louis R. Harlan, *Booker T. Washington: The Wizard of Tuskegee, 1901–1915* (New York: Oxford University Press, 1983); Judith Stein, *The World of Marcus Garvey: Race and Class in Modern Society* (Baton Rouge: Louisiana State University Press, 1986).

Kenneth M. Hamilton, *Black Towns and Profit: Promotion and Development in the Trans-Appalachian West, 1877–1915* (Urbana: University of Illinois Press, 1991), is one of the few studies that analyzes black boosters as such. Hamilton argues that "economic motives, rather than racism, led to the inception of western black towns. Their founders were speculators aiming to profit by fostering a migrant population's quest for social equality and financial security" (p. 1); and that "developers of the predominantly black townsites seemed to differ from promoters of white towns only in that they attempted to capitalize on race to secure inhabitants. Yet even this specialty matched that used by other promoters to attract ethnic groups or members of dissatisfied religious sects from the East. Essentially, the promotional process used by new predominantly black towns paralleled those used by promoters of new white towns in the Trans-Appalachian West" (p. 4). While we would agree with Hamilton that boosterism is racialized (i.e., it seeks to attract and to exclude specific racial or ethnic groups), we would contend that Hamilton's distinction between economic motives and racism is too sharply drawn. Surely the racism suffered by African Americans profoundly influenced the economic motives of the black-town promoters, as well as the economic (and social, and political) outlooks of the blacks who moved to those towns.

45. The effort to write blacks into the western narrative was a constant in California's black boosterism. Examples include: the 1892 *Souvenir History and Guide of the Pacific Coast* (California pamphlets [microfilm], vol. 23, Bancroft Library), which insisted that black '49ers were a vital part of California's glory and freedom: "[Their] work is approved by heaven. . . . The Eagle of freedom Floats over one and all which was brought about by their united efforts and palsy be the hand that would dishonor them"; Bass, *Forty Years*, Foreword and 1–6; and the early twentieth-century recollections of pioneer Angeleno C. C. Flint, who wrote romantically of the "days of the grand period of the golden West" [ca. 1870–1900] and the cordial

relations that existed between black and white pioneers. Flint's recollections are in J. McFarline Ervin, "The Participation of the Negro in the Community Life of Los Angeles" (Ph.D. diss., University of Southern California, 1931), 2–5.

46. Delilah L. Beasley, *The Negro Trail Blazers of California* (Los Angeles, 1919). Chapman's review in *Grizzly Bear Magazine*, reprinted in the Los Angeles *Citizen Advocate* (an African American newspaper that also praised the book), January 1, 1921. Another example of local black reception is Thompson's view of Beasley's work in "California: The Horn of Plenty," 215.

47. In addition to works cited in note 29, see also David G. Gutiérrez, *Walls and Mirrors: Mexican Americans, Mexican Immigrants, and the Politics of Ethnicity* (Berkeley: University of California Press, 1995); Patricia Nelson Limerick, *The Legacy of Conquest: The Unbroken Past of the American West* (New York: Norton, 1987), chaps. 6–8; White, "*It's Your Misfortune and None of My Own*"; Roger Daniels and Spencer C. Olin, Jr., eds., *Racism in California: A Reader in the History of Oppression* (New York: Macmillan, 1972); Camarillo, *Chicanos in a Changing Society*; Alexander Saxton, *The Indispensable Enemy: Labor and the Anti-Chinese Movement in California* (Berkeley: University of California Press, 1971; reprint, 1995); George J. Sánchez, *Becoming Mexican American: Ethnicity, Culture, and Identity in Chicano Los Angeles, 1900–1945* (New York: Oxford University Press, 1993); Ricardo Romo, *East Los Angeles: History of a Barrio* (Austin: University of Texas Press, 1983); John Modell, *The Economics and Politics of Racial Accommodation: The Japanese of Los Angeles, 1900–1942* (Urbana: University of Illinois Press, 1977).

48. Du Bois, "Colored California," 193–94.

49. Fisher, "A History of the Political and Social Development of the Black Community in California," 174.

50. *New Age*, March 26, 1915. On Roberts's activist rhetoric, see the surviving issues of 1914–16 (at the University of California, Berkeley).

51. *New Age*, July 23, 1915.

52. Charlotta Spear arrived in Los Angeles in 1910 and took over the *Eagle* in 1912; Joseph Bass arrived about that time, having previously edited black newspapers in Topeka, Kansas, and Helena, Montana. See Bass, *Forty Years*, 27, 32; *Eagle* quote, December 17, 1921. A good example of Joe Bass's anti-Eastern rhetoric (playful but nonetheless pointed) can be found in *Eagle*, November 23, 1918, when Frederick M. Roberts of Los Angeles became the first black elected to the California statehouse: "We note that the Eastern race papers are not taking cognizance of the fact that a race man was elected to the Assembly from this city. . . . But they had just as well wake up to the fact that the Negroes of the [West] coast are attending to Business, and even though they [Easterners] are so narrow as not to see things so far away, we are going right along progressive lines and outdo anything they have accomplished

along the lines of real progress. We are alive to the fact that the boys over the mountains hold us in the same estimation that the Kaiser held America, but now they will be compelled to sing another song."

53. *Western Dispatch*, October 6, 1921.

54. Bass, *Forty Years*, 6–7.

Recasting Identities

American-born Chinese and Nisei
in the Era of the Pacific War

CHRIS FRIDAY

In 1933, two all-star football teams, one made up of American-born Chinese, the other of Nisei players, met in San Francisco for the annual informal "Oriental Championship of the Bay Area." They did so after a two-year hiatus brought on by Japan's imperialist thrust into Manchuria and north China. In 1937, Japan's invasion of China led, not to cancellation of the game, but to an intensified rivalry. One report of the 1937 competition noted: "Instead of cannon balls, these battles will use [a] 'less dangerous' ball wrapped in pigskin." At the 1938 game, hundreds of spectators created "a veritable human fence around the field. . . . [It was] a game of international importance . . . played out on a sandlot." The Seattle *Japanese American Courier*, in its report on the game, pointedly noted that the "bigger" Chinese had lost 14 to 6. Whether intended or not, the allusion to a hulking but weak China and a small but strong Japan in the context of the emerging Pacific War is striking.[1]

The reporting of the sandlot football games captured the essence of these ethnic identities. References to the "human fence" remind us of how intertwined American-born Chinese and Nisei lives could be in the Far West's cities and towns. They crowded up against each other in both literal and figurative ways in those urban landscapes. Moreover, the kith and kin who pinned their hopes for victory on the teams from their communities were struggling with sometimes contradictory ideas about who and what the players should be, and saw themselves refracted through the actions of those athletes. For their part, squad members no doubt tried to live up to their fans' expectations and their own personal aspirations to play the game well and be victorious on and off the field. Their shared assumptions about good and just behavior illustrate some of the central features of ethnic identity, about the interplay between the personal and the community sense of self. Because identity is so often measured against political and social opponents, sport matches defined as "Oriental Championships" also provided a significant opportunity to mark off the "other" in order to define one's own group. At the same time, the concession that these were "Oriental" implies a recognition, or tacit acceptance, of a racial hierarchy in which American-born Chinese and Nisei might struggle against each other for social position, but which was dominated by "whites." Yet identity was not solely linked, as the sandlot war demonstrates, to local circumstances. Transnational connections and events impinged on ethnic identity, especially at specific historical moments.

During the 1930s and early 1940s, then, American-born Chinese and Nisei struggled with each other, their generational position, international events, and a racialized social order in their attempts to create, maintain, and modify separate ethnic identities in a dynamic interplay of resistance to, acceptance of, and domination within a shifting social order.[2] The contradictory identities of Nisei and American-born Chinese developed respectively in the 1930s and early 1940s thus reveal "power" in what anthropologists Jean and John Comaroff characterize as its "agentive" and "nonagentive" modes.[3] The Comaroffs argue that agentive power refers specifically to the ability of individuals or groups to bring influence to bear "in specific historical contexts"—amply illustrated by the way the ethnic press cast these sports competitions in light of the Pacific War. For the Comaroffs, nonagentive power comes in the form of "constraints," "conventions," and "values" that most often exist in the realm of "unspoken authority of habit," and require little or no direct coercion to implement. The human fence surrounding the playing field was emblematic of social boundaries and community expectations.

The assertion of an ethnic identity is thus an exercise of power. American-born Chinese and Nisei did not have complete free "agency" to articulate who and what they believed themselves to be. Their parents, extended families, friends, "ethnic" communities, the nation-states of their ancestors, and a "white"-dominated host society that "naturalized" a racial hierarchy contributed to a cacophony of directives on what second-generation identities should be. How these two groups came to view themselves as a cohesive cohort within their respective ethnic communities and within the United States illustrates how they sought to influence the social order to meet their desires. Wielding agentive power but forced to interact with other agents and with nonagentive power, American-born Chinese and Nisei tried to recreate a place, a social space for themselves. Whether in Seattle, San Francisco, or some other location, how these two groups tried to create, modify, and maintain identity in order to make a place is at the center of this study.

Popular and academic notions of Nisei and American-born Chinese frustrate serious, extensive examination of identity for the period under consideration. Two contradictory images of Nisei have dominated the narrative: some authors hold that they were simply too young to have had an identity; others argue that they were 100 percent Americans who, though unjustly interned, remained bent on a quite diligent mission to climb to the top of the social ladder.[4] Both of these images are incomplete and ahistorical. Even those who admit that Nisei developed complicated identities shy away from discussing cultural nationalism for fear of condoning or excusing internment. Internment was not justified but neither is the erasure of a complex and contradictory human history for Nisei before the war. (Postwar reluctance of Nisei to claim a "nationalist" identity, understandable as it was, should not be read back into the prewar period.) The result is that prewar Nisei identity has remained largely unexplored.[5]

The imagery of nineteenth-century "bachelor" Chinese sojourners,[6] so ardently espoused by anti-Chinese activists and by subsequent generations of scholars (albeit with different political interests), has rendered moot the examination of the twentieth century as well as the American born. Because both aspects have been grossly understudied, most scholars have not been concerned with how American-born Chinese wrestled with reconciling their Americanism and their sentiments toward China.[7] They were not interned and so virtually no debate emerged among "outsiders" as to who they were. With the notable postwar exception of possible connections to the Chinese Communist Party, they have not had to bear the same heavy burden of a negative association to their ancestral homeland that Nisei had to shoulder. From the 1930s to the mid-1940s, China never represented the "threat" to the United States that Japan did.[8] American-born Chinese constructed an identity that bridged the Pacific and was uninterrupted, even enhanced, by the war. Nisei tried to construct a bridge too, but the war smashed it and only recently has any portion been recognized or partly rebuilt.[9]

This topic is important, not only because of the illustration of the political link to the homeland, an aspect well covered in the literature for the immigrant generation,[10] but also for how collective memories of the 1930s and the years that followed have been reconstructed to remove much of the critical debate from the picture (the nonagentive articulation of power that has obscured the creation of complex identities). Setting these two groups side by side offers reflections on how distorting collective memories of the past can be,[11] and how misleading assimilation theory and the "frontier" thesis can be.[12] More important, it offers a window into how power is wielded as ethnicity and is "invented" in "moments of social crises" such as wars, depressions, generational shifts, and in the relative proximity of one group to "others."[13]

Attention to the gendered nature of identity, power relationships within a group,[14] and with other groups, as well as setting discussion to a historical dynamic, allows for a complex, rich, and human history of Nisei and American-born Chinese to emerge. Furthermore, a focus on Seattle and San Francisco, with some reference to other locales, reveals the interplay of international and local concerns in constructing ethnic identities for both groups in an era of great conflict. The *Chinese Digest* (a magazine) and the *Japanese American Courier* (a newspaper), in spite of their many limitations, provide ample evidence for this discussion.[15]

In the 1930s the war in Asia, provoked by Japan's invasion of Manchuria and then China, sent waves across the Pacific that forced many Nisei and American-born Chinese to confront, head on, their political and cultural perspectives as children of Asian immigrants with U.S. citizenship. During 1935, Thomas W. Chinn founded the *Chinese Digest* in San Francisco with those local and international tensions in mind. He announced in the first issue that the magazine's writers would combat the stereotype of "the Chinese [in the United States] as a sleepy Celestial enveloped in mists of opium fumes or a halo of Oriental philosophy, . . . [while keeping] alive the culture of the old world." He also sought to highlight the economic and social welfare of U.S. Chinatowns. Chinn wanted the *Chinese Digest* not merely to "chronicle the present-day life of the Chinese in America" but also to cover "Far Eastern news and events" in order to "give the truth on the Far East fearlessly and directly."[16]

In Seattle, the *Japanese American Courier*, established in 1928, had grown out of its editor James Sakamoto's desire to advocate "Americanisms," but by the 1930s many of its contributors were discussing how Nisei might contend with international events. For example, Minori Yasui of Portland, Oregon, noted: "I have been asked the point blank question: 'Do you, today, encounter difficulties in your personal life because of the war in the Orient?' " During the "Manchuria and Shanghai crisis," Molly Oyama observed that the average Nisei, "whether he wished to be drawn into the discussion or not, . . . was continually surrounded by those who wanted his opinion on the matter. . . . It was hard to remain neutral." Confirming Oyama's claims, in 1934, the president of the University of Washington's Japanese Students Club, a Nisei fraternal organization on campus, felt compelled to protest to the dean of men that the article in the student paper, "Japanese Control of Asia Curtains for U.S." by Cheng H. Wu of the Chinese Students Club, would "prejudice American students against the Japanese on campus while it would also tend to keep the breach open between the Chinese and Japanese students."[17]

The concerns about the "place" of American-born Chinese and Nisei in the United States, and subsequently the trauma that international events rendered, had their beginnings in the rise of an American-born population after the 1920s and in the 1924 immigration law that led to a two-decade ban on Asian immigration to the United States. In one fell swoop, years of lobbying by Chinese and Japanese for changes in immigration laws and naturalization policies came to naught. Increasingly, the fate of the American-born children thus became the focus of immigrant Chinese and Japanese parents. Especially in urban centers and small towns, parents sent their children to evening or weekend language schools. Jade Snow Wong recalls in her autobiography that her parents believed such schooling enhanced their children's understanding of Chinese culture. Her parents, too, understood that keeping the door open to reverse migration was important for the second generation, because racism in American society might prevent them from attaining an occupational mobility that matched their training and skills.[18]

In contrast to the rewarding experience that Chinese school offered Wong, Nisei Monica Sone came to remember her afternoon Japanese-language school as less than effective. Still, even Sone's narrative of resisting that socialization tells of certain students who excelled and thrived as Wong did.[19] Postwar assessments of Japanese- and Chinese-language schools have been filtered through the lenses of internment and assimilation, and scholars have been too quick to present one individual's experiences as representative. Without systematic investigation, the verdict must remain out, but the evidence is compelling that Chinese and Japanese immigrant parents wanted their children to be engaged in their ancestral cultures while also joining in what they and their children consistently labeled as "American" affairs.[20]

Along those lines, Chinn noted in the *Chinese Digest* that American-born Chinese should concentrate on "Bridging the Pacific." He argued that "without Chinese heritage, Young China here is nothing. With it he is a representative of the oldest civilization on earth. . . . Enlightened American-ism demands that we keep alive the culture of the old world . . . [through] Chinese language and literature." Columns highlighting prominent visiting Chinese intellectuals who urged similar programs, reviews of books, and attention to cultural affairs in other Chinatowns were regular fare in the publication, reinforcing the image of the American-born as a bridge.[21]

Similarly, parents of the Nisei, the Nisei themselves, and even visiting Japanese dignitaries urged Nisei to take up a "bridge" position through which they could explain America to Asia and Asia to America.[22] While other attitudes existed, the cultural bridge role prevailed but the arrange-ments were complex. In January 1934, Fred Hirasuna wrote in the *Japanese American Courier* urging Nisei to "bring to American civilization the best features of the civilization of our parents," but also to be "meticulous in choosing the best in civilization and culture of our native land [the United States]." James Sakamoto, the editor, explained in 1936 that Nisei should strive toward a "true nationalism" that was "the flowering of all that is best in the life of each nation of the globe . . . , [a] true internationalism."[23] In spite of the fact that Nisei adhered to the claims that the Japanese empire dated back nearly 2,600 years (highly problematic as a historical reality), they were also conscious that Japan, as one Nisei writer noted, "has not been hampered in her march of progress by deteriorations [sic] which has seeped into the institutions and moral fabric of many old nations."[24] The allusion to China is undeniable. Japanese American press reports of China acknowl-edged the past glory of the culture, but portrayed twentieth-century China as deeply divided and corrupt. Nisei visitors to Japan, however, reported that the country was "young" and "vibrant," while it successfully knit the older traditions with modern society.[25] A great many people and institutions thus encouraged Nisei to believe that linking Japanese and American interests was the logical outgrowth of "progress" and "modernization."

Issei parents, however, feared that Nisei would not automatically "feel the natural pride of their race origin." Not only was the cultural bridge at stake for the parents, but also the possibility of "any mutual understanding between father and son or daughter" (but not mother). In the late 1920s and first several years of the 1930s, Nisei were generally quite young. According to Molly Oyama, a Los Angeles transplant to the Pacific Northwest, while the Nisei "were children, they did not care, but as soon as they moved into the middle adolescent period, which is the threshold of young manhood and young womanhood they awoke to the utter responsibility of more knowledge of things Japanese. . . . Within the last year [1933–34], all up and down the coast, young people everywhere are plunging in earnest into the study of reading, writing and speaking the mother tongue." Oyama noted two key features, timing and gender. The timing was important, for Japan had established its presence in Manchuria firmly by that point. Indeed, some Nisei considered the possibility of pioneering the Manchurian "frontier" as their parents had the American West. The prospect, distant though it might be, was attractive because life under the Japanese government increasingly seemed more appealing than their lot in the Depression-ridden, discriminatory America to which they had been born citizens but were not allowed to join. Throughout the 1930s, "discouraged and disappointed" Nisei were "becoming more Japan-conscious."[26]

Oyama's comments on young men and women were also telling, because Issei sought to cultivate a better appreciation for Japan and Japanese culture among their children in a particularly gendered fashion. In 1925, Nisei women at the University of Washington formed a branch of the Fuyokai, or Women's Club, to bring "Japanese women" together, "to aid them in attaining a better understanding of the highest ideals of Japan and America," and to stress among members "Japanese womanhood." For club members that meant courses on Japanese flower arranging and receptions for visitors from Japan. "The American side," club officers explained, "was not neglected," and the women hosted "speeches on manners, etiquette, leadership, [and] fall fashions . . . presented by experts."[27]

Such lessons were not purely attempts to ensure "Americanization."[28] In 1939, when Nisei beauty-shop owner Hisae Yoshitomi spoke on Beauty Culture ("the care of the hair, fingernails, and other matters") to the Young Matrons club (an outgrowth of the Fuyokai), she took care to distinguish notions of traditional Japanese beauty from those concerning modern urban Japanese women. She focused on the latter. Issei parents played up the idea of *modern* Japan to their daughters. In 1936, the *Japanese American Courier* assured Nisei girls that marriage in Japan was an attractive option, listing several women who had recently entered into such unions. Potential brides need not worry about fitting into Japanese culture because of "Japan's modern day progress," the editor declared. Nisei girls and women, with the encouragement of their parents and peers, thus constructed or invested an ethnicity that was neither purely "traditional Japanese" nor "American." It was a dynamic, shifting amalgam that represented a new cultural identity.[29]

Issei and Nisei alike assumed that women and girls should, however, take up a greater burden of carrying what they believed to be "traditional" culture than the boys and men, especially in the many community plays, musicals, and even "ethnic" radio broadcasts common to the period.[30] While the contemporary political and cultural aspects of those performances sometimes took on very pointed meanings, by design or accident, the use of Nisei girls to deliver the messages was quite effective. In one mid-1930s case, for example, an all-girl cast presented several acts from *Chushingura* (*The Forty-seven Ronin*), a highly nationalistic Kabuki play that stressed loyalty to one's feudal lord at all costs.[31] The editor of the *Japanese American Courier* noted of the play: "While the girls . . . are all of a true American background, they will doubtless profit much from their participation. . . . It will make them more aware of the double cultural background that is theirs if they will but take it." The Issei sponsors and Nisei directors of that "recent hit" in Seattle had much more in mind for the actors and audiences than presenting an opportunity to realize a "double cultural background." They wanted to impress Nisei with Japanese "loyalty."[32] That they did so through girl actors must have made the play less challenging to those, both within and "outside" the Japanese American community, who might have been made uncomfortable by a masculine display of such obviously "Japanese" themes.

Women and girls in Chinese American communities, like Nisei, expressed cultural nationalism; but because white Americans did not perceive China as a threat to the United States internationally, their activities could be more overt than those of the Nisei. In March 1938, the Chinese Women's Club members in Seattle sponsored a two-night "Classical [Chinese] Drama" series as part of their efforts to raise funds for war-stricken China. Donations through ticket sales and foodstuffs sold at the event pulled in $2,000, and "capacity crowds attended the performances, coming from all sections of Seattle." The editor of the *Chinese Digest* highlighted the merits of the event for readers.[33] In San Francisco, the support of American-born Chinese for the war effort dovetailed with many agendas. Jane Kwong Lee, though born in China of a wealthy family and educated in a Presbyterian mission, epitomized and spearheaded much of the American-born agenda in San Francisco. She had immigrated to the United States and attended Mills College, then married and settled in the Bay Area. Ultimately, she landed a position at the Young Women's Christian Association (YWCA) in 1933 on a part-time basis and then moved into full-time employment there in 1935 as a community worker. As historian Judy Yung has aptly noted, Lee embodied what was supposed to be the "modern" Chinese woman—an image embraced by many American-born Chinese. She was highly visible outside the house but managed to maintain a family as well. Moreover, in the context of the Pacific War, Lee led the way for many Chinese American women through her writings and her YWCA-related activities.[34]

Writing in the *Chung Sai Yat Po* (*Chinese American Daily*), Lee argued that "American women" had attained their relatively high status because they had proven their worth along the way. Following that logic, she explained that if Chinese American women did their part for the war effort, "Who will dare say women are not equal to men?" She believed that they should act as a bridge to American society at large to generate support for the war. In her capacity at the YWCA and as a member of the Chinese War Relief Association (the overarching body made up mainly of elite male personalities of the Chinese community), she hosted Chinese dignitaries, sponsored speakers, wrote newspaper articles in English and Chinese, and even wrote, directed, and acted in plays. In all of this, she highlighted the heroic roles that Chinese American women could play as American citizens and Chinese nationalists. In *Boycott Silk Stockings*, Lee urged these women to wield their purchasing power. In *Blood Stains Rivers and Mountains*, she told the story of two Chinese American college women who trained as pilots, traveled to China, and lent their new skills to the war of resistance. American-born Chinese expressed nationalism more directly and openly than their Nisei counterparts, for they presented the war dramas to a wide audience without fear of criticism or retaliation.

But public performances did not have to be so overtly "nationalistic" as those of *Chushingura* for Nisei or *Blood Stains Rivers and Mountains* for Chinese Americans. Although seemingly mundane, the cultural "responsibilities" thrust upon American-born Chinese and Nisei girls and women suggest that costuming and public display of custom must have had a significant, if unconscious, effect on the claiming of space, on inventions of ethnicity.[35] Issei in Seattle, for example, consistently called upon Nisei girls to dress "in the native costumes of the Island empire" to serve teas and perform dances, especially at Christian church functions ranging from local meetings to national conventions. Similarly, Fuyokai members asked "an expert instructor [to] . . . teach them the intricacies of Japanese etiquette." That, the *Japanese American Courier* editor enthused, "will be of great value to club members in the years to come."[36] Chinese American women and girls carried out similar activities.[37] In this fashion, a foundation was laid on which to build more explicit notions of cultural identity at some future date.

So long as international events did not force Nisei or American Chinese to take sides, they remained content to operate in the contradictory but innovative gray area between an imagined culture of the "homeland" and their vision of America. For women and girls, the sites of cultural negotiation over place remained different from those of men and boys. At a July 4 celebration in Seattle, Japanese girls and women performed a "street odori, . . . a Japanese dance with hundreds of women and girls [lasting] . . . two evenings." The boys, on the other hand, played in a baseball tournament. In Yakima, Washington, for the town's 1935 Pioneer Days celebration, local Japanese businessmen sponsored a "Tea Garden" in which "Nipponese maidens dressed in classic kimono" served tea. Japanese men and boys, "not to be outdone," wore "10-gallon hats, derbies, cutaways and highwater trousers" and adhered to the town law that no men shave for a month before the festival in order to take on pioneer personas.[38]

Donning "Western" wear and playing baseball may not appear to have any "Japanese" components, but such was not the case. Press reports appraised Nisei boys of the "frontiers of Hokkaido and Manchuria," telling them: "Perhaps the future will see Washington-born Japanese developing rich agricultural resources of Manchukuo, pioneering a new land, even as their fathers were pioneers in a frontier state."[39] "Americans," as Nisei always labeled whites, had no corner on a pioneering spirit. It could be had on either side of the Pacific. Posturing as frontiersmen was less a sign of "assimilation" to American "norms" than it was a masculine invention of what was thought to be a "modern" adventurous identity for both Americans and Japanese.

For men and boys, the sports arena provided another site for the negotiation of place. As historian Samuel Regalado has argued, many Issei and Nisei liked baseball and other team sports because they believed participation on teams carried "the implication of American values . . . [and] democracy" and bound them up with "the attributes of courage, honor, and 'physical toughness' . . . that were part of the samurai tradition." Team sports also represented the cooperative skills necessary for confronting racism in America as well as serving as an emblem of "the collectivist ideal and fighting spirit" of Japan as a nation.[40] Japanese immigrants and the American-born combined transnational components of identity with local elements.

For Nisei boys in Seattle, sports more than frontier farming occupied the center of their world. In 1940, for example, the *Japanese American Courier* Courier Basketball League, which encompassed teams in the greater Seattle area, had 634 players in 53 teams spanning five different divisions. (Seven were girls teams.) The players alone may have accounted for as much as 20 to 25 percent of Nisei between the ages of fourteen and twenty in the area encompassed by the league. Nisei boys also regularly participated in baseball and football games as well as judo, kendo, and occasional sumo matches.[41]

Courier League basketball involved mostly Nisei athletes and teams, but did include a few American-born Chinese players and teams, and the competition between the two groups is instructive. Between 1925 and 1929, the Seattle Chinese Athletic Club basketball team dominated the city's "Oriental" teams, not losing a single game. By the 1930s, one or two Chinese teams regularly participated in the Courier League. At first the matches between Chinese and Japanese teams generated mutual respect, but by the late 1930s, international events tested interethnic understandings. In Seattle between 1937 and 1939, very few individual Chinese players and no Chinese teams participated in the Courier Basketball League, and all evidence suggests that Japan's invasion of China was the cause.[42]

In San Francisco, tension in sports competition because of the war was more overt than in Seattle. Those annual meetings for the "Oriental Championship of the Bay Area," in which the sandlot served as the surrogate war zone, provide a telling example. Sports matches did not have to pit American-born Chinese against Nisei in order to connect to international events. The 1938 football game between the San Francisco Chinese All Stars and those from Los Angeles is a case in point. The "game draws more than common interest," ran news reports, "for it brings together not only the best of football material but gains for a worthy cause, . . . the Chinese War Relief Association."[43] Where American-born Chinese girls and women sponsored classical Chinese theater for the sake of China, men and boys played "American" games much as did their Nisei counterparts.

The bombing of Pearl Harbor brought new problems into the sports arena. On December 19, 1941, the Chinese Clippers in Seattle "requested to be dropped from the Courier [Basketball] League" because its members faced "a rising wall of pressure from their homes." Team captain Harry Eng submitted the request and asked "that there be no ill feeling." There was not enough ill feeling or pressure from families to prevent an "Oriental Championship" game in late March 1942 between the Chinese All Stars and the Courier League championship team. Whether mutual respect or some desire to prove the "better" side brought the teams together, Nisei claimed one last victory by beating the Chinese 61 to 44.[44]

Especially for Nisei, sports events were much more than local activities, more than "proving" one's individual or (ethnic) team prowess, generating mutual respect, or raising funds for the defense of an ancestral homeland at war. In Seattle during 1926, Nisei associated with the Nichiren Buddhist

Church formed the Taiyo Athletic Club. In 1932, the club organized a *kengakudan*, or "study tour," of Japan for its members. It included visits to historical and cultural sites, steel mills and naval shipyards, and even Manchuria, as well as meetings with prominent military and governmental officials. Nisei boys on those trips also played exhibition baseball and basketball games, though the girls who made the trip were expected to be "personal" rather than "baseball" diplomats. Issei believed the trips would help Nisei "gain a knowledge of questions . . . which concern the native land of their parents" and "acquaint second generation Japanese in the Northwest with Japanese culture and things Japanese."[45]

The *kengakudan* trips had a tremendous impact on the individuals who went and on the larger Nisei community. On their return, the members invariably gave speeches, showed pictures, encouraged others to go, and attended receptions for visitors from Japan. Those presentations revealed the cultural "bridge" concept at work as Nisei tried to explain to U.S. audiences Japan's activities in Asia. Nisei consistently highlighted the industrial and agricultural advances in Manchuria as evidence of Japan's assistance. For those concerned about the role of the military, *kengakudan* students like William Takahashi justified Japan's military buildup as a response to Chinese and Russian activities. "Admittedly it [Japan] is arming itself to the teeth," explained Takahashi, "but, then, so is every other Nation." Nisei used the Monroe Doctrine as an intellectual device to argue that Japan's "East for East" policy differed little from U.S. involvement in South America. As University of Washington student Fred Uyeminami put it: "Japan is not militarizing for aggression, [but] . . . purely for protection . . . if and when any foreign nation tries to interfere."[46]

Though they began in the middle and late 1920s, *kengakudan* did not cease with Japan's invasion of China in 1937. If anything, they became more critical as a part of Issei *and* Nisei efforts to maintain a bridge of understanding between the United States and Japan, particularly given Japanese fears that U.S. public opinion was too tightly aligned with China. Henry S. Tatsumi urged Nisei to "get out the true story" of Japan's "sincere" efforts at creating a stable, unified China to counter what he believed were misleading statements by pro-Chinese forces. The *kengakudan* continued into 1940 and early 1941. Their regular occurrence for more than a decade was essential in keeping Japan immediate, close, and real for Nisei rather than as some distant, vague origin of cultural heritage. Japan's circumstances had saliency for Nisei who were similarly struggling to find a place in a hostile world.[47]

Not every Nisei could visit Japan, of course, and other trips sufficed to expose them to Japanese culture. In 1940, the Wapato, Washington, Japanese-language school graduates earned "the treat" of "seeing Seattle." On this modified *kengakudan*, the group visited Seattle's Japanese community and the city's mayor as well as the Japanese consul and his wife at their residence.[48] The trip also reflects the strong ties between rural and urban Japanese communities. Spatial relationships are important in shaping ethnicity, but so too are networks of association. Urban Nisei may well have been more "Japanese," or have had a greater sense of cultural nationalism than their rural cohorts, but farm and small-town Nisei were not exempt from nationalistic influences.

Throughout the early and mid-1930s, parental and peer-group assumptions, the Depression, and American racism imposed on American-born Chinese and Nisei abilities to freely define themselves. By the late 1930s, the Pacific War became the overriding concern and forced them to more clearly define their identities. The incidents that began in mid-December 1938 aptly illustrate the point. On December 16, some 200 Chinese from San Francisco assembled at the corner of Stockton and Clay Streets. From there they marched to Pier 45 on San Francisco's waterfront with 300 other protesters—among them "Americans, Greeks, Jews, and other volunteers of many nationalities"—to picket the SS *Spyros*, a Greek freighter loading scrap iron for Japan. That scrap iron, the demonstrators claimed, was for "implements of death . . . , for the bombs of Japan!" Their protests halted the loading of the vessel. In San Francisco's Chinatown over the next four days, an estimated 5,000 Chinese, some from outlying Chinese settlements, continued the pickets. A committee from the Chinese community met with the Waterfront Employers' Association and the International Longshoremen and Warehousemen's Union to negotiate a boycott of ships loading materials bound for Japan. While their efforts gained sympathy from union officials who agreed to study the problem, the committee reached no agreement with the shippers. After five days, the Chinese pickets withdrew from the waterfront and in a mile-long string marched to Chinatown. There they held a "mass meeting" that initiated "a national campaign for an embargo on war materials for Japan."[49]

The protest began as an enterprise "for the good of China," according to Lim P. Lee, writing for the *Chinese Digest* shortly after the demonstration, and it represented a significant battle in "the Sino-Japanese war on San Francisco's waterfront."[50] It was part of the competition for social space, for a place that reached beyond San Francisco at a time when Chinese American residents of other West Coast port cities were engaged in their own boycotts of Japan-bound ships. These boycotts, as jubilantly as they may have been greeted in Chinese American communities, irritated some residents of Japanese American communities. Referring to a February 24, 1939, picket of a Japanese ship in Seattle, the *Japanese American Courier* used a letter from "well-known first generation" member Toshihara Kambe to argue that "surely these jubilant children were not picketing of their own accord; some un-American group was behind the propaganda and the act itself of taking the children from school is un-American, and the display of such conduct should certainly be stopped."[51] The un-American label worked nicely because it encompassed potential "communist infiltration" of organized labor, which supported the boycotts, while it also implicitly indicted any Chinese association with the protest. For most Issei, such a display of Chinese patriotism was inappropriate. Yet Issei and Nisei were not beyond their own exhibition of cultural nationalism, though it might not have been quite as public as that of the Chinese protesters at Pier 45 in San Francisco.

From the early 1930s to World War II, Nisei wrestled with the meaning of the war in Asia and its impact on their lives in Seattle. Monica Sone recalled the trauma for Seattle's Japanese Americans when Japan invaded China:

> Gradually I learned . . . the terrible curse that went with having Japanese blood. As the nations went, so went their people. Japan and the United States were no longer seeing eye to eye, and we felt repercussions in our daily lives. . . . City officials, prominent men and women . . . all shouted for punishment and a boycott on Japanese goods. People stopped patronizing Japanese stores. The Chinese who were employed by Japanese resigned their jobs. . . . I dreaded going through Chinatown . . . [because the Chinese there] invariably stopped their chatter to give me pointed, icicled glares.

Caught in the riptide of international events with discernible local consequences, Nisei divided over potential courses of action. Some took this as the final sign that there was no place for them in American society; others joined in the boycotts to argue that they were "Americans" first and not "Japanese."[52]

As the war swelled, Nisei remained uncertain and ambivalent. At first in 1937, Japanese American Citizens' League (JACL) leaders declared that their organization "definitely takes no stand on the Far Eastern situation," but did condemn Chinese sponsorship of boycotts on Japanese imports because the boycotts hurt Issei businesses and their Nisei employees. Still, a great many

Nisei wanted to see Japan as a benevolent colleague among Asian nations. In 1940, when Bill Hosokawa toured China, Korea, and Manchuria, he noted that "there is little of the imperial exploitation which one would connect with [the] progress" that Japan had made there.[53]

By 1939, at least a few Nisei in the JACL were beginning to urge disassociation with Japan and abandonment of the bridge concept. National JACL president Walter T. Tsukamoto claimed to hear the "rumblings of a not too distant organized effort on the part of certain groups to attack the Nisei in this country." To head it off, Tsukamoto urged Nisei to "expatriate themselves," to denounce any claim to Japanese citizenship. By 1941, the JACL extolled its expatriation drive as one of its "major projects." Ironically, on December 5, 1941, just two days before Pearl Harbor, the *Japanese American Courier* claimed that the JACL expatriation program was one of the key features that helped convince the American public and politicians of Nisei loyalty to the United States.[54]

Not only were JACL claims of its success in winning public support not borne out by subsequent events, but the degree to which the JACL represented Nisei deserves examination. The JACL was formed in the late 1920s, and in Seattle its rolls listed only slightly more than a hundred people. Membership grew in the 1930s, but only in fits and starts. Several months of heavy lobbying in 1941 drummed up some new members, but by all appearances the JACL's membership on the eve of internment amounted to only 10 to 15 percent of all Nisei. (Recall that sports leagues involved as much as 20 to 25 percent.) JACL expatriation drives and other "100 percent Americanism" programs must be examined with the realization that the organization did not encompass or even represent a vast majority of Nisei.[55]

In the late 1930s and early 1940s, the showing of *bushido* films and Japanese newsreels, as well as the performance of pro-Japanese plays and the delivery of speeches defending Japan by Nisei to packed crowds at Christian churches and the Nippon Kan (Japanese Community Hall), probably had as much influence on Nisei as did the JACL.[56] Parents pressured their children to take up the "opportunities" to act as a bridge between Japan and the United States, to represent what they believed the "true Japan" to be. Some of the children balked, some sat on the fence, but international events forced many to confront questions of Japan's role in Asia and correspondingly their own role in the United States at schools, at sports events, and on the streets. That many chose to support Japan and saw no contradiction in claiming political allegiance simultaneously to the United States is important and instructive. In January 1941, Seattle JACL president Takeo Nogaki noted: "The young people are proud to be descendants of the Japanese race."[57] This from the same organization that urged expatriation.

For Chinese Americans in San Francisco, the advocacy of a "bridge" role did not cease with the advent of war in China proper. It increased dramatically. Between 1937 and 1941, Chinese in the city staged a series of Rice Bowl Campaigns to raise funds for war relief in China. Previous to the campaign, they stood divided over their futures. The 1936 *Chinese Digest* essay contest theme, "Does my future lie in China or in America?" reveals that one group of American-born Chinese believed that a return to China was the most viable option given American racism and the dismal economic circumstances. In China, so the argument ran, one might at least help "save China's millions" and thereby reach for some "higher aim" in life. Those sentiments persisted during the war. In 1940, as commencement speaker at her junior college graduation, Jade Snow Wong told the crowd: "The Junior College has developed our initiative, fair play, and self-expression, and has given us tools for thinking and analyzing. But it seems to me that the most effective application that American-Chinese can make of their education would be in China, which needs all the Chinese talent she can muster." Still, most American-born Chinese believed that China and the individual might be better served by remaining in the United States to work on establishing good relations with "Americans." Indeed, Wong herself took this position during the war. No matter where they stood on the issue, both sides agreed that China needed their assistance.[58]

Although the Rice Bowl Campaigns held China's salvation at their center, they also became the "catalyst for the development of a general [American-born Chinese] political and social consciousness."[59] Events in the campaigns included rallies and speeches, fashion and variety shows, parades and pageants in Chinese communities throughout the United States, but the largest were in San Francisco. The *Chinese Digest* noted that the 1938 San Francisco festivities included the standard songs, dances, and parades. "An air raid at midnight," though, momentarily transported all in attendance to the war that raged thousands of miles to the west. Admission to the festivities also stood as a reminder. "Chinatown was blockaged [sic]," one story ran, "and entry could only be made by the purchase of 'Humanity' badges at fifty cents each." Those badges symbolically labeled each tourist who came as a supporter of China in its efforts to combat Japan's invasion.[60]

At issue, too, was the economic well-being and autonomy of Chinatown, on which a majority of American-born Chinese believed their future relied. Before the campaigns, the writers in the *Chinese Digest* had been much exercised about the "outsider invasion" of Chinatown by "Eastern capital-ists," by whom they meant Japanese immigrants and Japanese Americans. This group of investors had purchased land in one corner of the district, intending to establish a competing tourist draw in anticipation of the 1939 world's fair. Chinese Americans felt much threatened by the move and tried to discredit the attempt while simultaneously taking up the call to "Keep Chinatown Chinese" by openly celebrating various "traditional" festivals, wearing "Chinese" clothing, building a public garden and pagoda, and keep-ing up a building code that emphasized identifiably Chinese architectural features. While the editors of the *Chinese Digest* held that their goals did not include making Chinatown "an exotic center of Oriental intrigue," their call for a more "Chinese" town played upon the images that European Ameri-cans had long used to separate and define the idea of a marginalized, other "Chinatown."[61] Defending place sometimes entailed reinforcing a subordi-nate position.

During the Rice Bowl Campaigns, however, the efforts to draw in tourist dollars were combined with war-relief fundraising, which promoted China-town and China. The *Chinese Digest* editors noted: "Chinatown kept open house all night till 4 A.M., with restaurants, teahouses, [and various] . . . association headquarters ablaze with lights to welcome all visitors." In the 1941 campaign, some 300,000 people reportedly attended.[62] The fearless-ness with which American-born Chinese publicly demonstrated their ties to China was increasingly unthinkable for Nisei.

While U.S. entry into the war ended the balancing act for Nisei at least temporarily, for Chinese it represented a high point. It opened the possibil-ity of fighting, once again, for the repeal of the exclusion acts. That fight was successful, in part because of wartime exigencies and lobbying by Chi-nese Americans. Kenneth C. Wing wrote to Washington State Congress-man Warren G. Magnuson, who had introduced the bill to place Chinese on the immigration quota system that ended exclusion. He and four other American-born Chinese "residents and voters" congratulated Magnuson for his "intelligent legislation." They argued that this was a significant signal to "our great and courageous Chinese ally." For Magnuson, support of the bill to remove Chinese exclusion was politically safe. The quota system allowed only 105 Chinese to enter the United States each year, thus curtailing any significant labor migration. Support of the bill, Magnuson believed, also curried favor from the "Chungking government" and "put [a] great dent in Japanese propaganda."[63]

In this vein, American-born Chinese called for the recognition of "Chinese, American friendship" and reveled in the ability to be unabashedly pro-China and pro-America. Early in 1942, San Francisco and Los Angeles Chinese American men formed short-lived Chinatown militia units and some joined the Fourteenth Air Service Group. The girls and young women marched in drum corps, enlisted in the Women's Auxiliary Army Corps (WAAC), and especially after Madame Chiang Kai-shek's U.S. tour in 1943, many participated in the New Life Movement, which was an effort to bring modernization and moral uprightness through a vague program of codified behavior set forth by Chiang Kai-shek. Both men's and women's activities placed them solidly in the ranks of Chinese and American patriots during World War II. As historian Scott Wong notes, World War II "was instrumental in the formation of a modern Chinese American identity as Chinese Americans were determined to defend China while claiming their place in America."[64]

During the war years, Chinese also took great pains to distance themselves from the Japanese. The Chinese American press and other organizations issued identification cards that certified one's Chinese ancestry to avoid any possibility of being labeled "Japanese." Some took to wearing a badge showing the Chinese flag on a white background with the word "China" boldly emblazoned across its face. The badge could be registered under a person's name to help certify its validity.[65] This public display of ethnic identity is a striking reminder of how different the possibilities had become for American-born Chinese compared with Nisei.

The same forces that drove Chinese to leverage themselves against Japanese had significant consequences for Issei and Nisei. Many years after internment, Nisei author Akemi Kikumura set about "peeling away the layers of secrecy, shame, and guilt" to get at her Issei mother's life history. That process forced her to "reexamine and reinterpret old beliefs" about her mother and herself.[66] In another example, sociologist Harry Kitano, an internee at Topaz, Utah, has recalled:

It was difficult to identify with America while in the concentration camps. . . . [T]here was also the reality of having "Japanese features" so that even if I was released, the outside white world would see me as Japanese. And there was also some pride that the tiny Japanese nation was challenging the might of the Western allies, so an identity based on nationality was not all negative. . . . [Upon release] I also knew that since my life and future was in the United States, I had to face the reality of eventually dealing with the mainstream society. My initial solution was to "pass," that is by changing my name to Harry

Lee, so that I would be mistaken for a Chinese. . . . I [was] . . . constantly afraid of being identified as a "Jap." . . . [A]t the time I did not realize the influence of this event [internment]. . . . At first it was negative; I repressed the memory, and even made believe that it had never happened. More recently, this period has become a target for discussion.[67]

Kikumura's and Kitano's comments drive home the point that internment significantly affected the collective Nisei psyche and has kept too many scholars from recognizing what Kitano describes as the "pride that the tiny Japanese nation was challenging the might of the Western allies" and that "an identity based on nationality was not all negative." During the Pacific War, American-born Chinese "loyalty" to the United States was not tested in the same way that it was for Nisei. They invented an ethnicity that became overtly "Chinese" as well as "American." Nisei tried to do much the same, but the entrance of the United States into the Pacific War drastically altered the contours of Nisei ethnic identity.

In its 1940 New Year's edition, the *Japanese American Courier* published a verse by Nisei Miyo Ishiwata that, as poems sometimes do, gave readers a simultaneous glimpse of the past, present, and future. She wrote:

> This Morning
> The turquoise skies
> And the warm sun
> Stirred light laughter,
> Faith,
> Fresh hope,
> In my heart:
> But alas at noon
> Foreboding clouds
> Gathered in the sky:
> The rains fell.
> And my pleasant joys
> Died.
> The somber hours
> Wrought pain within my soul,
> Until the solemn stillness
> Of midnight
> The clouds parted
> Allowing the satellite's rays

To stream into my room;
She lit my bosom
With her cold placid glow
Sad sensations
Flickered in my heart.
This morning's glory
Like my past,
Met sorrow at noon;
I changed.
New tomorrow's
Sun will
Never be the same.[68]

These lines of poetry capture, if unintentionally, the essence of the transformations in Nisei and American-born Chinese identities: that international and local events forced both groups to face difficult decisions as to who they were at a critical stage in their lives, and that events of the 1940s and beyond have shaped the reconstruction of memories, of the past itself.

The creation, maintenance, and modification of ethnic identity involves exercises of power to claim a place, to influence the social order even when that entails accepting certain aspects of one's subordinate position. For both groups, identity in its creation was an articulation of agentive power, though their parents tried to instill and encourage the conventions and values that were for them the nonagentive components of their respective ancestral homelands. The immigrant generation and their American-born children also recognized the problematic of a "traditional" world, for they knew well that both the lands from which they emigrated and the one to which they had come were in the midst of rapid cultural changes. In this transnational and transgenerational milieu, Nisei and American-born Chinese, along with their parents, hoped to forge an identity that was the best of both worlds.

In the North American West, the multiplicity of positions in the racialized social hierarchy fostered what social theorists Michael Omi and Howard Winant, drawing on Antonio Gramsci, have called a "racial war of maneuver . . . in which subordinate groups seek to preserve and extend a definite territory [a place], to ward off violent assault, and to develop an internal society as an alternative to the repressive social system they confront."[69] While the ambiguous and shifting social system of the region allowed for a discussion of where various groups of people might be located, changing local, national, and international historical contexts recast possibilities for the application of agentive power and the boundaries of non-agentive power.

For a great many racialized peoples in the region, transnational and transgenerational factors (along with class and gender) significantly affected how they got access to and articulated power to claim place. Mexican Americans, for example, labored to contend with conflicting pressures that allowed some to claim American citizenship and even occasionally to become "white," while others more regularly dealt with those who wanted to treat them as "aliens."[70] Similarly, the post–Spanish-American War occupation of the Philippines by the United States made "U.S. nationals" of Filipinos, only to have the Tydings-McDuffie Act of 1934 reinstate that "alien" status; and then Japanese occupation of the islands jettisoned Filipinos from alien labor to wartime allies.[71] Native Americans tried to balance the contradictory pressures to assimilate culturally and politically into the "white" system, while tribal governments established under New Deal auspices unevenly strove toward sovereignty.[72] Even African Americans, to some degree, recognized these same tensions. In the North American West, they, like other peoples of color, maneuvered for position not only against whites, but also against other peoples of color. Even among themselves, the fight for control over the cultural and political agenda between the older, urban, "Victorian" blacks and the "new" African American migrants of the 1940s created many tensions.[73]

What Nisei and American-born Chinese or the immigrant generations faced was thus representative of the "maneuvers" for place that so characterized the North American West in the second quarter of the twentieth century. No "frontier" assimilating experience, or "bumpy line" assimilation theory, adequately pins down the dynamics involved in the struggle for power and place.[74] Moments of crisis do, however, reveal how historical contingency, spatial relationships, human agency, and structural constraints combine to create complex human stories, not two-dimensional history.

NOTES

The author wishes to thank Valerie Matsumoto, Brian Hayashi, Katherine Morrissey, Alan Gallay, and Nancy Van Deusen for their insights, comments, and suggestions on this topic, and Katie Walker for reading too many drafts.

1. *Japanese American Courier* (Seattle), December 23, 1933, 2; December 4, 1937, 3; October 1, 1938, 3.

2. Sherry B. Ortner, "Resistance and the Problem of Ethnographic Refusal," *Comparative Study of Society and History* 37, no. 1 (1995): 173–93.

3. Jean Comaroff and John Comaroff, *Of Revelation and Revolution: Christianity, Colonialism, and Consciousness in South Africa* (Chicago: University of Chicago Press, 1991), 22.

4. Jere Takehashi, "Japanese American Responses to Race Relations: The Formation of Nisei Perspectives," *Amerasia Journal* 9, no. 1 (1982): 29–57; and Eileen H. Tamura, *Americanization, Acculturation, and Ethnic Identity: The Nisei Generation in Hawaii* (Urbana: University of Illinois Press, 1994), are notable exceptions, though the expression of Japanese ethnic identity in Hawaii may have been closer to that of Japanese in Brazil than in the mainland United States. For a discussion on Japanese in Brazil, see Christopher A. Reichl, "Stages in the Historical Process of Ethnicity: The Japanese in Brazil, 1908–1988," *Ethnohistory* 42, no. 1 (1995): 31–62. Scholars of Asian American literature, especially that written by women, have been quicker to recognize complexities of identities than most. For examples, see Shirley Geok-Lin Lim, "Japanese American Women's Life Stories: Maternality in Monica Sone's *Nisei Daughter*; Joy Kogawa's "Obasan," *Feminist Studies* 16, no. 2 (1990): 289–92; and Sau-ling Cynthia Wong, *Reading Asian American Literature: From Necessity to Extravagance* (Princeton: Princeton University Press, 1993), esp. 3–12, on theoretical issues.

5. Among the few studies that deal directly with nationalism among Japanese immigrants and Japanese Americans in the prewar period are Yuji Ichioka, "Japanese Immigrant Nationalism: The Issei and the Sino-Japanese War, 1937–1941," *California History* 69, no. 3 (1990): 260–75; Brian Masaru Hayashi, *"For the Sake of Our Japanese Brethren": Assimilation, Nationalism, and Protestantism Among the Japanese of Los Angeles, 1895–1942* (Stanford: Stanford University Press, 1995). For the contrasts with Chinese immigrants and Chinese Americans, see L. Eve Armentrout Ma, *Revolutionaries, Monarchists, and Chinatowns: Chinese Politics in the Americas and the 1911 Revolution* (Honolulu: University of Hawaii Press, 1990); and Judy Yung, *Unbound Feet: A Social History of Chinese Women in San Francisco* (Berkeley: University of California Press, 1995), esp. 223–77.

6. Renqiu Yu, *To Save China, To Save Ourselves: The Chinese Hand Laundry Alliance of New York* (Philadelphia: Temple University Press, 1992), 3–5, offers a succinct review and critique of the sojourner thesis.

7. Marjorie Lee, "*Hu-Jee:* The Forgotten Second Generation of Chinese America, 1930–1950" (M.A. thesis, Asian American Studies, University of California,

Los Angeles, 1984), 50 and 162; and idem, "On Contradiction: The Second Generation," in *Origins and Destinations: 41 Essays on Chinese America* (Los Angeles: Chinese Historical Society of Southern California and UCLA Asian American Studies
Center, 1994), 103–10. Lee, as the title of her thesis indicates, rightly notes this hole
in twentieth-century studies. Several other historians have taken up the assessment
of Chinese Americans between the 1924 immigration law that permanently excluded all Asians and the 1965 act that finally removed the ban on Asian immigration, though some had been allowed to enter in the context of World War II and the
Cold War. See Yung, *Unbound Feet*; Him Mark Lai, "To Bring Forth a New China,
to Build a Better America: The Chinese Marxist Left in America to the 1960s," in
Chinese America: History and Perspectives (San Francisco: Chinese Historical Society
of America, 1992), 3–82; Xiaojian Zhao, "Chinese American Women Defense
Workers in World War II," *California History* 75, no. 2 (Summer 1996): 139–53,
182–84; K. Scott Wong, "Defending China, Claiming America: San Francisco
Chinatown During World War II," paper presented at the 1994 annual meeting of
the Western Historical Association, Albuquerque, New Mexico; and Chen Yong,
"China in America: A Cultural Study of Chinese San Francisco, 1850–1943" (Ph.D.
diss., Cornell University, 1993).

8. I am grateful to Brian Hayashi for providing me with a copy of Joseph Yu
Kuo's seminar paper, "The Rise and Fall of the Chinese Six Companies: An Analysis
of the Factors Behind the Political Consolidation and Later Decline of the
Chinatown-San Francisco Kuomintang Establishment from 1950 to 1975." Kuo
suggests that in the 1950s the Kuomintang used the imagery of internment to
browbeat political opponents and maintain its power in Chinese American communities, threatening that Chinese could also be interned if they moved toward leftist
politics. Karen J. Anderson, "The Idea of Chinatown: Power of Place and Institutional Practice in the Making of a Racial Category," *Annals of the Association of
American Geographers* 77 (1987): 580–98, examines attempts to impose a racial
hegemony in spatial terms; while Sucheng Chan, "European and Asian Immigration
into the United States in Comparative Perspective, 1820s to 1920s," in *Immigration
Reconsidered: History, Sociology, and Politics*, ed. Virginia Yans-McLaughlin (New
York: Oxford University Press, 1990), 37–75, reveals how the international standing
of the homeland can also affect the conditions immigrants and their children face.
David R. Roediger, *The Wages of Whiteness: Race and the Making of the American
Working Class* (London: Verso, 1991); and Alexander Saxton, *The Rise and Fall of the
White Republic: Class Politics and Mass Culture in Nineteenth-Century America* (Lon-
don: Verso, 1990), discuss the matter of "whiteness" in great depth.

9. Takehashi, "Japanese American Responses to Race Relations"; and Samuel

O. Regalado, " 'Play Ball!' Baseball and Seattle's Japanese-American Courier League, 1928–1941," *Pacific Northwest Quarterly* 87, no. 1 (1995/96): esp. 30–31.

10. Ichioka, "Japanese Immigrant Nationalism"; and Ma, *Revolutionaries, Monarchists, and Chinatowns*. Outside those studies, Europeans have received much more attention. For examples, see the essays in Dirk Hoerder, ed., *"Struggle the Hard Battle": Essays on Working-Class Immigrants* (DeKalb: Northern Illinois University Press, 1986), especially the one by David Montgomery, "Nationalism, American Patriotism, and Class Consciousness among Immigrant Workers in the United States in the Epoch of World War I," 327–51. Kerby A. Miller, "Class, Culture, and Immigrant Group Identity in the United States: The Case of Irish-American Ethnicity," in *Immigration Reconsidered*, 96–129, has suggested that class hegemony directed nationalism in the creation of Irish American identity. The role of the merchant entrepreneurial elite among Chinese and Japanese in directing the construction of those respective ethnic identities was important, as Robert M. Jiobu, "Ethnic Hegemony and the Japanese of California," *American Sociological Review* 53, no. 3 (1988): 353–67, has demonstrated. Still, Yu, *To Save China, To Save Ourselves*, and Lai, "To Bring Forth a New China," and idem, "A Historical Survey of the Chinese Left in American Society," in *Counterpoint: Perspectives on Asian America*, ed. Emma Gee et al. (Los Angeles: Asian American Studies Center, University of California), 63–80, argue that working-class Asian Americans were not completely co-opted by elites. Such a discussion, though, is beyond the scope of this article.

11. Most helpful in my thinking on this matter are: Virginia Yans-McLaughlin, "Metaphors of Self in History: Subjectivity, Oral Narrative, and Immigration Studies," in *Immigration Reconsidered*, 254–90, who studies personal narratives "at the symbolic level . . . for the ways in which memories themselves are structured"; and Harry H. L. Kitano, *Generations and Identity: The Japanese American* (Needham Heights, Mass.: Ginn Press, 1993).

12. A thorough review of the vast literature regarding assimilation theory and of the "frontier" in American history is not practical here. For a helpful starting point regarding assimilation theory and its critics, see Ewa Morawska, "The Sociology and Historiography of Immigration," in *Immigration Reconsidered*, 187–238; and Kathleen Neils Conzen, David A. Gerber, Ewa Morawska, and George E. Pozzetta, "The Invention of Ethnicity: A Perspective from the U.S.A.," *Journal of American Ethnic History* 12, no. 1 (1992): 3–41. On the frontier, see Shirley Hune, "Pacific Migration Defined by American Historians and Social Theorists up to the 1960s," in *Asian American Studies: An Annotated Bibliography and Research Guide*, ed. Hyung-chan Kim (Westport, Conn.: Greenwood Press, 1989), 23–24; Patricia Nelson Limerick, *The Legacy of Conquest: The Unbroken Past of the American West* (New York: Norton, 1987); and

Peggy Pascoe, "Western Women at the Cultural Crossroads," in *Trails: Toward a New Western History*, ed. Patricia Nelson Limerick, Clyde A. Milner II, and Charles E. Rankin (Lawrence: University Press of Kansas, 1991), 40–58.

13. Conzen et al., "Invention of Ethnicity," 13–16; and Werner Sollors, *The Invention of Ethnicity* (New York: Oxford University Press, 1989). Important in rethinking the standard notion of assimilation theory is Miller, "Class, Culture, and Immigrant Group Identity." The Asian American literature lags behind other fields in examining this issue. The studies tend to be of single groups and still attempt to measure identity along a linear line between assimilation and ethnic resilience. For the best recent study that follows this theory, see Tamura, *Americanization, Accultura- tion, and Ethnic Identity*. For a vigorous and brief defense of modified assimilation theory, see Herbert J. Gans, "Comment: Ethnic Invention and Acculturation, A Bumpy-Line Approach," *Journal of American Ethnic History* 12, no. 1 (1992): 42–51. I believe George J. Sánchez, *Becoming Mexican American: Ethnicity, Culture, and Identity in Chicano Los Angeles, 1900–1945* (New York: Oxford University Press, 1993), provides one of the best recent models to follow.

14. This essay, by default, is a study of a largely middle-class population of landholding, hotel- and restaurant-operating families. These were the people who could "afford" as immigrants to reproduce families in the United States. Class rela- tionships, especially the power wielded by community leaders, are operative but a thorough examination of them is beyond the scope of this essay.

15. For a discussion of the two periodicals, their editors, and interpretive limita- tions, see Yuji Ichioka, "A Study in Dualism: James Yoshinori Sakamoto and the *Japanese American Courier*, 1928–1942," *Amerasia Journal* 13, no. 2 (1986–1987): 49–81; Julie Shuk-yee Lam, "The *Chinese Digest*, 1935 to 1940," in *Chinese America: History and Perspectives, 1987* (San Francisco: Chinese Historical Society of Amer- ica, 1987), 119–37; and Lee, "*Hu-Jee*."

16. *Chinese Digest*, November 15, 1935, 3; and January 1938, 2. The *Japanese American Courier*, November 23, 1935, 1, also noted Chinn's call in that first issue of the *Chinese Digest*.

17. *Japanese American Courier*, February 10, 1940, 1 (Yasui); October 20, 1934 (Oyama); February 3, 1934, and April 14, 1934, 1 (Japanese Students Club).

18. Yuji Ichioka, "*Kengakudan*: The Origin of Nisei Study Tours of Japan," *Nichi Bei Times*, January 1, 1992, pp. 1, 7–8, and 15. This same article appears in *California History* (1994). The lobbying on immigration did not, however, completely end, as scattered articles in the *Japanese American Courier* between 1928 and 1930 reveal. Jade Snow Wong, *Fifth Chinese Daughter* (1945; reprint, Seattle: University of Wash- ington Press, 1989), 33–34, 94–96, and 135.

19. Monica Sone, *Nisei Daughter* (1953; reprint, Seattle: University of Washing-

ton Press, 1991), 20–26. For more background on Wong and Sone, see Lim, "Japanese American Women's Life Stories," 289–312; and Elaine H. Kim, *Asian American Literature: An Introduction to the Writings and Their Social Context* (Philadelphia: Temple University Press, 1982), 66–81.

20. The degree to which Nisei and American-born Chinese consistently referred to themselves as "Japanese" and "Chinese," respectively, in distinction to "Americans," by whom they meant whites, is striking. Even the quickest reading of such publications as the *Japanese Courier* or the *Chinese Digest* brings this point home. Quite clearly, racism effectively shaped their consciousness to the point that they internalized these labels that so marginalized them in the U.S. context.

21. *Chinese Digest,* November 13, 1936, 13; November 6, 1936, 11; and July 24, 1936, 10. For additional listings, see the *Chinese Digest* annual indexes in the January 1937, 1938, 1939 issues.

22. References appear repeatedly in the *Japanese American Courier*—see April 7, 1928, 1, May 24, 1930, 1; January 5, 1935, 4; April 27, 1935, 2; April 11, 1936, 1; and January 1, 1941, 9. For a discussion of the concept in secondary literature, see especially Takehashi, "Japanese American Responses to Race Relations."

23. *Japanese American Courier,* January 1, 1934, 9; and March 28, 1936, 2.

24. Jay Esse, "Japan Fusing True Spirit of Eastern, Western Cultures," *Japanese American Courier,* July 4, 1931, 1.

25. *Japanese American Courier,* October 24, 1931, 1; September 18, 1937, 2; and May 3, 1941, 1. Sone, *Nisei Daughter,* 90, reveals that Japanese sensibilities of what was modern could be quite different from those held by Nisei. Visiting Japan with her family, she saw a "genteel-looking elderly woman wearing a *marumage* pompadour coiffure, [bi]cycling along." For Sone, these were contradictory expressions of modernity.

26. *Japanese American Courier,* August 17, 1929, 2 (mutual understanding); the issue of June 3, 1933, 1, lists the average age of Nisei in Seattle as ten to twelve years of age; March 31, 1934 (Oyama); January 13, 1934. For several telling examples of Nisei disillusionment with the United States, see the issues of April 5, 1930, 1; February 1, 1936, 2; and June 1, 1940, 1.

27. *Japanese American Courier,* January 1, 1928, 4; January 1, 1934, 8; January 1, 1931, 5.

28. Here I agree with Vicki Ruiz, "The Flapper and the Chaperon: Historical Memory Among Mexican American Women," in *Seeking Common Ground: Multidisciplinary Studies of Immigrant Women in the United States,* ed. Donna Gabaccia (Westport, Conn.: Greenwood Press, 1992), 141–57, who argues that women can create identities that break from "tradition" but need not be categorized as Americanized or assimilated. Identity represents a unique blending of cultures, a new amalgam.

This is, in essence, what Miller, "Class, Culture, and Immigrant Group Identity," argues for Irish Americans. Both Ruiz and Miller reject simplistic assimilationist theory.

29. *Japanese American Courier*, January 7, 1939, 4; June 24, 1939, 1; and February 29, 1936, 4.

30. Ichioka, "Japanese Immigrant Nationalism," suggests that the ideas portrayed as a constant regarding "traditional" culture were linked to the Japanese imperial policy of transforming immigrants into imperial subjects. For a discussion of ethnicity and gender in a similar context, see Micaela di Leonardo, *The Varieties of Ethnic Experience: Kinship, Class, and Gender Among California Italian-Americans* (Ithaca, N.Y.: Cornell University Press, 1984), esp. 218–19; and Evelyn Nakano Glenn, *Issei, Nisei, War Bride: Three Generations of Japanese American Women in Domestic Service* (Philadelphia: Temple University Press, 1986), who notes the ways in which a gendered division of labor simultaneously supported "traditional" patterns while the tenuous life in prewar America sometimes forced Japanese women and men to rethink and reorder their gendered roles.

31. For a discussion of the play, see J. Thomas Rimer, *A Reader's Guide to Japanese Literature from the Eighth Century to the Present* (Tokyo and New York: Kodansha International, 1988), 77–79; and James R. Brandon, ed., *Chushingura: Studies in Kabuki and Puppet Theater* (Honolulu: University of Hawaii Press, 1982).

32. *Japanese American Courier*, February 16, 1935, 2; March 16, 1935, 4; and April 27, 1935, 4.

33. *Chinese Digest*, March 1938, 12.

34. Yung, *Unbound Feet*, 235–37.

35. Conzen et al., "Invention of Ethnicity," 15; and Susan G. Davis, *Parades and Power: Street Theatre in Nineteenth-Century Philadelphia* (Philadelphia: Temple University Press, 1986), 3–20.

36. *Japanese American Courier*, May 30, 1936, 4; August 1, 1936, 4; and September 30, 1933, 3.

37. Lee, "*Hu-Jee*," 105–7, and 119. The most significant discussions of Chinese American women's activities are in Yung, *Unbound Feet*; and in Asian American Studies Center, University of California, Los Angeles, and Chinese Historical Society of Southern California, *Linking Our Lives: Chinese American Women of Los Angeles* (Los Angeles: Chinese Historical Society of Southern California, 1984).

38. *Japanese American Courier*, June 22, 1935, 4 (street odori); May 11, 1935, 1 (Yakima).

39. *Japanese American Courier*, August 5, 1933, 1; November 23, 1935, 1; and September 21, 1940, 1 and 4.

40. Regalado, "Baseball and Seattle's Japanese-American Courier League," 30–

31. Gail M. Nomura, "Beyond the Field: The Significance of Pre–World War II Japanese American Baseball in the Yakima Valley," in *Bearing Dreams, Shaping Visions*, ed. Linda A. Revilla et al. (Pullman: Washington State University Press, 1993), 15–31, also provides a broad discussion of baseball's place among Japanese immigrants and their children.

41. On the Courier Basketball League, see *Japanese American Courier*, January 13, 1940, 3. For the origins of the girls teams, see *Japanese American Courier*, January 18, 1930, 2. Girls basketball teams had been organized as early as 1928, but were not included in the Courier League until 1930. The percentages cited are only a rough estimate; see *Japanese American Courier*, February 23, 1935, 4, and September 12, 1941, 1.

42. *Japanese American Courier*, March 16, 1929, 3; January 1, 1940, sec. 2, p. 12; and October 26, 1940, 3.

43. *Japanese American Courier*, December 23, 1933, 2; Lee, "Hu Jcc," 102 (quotation).

44. *Japanese American Courier*, December 19, 1941, 3; March 27, 1942, 3.

45. *Japanese American Courier*, September 6, 1930, 4; January 1, 1931, 6; February 20, 1932, 4; September 2, 1933, 4; and September 30, 1933, 4 (study tour); November 9, 1935, 4; and December 21, 1935, 4 (girls on the tour). Japanese teams also toured the United States and played exhibition games against Japanese American community teams as well as U.S. professional and semiprofessional teams (for examples, see the issues of April 11, 1931, 2; April 18, 1931, 4; and April 20, 1935, 3). *Japanese American Courier*, August 17, 1929, 3; and February 20, 1932, 4 (quotations).

46. Ichioka, "Kengakundan," 15. *Japanese American Courier*, September 30, 1933, 1; January 20, 1934, 2; and February 24, 1940, 4.

47. *Japanese American Courier*, September 27, 1937, 2 (Tatsumi); April 20, 1940, 2; and January 18, 1941, 3.

48. *Japanese American Courier*, May 25, 1940, 4.

49. *Chinese Digest*, January 1939, 10.

50. Ibid.

51. *Japanese American Courier*, January 20, 1940, 4.

52. Sone, *Nisei Daughter*, 118–19, 120–24.

53. *Japanese American Courier*, November 13, 1937; for the overall position of the JACL, see articles of April 7, 1928, 1, and January 5, 1935, 4. Hosokawa quotation from the issue of August 31, 1940, 1. For the other articles in the series, see issues of August to October 1940, passim, but especially September 7, 1940, 1 and 4, September 21, 1940, 1 and 4, October 12, 1940, 1 and 4. On Japanese expansion in Asia and the role of Japanese constructions of "race" in that context, see John W. Dower, "Race, Language, and War in Two Cultures: World War II in Asia," in *The*

War in American Culture: Society and Consciousness During World War II, ed. Lewis A. Erenberg and Susan E. Hirsch (Chicago: University of Chicago Press, 1996), 169–201; and Dower, *War Without Mercy: Race and Power in the Pacific War* (New York: Pantheon Books, 1986).

54. *Japanese American Courier*, June 17, 1939, 1; March 8, 1941, 2; and December 5, 1941, 2.

55. *Japanese American Courier*, March 15, 1941, 1; April 5, 1941, 1; and July 12, 1941, 1.

56. Examples of these events are numerous; see *Japanese American Courier*, November 8, 1930, 4; November 27, 1937, 4; March 11, 1939, 4; January 6, 1940, 4; April 5, 1941, 4; and November 14, 1941, 4.

57. *Japanese American Courier*, January 1, 1941, 9.

58. Wong, *Fifth Chinese Daughter*, 134–35, 188 ff. *Chinese Digest*, November 15, 1935; May 22, 1936, 11 and 15; May 15, 1936, 3. Lee, "Hu-Jee," 83, 86, and 90.

59. Lee, "Hu-Jee," 96; Yung, *Unbound Feet*, 239–40.

60. *Chinese Digest*, July 1938, 12; Lee, "Hu-Jee," 98.

61. Lee, "Hu-Jee," 92–95, 98. For a discussion of the ways European Americans defined a Chinatown as a social space, see Anderson, "Power of Place."

62. *Chinese Digest*, May 2, 1941, 2; Lee, "Hu-Jee," 97.

63. Kenneth Wing to Warren G. Magnuson, [n.d.], box 58, folder 23, Warren G. Magnuson Papers, Accession 3181–2, Manuscripts and University Archives Division, University of Washington Libraries, Seattle. Magnuson to C. J. Heagerty, 29 September 1943, box 58, folder 25, Magnuson Papers.

64. Yung, *Unbound Feet*, 252–60. Wong, "Defending China, Claiming America," 1; Peter Phan, "Familiar Strangers: The Fourteenth Air Service Group Case Study of Chinese American Identity During World War II," in *Chinese America: History and Perspectives* (San Francisco: Chinese Historical Society of America, 1993), 75–107; Norine Dresser, "Chinatown Militia Units–1942 Los Angeles and San Francisco," *Gum Saan Journal* 15, no. 2 (1992): 16–25; Marjorie Lee, "Building Community," in *Linking Our Lives*, 94–99; and Lee, "Hu-Jee," 105–7. I am grateful to Scott Wong for agreeing to share his work-in-progress with me. His interviews of Chinese American veterans of World War II promise to add significantly to the scholarly and popular understanding of Asian Americans in this period.

65. Lee, "Hu-Jee," 109–10, 120.

66. Akemi Kikumura, *Through Harsh Winters: The Life of a Japanese Immigrant Woman* (Novato, Calif.: Chandler and Sharp, 1981), 7.

67. Kitano, *Generations and Identity*, 52, 70, and 164–65.

68. *Japanese American Courier*, January 1, 1940, sec. 1, p. 5.

69. Michael Omi and Howard Winant, *Racial Formation in the United States from*

the 1960s to the 1990s, 2d ed. (New York: Routledge, 1994), 81. I am in the process of refining this argument in "Engaging the Narratives of Race and Place," in *Race and Racism: Toward the 21st Century*, ed. Paul Wong et al. (forthcoming).

70. For example, see Sánchez, *Becoming Mexican American;* and David G. Gutiérrez, *Walls and Mirrors: Mexican Americans, Mexican Immigrants, and the Politics of Ethnicity* (Berkeley: University of California Press, 1995).

71. Harry H. L. Kitano and Roger Daniels, *Asian Americans: Emerging Minorities* (Englewood Cliffs, N.J.: Prentice Hall, 1988), 82–83; and Fred Cordova, *Filipinos: Forgotten Asian Americans, 1763–circa 1963* (Dubuque, Iowa: Kendall/Hunt, 1983), 217–27, provide a good starting point.

72. Alvin M. Josephy, Jr., "Modern America and the Indian," in *Indians in American History*, ed. Frederick E. Hoxie (Arlington Heights, Ill.: Harlan Davidson, 1988), 251–74, provides a quick overview of policy. See also Donald L. Fixico, *Termination and Relocation: Federal Indian Policy, 1945–1960* (Albuquerque: University of New Mexico Press, 1986); and Ned Blackhawk, "I Can Carry on from Here: The Relocation of American Indians to Los Angeles," *Wicazo Sa Review* 11, no. 2 (1995): 16–30.

73. Douglas Henry Daniels, *Pioneer Urbanites: A Social and Cultural History of Black San Francisco* (Philadelphia: Temple University Press, 1980); Albert S. Broussard, *Black San Francisco: The Struggle for Racial Equality in the West, 1900–1954* (Lawrence: University Press of Kansas, 1993); Gretchen Lemke-Santangelo, *Abiding Courage: African American Migrant Women and the East Bay Community* (Chapel Hill: University of North Carolina Press, 1996); and Quintard Taylor, *The Forging of a Black Community: Seattle's Central District from 1870 Through the Civil Rights Era* (Seattle: University of Washington Press, 1994), all speak to this issue.

74. Gans, "Comment."

PART III

ENVIRONMENT AND ECONOMY

Tourism as Colonial Economy

Power and Place in Western Tourism

HAL ROTHMAN

Near the end of her forty-three years in Sun Valley, Idaho, Dorice Taylor, the self-proclaimed dowager queen of the town, who had been the first guest in the Challenger Inn and later spent sixteen years running the Sun Valley publicity department for the Union Pacific Railroad, opened her memoir by announcing: "You could easily form a platoon of pre–Sun Valley natives to drive out all the newcomers; or a battalion of residents, here when Sun Valley was owned by the Union Pacific Railroad, to drive out all the Johnny-come-latelies; or a regiment of present inhabitants to man the mountain passes and roll rocks down on the hordes of Californians invading the highlands of Idaho."[1]

In this seemingly off-the-cuff but prescient statement, Taylor captured a number of the conflicts inherent in the evolution of tourist-based economies throughout the world: problems of power and place that permeate an industry in areas with prior, less economically viable histories and ways of life. In her characterization of Sun Valley, successive waves of residents arrived, fashioned a meaningful and pleasant existence—developing an identity grounded in place and worth protecting—and saw it transformed by changes in ownership, increases in visitation, and a host of other phenomena. Their response has been anger, alienation, and nostalgia, as well as the kind of arrogance and self-righteousness embodied in the unsolicited advice that made developer William Janss, who purchased the resort from the Union Pacific Railroad in 1964, moan: "Every person I talk to thinks he owns the place."[2]

These are symptoms of the changes in scale and scope wrought by the tourism industry in any of its successful incarnations. Tourism in the American West is at its core colonial, grafting new sources of power and financing atop existing social structures, bringing idealistic and romantic value systems supported by outside capital to places where the majority of residents have yet to experience material prosperity, and promising an economic panacea but delivering it only to privileged segments of the public. When it succeeds, tourism changes the economic structure of communities and surrounding regions, redistributes power from local people to outsiders with capital, and packages and transforms the meaning of place to successive waves of people, from "old-timers" to the newest "neo-native" arrivals, who seek to pull the figurative door shut behind them. The result is often the transformation through overuse and overpromotion of what is exceptional about any place. This engenders considerable after-the-fact resentment and wistfulness for the "way things used to be," as well as a sense of displacement for those with an investment in earlier psychic constructions of community and economy. Sawtooth Valley, Idaho, native and writer John Rember expressed this sentiment best when he wrote of his return to the area: "I am finding what once was familiar [is] unfamiliar, what once was real is no longer real." More reflective than most, Rember found himself "trapped by the indenture of memory."[3] The world in which he had vast psychic investment looked much the same, but had become substantially different.

In this way and others, tourism is a devil's bargain for much of the West. It may seem the best option to rescue places from the economic doldrums, but it carries unanticipated costs that often make people wonder, long after it is too late, if the change was worth the effort. Many western places have wholly formed self-images; they see their identities as stemming from substantive industries such as ranching and mining, from long history in a place, from patterns of behavior and living, and from the special characteristics of the land around them. They are Wallace Stegner's "stickers," now facing the onslaught of visitors and newcomers who seek to make this solidly formed core into something malleable and receptive to the whims of bicoastal America, of suburbs throughout the nation, of trendy fashions. Often this choice becomes galling, as it pits deeply held values against the possibility of economic revival and success.

In the process, an internal transformation and dislocation occurs.[4] At first it is subtle and embraced, but over time it becomes threatening and stultifying, burying the locals' sense of place within the reformed space of the visitors' construct. Few of the residents of any tourism-based community and its surroundings are exempted, and even participation in one form of a tourist economy does not guarantee success in a subsequent incarnation. Rents and land prices rise, places defined by one set of externalities are redefined by new forms of power, and a new world emerges, shaped by different standards and responding to a different constellation of forces. Most often locals stay in their transformed community, seeking some kind of accommodation, while resident visitors migrate to the next fashionable place, having initiated change but leaving its consequences to those who have greater commitment to the particular place or lesser ability to flee catalytic processes of change. Those who remain are left to fend for themselves. Throughout the twentieth century, thousands across a changing West have experienced the social, cultural, and economic consequences of such transformations.[5]

As a historic American form of economic endeavor, tourism is unusual. Like manufacturing, agriculture, or stock-raising, tourism creates a product that can be purchased, but unlike those industries, what it offers is barely tangible. Tourism is the marketing of experience, of meaning, of relaxation, of affirmation, and increasingly of status. Like other industries in the era of transportation networks, tourism depends on a nationwide market; but unlike those industries, its product cannot be delivered. People have to leave their homes and communities to partake of it, creating the possibility of a two-way exchange of culture, ideas, and behavior that no store-bought commodity from afar can offer. As in other industries, consumers select from many varieties of the tourism product; unlike other industries, communities that court tourists have to sell something unique and exciting—history, culture, scenery, recreation, sport, or entertainment. But rather than an exchange of cultures that transforms the visitor, more often the result is that the "visited" bear the brunt of change as they seek to fashion themselves in the image of what visitors seek in the competition for the dollars that tourists bring.

The process of inventing and reinventing that special commodity in changing cultural environments holds the intersection of power and place. Ownership of resources—ski areas, hotels, lakes, and historic properties—confers an extraordinary ability to reshape not only the attractions and their meaning but the entire system that depends on them, from local and regional government policy down to dishwashers and chambermaids. Yet such a transformation may be threatening to an existing dependent community precisely because its psychic and economic investment has become the local status quo, fickle, ever transitory, ever responsive to the vagaries of the marketplace of packaged meaning. In communities defined by amenity, long-standing presence is as important as ownership and wealth in the formation of local ideology and identity. Presence over time, not wealth, often lends genuine authority to year-round residents.[6]

This creates generations within communities. These are people for whom the meaning of previous incarnations has not died while their position in the community has been irrevocably altered by the appearance of fresh capital disguised as vision. New conceptions of the market, changing public images of activity, or new perceptions of the significance of a specific place play crucial roles. Technology and transportation are also critical in defining generational boundaries, as is the change in ownership of a resort, a repackaging of a place to a new and broader, or even older and smaller, constituency, a rise in the local or regional cost of living, and countless other factors.[7] In each community, these moments become demarcation lines between different cultures that inhabit the same physical but not always the same conceptual space. Such worlds "look" the same but, as John Rember suggests, "feel" quite different.

This is a process repeated throughout the American West, time and again, in national parks and historic communities, in ski resorts and towns that depend on hunting, fishing, or river-rafting, and it is especially apparent in Las Vegas and Disneyland, which seek to hold up a mirror to visitors, clean that glass regularly, and reflect upon tourists exactly what they want to see. In this, tourism blurs experience, refracts it, and makes it appear and become something entirely different. No place in the West or in the world remains the same after it shifts to depend on tourism or even to acknowledge how necessary tourism already is in its economic equation. People may have felt comfortable selling the wealth hidden in their ground or cutting the timber of their forests, but making an identity transformation is more problematic, especially in the West, with its mythic connotations and its formative place in America's self-definition. On a psychic level, the meeting of national mythology and resort transforms even more comprehensively; it takes from what you are and replaces that with an overlay and interpretation that connects with outside values.[8]

Sun Valley, Idaho, offers a dramatic example of the problems of tourism even in invented places, as well as of the complicated relationship between "neo-native" generations initiated by the invention of a successful tourist industry. Through three postinvention incarnations, each with different characteristics that have been obliterated because of changes made by subsequent regimes, Sun Valley has retained the special status and symbolism that came from being the first ski area in the West conceived for a national upscale audience. It has stood alone, even when packaged identically with other resorts owned by the same developer. Each of its transformations has had consequences; each version of the community has offered new advantages and each has alienated some portions of the existing community, pretourist and visitor-driven alike. Each has spread concentric rings of influence farther from the community itself, in effect colonizing a wider hinterland for its human, natural, and psychic resources. Each incarnation has redefined the essence of Sun Valley, in the process changing those characteristics that attracted that largest group of previous residents—neo-natives— and altering the entire area that depended on the tourism industry.

Sun Valley was the invention of W. Averell Harriman, the owner of the Union Pacific Railroad, and his publicity agent, Steve Hannagan. Equal parts enthusiast and businessman, Harriman wanted to increase passenger traffic on his rail line. The popularity of skiing in the aftermath of the 1932 Winter Olympics at Lake Placid, New York, offered a mechanism. At places such as Killington in Vermont, skiers dotted the slopes in unheard-of numbers, but Harriman's rail lines were closer to western mountains than the already crowded hills of the East. He sought to invent a place that was far enough from western cities and close enough to the main line of his railroad to create captive populations and ensure a healthy passenger trade in the winter.[9]

Before the coming in December 1935 of Count Felix Schaffgotsch, an Austrian hired by the railroad to find a location for a ski resort along its lines, Sun Valley was merely Ketchum, a mining town in the Wood River Valley at the base of the Sawtooth Mountains that had declined from its peak population of more than 2,000—served by thirteen saloons and a general store—in the 1880s to approximately 270 in 1935. Although the sheep industry had kept some vestige of a community there between the 1880s and the 1930s, Ketchum had clearly been passed by. Only freight reached the nearly abandoned town on the old Oregon Short Line, built to carry silver. Passenger service could be found at the rail stop sixty miles away at Shoshone, and as many local residents as could "went out," departed the region, for the winter. Until the community caught the eye of the Union Pacific, it had little future.[10]

With the place selected, Harriman set out to create a national image. He hired Hannagan, a man who hated winter and could not conceive of the pleasure of skiing but whose previous accomplishment was the creation of the mythic Miami Beach for the northeastern public. On a spectacular sunny March day in 1936, Hannagan found himself sweating in the snow of Ketchum and promptly named the area "Sun Valley." Harriman had planned a medium-sized establishment, but Hannagan returned to New York bursting with plans for a million-dollar luxury hotel where the famous and wealthy would become part of the spectacle. The public relations specialist bombarded Americans with the image of a young man, muscular, handsome, and stripped to the waist, skiing through the powdery snow of Sun Valley. Although the advertisement was photographed in a Manhattan studio, it represented the ambience that Hannagan sought to promote. The 250-room lodge, built to rival the chalets of the Swiss Alps, was filled for the grand opening in December 1936. Errol Flynn, Robert Young, Melvyn Douglas, Claudette Colbert, David O. Selznick, and numerous other celebrities attended the affair, dining on an exquisite menu of Brioche au Caviar, Supreme of Sole au Champagne, and Tournedos Sauté Chatelaine. A lack of snow almost ended the festivities, but when it fell on New Year's Eve, Sun Valley became the Saint-Moritz of America. "The whole country was crazy about skiing and where skiing was concerned, Sun Valley was IT," Dorice Taylor recalled in an interview shortly before her death. "If you had the money to ski, you came here." Hannagan made Sun Valley into the place where guests could "rough it in luxury."[11]

The image of Sun Valley received crucial authentication with the appearance of Ernest Hemingway. In September 1939, he arrived with his companion, Martha Gellhorn, staying two months and returning in each of the subsequent two years to hunt and fish. Harriman recognized the importance of a persona such as Hemingway, who fit the celebrity profile of the resort and whose own iconographic significance attracted a constituency different from the skiers who swarmed to Sun Valley in the winter. Associated with hunting and fishing, Hemingway had the potential to fill the lodge during another season, historically the time of year Sun Valley attracted few visitors. When Harriman found that Hemingway had moved from a suite at the main lodge to the less expensive Challenger Inn at the start of the 1939 ski season, he brought the author back at no charge—to the suite with the patio where he reviewed the galleys of his masterpiece, *For Whom the Bell Tolls*.[12] Hemingway embodied the image Harriman sought to promote.

All of this created a place quite different from the Wood River Valley that preceded Sun Valley. The Union Pacific became the only game in town. Before the invention of the resort, its few businesses and Basque sheepherders had little claim on the transportation technologies of the twentieth century; most of the people who lived in the town were relics of earlier economies. With the exception of a few ranchers who owned their land outright, employed a significant number of herdsmen, and depended on the price of beef, wool, and mutton for their livelihood, locals eked out a marginal economic existence. Building the resort meant opportunities in construction and created a new kind of accessibility for the community. After the resort opened, a branch line to Ketchum made Sun Valley easily accessible to any Union Pacific passenger. Harriman paid a little more than one dollar per acre (for 3,881 acres) to Ernest Brass, a rancher who had lost his cattle to poisonous larkspur weeds and his sheep to the plummeting prices of the Depression and whose daughters, Roberta and Marjorie, had served as guides for the Austrians assessing the region.[13] The economic structure of the future resort was reflected in that initial transaction.

Local merchants experienced the same transformation. Jack Lane of Lane's Mercantile, one of the primary businesses in Ketchum, found limits to the opportunities available under the new regime. The Lane family had been the sustaining business in Ketchum, the source of capital and supplies for most of the sheepherding outfits in the Wood River and Sawtooth Valleys. Its cachet with local people did not carry over to the resort. Although Lane had been instrumental in providing material, labor, and supplies, and Lane's Mercantile had been the headquarters for railroad men, contractors, architects, and engineers during the construction of the resort, Lane was bypassed when postconstruction plums were handed out. The ski shop in the Sun Valley Lodge, the top-of-the-line hotel in the resort, was initially run by Saks Fifth Avenue and later by a French designer of women's ski clothes, Henri Picard. Even the sale of sundry items was handled by the economic elite, and Lane's remained what it had been—the economic center of the local community, but greatly diminished in importance by the opening of the resort. Only after the Challenger Inn, with its more modest accommodations and clientele, opened a year later, did Lane win a contract for the ski shop there from the Union Pacific.[14] The change in Lane's position reflected the iconography of Sun Valley and its pretensions to status as well as the role defined for locals in the postresort world.

In employment, a similar superstructure existed. Hans Hauser, an Austrian ski champion, his "corps of bronzed young Tyrolese instructors," and other expatriate Europeans ran skiing at Sun Valley. These included Florian "Flokie" Haemmerle, a Bavarian who doubled as an artist and local philosopher; Freidl Pfeiffer, an Austrian who later went on to fame as the man who brought nationally marketed skiing to Aspen, Colorado; and Sepp Froelich, another Austrian ski racer, who married Natalie Rogers, a member of the Warburg banking family. The chefs in the hotel were French, the waiters

German, and local women worked as chambermaids. Another German, Frederich Blechmann, ran room service and later became captain of the dining room. Organized crime had a piece of the local action. George Weinbrenner of the Detroit "Purple Gang" was the reputed owner of the fashionable gambling establishment in Ketchum, the Christiannia Club. Even the perceptive Dorice Taylor played a part in the transformation. She and her husband, Everett "Phez" Taylor, an Ivy League–trained lawyer, left New York and became part of the fledgling community. He joined a local law firm, specializing in what was then the province of the rich—divorce—while she ran the publicity division at the resort.[15]

The advent of the resort brought significant changes in both the population and the distribution of its foreign-born residents. By 1940, more than 5,295 people lived in Blaine County, compared with 3,768 in 1930, a whopping 40 percent increase, exceeding that of any other rural Idaho county during the same period. In 1920 and 1930, less than 10 percent of the population in the county was foreign-born. Of the 298 Blaine County residents in 1930 who were born outside the United States, 137 were fifty-five or older, and another 69 were between forty-five and fifty-four. Although foreign-born residents shrunk in percentage as a result of the growth that followed the resort, their demography reflected the change in occupational structure in the county. By 1940, the foreign-born population had become dramatically younger, as foreigners played an important role at the ski resort: 107 were between twenty and forty-five, up from 38 residents recorded in the 1930 census who were in that age group.[16]

The agricultural economy, the mainstay of the county, also experienced dramatic change. In 1935, 1,647 people lived on farms in Blaine County, roughly 40 percent of the population. By 1939, farm income had dropped significantly in every category of production, from livestock to crops, at a rate faster than that of other Idaho counties of comparable size. Adjacent Camas and Butte Counties, one to the east and the other to the west of Blaine, both showed income drops typical of rural northern states during the Depression decade, but Blaine County exceeded those income levels by as much as 50 percent. Replacing agricultural income in what was a modestly more prosperous county than it had been in 1935 were the wages of 284 hotel and lodge workers at Sun Valley, making up more than 17 percent of the 1,839 workers in the county. In all of Idaho, only Ada County, which includes the state capital of Boise, had more hotel workers; but in Boise more than half of these workers were women. At Sun Valley, 210 of the 284 hotel workers were men, reflecting the predominance of resort workers in the county economy.[17] A new economic niche in rural Idaho had opened up with different gender segmentation than was common elsewhere in the state and nation.

In 1930, Blaine County mirrored other predominantly rural counties in Idaho; but by 1940 the total population, as well as its distribution by age, place of birth, and occupation, was significantly different. Besides showing unparalleled growth during the 1930s among rural counties in Idaho, Blaine County developed new segments in the labor force. No other rural counties included a significant percentage of service occupations, nor did they show as high a percentage of renters of land and housing. The percentage of farmers in the county population declined from about one-half to one-third of the total, while the number of people who lived on farms remained constant. The founding of the resort quickly transformed the economic and demographic structure of the county.

This economic structure left most prior inhabitants out of the opportunities brought by skiing. The people who departed area farms were marginal candidates for permanent employment at the resort. Their main economic resource became the land they owned, not their labor. Local landowners found that their property had renewed value, yet unless they were young and willing to work in service occupations, there was little for them to do. Those who did not own businesses benefited most from the improved transportation. No longer cut off from the outside world in the winter, they remained wage workers who lived in small homes while the rich and famous celebrated at nearby lodges.

The Taylors themselves were exempla of the first incarnation of Sun Valley, much like the Lanes in pre–Sun Valley Ketchum. Their tenure depended on the largesse of outsiders. As long as the Union Pacific ran the resort, the Taylors' position, status, and indeed cosmology were safe. Despite the husband's law practice, they needed the protectorate created there by the Union Pacific. Natives after a fashion, they were tuned to the rhythms of the place Harriman and Hannagan invented.

Sun Valley was enticing to more than just the Taylors. "There was a great sense of informality," Jack Hemingway remembered, describing a place where the "help mingled with the high and mighty." Larger-than-life personalities dominated the horizon, from Pat "Pappy" Rogers, who managed the resort for the Union Pacific from 1938 to 1952, to celebrities like Louis Armstrong and television comedienne Ann Sothern. Residents at the time remembered the place as egalitarian, fun, and surprising. Skiing down the mountain with a dishwasher, one might discover, in the words of longtime resident Johnny

Lister, that the person "had a doctorate from MIT." A charismatic openness existed that seemed to encourage people to be themselves, and residents and visitors of the time fondly recalled that quality.[18]

This view of a halcyon era exists in almost every resort community. It often coincides with carefree or seminal times in the lives of the people who recount such moments, and even more frequently closely mirrors the time when respondents entered such communities. They and the community they joined were younger, freer, somehow less tainted or jaded. Such moments uniformly have social rituals closely attached to them; in Sun Valley, Pappy Rogers's summer softball games served as a unifier within the resort community and a clear distinction from the world of visitors. The games made workers feel part of something special, a feeling they recalled with relish. Part nostalgia, part memory of a more innocent time in life, and part resistance to change, such attitudes permeate local perceptions of life in a tourist community. People who hold this view are often almost antimodern in their outlook on the world, finding a perfect moment in the past and seeing a fallen world based in the changes since. Such a view often reflects changing values in the community, and frequently appears as a result of growth and expansion of resort amenities.[19] Yet such perceptions, real or not, form an important component of the matrix of tourism-based communities.

Besides visitors, the Union Pacific's Sun Valley attracted two distinctly different categories of people. One large contingent mirrored the Taylors and Johnny Lister; like these transplanted easterners, such arrivals came from the world of the visitors, shared its assumptions and values, and found in the experience of living in Sun Valley a pleasant diversion from typical upper-middle-class American life. People from the surrounding region were drawn by the economic opportunities the industry offered. For many in this agriculture- and ranching-based part of the West, the chance at even seasonal employment offered a potential solution to the economic problems of rural life. For these local people, the resort economy had economic advantages that almost always carried social and psychic costs.

Before Sun Valley, little market existed for hunting and fishing guides and ski instructors. Under the Union Pacific, resort officials spent much time drumming up summer business, transforming the meaning of local skills from subsistence to market value. During the 1950s, John Rember's father served as a hunting and fishing guide during summers in the Sawtooth Valley, about sixty miles from Stanley, itself an hour north of Sun Valley. In the winter, he drove a ski bus at the resort while his wife worked as a nurse. The family catered to a constant stream of visitors to the house during the summer; after the road through the valley was paved in 1957, 4:00 A.M. arrivals for "sourdough pancakes and strong black coffee" before a day of fishing or hunting became common in the Rember household. "It was a kind of paradise we lived in," Rember recalled. "By winter, our southern freezer was full of venison and elk and the french-bread shapes of salmon, and you only had to look at your plate to realize where you were based, where your sustenance lay."[20]

The kind of sustenance Rember recalled was both illusory and insular. Tourists provided most of the family income, and his parents worked in the industry in various capacities. Their livelihood required uprooting the family twice a year—first to move to the Sawtooths and then back to Sun Valley for the winter season. They lived a migratory existence, offering a child a wonderful view of the world, but exacting a toll on the parents. While they had a kind of independence, the Rembers had little opportunity either for upward mobility or for anything more than an illusory sense of rootedness. Living as much as 100 miles from Sun Valley, they were bound to it by a web of connections that determined where and when they lived in various locations. They were as much a part of the Union Pacific's structure as the Taylors, albeit in a more indirect fashion.

This world had clear limits in time. Internal rhythms did not drive its transformation; the larger world beyond the borders of Idaho dictated the changes. The "paradise" John Rember fondly recalled "lasted long enough for me to be raised in it."[21] The railroad spur of the 1930s was augmented by the paved road from Stanley in the 1950s, and this web of connections brought the Rembers and the stream of executives who envied them at the breakfast table in ever closer contact. Those ties were an essential part of the transformation the greater region underwent.

Rember, Taylor, and Johnny Lister all were nostalgic for a way of life that disappeared with their experiences as changes swirled around them over which they had no control. Rember's childhood, Taylor's move to Sun Valley, and even Lister's fond remembrance reveal a vision of place intertwined with the formative experiences that shape identity. All of these individuals had grown up, had become new versions of themselves, in this variegated place; all were shaped by it, and all had deep emotional ties to it. Changes, even ones that may have been economically positive, also had the potential to disrupt those carefully constructed worlds.

From New Year's Eve 1936 until 1964, Sun Valley remained a Union Pacific resort. It had a checkered history within the company, for after Governor C. A. Robins cracked down on gambling in the state in 1945, the resort consistently lost money. The focus of the Union Pacific shifted from passengers to freight as Americans began to use automobiles for personal travel, decreasing the importance of the resort. The opening of newer and more easily accessible ski areas throughout the West and the advent of air travel made Sun Valley's preeminence even more tenuous. Squaw Valley at Lake Tahoe in California hosted the 1960 Winter Olympics; David R. C. Brown's leadership of the Aspen Ski Company catapulted Aspen to the forefront of skiing; and Sun Valley remained as it had been. After Harriman ceased day-to-day management of the railroad, Union Pacific officials could no longer reconcile the meaning of the resort and its bottom line. Sun Valley seemed to have lost some of its appeal to the traveling public. Although both Ketchum and Sun Valley were incorporated as villages in 1947, between 1940 and 1950 the population growth slowed in the county to 1.7 percent, and a precipitous decrease followed. By 1960, the population of Blaine County had fallen more than 14 percent from its 1950 level, to 4,598. In the words of one observer, Sun Valley had "gotten kind of old and stodgy." Arthur Stoddard, the president of the railroad, had supported the resort, but in the 1960s, with consultants suggesting a $6 million facelift, he decided to sell.[22]

In 1964, William Janss, a former American Olympic skier and the primary developer of the Snowmass resort then under construction near Aspen, and his partners in the Janss Corporation purchased Sun Valley. The Janss company had undertaken the survey that discouraged Union Pacific officials, but Janss believed his company had the expertise and capital to refurbish the old resort. With a stated philosophy that the critical aspect of a ski area was to own enough land to "preserve options for future development," Janss planned to become, in the words of journalist Philip Fradkin, "the Henry Ford of ski developers, with overtones of Cadillac styling and Pentagon computer techniques."[23]

An outstanding skier and experienced developer, Janss became the transformative developer of western resorts. He had an entirely new conception of what a resort should and could be, and his vision shaped the post-1970 resort West. A cattle rancher and construction magnate who had been instrumental in creating Thousand Oaks, California, a 45,000-person planned community in Ventura County, near Los Angeles, Janss forged a "new vision" both in Sun Valley and at Snowmass, outside of Aspen, that came to typify western resorts. His insight was the creation of a second-home market in what had previously been hotel-room–based resorts. He expanded his resorts from the room-rental business, structuring every aspect of the communities he built or bought. In this formulation, he initiated a new stage of development that became the standard throughout the industry.

Janss had his own ideas for Sun Valley. When inspecting the physical plant, he looked into a cavernous basement area that had once been the boiler room and announced that it would become the resort's new discotheque, The Boiler Room. Such decision making was Janss's signature, and he was a canny individual with an understanding of how to please the public. Condominiums, another Janss innovation, were so new in Idaho that they required a change in law to be legal. The town began to look physically different. Some of the condos, particularly near the upscale lodge, were attractive, but the second and third developments were prefabricated and ordinary; one of the complexes earned the sobriquet "Camp Janss." Janss himself even referred to them as "cookie-cutter houses."[24]

Condos became big business in Sun Valley. Late in 1967, new projects opened, housing more than one hundred families, "several of them Idahoans," by one newspaper account. Built by Boise-Cascade, an Idaho-based company, and the Janss company and located between Dollar Mountain and the Challenger Inn, these "ateliers" were modular units, which helped lower the extraordinarily expensive $19 per square foot average building cost to a more reasonable $14. This inexpensive construction, and plans for developments such as the 3,000-bed Elkhorn Village, prompted a regional construction boom that altered the face of the community.[25]

Upscale houses followed. Along Trail Creek and the golf course, luxurious homes for the wealthy and famous sprouted. Russell Stewart, senior vice-president of Field Enterprises and a devotee of cooking, built a house with five kitchens; Walter Annenberg built a typical home along the golf course. Others such as Steve McQueen, Tom Hormel of Hormel's Meats and his wife, actress Janet Leigh, and William W. and Mignon Winan added a personal touch as they built an enclave of homes that reflected sheer wealth and the revived mystique of Sun Valley. By 1970, Janss had succeeded in reinventing the resort; even the *New York Times* pronounced Sun Valley "neat again."[26]

But Janss's Sun Valley was not the same as the Union Pacific's. Although it contained the same primary attractions, spectacular skiing and the aura of wealth and fame, it was governed by a different set of economic and cultural premises. While Sun Valley remained the "social center of the ski world," the rules and relationships set up under Union Pacific administration and nurtured by its benign neglect no longer held. What ensued was a more bottom-line–oriented institutional structure, more rigidly controlled from the top. Janss's developments at both Sun Valley and Snowmass, which he designed from the ground up, were "Southern California come to the Rockies," wrote Fradkin. "The two lifestyles meet, and the resulting compromise preserves little of the two components."[27]

This generational shift dislocated even Dorice Taylor. In her memoir, she entitled the chapter about the sale to Janss: "We Are Dumped." This identification with Sun Valley as a place suggests the depth of neo-native proprietary feeling. Her memoir reads as if the railroad had no right to sell the resort. Even though she retained her position as publicity director, the new Sun Valley felt different to her and longtime locals. Janss's plans upset existing convention, angering some in the town who gave "loud yowls of grief" every time a new condominium project went up. The population grew dramatically between 1960 and 1970; 5,749 people were recorded in the 1970 census, a 25 percent increase over 1960. One resident, John E. P. Morgan, immortalized the changes in poetry: "The mountains are now like a city; with pandemoniums at prices pretty."[28]

By 1970, Janss's efforts had accelerated the pattern of change in the distribution of occupations in Sun Valley and Blaine County. Farmers decreased from 1,647 in 1935 to 1,312 in 1950, 1,166 in 1960, and 877 in 1970. At the same time, hotel and other service workers increased as a percentage of the working population of the county. Of 2,295 workers in 1950, 481 were identified as participating in service occupations. Forty-two percent of female workers in the county were in such capacities, the highest recorded percentage for female workers until that time. The gender segmentation reverted to more typical resort structure as growth created employment for women in positions such as maids at a much faster rate than predominantly male ski instructors were hired. At the nadir of resort development in 1960, fully 15 percent of male employees and 34 percent of female employees in Blaine County remained in the service industry. The initial years of the Janss era masked the growth in service as a percentage of the work force, for construction jobs made up a large percentage of growth in the late 1960s. Subtracting construction employment above the level of 1960, the early years show an increase to almost 25 percent of male workers in the country in service occupations; female service workers remained constant as a percentage of female employment; and there was a dramatic increase in self-employed individuals.[29] Janss created a structurally and economically different community that catered to outsiders more than to local people.

A backlash against Janss's activities emerged in the mid-1970s. The extensive Sun Valley building boom had spilled over to nearby Hailey and Ketchum, extending the tentacles of the resort, and a master plan for the region was under way. A questionnaire about development in Ketchum circulated to local residents, who expressed clear dislike for those responsible for the changes. Antidevelopment and antioutsider rhetoric dominated the responses. One respondent advocated "no more developers, no more condos, just private homes." "Stop advertising Idaho," read another. A third bemoaned the fate of the creek in which he had fished as a child, now muddied by upstream construction.[30] The feelings of the neo-native elite had become common across a broad spectrum of the local population.

Far from capitulation, Taylor, Morgan, and the others who responded with their opinion about the changes engaged in a negotiation with the new realities. Under the Union Pacific, they had felt themselves part of a community and a place that, while designed for visitors, also sheltered them and not incidentally granted them special status. Janss's changes fundamentally altered their situation; he fashioned a different kind of town with its own self-contained importance, and his power ensured that his vision would prevail. Janss brought his own people and placed them in positions of status. Even those he retained, such as Dorice Taylor, found their responsibilities altered, their decision making curtailed, and their status different. Located in this place and with little desire to leave it, the first generation of neo-natives had to reach an accommodation with a new and powerful force that inadvertently or intentionally devalued their presence. Grumbling disguised as social critique combined with reluctant participation in the new situation.

The results of Janss's plan were even more pronounced at Snowmass, which the Janss company built from the ground up. Like nearby Vail, the progenitor of the residential ski community, Snowmass had important features that differentiated it from existing ski areas. Quietly purchasing 3,400 acres of land in Brushy Creek outside of Aspen at $500 to $600 per acre, Janss fashioned a community where first the upper class and then the middle and upper-middle class could buy a second home to use for recreation.[31]

The initial development at Snowmass, West Village, was aimed at an affluent constituency. "At last you see the village," one reporter wrote, confirming the image Janss sought to put forth. "Unexpected. Compact. Intimate. Honey colored windows beckon through the night." Janss's developments, from Westwood and Thousand Oaks in California to Sun Valley, had always borne this imprint. Janss financed the project with a $4.5 million investment from the American Cement Company. At $10,000 to $30,000 per residential site, a substantial increase from the price Janss paid for the land, and with apartments that sold in the $46,000 range, West Village bore some of the aura of Sun Valley and the gentrifying nearby Aspen, as well as all of the amenities of modern suburbia. It cost Janss $250,000 to bury all the utility lines in Snowmass, mirroring a pattern perfected in Scottsdale, Arizona, where the visibility of all signage was regulated. He understood that total control of the features of a resort guaranteed the preservation of its desired ambience, declining offers from both the Playboy Club and Howard Johnson's to build in the resort. Snowmass marketing manager John Cooley, a member of a southern California shopping center development company family, best expressed this sentiment: "We want the effect [of the resort] to be one of total harmony."[32]

Flush with success, Janss built a second community at Snowmass designed to entice ordinary suburbanites. "Superb Snowmass homesites especially designed for middle income families," the advertising brochure trumpeted. Owners could enjoy a vacation home, "with Dad joining them on the weekends. Many offer their property for rent when they aren't using it." With lots starting as low as $6,000 at Meadow Ranch and $7,000 at Country Club, less than half the initial price of lots in Phase I development at West Village, and condos built in a style identical to the Elkhorn development adjacent to Sun Valley, Snowmass II was genuinely affordable for much of the upper-middle class.[33]

Business ownership at Snowmass followed the pattern typical of resorts. One restaurant, Cyrano's, was imported "lock, stock, and barrel" from Sunset Strip in Los Angeles. Southern Californians John Cooley and project manager Roland Herberg had positions of responsibility in management; Norwegian Stein Eriksen ran the lucrative ski school; and most of the bars, restaurants, and lodges were owned by outside interests. Even locals who ran lodges were transplants. Arthur Preusch, owner of the Norway Lodge in Aspen and the forty-five-unit Snowmass Inn, moved to Aspen in 1965. Jack Kemp, the quarterback-later-turned-politician, and Phillip Battaglia, Ronald Reagan's chief assistant, were investors in other properties. Locals were relegated to characteristically low-level positions at the resort.[34]

Janss's kinds of development clearly separated generations within resort communities. Prior to the arrival of Janss, both Aspen and Sun Valley had been hotel-based resort communities. In Sun Valley, only the wealthiest owned vacation homes; and Aspen had a ski-bum, Aspen Institute–oriented local culture. Aspen's focus had been culture when Walter Paepcke, the head of the Container Corporation of America, and his wife, Elizabeth Nitze

Paepcke, revived the old mining town, but skiing soon took over. Only the wealthiest guests—Gary Cooper, for example—owned property, buying ranch-like estates around town. Into the 1960s, most local homes were owned by people who, wealthy or not, resided in Aspen most of the time.[35]

With Snowmass, Janss had created a new constituency for second homes in the greater Aspen area. Unlike the proto-trophy homes of the wealthy, these more modest, "cookie-cutter" structures could be marketed to a mass audience. They were also interchangeable; built as modifications on a minute number of floor plans, they all looked the same. More threatening to the idiosyncratic culture of such locales, these planned developments raised the profile of the communities in question, increased the local population, and set the stage for a clearly distinguished hierarchy within communities.

Janss's form of development became a threat to nearly everyone who inhabited a resort community and felt at home there. The influx of people who were not wealthy, famous, or committed to the concept of a skiing community changed the nature of the place. When anyone could own a middle-class "cookie-cutter" condo or second home, the Victorian homes in Aspen and the more modest and sometimes ramshackle homes in Ketchum acquired a new significance. They were unique—at least compared with modern homes. Instead of escaping attention and remaining the province of older local families transformed into resort help, they became a desired acquisition for those who saw a home as reflecting their individuality or longtime resident status in a community deeply involved in the next wave of trendsetting.

Even more telling, in both Snowmass and Sun Valley, the availability of "pandemoniums" and middle-class homes changed the character of the local population. Instead of the Annenbergs and other moguls, more affordable vacation homes brought a constituency seeking status by association. This created a fierce new demand for existing residential structures, the plums of the local real estate acquisition derby, as well as for newly built condos and homes. The new-found desirability of existing homes spurred a rapid rise in real estate prices in these towns. Advertisements for residential properties in the Aspen area between 1964 and 1970 show approximately 12 percent annual increases in asking price between 1964 and 1968, and increases in the 20 percent range in 1969 and 1970. Beginning early in the 1970s, Sun Valley real estate began to soar as its population doubled to nearly 3,000 people. By the middle of the 1970s in Sun Valley, average home prices ranged from $129,000 to $320,000, with a few homes in the $500,000 range. Homesites of one-half to three-quarter acres ranged between $35,000 and

$120,000, depending on the view. By 1976, Sun Valley had once again become, in the words of a financial reporter, the "hottest and most high-priced land development spot in the Northwest."[36]

Proximate and quaint, older homes in such towns acquired an iconographic meaning that belied their size, location, and level of amenities. Ownership of an older house in a town given over to tourists conferred de facto "old-timer" status, granting owners a claim on neo-native pioneer status in the rapidly changing resort community. As prices rose, the initial rapid inflation of real estate values in western resort towns took shape. Combined with the zoning of such communities and the tax hikes that paid for needed infrastructural improvements and amenities, the increase in property cost drove some older families from their homes and placed most property beyond reach of longtime local residents as well as the average resort worker.

Janss developed an understandably proprietary feeling about his communities that prior residents simultaneously appreciated and resented. When asked about homes built on Sun Valley hillsides before the era of Janss-planned development, he announced: "There won't be any more of that."[37] This autocratic sense of ownership offended locals such as Dorice Taylor, who felt the community was hers as much as Janss's, but she and others like her appreciated that he sought to preserve the vistas of the community. It was a typical predicament for locals, faced with a powerful force that dictated terms to them. They understood and appreciated the effort, but wished for the greater input that they remembered, accurately or otherwise, from the days of the Union Pacific.

The goals of Janss's program at Sun Valley and Snowmass had unintended consequences. "Aspen will be one of the great skiing cities," Janss predicted in newspapers as he prepared to open Snowmass. "It will never return to being the pleasant small skiing town." To Janss, this was a good thing; to others, it was an implicit threat to their way of life. Janss's declaration meant that the captive constituency who had been working in the town would have to adjust to new realities. He implemented the same rigid control of development in Sun Valley, creating what one newspaper reporter in 1976 called its "enviable position." By then, Janss had master-planned and zoned his community, advocating "slow orderly growth" limited to about fifty condominiums a year. Only 15 percent of the land Janss held was scheduled for eventual development. The rest was to remain open space. Outside of the area he owned, people looked to his operation to provide a healthy portion of their yearly income. The buffer zone of land he owned around the resort ensured that he could implement his vision; the economic dependence on Sun Valley of the surrounding region guaranteed no less than grumbling compliance with his needs.[38] But Sun Valley was no longer the Sun Valley that the devotees of the Union Pacific era had known, and the new Aspen—with Snowmass—continued its transition from cultural center with skiing attached to ski town playground of the rich and famous.

In Sun Valley, there was considerable ambivalence about the changes, even from direct beneficiaries. Howard Richards, a broker for Ketchum Realty, reported increases in the cost of housing that averaged 6 to 10 percent annually throughout the early 1970s. Although clearly prospering as a result, he reported "mixed feelings" about the area's growth during his eight years in Sun Valley. He was "a little fearful" about the consequences of growth, but thought it brought advantages. "When I first came here there were hardly any permanent residents. It was a transient population," he reported. "Now people are staying and buying their own homes." To Richards, this suggested permanence, despite the reality that more than 70 percent of homes were inhabited on a seasonal basis.[39]

While beneficiaries could see positive aspects of the accelerated changes, Janss's developments were the subject of scathing critiques by those who had invested in a different kind of community. Prominent among them was *Aspen Times* columnist Peggy Clifford, who lived in Aspen from 1953 to 1979. At Brushy Creek, where the Snowmass development was located, "mountains, men, and machines came together in a very sophisticated way," Clifford wrote. What resulted was a village "that would serve the needs of skiers at [a] cost-profit ratio that the computer approved." In her view, Snowmass "exemplified qualities that Aspen had itself eschewed—large scale, efficiency, group think, and a no-nonsense cost-profit ratio. It was an anomaly in the landscape . . . [that] looked not unlike a prison." Culturally, it promoted "endless fun, comfort, and surprises that were uniformly pleasant. . . . It was not a town but a good-times machine, and the good times were organized and codified. They were also unreal."[40]

Like Dorice Taylor in Sun Valley, Clifford represented an earlier generation in Aspen. Her ideal was the antithesis of the Snowmass development so widely praised in business circles, but with resignation she recognized the inevitability of the transformation of her community, which had "turned its back" on America in the postwar years, "celebrating art and sport over money and goods." Aspen had been different from the rest of the nation, attractive in an intangible way. But for Clifford and others of her genera-

Sounds like
David Orr

tion, such as writer and pianist Bruce Berger, the Janss development made Aspen culturally common. "The eccentric's hideout was becoming affluent America's playground," Clifford pompously mused. "We hated and feared America, but it was still in love with us, for we were everything it was not." Berger became so alienated that he began to spend his winters—still the prime season in Aspen—in Phoenix.[41]

But words were all that the detractors of Bill Janss found available. His philosophy generated a maximum level of control over his resorts, and only businesses and employees in line with his views could find a place in these systematized organizations. To Janss, people such as Dorice Taylor and Peggy Clifford provided local color. They were eccentrics whose stories entertained visitors in the manner of old prospectors and their mules in hotel lobbies in 1930s Las Vegas.[42]

Although he sold Snowmass soon after it opened, Janss owned Sun Valley until 1977, when R. Earl Holding of the Little American Corporation purchased the resort. A Utahan by birth, the thrifty, determined, and "decidedly Yankee" Holding developed a different kind of western empire than Janss's. Little America, a chain of hotel/motels and truckstops, catered to the very center of the vast American middle class. Only when he purchased the luxurious Plaza Hotel in San Diego did Holding begin to serve the class of people to whom Sun Valley had once appealed.[43]

Holding's purchase began anew the process that Sun Valley experienced when Janss bought the resort. Holding "decidedly changed the guard" as he implemented "an extensive house-cleaning" of Sun Valley. Using the original Union Pacific objectives as his guidelines, he sought to restore the chic image and cultural cachet of the resort. First he stopped the sale of company-owned land for additional private homes, preventing any further development that would detract from the overall ambience of the resort and de facto increasing the value of existing privately held properties. Then he began renovations of some of the more spectacular parts of the original lodge, in particular the formal dining room. He also invested in recruiting Idahoans to visit their state's premier resort, changing the image of the resort. His Sun Valley accommodated ordinary skiers as well as experts.[44]

The entire program cost more than $5 million, and caused a spillover of construction to surrounding areas such as Ketchum and Hailey, as well as a new boom in Sun Valley proper. During 1979, over $15 million worth of construction slated to become 169 residential units began in Sun Valley, more than 40 percent above the previous record year of 1978. Ketchum and Hailey experienced a larger percentage growth in the dollar valuation of construction, reaching $12.3 million and $4.36 million respectively. Ketchum began to blossom with new galleries, Holding and his family personally planted 2,000 trees, and the golf course was renovated.[45]

Holding also sought the long announced but seemingly unreachable goal of making Sun Valley a year-round resort. A consistent flow of tourism throughout the year would ensure a profit for the resort; the Union Pacific had worked to make Sun Valley an attractive summer resort from the moment it opened. Beginning with Hemingway's association with the resort, rodeos, hunting, fishing, wilderness, and other activities were trumpeted, but with little long-term success. Steve Hannagan, who hated winter, fished the Sun Valley area in the summer, but even his remarkable promotional skill could not attract a wider summer constituency. Using Sun Valley as the summer training camp for the Brooklyn Dodgers and the Baltimore Colts of the All-America Football Conference, which began in 1946 and merged with the National Football League in 1950, did not develop a basis for summer tourism. An effort to develop a summer music camp patterned on Aspen made summer visitation slightly more diverse, but even the appearance of the Sun Valley Porsche Parade in 1971 did little to enhance summer visitation rates.[46] While the mountains at Sun Valley made its skiing extraordinary, its hunting, fishing, and other amenities were quite ordinary.

Efficient and quiet as opposed to Janss's more ebullient style, Holding sought to enhance this previously underdeveloped dimension of the local tourist industry. In cooperation with the Sun Valley Chamber of Commerce, which issued a brochure that touted the area as "The West's Year-Round Vacation Land" in 1982, Holding sought to improve upon the 32 percent annual occupancy rate and particularly the $17 average daily expenditure of summer visitors. "We want that person who is casually traveling through the Sawtooths," noted Wally Huffman, Sun Valley Company general manager. "We want to remind him that [in the summer] there is always room here." Unlike winter skiers, who came for a week at a time, summer visitors often merely passed through. Gasoline and food were generally their largest expenditures, but even combined the total expenditures of summer visitors averaged well below the food, lodging, transportation, and recreation averages for winter visitors. Attracting summer visitors who spent money posed a problem for Holding, as it had for every incarnation of Sun Valley before his.[47]

Although the nearly eighty-year-old Dorice Taylor, retired for more than seven years at the time of Holding's purchase, offered only a few caustic comments, others watched with a combination of interest and trepidation.[48]

The latest transfer of power was only marginally different from its predecessors. The stalwarts of the Union Pacific era were retired, and those who had made the community their home during Janss's era were more sanguine. Yet the transformation as a result of the sale again carried the risk of alienating the classes of people who made the town function.

That alienation is endemic, part and parcel of the process of self-selection that leads people to the inherent powerlessness of neo-native status in a community dependent on cheap labor and outside dollars for its economic sustenance. In his fiction, John Rember has best captured the character of what he calls the "Post-Ironic Recreational West," with its substitution of wealth for human spirit and narcissism for human relationships. Writing of the fictional town of Gomorrah in the shadow of Mount Mammon, a thinly disguised Sun Valley, Rember chronicles refugees from life who seek solace in hedonism, and meaning in the most bleak of gestures. Human, yet consumed by a search for humanity, they represent the social and ultimately personal powerlessness of people who cannot muster the energy to defend what is meaningful to them. Extensions of people like Dorice Taylor, who could fight back and negotiate accommodation, Rember's protagonists, the fictional cheerleaders from Gomorrah in the Lycra Archipelago, drift along from meaningless pleasure to subsequent encounter.[49]

Rember's memories meld with his fiction to offer a poignant view of the transformations caused by tourism. Many locals become materially better off as a result of the tourist industry, but the benefits are often negated by the changed perceptions of themselves and their community. "Trouble with unreality is preferable to trouble with reality," Rember wrote of his experience of coming home. This complex attitude—a mixture of resignation, nostalgia, genuine feelings of dislocation, and other emotions—is an integral part of the devil's bargain that tourism, for all its benefits, has become for many communities. When place and power intersect in the American West, something must give. In Sun Valley and the Sawtooth area, in Aspen and Snowmass, and elsewhere across the historic-, recreational-, and entertainment-based West, community identity and values have yielded to the demands of intra- and extra-regional capital, visitors, and incoming residents. The result has been communities that look quite similar but become inherently different. "There are worse lives than those lived in museums," Rember mused about his own fate, "worse shortcomings than a lack of authenticity."[50] This epitaph neatly encompasses the impact of tourism and the force of the powers that change place.

NOTES

1. Dorice Taylor, *Sun Valley* (Sun Valley, Idaho: Ex Libris Sun Valley, 1980), 5. Raymond Williams, *Marxism and Literature* (Oxford: Oxford University Press, 1977), 122–23, has coined the term "residual cultures" to describe such situations; see also Williams, "Base and Superstructure in Marxist Cultural Theory," *New Left Review* 82 (1973): 3–16.

2. Taylor, *Sun Valley*, 5.

3. John Rember, "On Going Back to Sawtooth Valley," in *Where the Morning Light's Still Blue: Personal Essays About Idaho*, ed. William Studebaker and Rick Ardinger (Moscow: University of Idaho Press, 1994), 82.

4. To date, geographers have explored the implications of tourist development more comprehensively than have historians. For an introduction, see Douglas Pearce, *Tourist Development*, 2d ed. (London: Longman Scientific and Technical, 1989), 1–151; for a specific analysis of what geographers call "ski fields," see P. Préau, "Essai d'une typologie de stations de sports d'hiver dans les Alpes du Nord," *Revue de Géographie Alpine* 58, no. 1 (1968): 127–40, and Préau, "Principe d'analyse des sites en montagne," *Urbanisme* 116 (1970): 21–25.

5. Hal Rothman, "Selling the Meaning of Place: Tourism, Entrepreneurship, and Community Structure in the Twentieth-Century American West," *Pacific Historical Review* 65, no. 4 (November 1996): 525–57.

6. Harlan C. Clifford, "Aspen: A Colonial Power with Angst," *High Country News*, April 5, 1993, encapsulates this problem. In this piece, Clifford writes of the Aspen town council, which rejected the donation of a public skating rink by billionaire David C. Koch because it did not want to encourage people to try to buy their way into the community.

7. Rothman, "Selling the Meaning of Place," 525–57.

8. Hal Rothman, *Devil's Bargains: Tourism in the Twentieth-Century American West* (Lawrence: University Press of Kansas, 1998).

9. Douglas G. Pearce, "Tourist Development: Two Processes," *Travel Research Journal* (1978): 43–45, describes such one-company developments as "integrated developments," one-owner developments that dominate a resource. He adds another category, "catalytic developments," to describe places where one major developer is augmented by the activities of others. The classic example is La Plagne in the French Alps; see G. Cumin, "Les stations intégrées," *Urbanisme* 116 (1970): 50–53.

10. U.S. Bureau of the Census, *Fourteenth Census of the United States: 1920*, vol. 1: *Minor Civil Divisions* (Washington, D.C.: Government Printing Office, 1921), table 53, "Population of Counties by Minor Civil Divisions: 1920, 1910, and 1900," 389, gives a population of 252 for the 1920 electoral precinct; "Tell the World All

About Sun Valley Ski Paradise in Shelter of the Sawtooths," *Hailey Times*, August 27, 1936; "Idaho's Winter Sports Mecca," *Idaho Sunday Statesman*, August 30, 1936; "World to Learn of Idaho: Union Pacific Plans Extensive Advertising Campaign Telling About Recreational Advantages of State and Nature of Famous Primitive Area," *Idaho Statesman*, September 2, 1936; Dick d'Easum, *Sawtooth Tales* (Caldwell, Idaho: Claxton Printers, 1977), 30–41, 97–100; Taylor, *Sun Valley*, 39–52; Maury Klein, *The Union Pacific: The Rebirth, 1894–1969* (New York: Doubleday, 1989), 310–16; Rudy Abramson, *Spanning the Century: The Life of W. Averell Harriman, 1891–1986* (New York: Morrow, 1992), 221–33; Carlos A. Schwantes, *In Mountain Shadows: A History of Idaho* (Lincoln: University of Nebraska Press, 1991), 210–14; Rodman W. Paul, *Mining Frontiers of the Far West, 1848–1880* (New York: Holt, Rinehart, and Winston, 1963), 144–49.

11. "Sun Valley, Winter Sports Capital, Ready to Open Monday," *Boise Capitol News*, December 19, 1936; "First Pictures at Sun Valley Since Snow Covered Sawtooths," *Idaho Statesman*, January 2, 1937; "East Goes West to Idaho's Sun Valley, Society's Newest Winter Playground," *Life*, March 8, 1937, 20–27; "Sun Valley Celebrates 50th Anniversary," *Rocky Mountain News*, February 9, 1986, 72; Taylor, *Sun Valley*, 45–46; Abramson, *Spanning the Century*, 222–30; A. Scott Berg, *Goldwyn: A Biography* (New York: Knopf, 1991), 287; Irene Link, "Early Arrival at the Inn," *Twin Falls Times–News*, April 2, 1980.

12. John Price, "Idaho's New Bonanza," *Travel*, February 1939, 32–33, 55–58; *Sun Valley Lodge at Sun Valley* (Union Pacific promotional brochure printed by Poole Bros., Chicago, ca. late 1930s), Sun Valley collection, Idaho State Historical Society, Boise; Lloyd R. Arnold, *Hemingway: High on the Wild* (1968; New York: Grosset and Dunlap, 1977), 1–33; Abramson, *Spanning the Century*, 225–30.

13. Doug Oppenheimer and Jim Poore, *Sun Valley: A Biography* (Boise, Idaho: Beatty Books, 1976), 21–33.

14. Taylor, *Sun Valley*, 40; "Owner of Sun Valley Ski Shop, John 'Pete' Lane, 60, Dies," *Idaho Statesman*, March 19, 1980.

15. Taylor, *Sun Valley*, 57–59, 69, 73, 115–21; Abramson, *Spanning the Century*, 228; "The Valley of Sun and Snow," *Saturday Evening Post*, n.d., circa 1937; Charlie Meyers, *Colorado Ski Country*, Colorado Geographic Series no. 4 (Helena and Billings, Mont.: Falcon Press Publishing Company, 1987), 38, 43.

16. U.S. Bureau of the Census, *Fifteenth Census of the United States: 1930*, vol. 3, part 1 (Washington, D.C.: Government Printing Office, 1932), 562; *Sixteenth Census of the United States: 1940, Population*, vol. 2 (Washington, D.C.: Government Printing Office, 1943), 415–30; *Census of Population: 1950*, vol. 2: *Characteristics of the Population*, part 12: *Idaho* (Washington, D.C.: Government Printing Office, 1952), 12–12; the 1930 numbers list 12 Chinese, down from 43 in 1910, 13 Mexi-

cans, and no Japanese living in Blaine County. Presumably the vast majority of remaining foreign-born individuals were European in origin and a large percentage of those were probably Basque.

17. U.S. Bureau of the Census, *United States Census of Agriculture: 1935*, vol. 2 (Washington, D.C.: Government Printing Office, 1936), 815–30; *Sixteenth Census of the United States: 1940, Agriculture*, vol. 2 (Washington, D.C.: Government Printing Office, 1942), 44–76; *Sixteenth Census of the United States: 1940, Population*, vol. 2 (Washington, D.C.: Government Printing Office, 1943), 432, 441.

18. Oppenheimer and Poore, *Sun Valley: A Biography*, 170–71; Taylor, *Sun Valley*, 97–105.

19. See T. J. Jackson Lears, *No Place of Grace: Anti-Modernism and the Transformation of American Culture, 1880–1920* (New York: Pantheon Books, 1981). Raye Ringholz's *Little Town Blues: Voices from a Changing West* (Salt Lake City: Peregrine Smith Books, 1992) provides an example of the kinds of sentiments locals express about change; see also Pearce, *Tourist Development*, 183–243, for an analysis of the impact of tourism in aggregate form.

20. Rember, "On Going Back to the Sawtooth Valley," 84.

21. Ibid., 85.

22. *Census of Population: 1950*, vol. 2: part 12, *Idaho*, 12–62; *1960 Census of Population*, vol. 1: *Characteristics of the Population*, part 14: *Idaho* (Washington, D.C.: Government Printing Office, 1963), 14–23; Oppenheimer and Poore, *Sun Valley: A Biography*, 165–69; Taylor, *Sun Valley*, 243–47; Leonard J. Arrington, *History of Idaho*, 2 vols. (Moscow: University of Idaho Press, 1994), 2: 203–4; Klein, *The Union Pacific*, 490–92.

23. Philip Fradkin, "King of the Mountains," *Los Angeles Times West Magazine*, January 29, 1968, 7–10; "Janss Corporation Buys Sun Valley," *Northwest Skier* 7, no. 2 (October 16, 1964); Paul Anderson, "Laying a Foundation for Snowmass," *Aspen Times*, January 29, 1967.

24. Taylor, *Sun Valley*, 244–48.

25. Dorice Taylor, "No Growing Pains for Sun Valley as 100 New Families Move In," *Idaho Sunday Statesman*, November 26, 1967; Steve Ahrens, "Imagination, Skill, Know-How Join Forces to Produce Sun Valley 'Ateliers,'" *Idaho Daily Statesman*, January 2, 1968; O. A. Kelker, "Ketchum Area's $6 Million Building Boom Is Really Something to Behold," *Twin Falls Times–News*, September 14, 1969; "Sun Valley Council Hears Plan for Elkhorn Village," *Wood River Journal*, December 16, 1971.

26. Martin Arnold, "To the Rich Who Ski by Day and Party at Night, Sun Valley's 'Neat' Again," *New York Times*, January 18, 1970, 38L; Taylor, *Sun Valley*, 244.

27. Fradkin, "King of the Mountains"; Steven Birmingham, "The Sun Valley Set," *Holiday*, November 1967, 62–66, 133–36.

28. U.S. Bureau of the Census, *1970 Census of Population*, vol. 1: *Characteristics of the Population*, part 14: *Idaho* (Washington, D.C.: Government Printing Office, 1973), 14–13; Taylor, *Sun Valley*, 245–48.

29. *Census of Population, 1950: Idaho*, 12–63, 12–75; *Census of Population, 1960: Idaho*, 14–129, 14–149; *Census of Population, 1970: Idaho*, 14–13, 14–238, 14–242.

30. Shannon Besoyan, "Ketchum Questionnaires Find Dislike for Developers, Population Growth," *Idaho Daily Statesman*, April 10, 1973.

31. Fradkin, "King of the Mountains"; "Snowmass-at-Aspen: Exciting New Shangri-la of Skiing," *Denver Post*, November 12, 1967, 17–20; Anderson, "Laying a Foundation for Snowmass." Snowmass offers a useful barometer of the changes Janss's ideas brought, precisely because it was built from scratch. At Sun Valley, Janss transformed the community just as thoroughly, but it is harder to discern the precise impact because of the existing superstructure that preceded his arrival.

32. Fradkin, "King of the Mountains"; Curtis Casewit, "Snowmass Shangri-La in Ski County USA," *Colorful Colorado*, Mid-Winter 1968, 64–70, 94. For Scottsdale, see Bradford Luckingham, *Phoenix: The History of a Southwestern Metropolis* (Tucson: University of Arizona Press, 1989), 264–66.

33. "Snowmass 67," Janss Development Company, Snowmass file, Aspen Historical Society, Aspen, Colorado; *The Snowmass Villager* 1 1 (October 23, 1967).

34. *The Snowmass Villager* 1 1 (October 23, 1967).

35. Malcolm Rohrbaugh, *Aspen: The History of a Silver Mining Town, 1879–1893* (New York: Oxford University Press, 1986); James Sloan Allen, *The Romance of Commerce and Culture: Capitalism, Modernism and the Chicago-Aspen Crusade for Cultural Reform* (Chicago: University of Chicago Press, 1983).

36. Tim Woodward, "Idaho's Most Famous Resort Area Maintains Western Flavor," *Idaho Daily Statesman*, October 3, 1976. See *Aspen Times* real estate advertisements of February 1, 1963; February 8, 1963; April 12, 1963; July 19, 1963; January 5, 1967; March 2, 1967; and October 29, 1967, for examples of the increase in asking price of similar properties.

37. Woodward, "Idaho's Most Famous Resort Area."

38. Anderson, "Laying a Foundation for Snowmass"; Woodward, "Idaho's Most Famous Resort Area."

39. Woodward, "Idaho's Most Famous Resort Area."

40. Peggy Clifford, *To Aspen and Back* (New York: St. Martin's Press, 1980), 105–9, 133.

41. Ibid., xi; Bruce Berger, *Notes of a Half-Aspenite* (Aspen, Colo.: Ashley and Associates, Inc., 1986).

42. For an analysis of western themes in Las Vegas gaming, see John M. Findlay, *People of Chance: Gambling in American Society from Jamestown to Las Vegas* (New York: Oxford University Press, 1986), 127–35.

43. "New Owner to Expand Sun Valley," *Idaho Statesman*, April 28, 1977; F. M. Hinkhouse, "Sun Valley: A Most European American Ski Resort," *Portland Oregonian Northwest Magazine*, January 28, 1979, 8NW–10NW.

44. Hinkhouse, "Sun Valley"; Bart Quesnell, "Sun Valley Shifts Marketing Emphasis," *Idaho Statesman*, December 11, 1977.

45. Lee Bellavance, "Sun Valley Boom Through the Roof," *Idaho Statesman*, February 3, 1980; Ron Zellar, "Sun Valley's Past Part of New Plans," *Twin Falls Times–News*, April 27, 1980, B1–B2.

46. Bart Quesnell, "Sun Valley Resort to Open Year-Round," *Idaho Statesman*, September 1, 1977; "Reveal Plan for New Summer, Winter Resort at Sun Valley," *Boise Capitol News*, March 15, 1937; "Second Annual Sun Valley Rodeo, Staged at the Gateway to America's Last Wilderness, August 12–14, 1938," Sun Valley file, Idaho State Historical Society, Boise; "Idaho State Trapshoot to Highlight July 4th Weekend," *Valley Sun*, June 1947; Dorice Taylor, "Per-SUN-als," *Valley Sun*, July 16, 1947; "Big League Football Comes to Sun Valley," *Valley Sun*, July 23, 1947; "Ashby Trophy Won by Manuel Enos of Fort Worth," *Valley Sun*, September 10, 1947; "Sun Valley Music Camp Brochure, 1965," Sun Valley Collection, Idaho State Historical Society; "Sun Valley Porsche Parade '71, Silver Sage Region, Porsche Club of America, July 6–10, 1971," Sun Valley Collection, Idaho State Historical Society. The *Valley Sun* was a Union Pacific promotional newspaper printed from about 1940 to 1964. Dorice Taylor frequently wrote for the paper.

47. John Dean, "Sun Valley Polishes Armor to Regain Ski Crown," *Idaho Daily Statesman*, September 2, 1982, 10a; Quesnell, "Sun Valley Shifts Marketing Emphasis."

48. Hinkhouse, "Sun Valley"; Taylor, *Sun Valley*, 257–59.

49. John Rember, *Cheerleaders from Gomorrah: Tales from the Lycra Archipelago* (Lewiston, Idaho: Confluence Press, 1994).

50. Rember, "On Going Back to Sawtooth Valley," 88.

Creating Wealth by Consuming Place

Timber Management on the
Gifford Pinchot National Forest

PAUL W. HIRT

In *The Pacific Northwest: An Interpretive History*, Carlos Schwantes claims that the region's geography and natural resources have profoundly shaped northwesterners' sense of place and distinctive identity. Particularly in his chapter "The Stumps of Enterprise," he argues that "no economic activity is today more closely identified in the popular mind with the Pacific Northwest than logging and sawmilling."[1] Part of the reason for this attitude toward logging is the legendary vastness of the region's forests, originally some 70 million acres of timber that had been growing for millennia. From the Cascade Mountains to the coast, Northwest forests 200 years ago represented the largest temperate rain forest on the planet, supporting many of the oldest and largest conifers in the world.[2]

Another reason for the popular association of the Northwest with the lumber business is the great controversy surrounding commercial logging in the region. The public has viewed the felling and marketing of these giant trees at times as heroic and at times as immoral. A century of logging has consumed all but about 10 percent of the native old-growth forests of the Northwest. The timber industry and the U.S. Forest Service, in their quest to generate jobs and wealth, have essentially consumed one of the defining characteristics of the region—its vast, ancient groves of Douglas-fir, red cedar, spruce, and hemlock. Controversy has accelerated most recently not only because of the increasing scarcity of old growth but because the rural economies dependent on harvesting that diminishing resource have been going bust—despite industry experiments with "tree farming" and Forest Service dedication to the principle of sustained yield.

Gifford Pinchot National Forest (source: U.S. Forest Service, "Analysis of Management Situation . . . ," 1985)

The dramatic decline of timber harvesting on the national forests of the Northwest in the 1990s begs for an explanation. For the national forests of Washington and Oregon, the harvest declined more than 85 percent from an all-time record high of 5.6 billion board feet (bbf) in 1987 to 0.87 bbf in 1995 (figure 1). The harvest is expected to remain below 1 billion board feet for the remainder of the decade at least. The Gifford Pinchot National Forest in south-central Washington, until recently the second highest timber-producing national forest in the country, experienced a total crash in

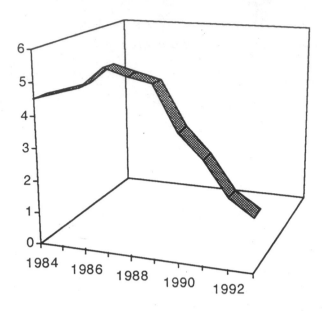

FIGURE 1. Forest Service timber harvests (billions of board feet),
Pacific Northwest Region, 1984–1993

its harvest from 514 million board feet (mmbf) in 1988 to 154.9 mmbf in 1992, and to 11 mmbf in 1996. This certainly does not reflect the much touted ideal of sustained yield that has supposedly guided federal forest management for the past century. As a result, the Forest Service finds itself the butt of sharp criticism from the timber industry and timber-dependent communities, as well as from environmentalists.

Since the early 1990s, the failure to sustain national forest timber yield has generally been blamed on the Endangered Species Act of 1973, especially old-growth logging restrictions designed to protect the northern spotted owl from extinction. In fact, the reasons are more complicated, have a much longer history than is usually supposed, and are far more interesting than "owls versus loggers." The timber bust resulted from conscious policies

TABLE 1. Gifford Pinchot National Forest timber harvest,
in millions of board feet, 1988–1994

Year	1988	1989	1990	1991	1992	1993	1994
Harvest	514 mmbf	444 mmbf	313 mmbf	286 mmbf	160 mmbf	155 mmbf	96 mmbf

and deliberate actions promoted by foresters and timber industry lobbyists, and adopted by the federal government during and after World War II. Moreover, these very decisions that undermined sustained yield also undermined multiple use and environmental protection policies, leading to growing dissatisfaction with the Forest Service among conservation groups. Politicians and foresters walked into this crisis with their eyes open. In fact, they have been traveling toward this destination for more than a generation. Yet those who are accountable repeatedly deny responsibility, making it difficult to assess where the problems lie.

While measures to protect the spotted owl appear to be the immediate cause of timber declines in the "westside" (west of the Cascades) forests of Washington, Oregon, and northern California, it must be remembered that Federal District Court Judge William Dwyer, who temporarily shut down logging in most remaining westside old growth, only did so as a last resort, frustrated by what he called "a deliberate and systematic refusal by the Forest Service and the U.S. Fish and Wildlife Service [under Presidents Reagan and Bush] to comply with the laws protecting wildlife."[3] This failure to comply with wildlife law represents a long-term failure to equitably balance resource development with resource protection.

Rescuing wildlife species from the brink of extinction is not a new problem nor a new policy. Declines in wildlife populations spawned conservation measures throughout the twentieth century, culminating with the Endangered Species Act. Compliance with wildlife protection laws, however, would have meant setting lower timber harvest goals decades ago, keeping logging levels on the national forests about 30 percent lower than the artificially inflated harvest levels attained from the late 1950s to the late 1980s. The lower harvest level could have been maintained in perpetuity while still protecting wildlife, recreation, watershed, and other values. But the Forest Service pursued a path of timber maximization that marginalized all other public values and uses of the forest land. Ironically, even the agency's plans for maximum sustained timber production were deeply flawed and destined for failure, with or without the intervention of environmentalists and the federal courts, as this chapter will show.

Tragically, the federal government and its appointed caretakers of the national forests have sidestepped full commitment to multiple use and sustained-yield principles for at least forty years in the Northwest while maintaining a facade of plausible deniability. Constructing that facade involved the adoption of grandly optimistic assumptions by scientists and technicians regarding their ability to control nature in order to maximize its productivity and usefulness. Disturbing side effects of intensive forestry, such as soil erosion and wildlife declines, loss of biological diversity, marred scenery, deterioration in water quality, and increased risk of destructive fire and pest infestations, have long posed challenges to this vision of efficiently engineered forests. But optimists maintained faith that such problems could be overcome with sufficient applications of technology, capital, and expertise, and that high levels of commodity production could be reconciled with environmental protection goals. A floodtide of scientific literature poured forth after World War II on how to manipulate natural systems to increase productivity. A corresponding swell of literature appeared on how to mitigate environmental impacts through more technological manipulation of natural systems. The dreamers would maximize production and environmental protection simultaneously, providing the greatest good to the greatest number.

But what may have been theoretically feasible turned out not to be practicable in the real world. As ecologist David Ehrenfeld says in a recent essay, "Down from the Pedestal—A New Role for Experts," traditional land management science adopted reductionist, closed-system theories of control over nature that "break down under the open-endedness imposed by biological complexity and by the interacting complexities of political, economic, and social factors."[4] The Forest Service in the 1940s and 1950s became overenthusiastic about how much timber production could be sustained over the long term—not to mention how much logging was compatible with other forest uses and with environmental protection mandates.

By the late 1950s and 1960s, federal timber inventories began to reveal that the burgeoning timber harvests on national forests in the Northwest were unsustainable. Additional studies in the 1970s corroborated this.[5] To avoid reducing logging, forest managers promoted an ever more implausible array of intensive management practices designed to squeeze greater productivity from the forests. One of those measures involved eliminating virtually all old growth from the national forests, regardless of its effect on wildlife, forest ecosystems, or recreationists. But biological complexity, technical limitations, lack of funding, unpredictable markets, political pressures, and other social and environmental obstacles foiled the cornucopian dreams. Failure was predictable and, indeed, forewarned. Only the exact timing and rapidity of the timber bust was surprising.

As Wenatchee National Forest timber sale planner Tim Foss acknowledged: "Even though field foresters have known since the mid-1970s that this day was coming, it still represents a major shock to our bureaucratic system."[6] The executive director of an economic development council for

Lewis County in southwestern Washington remarked in 1992, "We knew we would have long-term challenges to deal with. But it's coming very, very quickly." *High Country News* quoted a logger from the Northwest that same year saying, "We knew for years and years that it wouldn't last. In 1979, we were talking, 'Hey, there's only a few more years left of old growth.' You knew eventually the well would run dry."[7]

This was not Washington's first timber bust. Others occurred in the early decades of the twentieth century after timber supplies on private lands began to run out. Historical geographer Michael Williams noted in his book *Americans and Their Forests* that in 1909 over a quarter of the forest land west of the Cascades in Washington had been logged and abandoned. Nearly half of the forested acres in Grays Harbor County, Washington, were clearcut between 1900 and 1920.[8] Richard White, in his environmental history of Island County, Washington, described how large lumber companies set up booming mills on Whidbey and Camano Islands at the turn of the century and proceeded to liquidate what was left of the forests there, largely completing the job by the 1920s and leaving behind pauperized ecosystems and defunct milltowns.[9] Total Washington State lumber production peaked in the 1920s and has generally declined ever since.[10] As a Forest Service report of 1920 ominously foreshadowed, "To the West only, of all our heritage of magnificent softwood forests, can the country look to an increasing cut; but even here there are already local evidences of depletion, warnings that the conclusion of the story will be the same as that of other regions and in far less time than has been estimated."[11]

The social dislocations and environmental degradation caused by this migratory pattern of private investment–depletion–divestment led the federal government, at the dawn of the Progressive Era a hundred years ago, to establish a forest reserve system and create the U.S. Forest Service to manage those reserves in the public interest rather than simply for private profit. The Forest Service was supposed to guarantee a sustainable and high quality flow of timber for communities, while protecting the essential integrity of the forest—something the private market economy seemed incapable of doing on its own. But the Forest Service itself soon became captured by a reductionist forestry orthodoxy and political and economic incentives that rewarded the agency for accommodating the timber industry. This is the story of how the Forest Service liquidated the centuries-old conifers of the Gifford Pinchot National Forest in a forty-year period, leaving behind a pauperized landscape and angry communities, all the while plausibly claiming to be acting in the public interest.

THE SETTING

Named for the nation's first chief of the U.S. Forest Service, who has been dubbed the "father of conservation," the Gifford Pinchot National Forest (GPNF) is located in the southern Cascades of Washington, an hour's drive from Portland and two hours from Seattle. The GPNF straddles the crest of the Cascades, with the Columbia River near its southern border and Mount Rainier National Park to the north. Situated in one of the most spectacular mountain regions of North America, the forest's topography ranges from nearly sea level on the Columbia River to 12,326 feet elevation on Mount Adams, the second largest peak (in height and bulk) in Washington. Influenced by the wet, temperate Pacific coastal climate, the area is heavily forested with mixed conifers dominated by Douglas-fir, a highly desirable commercial species for lumber. Forty to one hundred or more inches of precipitation drench the forest annually and give rise to three significant tributaries of the Columbia River, countless smaller streams, and nearly a hundred alpine lakes. The biological resources of this national forest are extraordinarily varied and their value incalculable.

The GPNF is preeminently a national forest of contrasts. Not long ago, it had the dubious distinction of being named "the first intensively-managed Forest in the country"—meaning intensively logged and replanted with commercial tree species.[12] In the recent past it produced the second highest output of lumber and pulpwood of the entire national forest system. (The Willamette National Forest in Oregon ranked first.) Through its timber sale program, GPNF managers have facilitated logging on 10 to 20 square miles of forest land *per year* since the 1960s, sending to local mills annually 400 to 560 million board feet of lumber (enough to build 40,000 to 56,000 three-bedroom homes each year), and generating gross receipts of $17–$20 million dollars per year from its timber sales.[13]

Clearly, this forest has substantial economic assets which the Forest Service has not been timid about developing. It also has equally substantial recreational, scenic, and scientific assets which, however, became increasingly secondary to economic production after World War II. Three of the Cascade range's famous volcanoes lie within or on the border of the GPNF: Mount St. Helens, Mount Adams, and Mount Rainier. The famous Pacific Crest Trail, a National Scenic Trail that winds its way from Canada to southern California, traverses the forest. Congress has designated several large wilderness areas, and the Forest Service has designated several Research Natural Areas on the forest. In the 1980s, thirty-four domestic water systems depended on streams from the forest for drinking water supplies. Wildlife is abundant, though declining (except for deer, which thrive on the early successional plant stages following clearcutting). In the mid-1980s, 11 percent of the forest was protected wilderness, another 6 percent became part of the Mount St. Helens National Volcanic Monument in 1981, and a few additional smaller areas have been placed off-limits to logging.

Development, however, clearly dominates the landscape. Other than the above-mentioned protected areas, the remainder of the forest has been dedicated to intensive timber management since World War II. Getting at the timber in the 1980s required 80 to 90 new miles of road construction and 40 to 50 additional miles of road reconstruction every year. In 1985, the GPNF calculated that two-thirds of its 1.4 million acres were "roaded," with 4,300 miles of roads. That translates to an average of three miles of road per square mile of forest in the developed areas.[14] Ancient conifers over 200 years old, so highly prized aesthetically as well as commercially, remained on only 9 to 14 percent of the forest in the late 1980s (depending on how one defines "old growth"). More important, according to forest ecologist Peter Morrison, only 30,000 acres of that old growth (2 percent of the forest) were in ecologically functional unfragmented blocks in 1988. The rest lay in small, isolated fragments. Wilderness designation protected only 8,000 acres of that old growth; the remainder was falling fast to the chain saws, and at 1980s harvest levels Morrison predicted the unprotected areas would be logged out by the year 2008.[15]

This was the situation conservationists, the timber industry, and politicians faced in 1991 when Judge Dwyer halted nearly all new timber sales in the remaining old growth on the GPNF—sales accounting for about half the forest's annual harvest at the time. The ban, which applied to most of the national forests on the west side of the Cascades in Oregon and Washington, would last until the agency came up with a credible plan to protect the threatened spotted owl, whose primary habitat centered on the rapidly dwindling remnants of ancient forest. As the two-year backlog of sold but uncut timber slowly ran out, the annual harvest in the region plummeted.

A battle raged between those who wanted to protect what was left of the ancient forests and those who felt that sustaining the high harvest levels for another decade or two was more important. The fate of the Endangered Species Act appeared to hang in the balance as bills to weaken the act were introduced yearly by allies of the timber industry. Acknowledging the importance of this issue, newly elected President Clinton sponsored a precedent-setting Timber Summit in Portland, Oregon, on April 2, 1993, only a few months after his first inauguration. Why did the president of the United States choose to assemble five of his cabinet members on the West Coast to address resource allocation problems that the Forest Service is allotted hundreds of millions of dollars a year to resolve on its own? The answer lies in the evolution of historical events mainly after World War II.

EARLY HISTORY OF THE GIFFORD PINCHOT NATIONAL FOREST

European exploration of the area now included in the GPNF probably began in the 1850s. Prior European settlement in the region had concentrated along the shorelines and river valleys, where transportation was easier. Trails, tentative wagon roads, and railroad spurs began opening up some of southern Washington's Cascade Mountains to homesteading, logging, grazing, and mining in the 1880s and 1890s, but this settlement concentrated in the wide, flat, heavily forested stream bottoms within easy reach of the Columbia River. The GPNF is a portion of what was originally the "Mount Rainier Forest Reserve" established in February 1897 by President Grover Cleveland just before leaving office. In 1907 the Forest Service divided Mount Rainier into two new administrative units: the Mount Rainier and Columbia National Forests. Then in 1949, in a formal dedication ceremony, the Columbia forest received its present moniker as a tribute to Gifford Pinchot, who had died a few years earlier.

Unlikely as it might seem for such a wet area, natural fires played an important role in the forest's history, helping shape both the species composition and their age distributions. Virtually all of the high annual precipitation in the area comes between the months of October and May. During the warm summer months, blue, cloudless skies are common. (Snowmelt in the high country keeps the rivers flowing, however, and dense canopied forest cover can keep the ground moist.) This prolonged drought season has allowed fires to sweep periodically across the landscape, mostly spreading along ridges where winds are more frequent while sparing the wetter valley floors. Some of these fires burned "cool" and consumed mainly ground cover, but some burned "hot" and destroyed the entire tree canopy where they spread, opening large areas to sunlight and attendant stages of vegetational succession. These hot fires came irregularly, with any given area experiencing a hot, "stand replacing" fire only once every two or three centuries.

Douglas-fir is a tree that likes sunlight and thrives in these fire-scarred openings. The fact that the entire forest belt running down the Cascade and Coast ranges from Canada to northern California is called by foresters the

"Douglas-fir region" is testament to the historic influence of fires, although Douglas-fir is not always the dominant species in westside forests. One of the largest and most damaging fires in Washington's recorded history occurred in 1902 and spread across portions of what is now the Gifford Pinchot National Forest. Called the Yacolt burn, it consumed 300,000 acres, half inside the national forest boundary and half outside, including thousands of acres of Weyerhaeuser land. Just after much of the area had regenerated a young forest, a second hot fire swept through in 1929, reburning a large percentage of the new growth. Fire suppression, one of the Forest Service's earliest and most important functions, began on the GPNF in the 1920s and became firmly and successfully established in the 1930s. In the two decades between 1912 and 1932 an average of 9,500 acres burned yearly on the GPNF (most were not "hot" fires, and many were human-caused). In stark contrast, between 1932 and 1952 an average of only 370 acres burned annually.[16] The purpose of this ambitious fire suppression was to save as much timber as possible for future logging. In fact, foresters would later argue that clearcutting merely mimicked natural fire regimes—a superficially plausible argument that did not in fact ring true for the large-scale, heavily ground-disturbing, nutrient-depleting, monocultural timber crop management implemented in the region after World War II.

The first timber sale on the GPNF, which is believed to be the first large sale of national forest timber in the Pacific Northwest Region, occurred in 1906. It involved six million board feet. The pace and scale of timber sales over the next thirty years remained quite modest, compared to what would evolve after midcentury. Private landowners—including railroads that had amassed huge empires from federal land grants in the nineteenth century, and timber and mining corporations that had acquired similarly vast holdings from other public land grant laws and through purchase and fraud— owned the most accessible, profitable timberland in the region. Most of the landowners were busy mining the bounties nature had created over millennia: the giant timber, the incomparable runs of Pacific salmon and steelhead, the fertile valley soils, lush grasslands, and subsurface minerals. The resources available on private land were usually ample to satisfy the entrepreneurial spirit of the relatively small number of white settlers in the region in the early decades of the century. But slowly, private supplies of timber and other resources declined to the point where investors began looking covetously at adjacent federal lands. Thereafter, logging activities gradually increased on the national forests in the Northwest until World War II, when they accelerated in a quantum leap.

A 1919 timber industry analysis of the Wind River District of the GPNF reveals this early historical context. In 1992, the Wind River District was one of about five subdivisions of the GPNF (districts and their boundaries have changed over time). It lies in the southern portion of the forest close to the Columbia River and thus it experienced commercial activity first, including the 1906 timber sale mentioned above. Just south and west of the forest boundary, in the lowlands sloping toward Portland, private landowners, including Weyerhaeuser, had been cutting out the old forest as rapidly as they could market the timber. After clearcutting the land, most owners, other than the huge Weyerhaeuser syndicate, sold or forfeited their land to the state for delinquent taxes.

An example of this type of commercial enterprise involved a large area of private land in the lower Wind River Valley adjacent to the national forest. The private forest land had been mostly cut out by 1918. Subsequently, about four square miles of it (in sixteen separate parcels) were sold at a bargain price to the enterprising Wind River Lumber Company, which then hired prominent forestry consultant H. D. Langille in 1919 to assess what was left and prepare a financial analysis and logging plan. Langille's report acknowledged that the previous company had "cut over the most accessible parts and passed on to more continuous stretches of national forest timber leaving patches and isolated small tracts." In sum, he stated, "The cream has been skimmed from the basin" (private holdings). Langille then concentrated his report on an analysis of the adjacent national forest lands that might provide profitable logging in the coming years.[17]

The most striking feature of Langille's report is its description of the national forest timber and soil resources which were judged to be of marginal quality at best. Geologically influenced by a long history of volcanism and glaciation, soils of the forest are generally coarse, porous, and unstable. Under a section titled "Soil & Geology," Langille described the numerous geologically recent lava flows from Mount St. Helens, Mount Adams, and lesser sources which caused inferior tree growth, and he pointed to glacial debris in many valleys that lacked the soil fertility of nonglaciated areas: "Over much of the District soil is so poor that it has not yielded the normal tree crop of the Douglas Fir region." His timber cruise, for example, revealed that the average stand held about 30,000 board feet per acre, whereas the industry average on nearby private land was about 50,000 per acre. The average tree on the national forest held about 1,600 board feet, while the average industry tree on private land yielded 3,300 board feet. Furthermore, only the stream bottoms and the first 100 feet of elevation above the streams held valuable, supersized

Douglas-fir, he said. On the higher slopes and at elevations above 1,500 feet, the trees grew "shorter, smaller, and coarser" and shifted toward less desirable conifers like western hemlock, considered an unmarketable "garbage" tree at the time. Nevertheless, there were several very attractive timber stands, especially in Trout Creek, where small groups of Douglas-fir grew as large as 200 feet tall and six feet in diameter. Langille felt there was enough there to sustain lumber mill operations for 1920 and 1921, and recommended the company sell its logged-off lands to employees and settlers. This exemplifies the migratory nature of the early lumber industry and shows why "sustained yield" on federal lands was such an important policy.

From Langille's description, one wonders how the Forest Service ever found 400–500 million board feet of lumber a year for the past three decades for forest industries to log. The effusive praise the Forest Service subsequently heaped on the GPNF's timber resources after World War II indicates how second best begins to look attractive when the best is gone. As the really big timber became scarce, timber purchasers looked increasingly to marginal lands to supply their needs, and thus the Forest Service could open up more of its lands to logging. In the 1950s and 1960s this became a serious source of trouble for the agency as it tried to log portions of previously designated "wild" or "primitive" areas that had suddenly become commercially viable. The agency seemed willing to support a "hands-off" management policy only where lands had no commercial value. With commercial viability changing along with market conditions, the Forest Service reneged on earlier promises to protect certain areas. Conservationists protested these "boundary adjustments" to designated wild areas. But the Forest Service, by then under intense pressure to maximize harvests, responded that "preservationists" were being unreasonable in opposing the development of such valuable properties.

TRANSITION TO INTENSIVE TIMBER MANAGEMENT
AT MIDCENTURY

World War II marked a watershed in national forest management. The peak of logging operations on *private* timberlands in the Northwest lasted from the 1890s to the 1940s. Washington's boom in production from private lands in fact peaked in the 1920s. Oregon's peaked two decades later. Thereafter, companies increasingly turned to the national forests to acquire timber. The Depression of the 1930s slowed demand for lumber, but increasing economic activity in the 1940s and 1950s led to an explosion in the demand for logs from federal lands. This rapid rise in demand propelled the agency out of its "custodial era" (named in hindsight) and into an era of intensive management. War production provided the initial impetus, but the postwar housing boom, baby boom, and general economic expansion that lasted into the 1970s continued the trend. In an oral history in 1986, veteran Forest Service employee C. Glen Jorgensen, who served as supervisor of the GPNF from 1957 to 1961, recalled the war years as follows: "Timber was king and you would drop everything—if any mill was out of timber, why, you would drop whatever you were doing and go put up some timber for sale to keep the mill running. Almost that simple."[18]

To fully understand the new pressures the Forest Service labored under in the 1940s and 1950s, and to fully comprehend the scope of changes that came to the national forests after World War II, it is instructive to compare timber production data for the forest from the early part of the century to the 1960s. Between 1906 and the beginning of World War II, only nineteen separate sales of timber occurred on the GPNF. Spread out over the thirty-four years, they averaged 8 million board feet of lumber per year. A veritable revolution occurred during the war, and by 1947 a Forest Service press release proudly announced that an average of 100 mmbf per year were coming off the forest. By the mid-1960s, the GPNF sold *hundreds* of timber sale contracts annually and exceeded 400 million board feet of harvests each year. This incredible increase in logging, from a few million board feet before the war to over 400 million board feet after the war (figure 2), dramatically transformed the entire nature of forest management on the Gifford Pinchot National Forest, and revolutionized the agency's employee base, its functions, and its incentive structures.

The GPNF was hardly prepared for this radical transformation. Its first timber management plans for the various districts on the forest were drafted between 1937 and 1949, and were often outdated within a year or two. The Forest Service essentially blundered forward making decisions based on minimal or nonexistent data and with an unseasoned work force that grew at the unmanageable rate of 20 to 40 percent per year.[19] And virtually everyone hired in this period was trained in silviculture (tree farming) or engineering (road building). The Forest Service only began hiring wildlife biologists at the regional level in the 1960s. There were none at the forest level at that time. Even then, the wildlife biologist's function was to assess tree seedling damage caused by wildlife and to develop wildlife damage control measures to support the timber program.

Road construction provided the essential physical infrastructure for the

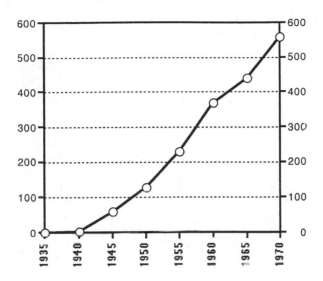

FIGURE 2. Timber harvests (millions of board feet),
Gifford Pinchot National Forest, 1935–1970

logging program. Thus road-building data provide an illuminating picture of forest management priorities and the transformation of the GPNF after the war. In 1947 the GPNF had 520 miles of roads on the forest and 1,990 miles of foot and horse trails. (The Civilian Conservation Corps had helped build or upgrade some of those trails in the 1930s.) This preponderance of trails and dearth of roads was completely reversed in the next few decades, as figure 3 shows.

The most environmentally damaging aspect of logging is road construction, which causes most of the erosion in timber harvesting areas. Foresters, especially in the Forest Service, often speak about the critical importance of minimizing soil disturbance in order to protect watersheds. Since 1897, watershed protection has been one of the two fundamental reasons for establishing national forests. Besides this protective function, soil stability is a crucial consideration for successful reforestation of logged land. If soil is highly erodible, regenerating forests becomes difficult. Soil loss also harms biological productivity and causes sedimentation of streams, which harms fish and ruins salmon spawning habitat. Agency regulations therefore have always emphasized that areas with unstable soils that cannot be effectively protected from erosion during logging should be excluded from the commercial timber base. But as the demand for timber pressed upon harvest ceilings

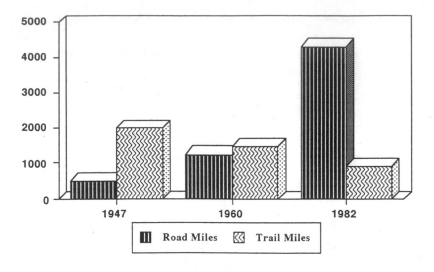

FIGURE 3. Miles of roads and trails, Gifford Pinchot National Forest

("allowable cut") established by forest managers, the road builders in the agency simply adopted increasingly optimistic assumptions about their ability to engineer safe roads in just about any soil type. Instead of a constraint, as originally intended, soil classification merely became a challenge requiring improved technical skill and more financial resources. This is exemplified in a 1961 Multiple Use Plan for the Canyon Creek District of the GPNF in which district managers identified timber production as the "dominant use" for 90 *percent* of the "working circle" (as they called timber management units at that time), while acknowledging that 75 percent of the district had "poor" or "very poor" soil stability.

In the face of market pressures and guided by a can-do technological optimism, soil stability became little more than a technical consideration attendant to the primary objective of laying out a timber sale. This is crucial.

TABLE 2. 1961 soil stability class for Canyon Creek Working Circle

Class	Excellent	Good	Fair	Poor	Very Poor	Total
Acres	6,292	510	16,110	67,454	1,040	91,406
Percent	6.88%	0.56%	17.62%	73.80%	1.14%	100%

Mainstream forestry after World War II completely adopted economic thinking, basing management decisions on commodity production goals with environmental quality and ecosystem integrity incidental. In other words, the Forest Service established production *ceilings* (and sought to raise them whenever necessary to meet market demands), while in contrast it set *minimum* standards for environmental protection. Many critics now argue, as many did a hundred years ago when Congress created the forest reserve system, that a conservation agency should reverse this order of priorities.

While economic thinking has always dominated the forestry profession, an environmentally sensitive breed of professionals gravitated to the Forest Service (as opposed to private industry) in its early years, including such major figures in the history of conservation as Aldo Leopold, Bob Marshall, and Arthur Carhart. After World War II, however, as custodianship of the national forests gave way to industrial-style logging, the voices of caution were overwhelmed by the institutional rush to maximize timber production. This transition to "intensive management" can be seen clearly by comparing a 1940 timber management plan for the Wind River District of the GPNF with a 1975 forestwide timber management plan. The authors of the 1940s plan were distinctly conservative in determining the district's annual allowable cut (AAC) of timber. They calculated the maximum sustainable yield (based on the standard mathematical Hanzlick formula), and then settled on less than half that amount for several explicit reasons: They wanted a "margin of safety" to buffer against likely losses due to fire or other unpredictable circumstances; they wanted to extend the period of old-growth liquidation to avoid a harvest reduction in the future while waiting for second growth to mature; they wanted to extend the amount of time large logs would be available so that mills and manufacturers would not suffer a sudden transition to small-diameter logs a few decades hence; and they did not automatically assume that lower quality second-growth timber would be commercially marketable as soon as the old growth on the district was gone.[20] All these considerations were calculated to preserve the sustainability of timber flows from the national forests so that local towns dependent on the logging economy would perhaps be spared the traditional boom and bust.

But entrepreneurs in the logging industry guided their investment decisions on much shorter-term considerations. Year-end bottom lines and five-year investment amortizations and annual market trends dominated their worldview. As long as lumber prices were rising, which they did dramatically in the 1940s and 1950s, the industry wanted access to more national forest timber—as much as the market could absorb. As harvest levels bumped against allowable cut ceilings, forest managers felt pressure to accommodate the increasing demand. Asked in the 1986 interview mentioned above about such pressures in the 1950s, Glen Jorgensen recalled: "The industry [let] their congressmen know and the committees know, that they needed more timber and the Forest Service wasn't selling enough timber, and so through the Secretary [of Agriculture] and otherwise, by committee investigations, the Forest Service got the message pretty clear." Reflecting economic thinking as well as the innocence-under-siege mentality central to the agency ethos, Jorgensen continued: "And that is probably one reason that this region has always been accused of having a timber management orientation. We were forced to it, you know. We were sitting on a pot of gold, so to speak, and it was too valuable to ignore, and we had to do something about it."[21] Note the implication that Congress is to blame for the agency's timber bias, the reference to uncut forests as a "pot of gold," and the revealing admission that the agency "had to do something" about this unutilized gold. And do something it did. Jorgensen was in charge in 1959 when the GPNF sold 554 million board feet at a time when the "annual allowable sustained yield cut" was only 397 million. From 1957 to 1959 Jorgensen presided over a 110 percent increase in timber sales.

Still dedicated to the *principle* of sustained yield, managers like Jorgensen had to find technical ways of justifying such huge increases in the harvest. So they revised the assumptions they used to derive the allowable cut calculation, such as those employed in the 1940 Wind River Plan mentioned above. Using purely mathematical calculations, the Wind River rangers in 1940 had determined that the district could support a maximum harvest of 34 million board feet indefinitely. Yet they settled on 15 million as an appropriate harvest ceiling to provide a safety net. That safety net would have to go. In 1950, harvests topped 15 million board feet on the Wind River District and demand remained strong. Wind River rangers then went to work on a new timber management plan. Published in 1953, the new plan incredibly raised the allowable cut to 55 million board feet, almost three times higher than the allowable cut ceiling of 1940, and well above 1940's theoretical maximum.[22]

How was this justified? Acreage in the "commercial timber base" of the district had expanded during that time, but only by a third. Two key calculations changed: managers eliminated the buffer and increased their estimate of available timber volume from about 800 million board feet to 4.4 *billion* board feet.[23] This new volume figure made the dramatic rise in the allowable cut seem reasonable, even conservative, but in fact the managers were pushing the forest ecosystem to its limits and beyond. Less than a decade later, in 1962, a Multiple Use Plan for the Wind River District acknowledged: "The present allowable cut seems unrealistic and needs to be recomputed when more reliable basic information is available." Unfortunately, the harvest level had reached 55 million board feet in 1956 and remained there. While forest managers could admit they had overestimated sustained yield, they lacked sufficient will to implement reductions.

In 1968, the Wind River District's allowable cut still hovered at the same level while forest managers warned in a second multiple use plan: "To maintain this harvest, prompt regeneration of harvested areas is required."[24] Such statements contain subtle messages identifiable to those familiar with organizational language. In this case, the implied message is that maintaining the harvest level over time looks doubtful, but might still be possible with increased investments of capital and labor, especially in reforestation. The usefulness of this organizational response should be obvious. If industry groups and politicians want maximum production *and* sustainability they simply have to fund the agency at higher levels. If the funding is not forthcoming, then the agency is not to blame for the inevitable production declines.

What happened on the Wind River happened on the other districts of the forest (and on other timber-producing forests, too). Managers on the Canyon Creek District of the GPNF, for example, had determined in the 1940s that the allowable cut should be 22 million board feet per year. By 1957, however, the harvest had exceeded that amount for several years, so in a revised timber management plan that year the district raised the allowable cut to 38 million. Just four years later (1961), the cut was bumping up against the harvest ceiling again. Likewise, the Packwood Ranger District established an optimistic allowable cut of 67 million board feet in 1957, but in a Multiple Use Plan written just a few years later forest managers explained that they were having "major timber problems": half the district had been classified in the lowest two categories of soil stability, requiring "some form of restriction placed on the activities allowed on them." Yet at the same time, the plan admitted: "To attain the present calculated allowable cut, areas of steep, low stability soils must be logged." In areas of low soil stability that had been logged recently, the district ranger said he was "experiencing difficulty in obtaining satisfactory regeneration." Consequently, reforestation was substantially below projected needs. To make matters worse, the plan further admitted that 20 percent of the timberlands included in the allowable cut calculations had been classified as landscapes

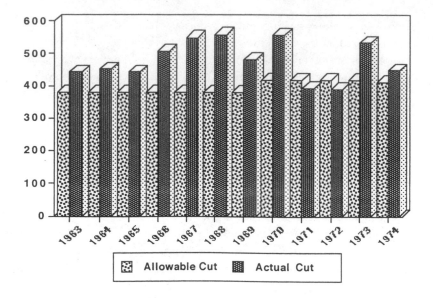

FIGURE 4. Allowable cut versus actual cut,
Gifford Pinchot National Forest, 1963–1974

of high recreational value; nevertheless, achieving the allowable cut required logging those areas, too.[25]

The GPNF as a whole simply reflected the sum of all these parts during the
postwar era. Allowable cut levels steadily increased forestwide, from 200
million board feet in 1949 to 313 million in 1956 to 381 million in 1962 to
410 million in 1974.[26] With each increase, the assumptions defining what
was sustainable became more optimistic and less realistic. As the harvests
increased, too, the impact on forest ecosystems multiplied along with the
dissatisfactions among other forest users.

But this is not the end of the problems. Even worse than overinflating
allowable cut determinations, GPNF managers allowed *actual harvests* to exceed the allowable cut through most of the 1960s and 1970s. This was in
large part the forest managers' own fault because they kept selling more than
the allowable cut every year (figure 4). Forest Service decision makers
strongly supported the idea of eliminating all old growth in order to convert
the forest into younger, fast-growing plantations that would maximize total
timber growth over the long run. Old-growth forests held huge amounts of
wood fiber but they did not provide much annual growth because the trees
were "mature" and in many cases beginning to decay. Managers dedicated to

the ideology of intensive management for maximum production firmly believed that natural decay in an old forest was wasteful and the sooner those "decadent" and "overmature" forests were harvested and replaced with Douglas-fir plantations the better.

Recognizing the need to get a handle on overcutting, the GPNF wrote a new timber management plan in 1975. It was a schizophrenic document that both waved the banner of intensive management and admitted that the forest was overextended and that adjustments needed to be made. It is a paradigm of the intensive management ethos, yet portions of it reveal a growing concern for the reliability of previous optimistic assessments. This is exemplified in the way the allowable cut determination was handled. Up front, the plan announced that the new annual harvest ceiling was being reduced slightly to 404 million board feet (from 410). At the same time, it claimed that a maximum sustained yield of 495 million might be possible under ideal circumstances with an essentially unlimited investment in silviculture. Note that the harvest levels had often exceeded even this higher figure. These numbers implied two things: (1) that the managers felt the forest *could* produce more than 404 million board feet with greater investments in intensive management, and (2) that the foresters felt this was nevertheless unlikely and wanted to reduce logging accordingly.

A much more revealing set of calculations, buried in subsequent technical discussions, added dimension to this problem of overcutting. Almost as an aside, the document mentioned that under current levels of silvicultural investment, the allowable cut should be set at 334 million board feet. That is, 404 million was really just a hopeful goal the forest managers were striving for over the next ten years that would require significant additional investments to achieve. Seven different intensive management activities (reforestation, thinning, weeding, pruning, etc.) needed to be accelerated two to ten times above current levels to achieve the modest goal of 404 million.

So why did the GPNF set the allowable harvest level at 404 million instead of at 334 where it belonged? Because the lower figure would have precipitated a veritable revolt in the local timber industry, and it would have made clear how overextended the forest already was, making the agency look bad. Expediency ruled the day. Buried in the back of the plan was one more revealing figure: *without* all these expensive, controversial, intensive silvicultural practices, the forest might be capable of sustaining as much as 292 million board feet per year in perpetuity (although that was still 50 percent higher than the allowable cut forest managers established in 1949). In comparison, the actual cut in the 1960s and 1970s consistently fell between 400 million and 550 million board feet—a disastrous two decades of overcutting.

Of course, the forest industry and its political allies sought to avoid any harvest reductions at all. Focusing on the hypothetical ideal of 495 million board feet, congressional representatives from the Northwest earmarked special funds to pay for additional silvicultural practices, the accomplishment of which automatically translated into increased allowable harvests the next year. Never mind that the theoretical increases in future timber volume could not be verified for decades hence. This practice of "buying" increases to the allowable cut by funding additional intensive management practices had been specifically sanctioned by the National Forest Management Act of 1976.[27] The players were gambling on future payoffs while cashing in on the present. The Forest Service got more money and the industry got more timber—a useful arrangement. But it was a sham, bearing little relationship to the real world, because the extra monetary infusions never "bought" more than small incremental increases to the allowable cut base of 334 million board feet. "Earned allowable harvest" increments never even brought the GPNF up to the hoped-for 404 million level, yet harvests remained in the range of 450 million to 500 million throughout the remainder of the 1970s and the 1980s. The spotted owl litigation brought this house of cards down, although it was destined to collapse on its own in due course.

THE END OF THE TIMBER BOOM

Events of the 1980s are reasonably familiar to anyone who has paid attention to natural resource controversies since the "Reagan revolution." Briefly, President Reagan appointed prominent timber industry leaders to key positions in his administration, such as John Crowell as assistant secretary of agriculture with oversight over the national forests. Crowell formerly served as chief legal counsel for Louisiana Pacific, the nation's largest corporate purchaser of federal timber. Douglas MacCleery, who worked for the National Forest Products Association, the nation's leading lumber lobby, was appointed deputy assistant secretary of agriculture. Crowell, MacCleery, and others sought to make federal natural resources more available to industry while relaxing environmental regulations. Crowell specifically sought to double timber harvests from the national forests and exempt the agency from sustained-yield mandates in order to quickly liquidate remaining old growth. He also directed the agency to place a priority on building roads

Just like Bush [handwritten margin note]

This is why we need David Orr. Type education! Econ + Ecol! [handwritten note]

into large roadless areas in order to eliminate them from potential future wilderness designation.

The 1976 National Forest Management Act had required the preparation of comprehensive management plans for each national forest in the nation, and this provided a vehicle for promotion of the Reagan agenda. As the first forest plans were being drafted in the early and mid-1980s, political appointees and agency heads applied considerable pressure on forest planners to maximize timber production. Forest planners adopted the most optimistic assumptions possible to justify ratcheting up the harvest. A wide variety of data manipulation hidden deep in planning documents could and did serve this purpose. Again, the GPNF provides an example. Rather than implement long-overdue reductions in the allowable cut (called allowable sale quantity—ASQ—by the 1980s), the forest planners renewed their faith that intensive management would accelerate future timber growth and consequently proposed an *increase* in old-growth harvests. To rationalize this plan, managers built into the computer planning model assumptions that significant future gains in timber growth would be realized from the planting of genetically improved "super trees," and from fertilization, thinning of undesirable trees, and stocking all timber stands to their optimum. The computer model that projected future timber yield also assumed there would be essentially no loss of soil productivity and nearly complete protection of the forest from disease, insects, fire, and wind (not to mention erupting volcanoes). Conservationist critics detailed the absurdity of these assumptions, to no avail. The arguments of the critics are interesting and instructive.

The GPNF planners assumed a 6 percent increase in timber yield over time from fertilization based on a 1983 report on experimental fertilization on the forest. But, curiously, the 1983 report indicated that response to fertilization varied widely; in fact, on four of ten soil types tested, productivity of the target species *decreased* after fertilization. Nevertheless, forest planners assumed optimistic benefits forestwide. The planners assigned a 15 percent increase in yields to improved genetics, beginning immediately, even though no genetically improved trees yet existed. Furthermore, the assumption that super trees would be available was (and remains today) scientifically insupportable. In fact, many of the nursery grown seedlings planted on the GPNF in the past seventy years were not genetically adapted to their sites and may result in a *decrease* in expected productivity.

Another 11 percent increase in future yields was ascribed to commercial thinning that would take place at intervals in the growing cycle of a timber stand. This assumed that enough money and an adequate staff would be available to accomplish this labor-intensive activity. Economic analyses of thinning, however, show it to be a money-losing effort in most cases on national forests. The cost of thinning exceeds the value of the added wood fiber, so consistent funding for such economically irrational practices cannot be counted on.

The plan assumes an incredible boost of another 28 percent in timber yield from replanting cutover areas immediately and restocking poorly stocked areas. But, again, these activities are usually not cost effective and have never been fully funded by Congress on a consistent basis. Furthermore, the plan assumed optimum stocking of 300 trees per acre, yet it required replanting efforts only if stocking fell below 125 trees per acre. The computer model also assumed each stand would be composed of 300 perfectly spaced, genetically improved commercial species like Douglas-fir, yet trees never grow perfectly spaced, nor are they all commercial species, nor are any genetically improved seedlings available. Mark Wigg, the main critic of these timber yield assumptions, pointed out in his critique that the U.S. General Accounting Office in 1978 found that the GPNF had overestimated by 100 percent the yield gains it could expect from replanting and restocking.

Finally, the forest plan assumed only minimal losses to soil productivity over time. No losses were assigned for accelerated soil erosion from all this additional logging and manipulation of the forest, or for soil compaction or nutrient depletion or changes in the watershed hydrology. Yet, ironically, the environmental impact statement for the forest plan acknowledged the likely occurrence of all these impacts.[28] Despite these rather devastating criticisms, the forest planners remained dedicated to their course—at least until the federal district court shut down logging in the remnant patches of old growth. The planning process, though supremely rational in appearance, was driven more by political objectives than by science or reason.

CONCLUSION

The forestry profession for most of this century has focused on producing commodities such as timber, water, and big game. Consequently, forest science theory emphasized narrow agronomic models of forest management designed to maximize desired commodities. A linear concept of sustained yield dominated the profession well into the 1960s: by manipulating inputs one could achieve desired outputs. Like farmers in the Midwest maximizing their corn crop, foresters in the Northwest would maximize yields of commercial wood fiber. This view ignored the complicated ecological interactions at play in natural forests and optimistically assumed that ecosystems could and *should* be dramatically simplified to maximize their utility.[29]

This instrumentalist management perspective tended to overestimate the productive capabilities of forests. Responding to various institutional and economic incentives, foresters placed exaggerated faith in the ability of new technologies (genetics, engineering, pesticides, fertilizers, etc.) to reconstruct the natural forest into a virtual wood fiber cornucopia. Certain that they were acting in the public interest, foresters sought to eliminate the old, inefficient natural forests and replace them with rapidly growing young timber planta- tions. This crusade to "maximize production" through "intensive manage- ment" unfortunately ignored environmental limitations, economic inefficien- cies, political constraints, and social dissatisfactions. Foresters dedicated to the vision of a fully regulated forest considered these obstacles technically surmountable.

The complicated forest management decision environment provided nu- merous opportunities for managers, politicians, and industry representatives to dodge responsibility for failures that resulted. When accused of over- cutting forests, industry claimed they were only catering to public demands for wood products. When accused of crippling forest ecosystems, foresters blamed Congress for inconsistent policies and inadequate funding, or blamed nature for behaving unpredictably, or claimed that a lack of informa- tion hampered good decision making. When accused of skewing agency budgets toward timber sales and away from environmental rehabilitation, politicians pointed to the federal deficit or to another branch of government or to the other political party as the culprit.

Claiming innocence is a ubiquitous feature of resource development cul- ture. In fact, Patricia Limerick argues in *The Legacy of Conquest* that the myth of innocence is central to the history of the whole American West: "Among those persistent [western] values, few have more power than the idea of innocence. The dominant motive for moving West was improve- ment and opportunity, not injury to others. Few white Americans went West intending to ruin the natives and despoil the continent."[30] Just so, few foresters intended to overcut their forests, silt up their streams, and cause the extinction of myriad species of wildlife. So why did it happen? How did the responsible decision makers allow things to deteriorate to the point where every interest group is dissatisfied and every core forest management policy seems to have been violated?

Part of the explanation, as mentioned above, lies in the fact that the panoply of decision makers have all been able to dodge responsibility for outcomes. Lack of attention to historical experience aided this. Forest managers carefully ignored recurrent obstacles to their dreams of production maximization, ignored their past inability to achieve consistent and balanced funding for multiple use management, ignored growing environmental deterioration and escalating public opposition. Historical precedent provided no wisdom or restraint on management plans. Perhaps this was because the lessons of the past and responsibilities to future generations were only weak abstract notions compared to the economic demands of the present. But the ideology of maximum production itself rested on weak silvicultural abstractions. Yet, those theories supporting industrial forestry had the power to clear whole forests while those defending social responsibility and environmental sensitivity remained unrealized.

The fact that generating wealth prevailed over forest protection and social equity should not surprise anyone. What is surprising is that forest managers plausibly claimed to be conserving forests and protecting the public interest all the while they were eliminating those forests in a forty-year boom and bust to benefit industry. Technological optimism and the ideology of intensive management provided a useful facade of rationality over what was essentially asset liquidation. The ancient forests that defined the Pacific Northwest's regional character at the turn of the century were consumed to generate wealth for an economic culture obsessed with growth and plagued by fears of scarcity and political vulnerability. In the end, this culture's actions produced the very conditions it hoped to avoid.

Forest managers and their industry clients and political sponsors all seemed to have an extraordinary capacity to rationalize "staying the course" on a troubled path. They did this by redefining covetousness as patriotic dedication to economic growth. The ideology of maximization simply obscured their unwillingness to accept limits. Defining logging as the essence of forest conservation completed the rationalization. Diligent, well-meaning professional managers effected this transformation in the name of progress and the public interest—all with a straight face and a clear conscience. And the American public cheered this process on in the early years of the post–World War II era, giving it enough momentum to withstand outside challenges in the 1960s and 1970s. By the time dissenters convinced a majority of the public that this program was faulty, the damage was done and the inevitable economic bust loomed just around the corner. Boosters, dodgers, and rationalizers searched for a plausible scapegoat. The spotted owl? Radical environmentalists? Liberals? Behind the oppositional rhetoric of loggers versus tree huggers, however, lay the indelible record of the decision makers themselves: millions of acres of former forests shaved bare, soil washing off steep hillsides, mile after mile of muddy streams choked of fish life, one species of wildlife after another drifting toward the brink of extinction, all reflecting a not-so-innocent "legacy of conquest."

NOTES

Portions of this chapter are drawn from the author's book A *Conspiracy of Optimism: Management of the National Forests since World War Two* (Lincoln: University of Nebraska Press, 1994).

1. Carlos Schwantes, *The Pacific Northwest: An Interpretive History*, rev. ed. (Lincoln: University of Nebraska Press, 1996), 215.

2. Elliott A. Norse, *Ancient Forests of the Pacific Northwest* (Washington, D.C.: Island Press, 1990).

3. This famous "Dwyer decision" in the spring of 1991 has been widely quoted and analyzed. An excellent discussion of the context and repercussions of the decision is found in William Dietrich, *The Final Forest: The Battle for the Last Great Trees of the Pacific Northwest* (New York: Simon and Schuster, 1992), chap. 13.

4. David Ehrenfeld, *Beginning Again: People and Nature in the New Millennium* (New York: Oxford University Press, 1993), 147–48.

5. For example, the Forest Service's *Douglas-fir Supply Study* of 1969 predicted that timber production would inevitably fall off after the liquidation of old-growth forests. When this would occur depended on future harvest levels and the intensity of management. At the levels of production that ensued in the 1970s, harvest fall-offs were predicted to begin at the turn of the century and to increase dramatically after 2030 under the most optimistic assumptions. USDA Forest Service, *Douglas-fir Supply Study: Alternative Programs for Increasing Timber Supplies from National Forest Lands* (Portland: Pacific Northwest Forest and Range Experiment Station, 1969), 14–16.

6. Tim Foss, "New Perspectives, Old Interpretation?" *Inner Voice* 3, no. 3 (Summer 1991): 13.

7. Quotations from Bridgid Schulte, "Busted Timber Towns Seek New Economic Foundations," *High Country News* 24, no. 16 (September 7, 1992): 4.

8. Michael Williams, *Americans and Their Forests: A Historical Geography* (Cambridge and New York: Cambridge University Press, 1989), 309, 325.

9. Richard White, *Land Use, Environment, and Social Change: The Shaping of*

Island County, Washington (Seattle: University of Washington Press, 1980, 1992), chap. 5.

10. Williams, *Americans and Their Forests,* 309.

11. USDA Forest Service, *Timber Depletion, Lumber Prices, Lumber Exports, and Concentration of Timber Ownership* [the Capper Report], U.S. Congress, Report on Senate Res. 311 (Washington, D.C.: Government Printing Office, 1920), 13–14.

12. USDA Forest Service, Gifford Pinchot National Forest, "Resume of Forest History, Gifford Pinchot National Forest" (Vancouver, Wash., 1982?), 2; pamphlet in the author's possession.

13. According to the Gifford Pinchot National Forest annual Multiple Use Reports, 7,000 acres were logged in 1962, 12,000 in 1965, and 13,500 each in 1966 and 1967 (640 acres equals one square mile). The annual cut for those years ranged from 430 million board feet (mmbf) to 510 mmbf. This harvest level remained consistent for the next 20 years, and so it can be assumed that the area logged similarly remained in that range. Timber sale revenues fluctuate widely and are really meaningful only in their historical context. The $17–$20 million figure comes from the Gifford Pinchot National Forest, "Resume of Forest History, Gifford Pinchot National Forest," written apparently in 1982.

14. USDA Forest Service, Pacific Northwest Region, *Analysis of the Management Situation, Gifford Pinchot National Forest* (Portland, 1985?), 119.

15. Peter H. Morrison, *Old Growth in the Pacific Northwest: A Status Report* (Washington, D.C.: The Wilderness Society, 1988), 27–28. Norse, *Ancient Forests of the Pacific Northwest,* chaps. 2 and 8.

16. USDA Forest Service, Northwest Regional Office, "Timber Management Plan for the Gifford Pinchot National Forest," 1953, 2–3. (The author received from the GPNF a copy of pages 1–3 of what appears to be the 1953 timber management plan—but at present this is unconfirmed.)

17. H. D. Langille, "General Report on the Timber Resources of Wind River Valley, Skamania County, Washington," 1919; in author's possession, available at Wind River Ranger District Office, Gifford Pinchot National Forest.

18. C. Glen Jorgensen, quoted in *Timber Management in the Pacific Northwest: Oral History of Five Region 6 Employees,* vol. 3, interviews conducted by Dennis Roth and Jerry Williams (Washington, D.C.: U.S. Forest Service History Unit, 1986), 190.

19. Data available for 1959–62, after the timber harvest level had peaked, show that full-time employees of the GPNF increased from 137 to 222, and part-time employees increased from 265 to 377; Gifford Pinchot National Forest, annual "Multiple Use" reports, 1959, 1962, formerly available at Pacific Northwest Regional

Office archives (warehouse), box A-1. (In 1995 these archives were all transferred to the National Archives regional center in Seattle.)

20. USDA Forest Service, Region 6, "A Plan for Timber Management, Wind River Working Circle, Columbia National Forest," April 20, 1940, 12–13; document in the author's possession, obtained from Gifford Pinchot National Forest, Supervisor's Office.

21. Jorgensen, in *Timber Management in the Pacific Northwest*, 213–14.

22. A summary of data from the 1953 timber management plan is contained in: Forest Service, Region 6, "Wind River Ranger District Multiple Use Plan," 1962, 12–14 and 36; in author's possession, available at GPNF Supervisor's Office.

23. "A Plan for Timber Management, Wind River Working Circle," 1940, 2; also "Wind River Ranger District Multiple Use Plan," 1962, 36.

24. Forest Service, Region 6, "Wind River Ranger District Multiple Use Plan," 1968, 10.

25. Gifford Pinchot National Forest, "Multiple-Use Plan, Packwood Ranger District, Gifford Pinchot National Forest," approved March 31, 1961, 3–4; in the author's possession, obtained from GPNF Supervisor's Office.

26. Allowable cut for 1949 taken from USDA Forest Service, press release, "Gifford Pinchot National Forest To Be Dedicated October 15," September 19, 1949 (for September 26, release), USDA 1993–49; in author's possession. Allowable cut for 1956 taken from USDA Forest Service, Washington Office, "Report on National Forest Timber Resource Operations," Forest History Society archives, Durham, North Carolina, National Forest Products Association records, box 54. Allowable cut for 1962 and 1975 derived from USDA Forest Service, Pacific Northwest Region, *Final Environmental Statement: Timber Management Plan, 1975–1984*, February 1975, 5.

27. See Charles F. Wilkinson and H. Michael Anderson, "Land and Resource Planning in the National Forests," *Oregon Law Review* 64, nos. 1 and 2 (1985): 125–28, 151–54, and 184–86.

28. The critique of the GPNF plan outlined in these paragraphs comes from two sources of comment on the draft plan: Mark Wigg's analysis, "Review of Managed Timber Yield Tables," in the collected comments provided to the Forest Service by the Gifford Pinchot Task Force, chaired by Susan Saul (in the author's possession); and Randal O'Toole's report, "Economic Analysis of the Gifford Pinchot Forest Plan and Draft Environmental Impact Statement" (Eugene, Ore.: Cascade Holistic Economic Consultants, November 1987), 8–11.

29. Arthur F. McEvoy discusses the impact of this old, flawed linear model of sustained yield on the California fisheries, noting how environmental deterioration led to a reevaluation of it in the 1970s. McEvoy, *The Fisherman's Problem: Ecology*

and Law in the California Fisheries, 1850–1980 (Cambridge and New York: Cambridge University Press, 1986), 6–7, 251–57. The Society of American Foresters at its annual convention in 1993 contentiously debated a Task Force Report, "Sustaining Long-Term Forest Health and Productivity," in which the authors suggested "sustained yield" had become outmoded and should be dropped as a forest management model in favor of "ecosystem management." See the proceedings from that conference, published in the spring of 1994 by the SAF.

30. Patricia Nelson Limerick, *The Legacy of Conquest: The Unbroken Past of the American West* (New York: Norton, 1987), 36.

"Politics Is at the Bottom of the Whole Thing"

Spatial Relations of Power in

Oregon Salmon Management

JOSEPH E. TAYLOR III

There is a dissonance between the way historians discuss the environmental history of salmon fisheries and the reality of how those fisheries evolved. Historians have tended to fixate on whether the "tragedy of the commons" is an apt metaphor to explain decline.[1] Calling the Columbia or any other Oregon stream a "commons," however, ignores the fishery's spatial and racial politics. The river was not an open field for all to enter freely, but neither was it effectively closed.[2] Fishers could claim exclusive use of sections of the river by forming snag unions, erecting barriers, or petitioning to exclude their competitors, but until the second decade of the twentieth century the number of nets continued to grow regardless of their efforts.[3] We need new ways of discussing the environmental history of fisheries without bogging down in inapt metaphors and impotent debates.

Spatial analysis suggests a more fruitful path. Geographer Edward Soja has criticized historians for too often producing "visions of a depoliticized economy that existed as if it were packed solidly on to the head of a pin." History, he writes, "has tended to occlude a comparable critical sensibility to the spatiality of social life," to seeing it as "being creatively located not only in the making of history but also in the construction of human geographies, the social production of space and the restless formation and reformation of geographical landscapes."[4] The unwillingness of historians to articulate the influence of space in the distribution of social power has left an oddly disembodied vision of the past. Yet as Allan Pred notes, "Power relations, while abstract and intangible, are always somehow associated with the concrete conduct of social life in place, always in some way involved with 'the capacity to organize and control people, materials, and territories.' . . . Thus, struggles, of whatever focus and scale, are always at some level struggles over the use and meaning of space and time."[5]

Examining the development of Oregon salmon management during the late nineteenth and early twentieth centuries from the standpoint of the effects of space on arrangements of power helps us see how such forces can be reincorporated into history. Analyzing early Oregon salmon management from this perspective reveals the tendency of society to understand rivers not as complete systems but only according to their relevant parts. It also shows how the disassembly of nature for social and economic convenience follows. During the nineteenth century, Oregonians intellectually and then physically transformed rivers into sluices for minerals, channels for irrigation, flumes for logs, spaces for fishing gear, nurseries for fish, mass for hydroelectricity, roads for barges, and sewers for civilization. As they came to associate usage with space, Oregonians fragmented watersheds into their socially defined constituent parts, and then insisted that they be physically managed to serve those uses. Rivers ceased to operate as purely natural systems.

The spatial reorganization of salmon streams unleashed a series of secondary political responses. The multiple uses of rivers created a kaleidoscopic vision of nature which simplified and truncated natural systems, but salmon adapted poorly to these changes. Rival economic interests tried to compensate to save salmon, but their responses reveal the limits of their concern. Oregonians embraced the chimera of artificial propagation as a political panacea, but when hatcheries failed to stem the decline, the solution was to claim and regulate the spaces of rival interests. In each case the rearrangement of existing natural and social space turned on the political game of assigning blame to other, more marginal groups. As a result, the physical and social spaces of the salmon fisheries remained in constant flux prior to World War II as Oregonians tried to have their salmon and consume them too.

Pacific salmon (*Oncorhynchus* species) have some of the most complicated life histories in nature. Because they are anadromous, these salmon breed and rear in freshwater environments but spend most of their adult lives traveling through the northeastern Pacific. They lay their eggs in gravel beds of main-stem rivers, tributary streams, small creeks, and lakes. After hatching, juveniles spend from a few days to two years (depending on the species) in these freshwater environments before migrating to sea. They then spend from one to six years (this also differs by species) growing to maturity before returning to their natal stream to breed and die. Only steelhead (*O. mykiss*) and an occasional coho (*O. kisutch*) and sockeye (*O. nerka*) survive to spawn a second time. Their movements defined a series of natural spaces throughout the region's river systems that became a vital component of human economies.[6]

Humans long ago recognized the patterned regularity of salmon life cycles and began to exploit their huge annual spawning runs as a convenient and dependable source of protein. By the early nineteenth century, aboriginal fishers harvested about 41 million pounds of salmon annually in the Colum-bia River Basin, but then diseases, wars, and social dislocation drastically reduced their consumption. Indians also initiated a commercial fishery early in the century to supply fur and fish traders visiting the region, but the industrial fishery did not begin until 1866, when several entrepreneurs built the first canning operation on the lower Columbia River. Other white fishers quickly migrated north from the troubled salmon fisheries on the Sacramento River. By the mid-1870s, Columbia River canneries were can-ning 25 million pounds of chinook salmon (*O. tshawytscha*) and shipping the "royal" salmon around the world.[7]

During these years industrial fishers used gillnets exclusively to catch salmon. They wove gillnets with linen twine and hung them with wood buoys and iron weights to create a vertical barrier that floated through the water with the current. Fishers sized the meshes so a salmon could swim only partly into the net. When the fish attempted to back out, its gill plates or fins became entangled. Weaving a net required great skill because mesh size was critical. An opening slightly too large or too small rendered the net useless. Fishing a gillnet was also demanding. Keeping the net taut and aligned properly in a current required years of practice, especially so because gillnets could only be fished at night or in muddy water since salmon avoided the thick-twined nets during daylight.[8]

As participation grew during the 1870s, fishers began to multiply the types of gear used to catch salmon. Canners encouraged the proliferation of seines, poundnets, and fishwheels to exploit additional areas of the river and to reduce their dependence on gillnetters. Laissez-faire rules of competition led to overcapitalization, however, and competition for finite fish and fish-ing spots raised concerns among observers. By 1875 the U.S. Commissioner of Fish and Fisheries was warning of imminent decline. The first signs of that decline came two years later when El Niño weather conditions contributed to a sharp drop in catches all along the coast. An alarmed federal investigator noted, "There is a very small run of Salmon this year in the Columbia. With twice the number of nets, the fishermen catch less salmon than last year."[9]

Solutions to this problem were not long in coming. Artificial propagation generated immense pubic interest during the late nineteenth and early twentieth centuries. By 1870 fish culturists had learned how to incubate fish eggs efficiently, and apparent successes at restoring shad and Atlantic salmon runs created a ground swell of support for fish hatcheries in New England. In 1871, Spencer F. Baird, soon to be the first U.S. Commissioner of Fish and Fisheries, used that popularity to persuade Congress to create what would eventually become a huge federal bureaucracy dedicated to replenishing America's streams through artificial propagation. The fish culture movement was further fueled by boosters such as Livingston Stone, who in 1872 proclaimed artificial propagation "to be *the one great work, above all others, in the restoration of salmon to the American rivers and lakes.*"[10]

Throughout the nineteenth century, fish culturists reinforced public confidence by making grandiose but unsubstantiated claims. Most boosters relied on a deductive arithmetic in which increases in hatch rates produced one-for-one increases in runs. In 1893, for example, salmon canner and fish culturist R. D. Hume claimed:

> Professor Baird often said that "one acre of water was worth seven acres of land, if properly cultivated," but I am convinced that the Professor erred only in this, that I believe one acre of the waters of any salmon stream in Oregon, if judiciously cultivated under favorable circumstances, and if not paralyzed by ignorant or vicious legislation, is worth more as a medium for the product of a food supply than forty acres of the best land in the State.[11]

Baird was a highly respected biologist, but he never possessed the practical experience with salmon to make such a claim; while Hume, who had no scientific training, was even less equipped to document such braggadocio. Nevertheless, by the 1890s fishery managers had elevated these claims to gospel, transforming dubious science into strategic panacea. In 1893, Oregon Fish Protector Hollister D. McGuire noted, "Artificial propagation alone can preserve the industry."[12] Technology would depoliticize management by alleviating the need to limit industry or control space. Hatchery workers would release young salmon from their fish factories, and the industry and the public would reap an inexhaustible bounty. Oregon managers mindlessly repeated this wisdom well into the twentieth century despite their lack of expertise and a growing amount of evidence to the contrary. In 1902, Oregon Master Fish Warden H. G. Van Dusen, a man with no background in fish culture, claimed, "It is now a recognized fact, even by the most skeptical, that the salmon product in our rivers can be limited only by the number of young fry liberated from our hatcheries."[13]

For a while it seemed to work. Catches rebounded briefly during the late 1870s and early 1880s, but in 1885 the industry entered its first prolonged crisis. Although the decline in harvest was probably triggered by a combination of factors, including accumulating damage to spawning grounds upstream and the return of El Niño conditions to the northeastern Pacific, the crisis itself was less environmental than structural. The number of nets on the Columbia reached an all-time high as gillnetters abandoned the collapsing Sacramento River fishery, but fishers were also competing against a growing assortment of gear. Gillnetters, who relied on slow-moving water to operate their nets, had to share the lower Columbia River with a mushrooming number of poundnets and seines, which also required slow currents to be effective. Farther upstream the number of fishwheels, which relied on faster water to turn their giant scoops, and seines, which exploited the eddies in the swift current, expanded similarly. The dividing line between the upriver and downriver fisheries, both in terms of the physical character of the river and the social composition of the fisheries, was the Cascades rapids at Bonneville.[14]

The rapid expansion of the fishery during the 1880s produced a watering-down effect on income. Individual catches diminished even as total harvest grew. Gillnetters in particular saw their standard of living decline precipitously. Once they realized that demand had outstripped supply, fishermen began to balkanize according to relations of production and spatial distribution. Gillnetters initiated the process in 1886 when they created the Columbia River Fishermen's Protective Union, the fishery's first effective industrial organization. Other groups soon followed with their own organizations, but restructuring didn't end until well after 1899, when the lower Columbia River's major canners consolidated as the Columbia River Packers Association, and upriver packers responded with the rival Association of Pacific Fisheries.[15] The restructuring process did not in itself resolve existing problems related to overfishing; rather, it created a social context of use groups that has dominated the contest to shape natural and social space for the past century.

As competition increased and ocean conditions deteriorated during the 1880s, rival fishing interests began to shape and appropriate the river's spaces to exclude their competitors. The scale and scope of these activities varied considerably. At the local level, small bands of gillnetters formed snag unions to clear debris from the river and claim prescriptive use of the resulting "drift." Poundnet and fishwheel owners did essentially the same thing by driving posts, hanging nets, erecting wheels, or building weirs. Such "improvements" monopolized river space by physically impeding the use of drift nets or other movable gear.[16]

Achieving the moral authority to exclude competitors required claiming and then defending first rights. "Corking" a rival's net (a term for placing a gill net in front of a competitor's so it caught nothing), vandalizing a rival's net or boat, or threatening and even committing violence against a person were all considered legitimate means. But actual contests reveal a complicated tableau. Employment in the fisheries often blurred what seem at first to be stark divisions between rival interests. Seine operators routinely refused to accept financial contributions from their laborers to help defray the costs of clearing a drift. They feared that the workers, who were also gillnetters, would then claim the right to fish the drift with their own nets. Similarly, the ethnic homogeneity of most snag associations and drift unions in an ethnically heterogeneous fishery provided a strain on gear solidarity. Such tensions further helped to fracture the river into a series of personally demarcated and exclusively allotted physical and social spaces.[17]

Unions and associations regularly sanctioned these practices, but they also operated on a broader front. In 1886 the gillnetters' union petitioned Congress to eliminate poundnets from Bakers Bay, protesting that rival traps and poundnets obstructed navigation and posed a safety hazard to netters. Gillnetters complained that traps had displaced them from the best fishing grounds onto the dangerous Columbia River bar, and that unmarked traps were responsible for the drowning deaths of several fellow netters. According to gillnetters, the issue was strictly one of safety. The Washington Fishermen's Association, a group of Bakers Bay trap owners, countered with equal disingenuousness. Poundnet owners deflected criticism by noting that gillnetters regularly wasted salmon by highgrading (continuing to fish after reaching a quota so as to replace smaller fish with larger ones to maximize profit) while they conserved salmon by selectively harvesting from their pens without undue mortality. The episode ended in a stalemate, neither side persuading investigators to exclude their rivals. Gillnetters did not quit, however, and in ensuing years they continued their campaign against rival forms of gear. In 1896, for example, the secretary of the Protective Union vowed, "Not until it is arranged to do away with small mesh gear, wheels, and traps can there be expected any protection to Columbia river fish." Such tactics would come back to haunt gillnetters in Oregon's 1908 initiative election.[18]

The struggle to control fishing space eventually encompassed whole states. Divisions within the industry were reproduced in both the Oregon and Washington legislatures as various factions vied to seize control or limit access to resources. Although many spoke of conservation, it was rarely the primary impulse. Social concerns were of at least equal importance when the Oregon State Board of Fish Commissioners noted in 1888: "Had the literal law been enforced this year private property to the amount of $200,000 would have been rendered worthless, and while owing to the wealth of the packers they could have borne the loss without serious hardship . . . it is not so with the fishermen who have their all in their fishing gear." Conservation was always contingent upon the political palatability of its social costs.[19]

Even when enforced, laws could be ineffective because of the division of the Columbia River into Oregon and Washington waters. Struggling fishers and canners, who were both symptom and cause in these problems, exploited the river's ambiguous jurisdiction in several ways. Gillnetters played one state against the other by buying licenses in whichever state charged less or gave more privileges. In 1904, gillnetters protested Oregon's attempt to impose a personal license by buying Washington net licenses instead. The boycott was successful, and Oregon rescinded the license the following year. Similarly, when Oregon's Master Fish Warden refused to grant licenses to itinerant California fishermen, they too exploited Washington's more lenient statutes and gained a repeal of the policy. Canners also exploited the lax enforcement of Washington wardens to circumvent conservation efforts by Oregon. On several occasions Oregon wardens spied canners transporting and processing salmon out of season, but the wardens were powerless to arrest violators in Washington's unpatrolled waters. Interstate tensions were further exacerbated by each state's tendency to change its fishery laws frequently and with little regard for its neighbor.[20]

Meanwhile fish culture continued to fail its promise. Salmon runs charted an uneven but inexorable decline despite massive investments in hatchery technology. This was not for want of trying. Hatchery workers attempted to process as many eggs as possible, but as the last in a long line of harvesters they found themselves at the mercy of an industry indifferent to self-restraint. In 1901, hatchery workers harvested nearly 60 million eggs from the Columbia River. When the fishing industry ignored closed seasons in 1903, however, hatcheries took only 18.5 million eggs. Even when enforcement resumed two years later, hatcheries harvested only 33 million eggs. The Commissioner of the Bureau of Fisheries blamed fishermen for not obeying the closed seasons and the Oregon Master Fish Warden for lax enforcement. The Warden in turn blamed the state of Washington for passing less restrictive legislation and then refusing to enforce even those laws. The political division of the Columbia allowed fishermen to cross abstract boundaries of social space to continue fishing the natural river in a desperately overcapitalized fishery.[21]

The way fishery managers responded to overfishing radically altered the spatial distribution of reproduction within river systems. During the nineteenth century, federal workers selected hatchery sites more for their accessibility to railways than for natural criteria. According to Livingston Stone, his instructions in 1875 were "to select a point for collecting salmon eggs which would be near the line of the Pacific Railroad, this precaution being necessary both for convenience in operating the station and for facility in distributing the eggs."[22] Consequently, the Clackamas, Rogue, and Little White Salmon Rivers remained the main hatchery streams until rails and roads expanded access after 1900.

But hatcheries hardly ensured stability. As runs declined and spawning beds went unused or disappeared under dams, fish culturists moved hatcheries farther downstream to compensate for declining egg harvests. Such tactics had the unintended consequence of setting in motion a vicious spiral that exacerbated the concentration of reproduction in the lower reaches of streams. The cycle worked like this: as egg takes declined, fish culturists moved farther downstream to compensate; abandonment reduced concern for upstream areas, since they were no longer deemed essential to reproduction; but abandonment also opened these areas up to damming, logging, and grazing; such activities further inhibited salmon populations both locally and farther downstream; and ensuing decline triggered a new cycle of concentration.

The Clackamas River serves as a case in point (see map). In 1877, Columbia River packers and Portland merchants formed a joint stockholding company, the Oregon and Washington Fish Propagating Company, and built the region's first hatchery on the Clackamas. The venture collapsed after four years due to lack of funds, and the building in another three due to lack of interest. But declining runs kept the idea of hatcheries alive. In 1887, the Oregon Fish Commission refurbished the Clackamas station, and the federal government assumed operations the following year. Thereafter one or more hatcheries operated on the river continuously, but as time

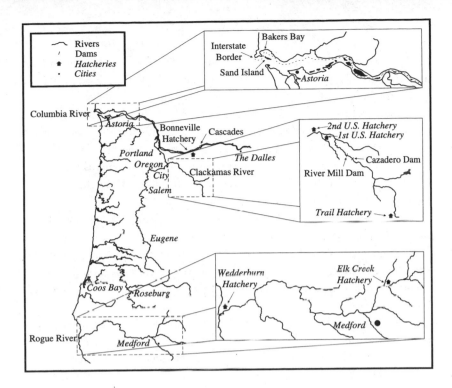

passed the number of fish reaching the Trail station on the upper river declined sharply. By the early 1900s the state had more or less abandoned the Trail station, while the federal government had moved its own operations downstream twice to stabilize its supply of salmon.[23]

Thus in 1904 when the Oregon Water Power and Railway Company announced they were going to build a dam on the Clackamas River at Cazadero, there was little reason for hatchery workers to oppose the development. But neither was it a case of simply surrendering to civilization. Rather, hatchery operators saw the dam as a potential benefit because of its ability to intercept returning fish. Hatchery superintendent Claudius Wallich noted, "The possibilities of an increased take at the site of the dam . . . are somewhat alluring and if the field in this direction is left to us, we think that some good steelhead work may eventually be done there." Wallich's replacement concurred: "Providing the fish will mature at this point it will be possible to increase the collections . . . by closing the fishway in the dam and securing the eggs at that point. The dam would act as a permanent rack and would shut off not only the [chinook] salmon, but later in the fall the silversides [coho] and in the early spring the steelheads."[24]

The experiment failed, and seven years later a second dam at River Mill further concentrated reproduction.[25] In hindsight these actions seem foolish and irresponsible, but at the time they *appeared* to be logical. No one wanted to destroy salmon runs, yet just about everyone did.

When decline continued, managers called for more drastic measures, recommending a ban on fishing in streams with hatcheries to protect the surviving brood stocks. In 1905, the chief of the Bureau of Fisheries' Division of Fish Culture argued, "The proposition to permanently close the Clackamas River will undoubtedly result in affording to the Bureau better facilities for taking a much larger number of salmon eggs than are now taken."[26] Yet "hatchery streams" represented a whole new plateau in the production of fishery space, one that signaled not the triumph of fishery management but its failure. Forced to contest space with the very groups they served, managers argued that eliminating fishermen would save the fishery. But cannibalizing the fishery only showed how absurd management had become.

The Columbia River fishery was hardly the sole arena for these spatial politics. By the early 1900s, salmon canner Robert Deniston Hume was locked in similar endgames with the state of Oregon and rival fishers for control of the Rogue River salmon fishery. At stake were Hume's monopolistic claims to the lower Rogue River and the state's power to tax his canning operations. Hume's battles highlighted both the environmental and social problems of managing Oregon's industrial salmon fishery and Hume's unusual solutions to controlling access and ensuring reproduction.

Hume was an ornery but highly successful businessman in southwestern Oregon. During the late nineteenth century, from his home in Wedderburn, Oregon, at the mouth of the Rogue River, Hume controlled operations scattered over two states and a territory. His business interests included fish and vegetable canning, lumbering, land speculation, shipping, and retail sales. He also played an intermittent but significant role in Oregon's Republican Party during the 1890s and 1900s. Hume's activities garnered him both ardent supporters and bitter opponents, the latter relationships often exacerbated by his tendency to imagine conspiracies and litigate at the drop of a hat.[27]

In many respects Hume epitomized the grasping capitalist of the period, yet he remained more than a self-styled "pygmy monopolist." Hume also understood the nature of salmon and the dynamics of an open access fishery. Raised on the Kennebec River, initiated on the Sacramento River, and seasoned on the Columbia River, he had witnessed the decline of once promising salmon fisheries three times over. He had been a favored member of a failed swidden fishery that was well on its way to depleting every salmon stream from Maine to Alaska. Yet unlike his competitors, Hume developed a holistic understanding of the fishery's problems.[28]

While most saw rivers only as avenues for fish, Hume understood the fishery as a system. He realized that the inability to limit fishing and ensure reproduction was the industry's fatal flaw. But he also saw that competitive tensions within the industry and the scale of environmental change on major rivers kept the industry, let alone any one individual, from responding effectively. Earlier than most, he recognized that the laissez-faire rules of fishing that had destroyed other streams would eventually doom even the mighty Columbia, so in 1877 he moved his operations to the Rogue (see map). The switch was more than a simple relocation. It represented a brave and brazen experiment in sustainable exploitation. By 1877, Hume believed he might avoid past mistakes if he could control all aspects of the salmon's environment, but he needed the right river. Ideally, it would have salmon runs large enough to obtain a handsome profit, yet not so large as to invite competition. Nor could civilization have yet undermined the natural river with dams, logging, or irrigation. In the Rogue, Hume thought he had found such a stream.[29]

Hume understood that success hinged on his ability to moderate society's impact on salmon and their environments, yet he realized he could not control human activity over the entire length of even this smaller river system. Instead, by devising a plan to control only those sections strategic to his fishery, he truncated the natural river into its constituent parts and monopolized or redesigned the important fragments to fit his needs. To control fishing along the lower river, he bought the tidal and shore rights to both banks for an extended distance upstream. He then lobbied state legislators to sanction this de facto monopoly by passing specious legislation designed to grant him "ancient rights" to the river. He also harried state and federal fishery agencies to police dams, irrigation ditches, and mining operations that threatened his fishery.[30]

As aggressive as he was in defending his claims, Hume realized that his control of the fishery remained incomplete, so he also invested tremendous sums of money and energy in artificial propagation. He built his first hatchery in 1877 to increase the river's disappointing runs. But to reduce transportation costs and rationalize reproduction, he located the hatchery not at the existing spawning grounds but next to his cannery at Wedderburn near the mouth of the river. This created new problems. Except for the economically unimportant chum (*O. keta*), most species of salmon are not ready to spawn the moment they enter a stream, but take up to six months before they reach sexual maturity. To solve this problem, Hume dug and enclosed a holding pond to retain the fish until they were "ripe."[31] He attempted to collapse the spatial requirements of salmon by eliminating their need to travel upstream to spawn, reducing in the process his own need to control nonfishing space.

Hume's hatchery became a central component for ensuring reproduction independent of upriver conditions. His dedication to this scheme was underscored when the initial hatchery failed to sustain the river's salmon runs. Instead of pulling up stakes and moving to Alaska like most of his competitors during the 1890s, Hume enlisted the help of the U.S. Fish Commission to build a second hatchery far upstream at Elk Creek. He even offered to underwrite construction of the new hatchery, but stipulated that one-third of the collected eggs be shipped to his private hatchery near Wedderburn.[32]

In so doing, Hume unintentionally began to expand the domain of his fishery ever outward. The journey the eggs took from the upper Rogue to his hatchery at the mouth required a less than obvious route. Federal employees first packed the eggs in wooden crates lined with moss and ice, then loaded them onto a wagon for the 30-mile trip to Medford. Because rugged mountains and rapids blocked the route between Medford and Wedderburn, the eggs were instead placed on a Southern Pacific railroad car and shipped to San Francisco, transferred to a steamer bound north for Coos Bay, transferred once more to a smaller steamer for the trip south to Wedderburn, before finally being loaded back onto a wagon for the last leg to Hume's hatchery. In all, eggs taken approximately 150 miles above the mouth of the Rogue journeyed over 1,000 miles to reach Hume's increasingly unnatural nursery. With time, the spaces of Hume's fishery expanded even farther, as federal agents began transplanting eggs from the Columbia to restore the Rogue's dwindling runs.[33] Through purchase, legislation, and science, R. D. Hume attempted to create and control an environmentally coherent political space conterminous with his fishery; yet despite his intentions, he fragmented nature as surely as his competitors.

Hume's uneasily contained space proved equally difficult to maintain. Rivals for salmon, water, or political supremacy fought him doggedly, and invariably these contests wound up in the newspapers and before judges. By 1908, his battles had dwindled to two lingering court cases. One involved a long-standing dispute over Hume's monopolistic claim to the Rogue River fishery; the other the state's power to tax his canning operations. Hume justified his monopoly of fishing space on a specious argument of "ancient rights" that had no legal precedent apart from a dubious state law passed at his behest in 1899. Rivals had challenged the monopoly in one way or another since the early 1890s, but as late as 1906 Hume appeared to be winning the fight. Unfortunately for him, this was less the result of judicial confirmation than his opponents' habit of dying before hearings could be held. Hume himself noted darkly, "It seems as if all the ones who oppose me here are bound to be drowned, and then fish improve."[34] Similar to the Columbia, battles to conserve Rogue River salmon devolved into so many struggles to exclude rival interests.

And as on the Columbia, the interests involved transcended the local and personal to include government. Hume's intransigence in the monopoly case was mirrored by his resistance to the Oregon Fish Commission's efforts to license his cannery. He initially objected to paying a license fee that supported state hatcheries, rightly noting that the only hatcheries operating on the Rogue were run by himself and the federal government, not the state. Why, he reasoned, should he be required to support activities that gave him no benefit? Over time the license issue expanded into a general debate whether the state or the federal government should manage Oregon salmon. By 1908 federalization had grown into a broad movement, and Hume's personal struggle drew support from elsewhere. Attorney W. C. Hale wrote: "I am in accord with your contention that the operation of hatcheries and control of fish industries and their protection should be placed in the hands of the United States Fish Commission, and would be pleased to render any assistance towards that result." Portland merchant J. O. Hawthorn concurred: "I hope that such will be the case. I, like yourself, think it is a matter that does not belong in politics, at all."[35]

Since the 1870s, Oregonians have engaged in a Promethean contest to create and control the social and natural spaces of salmon streams. They have fought over who would have access to these streams, where and how fish should be caught, where and how fish would reproduce, and who would benefit. But rarely have contestants articulated their agendas so plainly. More often they spoke of property rights, onerous taxes, or the relative morality of fishing methods. In 1907 Hume succumbed to this kind of obfuscation when he crowed to a nephew: "Whichever way it goes whoever attempts to fight us will come out the little end of the horn. Politics is at the bottom of the whole thing."[36] That party politics was a factor is undeniable, but arguing that it was strictly about politics, at least in the conventional sense of the term, only denies the complexity of events.

Hume and his competitors articulated their concerns differently, but in the end claiming space—in this case sections of a river—remained the fundamental goal, whether that meant controlling a sustainable fishery, preserving state sovereignty, or preventing incipient feudalism. Hume complained about the "meanness" and cowardly incompetence of the Master Fish Warden. He called the Oregon governor a "dirty scrub and a liar" and another opponent "a sneaking, cowardly rascal." Hume and his allies painted pictures of faceless individuals, "crowds," and "gangs" all conspiring to destroy his work. Meanwhile, his rivals called him "Millionaire Hume" and "Lord Hume" and likened him to "a feudal baron" motivated by greed and narrow interest. Inside the courtroom, lawyers obscured issues even further by speaking of rights, privileges, and sovereignty in the impenetrable language of law.[37]

Beyond the words lay the more fundamental question of who would shape and control the natural and social spaces of the Rogue River. R. D. Hume's monopoly was certainly self-serving, but it was also a rational response to the overfishing and environmental degradation plaguing salmon rivers everywhere. Federal administrators usually refused to be dragged into the grudge fights that passed as state politics, but in this instance they applauded Hume's efforts. The chief of the Division of Fish Culture went so far as to call Hume "the most public spirited of all the fishermen on the Pacific Coast."[38] Such high praise counted for little within Oregon. Opponents and the general public understood Hume in quite different terms, partly because the personal rivalries were so intense, but also because the Rogue fishery was not and could not be a battle unto itself. The connection with concurrent struggles to control the spaces of the Columbia River fishery was unavoidable, and as such Hume's defeat was probably inevitable. The contest to control fishery spaces had transcended the local. Not only were rival governments involved but the public as well, especially as a result of the growing influence of voters and urban anglers. Between 1906 and 1910, political power in the salmon fisheries shifted decisively away from the personal to the state, and from industrial fishers to sports fishers.

Spatial rivalries on the Columbia began to boil over in 1906. Tensions surfaced first between Oregon and Washington during a dispute over their border along the river. The location of the "main channel" was the central point of contention. When Oregon achieved statehood in 1859, the Columbia emptied into the Pacific from two separate mouths in the shifting sands of Clatsop Spit. The state charter established the border along the "main channel," which followed past the north side of Sand Island; but after the Army Corps of Engineers constructed the south jetty, sealing the southern entrance, the river's flow altered and the north channel began to shoal. Shipping traffic instead flowed south of Sand Island.[39]

The ambiguous language of Oregon's charter provided Washington an opportunity to contest fishery space. Washington opposed a policy allowing canners to lease seining rights on Sand Island from the federal government after Oregon canners won most of the bids. Washington contested the government's right to lease the land. According to the Seattle-based *Pacific Fisherman* in 1905, "The island reserved [by the federal government in 1860 for military use] and the island of today are not one and the same." Washington used the shifting sands to argue that the border should be redrawn to reflect the change in traffic. Oregon insisted that the border ran along the north channel regardless of where the "main channel" now existed. At stake was control of the lucrative seining operations at Sand and other islands and shoals along the lower river, but monetary considerations were only one part of the equation. With jurisdiction also went managerial control of the fishery. As boundary commissioner C. C. Dalton noted after the U.S. Supreme Court ruled in 1908 in Oregon's favor: "The decision is a great loss in territory and jurisdiction to the State of Washington. It gives to Oregon nearly exclusive control of the salmon fisheries and islands of the Columbia River."[40]

More than any other trope, "conservation" dominated the political rhetoric of salmon politics, but its invocation was far from universally persuasive. Like so much else, its appeal was contingent on spatial perspective. Viewed from Astoria, Bakers Bay, or The Dalles, conservation could be a legitimating sign for local interests. From Portland, Salem, or Olympia, however, the claims of rival fishing interests or legislatures tended to ring hollow. As early as 1887, an Oregon legislative committee judged conservation practices to be little more than synonyms for the gear a particular group used. "Many fishermen," the committee noted, "judge . . . the question solely with a view to what is most advantageous to them." The spectacle of fishermen fighting over the title *most worthy protector* only compounded public cynicism. Many despaired of finding a solution so long as the salmon fishery went unchecked. Newspaper editors repeatedly criticized the industry for manipulating the political system rather than solving its problems. "The real cause of the industry's serious plight," the Portland *Morning Oregonian* insisted, "is in a deadlock as to really protective legislation."[41]

Some Pacific Northwesterners eventually saw federal assumption of management as the only way to break the deadlock and save the fishery. In March 1908 the *Morning Oregonian* reported growing support for the idea among canners and the Secretary of Commerce. In June, Miller Freeman, publisher of the highly influential *Pacific Fisherman*, wrote the Commissioner of the Bureau of Fisheries: "I am becoming more convinced than ever that the only solution of the problem in such districts as the Columbia is proper administration under a single control; namely, the United States Bureau of Fisheries."[42] R. D. Hume's battle against the state merged with a much larger movement. Growing doubts about Oregon's ability to manage its fisheries produced a political climate in which public and state eclipsed private and local.

Meanwhile the triage-like decisions fishery managers had made to save "hatchery streams" inadvertently introduced a new destabilizing factor. By legitimizing the idea of closing streams to conserve runs, they unwittingly handed gillnetters a new rationalization in their fight against upriver competitors. Oregon's Master Fish Warden H. G. Van Dusen, a native Astorian and open supporter of gillnetters, began criticizing poundnets and fishwheels as early as his 1904 annual report, recommending: "Under no circumstances should a fish-trap or a fish-wheel be permitted at the mouth of a salmon-breeding stream or within miles of one." By 1907 he was calling for more drastic measures. Noting that "a sacrifice has to be made some place," Van Dusen recommended extending to the Columbia a law restricting commercial fishing to tidewater in Oregon's coastal streams. "The Columbia River should have been included in this measure at the time it was enacted," he noted, ". . . but the influence brought to bear by the upper river interests was too strong."[43]

Van Dusen had deftly created a situation in which fishwheel owners and the state legislature were obstructing a scientifically legitimate spatial approach to conservation. In 1907, gillnetters seized the opportunity by drafting an initiative bill to close the Columbia to fishing above tidewater near the Cascades. The bill would have effectively ended the use of fishwheels by eliminating access to the fast water needed to operate the devices. Upriver fishermen responded with a two-pronged counteroffensive. One thrust attempted to dilute or confuse the gillnetter initiative by introducing a rival measure that would have eliminated gillnetting by restricting fishing to daylight hours, when nets were least effective. The other sought replacement of the Master Fish Warden.[44]

Behind the scenes, a third group of Oregonians tried to moderate the conflict. At the heart of this quiet effort were nonlegislative government officials from the courts and the Oregon Fish Commission, the publishers of the Portland Morning Oregonian, and a few discreet salmon canners. Fearing the threat of federalization, they attempted to defuse the spatial tug-of-war between upriver and downriver interests, and with it public dissatisfaction of fishery management. Their solution was to assert state hegemony over the fisheries. They began in the summer of 1907 with back-room negotiations to find an "impartial" replacement for Van Dusen.[45]

By mid-March of 1908 the Fish Commission believed they had found such a replacement in Herman C. McAllister, a traveling salesman with no experience in the fisheries. But as the *Morning Oregonian* of March 11 noted: "Technical knowledge of the fishing industry is not regarded as an essential qualification for the position, and the Board will select a man with particular attention as to his executive ability as well as a disposition to be impartial and treat all sections and interests alike." McAllister didn't disappoint. He knew nothing and did little, but one of his first acts was to move the warden's office from Van Dusen's home of Astoria to the supposedly neutral turf of Portland.[46]

The moderating impulse continued with final rulings in R. D. Hume's lawsuits. As Hume's biographer noted, it was "the jurist, not the vigilante" who ultimately shaped the social geographies of the Rogue River. In May 1908 the Oregon Supreme Court rejected Hume's protest against the state license fee. The court followed in August by ruling that the state, not private citizens, retained ultimate authority over its waters. The rulings asserted state sovereignty in unequivocal terms and effectively ended Hume's thirty-year battle to protect Rogue River salmon. Discussion of these cases has focused on antimonopoly sentiment and the shortcomings of Hume's legal arguments, but such interpretations abstract these cases from the vital context of Oregon's fish fights during the early twentieth century.[47] Hume's legal defeats need to be understood as part of a widespread retaliation by the state and the public against what was perceived as a greedy, irresponsible industry.

Finding a way to defeat both fishing initiatives proved more difficult, especially after the successful replacement of Van Dusen. Having lost a key ally in government, gillnetters grew more determined to destroy their competitors, while wheel owners tried to capitalize on the netters' loss of political influence by publishing caustic newspaper advertisements. In late May 1908, wheel owners concluded their campaign with a provocative ad that mixed numbers and images to create a thoroughly alarming scenario. Under a heading in capital letters crying "Protect Our Salmon," the ad argued that gillnets and seines were the true villains, and that most of them were located in a highly congested area around Astoria: "In 10 miles by 5 miles are 570 miles net, 80 miles seines, catching 95% of salmon." By contrast, wheels on the upper river were located "1 to 5 miles apart." In case the reader didn't get the picture, they drew one. The ad showed a river mouth dotted with nets contrasted against a capacious, sparsely fished upper river.[48]

Gillnetters followed the next day with their own inflammatory ad offering the "Last Word" on the election. They claimed that migrating salmon could not reach their spawning grounds because of the wheels, and invoked no less an authority than Stanford University president and famed ichthyologist David Starr Jordan to prove that "wheels and all stationary traps are especially pernicious . . . and should be everywhere prohibited." Gillnetters drew their own picture, portraying a gauntlet of fishwheels relieved only by a distortedly narrow open river filled with impassable rapids. "No salmon," the caption warned, "can now get into upper Columbia and tributaries to spawn."[49]

Against this backdrop the *Morning Oregonian* tried in vain to counsel restraint. As early as February the paper criticized both bills for being "silent on the most important element of salmon legislation—extension of closed season in months when fish need protection most and when greed of salmon men is keenest." But by May the paper had not elaborated its position any further than a simple negative. In an editorial deriding the surfeit of voter-sponsored initiatives on the June ballot, the paper stated simply: "Two bills are presented by opposing interests with a view to regulating the taking of salmon in the Columbia, neither of the bills being drawn with a view to fair and reasonable regulation, but each attempting to serve a selfish interest." The paper recommended against both bills and even published a post-election image of two greedy trolls locked in a tug-of-war over a very distressed-looking salmon, but moderation in this instance had always been a remote possibility.[50]

Netters, wheel owners, and moderates had all tried to wield the rhetoric of conservation to their advantage, but the discourse remained open to other interpretations. Against the intensity of the public's disgust, the *Morning Oregonian*'s efforts amounted to little more than impotent griping. In promising conservation through more hatcheries and better enforcement of closed seasons, the paper offered only warmed-over failures. They satisfied no one, especially voters. As early as February the newspaper had noted presciently, "A great many people would take pleasure in enactment of both bills. . . . perhaps this is the opportunity."[51] When Oregonians went to the polls on June 1, they did pass both measures, effectively killing the entire river fishery.

Between late March 1908 and the fall election of 1910, the fallout from the campaign and election radically altered the natural and social geography of

Oregon's salmon fisheries. The first change came when Warden McAllister relocated his office from Astoria to Portland in May 1908, and then to Salem the following year. The moves contained a class bias that placed gillnetters at a logistical disadvantage. Distance and the time constraints of gillnetting, which binds fishermen to the river by the cycle of tides, discouraged gillnetters from making the long trek to Salem to meet legislators and administrators. Wealthier wheel owners experienced no such hindrance, but they suffered their own serious setback as a result of the election. Passage of the rival bills initially hurt them more than gillnetters, because the courts ruled that the new laws pertained only to waters within Oregon's jurisdiction. That arbitrary division of river space allowed gillnetters to cross an imaginary line and continue fishing under Washington licenses while Oregon fishwheels stood idle.[52]

Squabbles between gillnetters and wheel owners throughout the summer only exacerbated public disgust. In late fall President Theodore Roosevelt responded to complaints in his state of the union address by suggesting that the best course of action was to federalize the entire Pacific fisheries. Even the *Morning Oregonian*, which adamantly opposed federalization, acknowledged the idea's wisdom:

> To stave off National control of Puget Sound and the Columbia River, it will be necessary for the conflicting Legislatures to agree right away on concurrent laws and afford needed salmon protection. They have tried this often enough in past years and just as often have failed, on account of the warring interests. It will hardly be disputed that it would be better to take fish control away from the States of Washington and Oregon and the Province of British Columbia, and place it in a higher authority, than to continue the destruction of salmon. It is, therefore, "up to" the lawmaking bodies of Oregon, Washington and British Columbia to "make good." This may be their last chance.[53]

The legislatures did make good, closing most loopholes in the following months and agreeing in principle and then fact to concurrent jurisdiction of the fisheries.[54] The states prevented federalization, but at a great cost to the industrial fishery. Having stripped the fishing industry of most of its political leverage by depriving it of the ability to play one state against the other, power devolved to whoever could control the state—nothing new there—but, as the June 1908 election demonstrated, that was no longer industrial fishers.

The industry's lack of influence manifested itself in various ways. In

September 1908, Master Fish Warden McAllister endorsed a plan drawn up by his predecessor to create a central hatchery at Bonneville. Van Dusen had proposed the hatchery as a way to achieve economies of scale by processing all the Commission's eggs at one location. Along with some of R. D. Hume's schemes, it was a classic example of trying to bend nature to economic reasoning. Sensing a flaw in this plan, wheel owners protested in court but only succeeded in delaying construction. When finished, the hatchery stood as a triumph of organization. Capable of incubating 60 million eggs and nursing 3 million more in retaining ponds, it was billed as the largest hatchery in the world. But when put into operation, the plant accelerated the concentration of salmon reproduction in the lower Columbia. Fish culturists collected eggs from all over the state, but when workers released the young salmon at Bonneville instead of their original spawning beds, the fishes' homing instincts were affected. Taking from Peter to pay Paul undermined upstream runs, hurting wheel owners and Indian fishers alike.[55]

The most significant legacy of the 1908 election lay in the new voting patterns. The election had signaled a seismic shift in the political landscape of fishery politics. While the gillnetters' initiative received over 7,000 votes more than the wheel owners', both groups discovered that a new force controlled the political fate of the salmon fisheries. In the realm of initiative politics, power shifted from cannery offices and union halls to urban ballot boxes. Over half of all votes came from the counties containing the urban spaces of Portland, Oregon City, Salem, Eugene, Roseburg, and Medford. Multnomah County alone accounted for over a quarter of the votes.[56]

The spatial implications of urban voter influence did not so much defuse tensions within the industrial fishery as thoroughly rearrange the balance of political power. Urbanites consume a large percentage of commercially caught fish, but they also fish. However, the way urbanites fish—angling— and the reason why—leisure—produced a cultural fissure between the interests of industrial fishers and those of Oregon's most significant voting block that physical distance only reinforced. Voters began to lose sight of the material connections between the industrial fishery and urban consumption. The resulting social myopia provided anglers with the political leverage necessary to ensure that they would be the ultimate political beneficiaries of the 1908 election.[57]

Following the 1908 election, anglers appropriated the conservation banner for their own campaign to control fishery space. Tapping into a sympathetic electorate in November 1910, Medford anglers persuaded Oregon voters to close the Rogue River to gillnets—again over the opposition of the *Morning Oregonian*. The death of R. D. Hume had been a critical loss to fishing interests on the lower Rogue. Without Hume, gillnetters possessed neither the talents nor the resources to refute the misinformation of their upstream opponents. In 1911, Oregon anglers institutionalized their political power in a revamped Board of Fish and Game Commissioners dominated by anglers. Gillnetters succeeded in reopening the Rogue three years later, but only by conceding to a series of humiliating compromises. Other fishers proved less fortunate. An angler-sponsored initiative closed the Willamette to gillnets in 1918. In 1926, anglers teamed with gillnetters to outlaw fishwheels, traps, and seines throughout Oregon, but thereafter anglers resumed their campaign against all nets. In 1927, they persuaded voters to close the Nestucca River, in 1935 the Rogue again, and in 1946 almost every other coastal stream. In less than four decades, anglers had succeeded in claiming almost exclusive access to Oregon's salmon fishing spaces.[58]

The 1908 election was a watershed moment in the spatialized politics of Oregon's salmon fishery. Anglers unleashed a potent political movement by tapping into public disgust with the industrial fishery, yet in their tactics, agendas, and results they essentially emulated their opponents. Anglers deployed the rhetoric of conservation with great facility, and they succeeded in claiming exclusive use of vast stretches of fishery space by displacing netters from most Oregon streams. But as the past half century has shown, such efforts did not result in conservation. If anything, decline accelerated. And the greatest human-driven agents of decline—overlogging, overgrazing, and dam building—were largely conducted to satisfy the consumption demands of the growing urban centers that were the political base of anglers. Yet despite their successes, anglers failed to kill the industrial fishery. They merely displaced it to the ocean, where it grew tremendously after World War II and remained essentially unregulated until the late 1970s.[59]

It is not enough to discuss environmental history the way Perry Miller talked about Puritans. The past did not occur on the head of a pin but across expansive, interconnected space. Abstract issues like gear rivalries, state jurisdiction, and artificial propagation produced physical effects. The act of defining borders shaped human activity and, by extension, the surrounding environment. Nature responded to such changes on its own terms, often causing humans to compensate in new ways. Social history and natural history informed each other reciprocally. The two cannot be disentangled. The spatial analysis that Soja, Pred, and others suggest makes such insights

Again David Orr

This editorial cartoon by Jack Ohman captures the hopelessly simplistic and circular arguments that still shape debates about the salmon crisis.
(*Oregonian*, September 5, 1994)

possible in ways standard narrative has not. This is not a call to abandon history for geography, but historians do need to expand their vistas.

The rapid decline of salmon stocks during the last 150 years cannot be adequately explained without addressing all the *interrelated* forces, yet Pacific Northwesterners continue to think about their history as discrete problems and events. They do so because it is functional to do so. In the spatialized politics of the salmon fishery, one must offer selective histories in order to play the Blame Game effectively. Anglers, industrial fishers, Indians, dam operators, aluminum smelters, barge owners, irrigators, grazers, miners, and loggers continue to accuse each other of endangering salmon in order to claim the title *most worthy protector*. This is how Kenneth Peterson, president of Columbia Aluminum, one of the largest consumers of electric power generated by Columbia River dams, could in the name of saving salmon institute a lawsuit to stop gillnetting and still keep a straight face.[60] It is why political solutions such as the 1992 ballot Measure 8, written by anglers interested in eliminating gillnets from the lower Columbia River and only barely defeated, remain political staples of fishery politics. Salmon management continues to resemble what Edward Soja has called "the restless formation and reformation of geographical landscapes." The contest is still about claiming space in order to control who will have access to and benefit from salmon and salmon streams; it is still a battle to produce space, to have salmon and consume them, too.

Thus the challenge is not to let R. D. Hume's tirade about politics become a reductive way of thinking about history. Hume's politics, like modern politics, existed within a spatial context, the implications of which are crucial to understand both the tensions and consequences of action. The process of transforming the natural spaces of rivers into social spaces produced myriad consequences to both people and fish. Hume's attempt to truncate nature on the Rogue was repeated throughout Oregon and the Pacific Northwest. His unchallenged claims about fish culture unleashed a giddy assault on salmon habitat, the results of which have been devastating to both salmon and the people who depend upon them.

In compensation for failure, Oregonians chose not to change their ways but to build a fine tradition of demonizing one social group after another in order to exclude them from fishery space, all so they could continue their own destructive ways. The list of intended victims can be ticked off by race and ethnicity: Indians, African Americans (by state constitution), Asians, and Austrians (during World War I); or by activity: purse seiners, trollers, seiners, trapmen, wheel owners, gillnetters, and trollers again. Oregonians systematically excluded each group in the name of conservation, yet protection did not follow. The solutions were and remain purely superficial. Eliminating gear deflected questions about overconsumption instead of addressing the underlying issues of markets, growth, and lifestyle. Such evasions will end only when historians succeed in changing the way society thinks about the past. Only by reincorporating time with space will the politics of R. D. Hume cease to be salient.

NOTES

1. Garrett Hardin, "The Tragedy of the Commons," *Science* 162 (December 13, 1962): 1243–48. For historical applications of the commons model, see Arthur F. McEvoy, *The Fisherman's Problem: Ecology and Law in the California Fisheries, 1850–1980* (Cambridge and New York: Cambridge University Press, 1986); and Louis S.

Warren, *The Hunter's Game: Poachers and Conservationists in Twentieth-Century America* (New Haven: Yale University Press, 1997). For opposing arguments, see Bonnie J. McCay, "The Culture of the Commoners: Historical Observations on Old and New World Fisheries," in *The Question of the Commons: The Culture and Ecology of Communal Resources*, ed. Bonnie J. McCay and James M. Acheson (Tucson: University of Arizona Press, 1987), 195–216.

2. For racial politics, see Chris Friday, *Organizing Asian American Labor: The Pacific Coast Canned-Salmon Industry, 1870–1942* (Philadelphia: Temple University Press, 1994); and Joseph E. Taylor III, "Who's in Charge Here Anyway?: Contested Federal Authority at Warm Springs Reservation in the Late Nineteenth Century," paper presented at the annual conference of the Pacific Northwest Historical Association, March 1993.

3. The number of gillnet boats on the Columbia increased until 1915; Courtland L. Smith, *Salmon Fishers of the Columbia* (Corvallis: Oregon State University Press, 1979), 107–8. Coastal rivers experienced similar patterns of congestion before 1920; John N. Cobb, *Pacific Salmon Fisheries*, Fisheries Doc. 1092, U.S. Department of Commerce, Bureau of Fisheries (Washington, D.C.: Government Printing Office, 1930), 565–70; see also the annual reports of the Fish Commission and Fish and Game Commission for the state of Oregon.

4. Edward W. Soja, *Postmodern Geographies: The Reassertion of Space in Critical Social Theory* (London: Verso, 1989), 32, 11.

5. Allan Pred, *Making Histories and Constructing Human Geographies: The Local Transformation of Practice, Power Relations, and Consciousness* (Boulder: Westview Press, 1990), 12. See also Denis Cosgrove, *Social Formation and Symbolic Landscape* (London: Croom Helm, 1984); Michel Foucault, "Questions on Geography," in *Power/Knowledge: Selected Interviews and Other Writings*, ed. and trans. Colin Gordon (New York: Pantheon, 1980), 63–77; Cole Harris, "Power, Modernity, and Historical Geography," *Annals of the Association of American Geographers* 81 (December 1991): 671–83; Henri Lefebvre, *The Production of Space*, trans. Donald Nicholson-Smith (Cambridge: Blackwell, 1991); and Soja, *Postmodern Geographies*.

6. C. Groot and L. Margolis, eds., *Pacific Salmon Life Histories* (Vancouver: University of British Columbia Press, 1991).

7. Randall F. Schalk, "Estimating Salmon and Steelhead Usage in the Columbia Basin Before 1850: The Anthropological Perspective," *Northwest Environmental Journal* 2, no. 2 (1986): 14–20; Joseph A. Craig and Robert L. Hacker, "The History and Development of the Fisheries of the Columbia River," *Bulletin of the Bureau of Fisheries* 49 (1940): 139–50; Smith, *Salmon Fishers*.

8. Irene Martin, *Legacy and Testament: The Story of Columbia River Gillnetters* (Pullman: Washington State University Press, 1994).

9. Livingston Stone to Spencer Baird, 14 June 1877, Letters Received from Livingston Stone, 1874–77, Record Group 22, National Archives, College Park (hereafter cited as RG 22, NA). See also Livingston Stone, "Report of Operations at the Salmon-Hatching Station on the Clackamas River, Oregon, in 1877," *Report of the Commissioner of Fish and Fisheries* (Washington, D.C.: Government Printing Office, 1877), 787; Taylor, "Who's in Charge Here Anyway?"; Spencer F. Baird, "Salmon Fisheries in Oregon," *Morning Oregonian* (Portland), March 3, 1875, 1; George N. Kiladis and Henry F. Diaz, "An Analysis of the 1877–78 ENSO Episode and Comparison with 1982–83," *Monthly Weather Review* 114 (June 1986): 1035–47; William H. Quinn, Victor T. Neal, and Santiago E. Atunez de Mayolo, "El Niño Occurrences Over the Past Four and a Half Centuries," *Journal of Geophysical Research* 92 (December 15, 1987): 14,451; Gary D. Sharp, "Fishery Catch Records, El Niño/Southern Oscillation, and Longer-Term Climate Change as Inferred from Fish Remains in Marine Sediments," in *El Niño: Historical and Paleoclimatic Aspects of the Southern Oscillation*, ed. Henry F. Diaz and Vera Markgraf (New York: Cambridge University Press, 1992), 379–417; Lawrence A. Mysak, "El Niño, Interannual Variability and Fisheries in the Northeast Pacific Ocean," *Canadian Journal of Fisheries and Aquatic Sciences* 43 (February 1986): 464–97; Thomas E. Nickelson, "Influences of Upwelling, Ocean Temperature, and Smolt Abundance on Marine Survival of Coho Salmon (*Oncorhynchus kisutch*) in the Oregon Production Area," *Canadian Journal of Fisheries and Aquatic Sciences* 43 (March 1986): 527–35; Smith, *Salmon Fishers*; R. D. Hume, *A Pygmy Monopolist: The Life and Doings of R. D. Hume, Written by Himself and Dedicated to His Neighbors*, ed. Gordon B. Dodds (Madison: University of Wisconsin, 1961), 46, 50.

10. Stone to Baird, 18 June 1872, vol. VII, Letters Received, 1871–74, RG 22, NA, p. 98 (italics in the original); Dean Conrad Allard, Jr., *Spencer Fullerton Baird and the U.S. Fish Commission* (New York: Arno Press, 1978); George Brown Goode, "Epochs in the History of Fish Culture," *Transactions of the American Fisheries Society* 10 (1879): 34–57; Livingston Stone, "Some Brief Reminiscences of the Early Days of Fish-Culture in the United States," *U.S. Fish Commission Bulletin* (Washington, D.C.: Government Printing Office, 1897): 337–43.

11. R. D. Hume, *Salmon of the Pacific Coast* (San Francisco: Schmidt Label and Lithographic, 1893), 22–23.

12. Oregon, *First and Second Annual Reports of the Fish and Game Protector to the Governor, 1893–4* (Salem: State Printer, 1894), 9 (the reports, published under many different titles, are hereafter cited as *Oregon Fish Commission Reports*); Baird to Stone, 31 May 1873, vol. 5, Press Copies of Letters Sent, RG 22, NA, pp. 108–9.

13. *Oregon Fish Commission Reports* (1902), 64; (1888), 3; (1899), 16; (1901), 8. Researchers would eventually learn that early hatcheries were at best no help, at

worst clearly destructive; Willis H. Rich, "A Statistical Analysis of the Results of the Artificial Propagation of Chinook Salmon," typescript in the reprint file of the library at the Northwest Fisheries Science Center, U.S. Fish and Wildlife Service, Seattle, Washington; R. E. Foerster and W. E. Ricker, "A Synopsis of the Investigations at Cultus Lake, British Columbia, Conducted by the Biological Board of Canada into the Life History and Propagation of Sockeye Salmon, 1924–1937," Pacific Biological Station, Nanaimo, British Columbia, December 1937, typescript in Fisheries Library, University of Washington, Seattle; Willis H. Rich, "Early History and Seaward Migration of Chinook Salmon in the Columbia and Sacramento Rivers," *Bulletin of the Bureau of Fisheries* 37 (Washington, D.C.: Government Printing Office, 1919–20): 68.

14. Robert C. Wissmar, Jeanette E. Smith, Bruce A. McIntosh, Hiram W. Li, Gordon H. Reeves, and James R. Sedell, "A History of Resource Use and Disturbance in Riverine Basins of Eastern Oregon and Washington (Early 1800s–1990s)," *Northwest Science* 68 (1994): 1–35; and Bruce A. McIntosh, James R. Sedell, Jeanette E. Smith, Robert C. Wissmar, Sharon E. Clarke, Gordon H. Reeves, and Lisa A. Brown, "Historical Changes in Fish Habitat for Select River Basins of Eastern Oregon and Washington," *Northwest Science* 68 (1994): 36–53. On El Niño see Quinn et al., "El Niño Occurrences Over the Past Four and a Half Centuries," 14, 451; McEvoy, *The Fisherman's Problem,* 72.

15. Smith, *Salmon Fishers,* 28–30, 48–49, 53–54; Friday, *Organizing Asian American Labor,* 45–46, 68.

16. For snag unions see Craig and Hacker, "The History and Development of the Fisheries of the Columbia River," 166–67; Martin, *Legacy and Testament,* 70.

17. Martin, *Legacy and Testament,* 70–71, 73, 83–99; Smith, *Salmon Fishers,* 91–93.

18. Smith, *Salmon Fishers,* 54 (quotation), and 30, 31, 91–93; W. A. Jones, *The Salmon Fisheries of the Columbia River,* Sen. Ex. Doc. 123, 50th Cong., 1st sess. (1887), 2510.

19. *Oregon Fish Commission Reports* (1889), 4 (quotation); Smith, *Salmon Fishers,* 83–85.

20. *Oregon Fish Commission Reports* (1904), 105, 109–11, 119–22, 134–35; "Sacramento Fishermen," *Pacific Fisherman* (Seattle), June 1905, 19; *Oregon Fish Commission Reports* (1905), 9.

21. Cobb, *Pacific Salmon Fisheries,* 570. *Oregon Fish Commission Reports* (1901), 62; (1904), 183; (1905), 122. George M. Bowers to Governor of Oregon, 16 January 1905, vol. 654, Press Copies of Letters Sent, 1871–1906, RG 22, NA, p. 6456. Concurrent legislation was a long-standing problem between the states; Jones, *Sal-*

mon *Fisheries of the Columbia River*, 5; *Oregon Fish Commission Reports* (1904), 109–11; Smith, *Salmon Fishers*.

22. Livingston Stone, "Explorations on the Columbia River from the Head of Clarke's Fork to the Pacific Ocean, Made in the Summer of 1883, with Reference to the Selection of a Suitable Place for Establishing a Salmon-Breeding Station," *Report of the Commissioner of Fish and Fisheries* (Washington, D.C.: Government Printing Office, 1883), 238.

23. Cobb, *Pacific Salmon Fisheries*, 233–34; Fish and Game Commission minutes, 8 June 1904, box 1, folder 1, Department of Fish and Wildlife papers, Oregon State Archives, Salem (hereafter cited as ODFW Papers), p. 114; J. N. Wisner to Commissioner, 16 December 1906, and Waldo Hubbard to Commissioner, 19 March 1907, box 4, Records Concerning Abandoned Stations, 1879–1931, RG 22, NA.

24. Claudius Wallich to Commissioner, 14 May 1904, box 4, Records Concerning Abandoned Stations, 1879–1931, RG 22, NA; Wisner to Commissioner, 1 August 1904, vol. 641, Press Copies of Letters Sent, 1871–1906, RG 22, NA, p. 1287; Henry O'Malley to Commissioner, 12 August 1912, box 8, Records Concerning Fish Culture Stations, 1875–1929, RG 22, NA.

25. Leonard A. Fulton, "Spawning Areas and Abundance of Steelhead Trout and Coho, Sockeye, and Chum Salmon in the Columbia River Basin—Past and Present," *United States Fish and Wildlife Service Special Scientific Report* 618 (Washington, D.C.: Government Printing Office, 1970), 5, 16.

26. Memorandum to Deputy Commissioner, Press Copies of Letters Sent, 1871–1906, vol. 657, RG 22, NA, p. 8118; Bowers to Governor of Oregon, 16 January 1905, vol. 654, Press Copies of Letters Sent, 1871–1906, RG 22, NA, p. 6456.

27. Gordon B. Dodds, *The Salmon King of Oregon: R. D. Hume and the Pacific Fisheries* (Chapel Hill: University of North Carolina Press, 1959); Hume, *A Pygmy Monopolist*; W. deC. Ravenal to S. W. Downing, 28 February 1900, vol. 532, and Ravenal to E. N. Carter, 2 July 1900, vol. 544, Press Copies of Letters Sent, 1871–1906, RG 22, NA, pp. 7188, 682.

28. Hume, *Salmon of the Pacific Coast*, 17–20; McEvoy, *The Fisherman's Problem*, 73.

29. Hume, *A Pygmy Monopolist*, 45–50; Dodds, *Salmon King*, 131; Patrick Spurlock, "A History of the Salmon Industry in the Pacific Northwest" (M.A. thesis, University of Oregon, 1940), 124.

30. *Morning Oregonian*, July 27, 1877, 3; Hume, *A Pygmy Monopolist*, 46–48; Dodds, *Salmon King*, 81, 107–9, 111–12; R. D. Hume to Robert McLean, 1 June 1896, vol. 84, R. D. Hume Papers, Special Collections, Knight Library, University of Oregon, Eugene (hereafter cited as Hume Papers), 582–91; Fish and Game Commis-

sion minutes, box 1, folder 1, ODFW Papers, p. 67; Bowers to R. D. Hume, 25 August 1902, vol. 591, Press Copies of Letters Sent, 1871–1906, RG 22, NA, p. 1141.

31. Dodds, *Salmon King,* chap. 6; Groot and Margolis, *Pacific Salmon Life Histories.*

32. Richard A. Cooley, *Politics and Conservation: The Decline of the Alaska Salmon* (New York: Harper and Row, 1963); Bowers to Wm. S. Crowell, 19 January 1900, and Bowers to R. D. Hume, 29 January 1900, vol. 529, Press Copies of Letters Sent, 1871–1906, RG 22, NA, pp. 5798, 5945.

33. R. D. Hume to Editor, 29 July 1907, vol. 90, Hume Papers; H. C. McAllister to R. D. Hume, 11 September 1908, and O'Malley to R. D. Hume, 12 September 1908, box 7, Hume Papers. Hume objected strenuously to shipping Rogue River eggs elsewhere, but had no qualms about reversing that equation; Ravenal to Downing, 13 December 1899, vol. 530, Press Copies of Letters Sent, 1871–1906, RG 22, NA, p. 6065.

34. R. D. Hume to Herbert Hume, 18 June 1906, Hume Papers, box 4.

35. Gordon B. Dodds, "Rogue River Monopoly," *Pacific Historical Review* 27 (August 1958): 267, 271–72, 278–79; *Oregon Fish Commission Reports* (1906), 152; Dodds, *Salmon King,* 150–52; W. C. Hale to R. D. Hume, 28 May 1906, and J. O. Hawthorn to R. D. Hume, 29 May 1906, box 4, Hume Papers.

36. R. D. Hume to Herbert Hume, 20 December 1907, box 7, Hume Papers.

37. Dodds, *Salmon King.* For "meanness," "scrub," and "gangs," see R. D. Hume to Herbert Hume, 27 August 1906, box 6, 24 November 1907 and 17 November 1907, box 7, Hume Papers. For "incompetence" and "Millionaire," see "Declines to Pay Taxes," *Recorder* (Bandon), 18 November 1906, 3; "About Those Fish Licenses," *Radium* (Wedderburn), 7 November 1907, 3; Bowers to Downing, 12 April 1900, vol. 535, Press Copies of Letters Sent, 1871–1906, RG 22, NA, p. 8473. For "crowds," "cowardly," "Lord," and "baron," see Dodds, "Rogue River Monopoly," 265, 276, 279; *Morning Oregonian,* November 21, 1907.

38. W. deC. Ravenal to Carter, 2 July 1900, vol. 544, Press Copies of Letters Sent, 1871–1906, RG 22, NA, p. 682. See also McEvoy, *The Fisherman's Problem,* 110. For a detailed but problematic discussion of Hume's hatchery work, see Gordon B. Dodds, "Artificial Propagation of Salmon in Oregon, 1875–1910: A Chapter in American Conservation," *Pacific Northwest Quarterly* 50 (October 1959): 125–33.

39. *Washington v. Oregon,* 211 U.S. 127–36 (1908); *Washington v. Oregon,* 214 U.S. 205–18 (1909); *Oregon Fish Commission Reports* (1908), 138–39; "Settle the Boundary Line," *Pacific Fisherman,* April 1905, 10; "State of Oregon Gets Sand Island," *Pacific Fisherman,* December 1908, 17; Lawrence D. Jackson, "Reminiscence: Lawrence D. Jackson on Sand Island Fishing," *Oregon Historical Quarterly* 89 (Spring 1988): 30–69.

40. "Sand Island Contest," *Pacific Fisherman*, June 1905, 18–19; "State of Oregon Gets Sand Island," *Pacific Fisherman*, December 1908, 17.

41. Oregon Legislature, *Report of Special Committee to Examine into and Investigate the Fishing Industry of This State* (Salem: State Printer, 1893), 4; "Fish Warden to Move His Office," *Morning Oregonian*, March 29, 1908, 8; "Analysis of Fish Bills," *Morning Oregonian*, February 25, 1908, 8; "Rival Salmon Bills," *Morning Oregonian*, March 9, 1908, 6.

42. "Save the Salmon," *Morning Oregonian*, March 20, 1908, 10; Miller Freeman to Bowers, 18 June 1908, box 1, Correspondence with Publishers of *Pacific Fisherman*, 1903–17, RG 22, NA.

43. *Oregon Fish Commission Reports* (1904), 115, 132; (1907), 6–7.

44. Ed. Rosenberg, "Says Fishwheels, Traps, and Seines Are Destroying Columbia Salmon Fishing Industry," *Morning Oregonian*, June 29, 1907, 12; *Oregon Fish Commission Reports* (1908), 129–33; for initiative handbills see box 1, folder 27, Frank M. Warren Papers, Oregon Historical Society, Portland; "Van Dusen May Lose His Scalp," *Morning Oregonian*, February 3, 1908, 10; "Laws on Salmon for Two States," *Morning Oregonian*, February 3, 1908, 15; "Governor After Van Dusen's Head," *Morning Oregonian*, February 5, 1908, 7; "Make Answer to Astoria Fishers," *Morning Oregonian*, February 22, 1908, 6.

45. Van Dusen's problems began well before his remarks against wheels and traps and extended to all corners of the fishery; Fish and Game Commission minutes, box 1, folders 1 and 2, ODFW Papers, pp. 100, 118–19; Samuel Elmore to R. D. Hume, 14 August 1907, box 8, Hume Papers; "Fish Commissioner Office Change," *Telegraph* (Portland), 4 March 1908; W. W. Ridehalgh to Frank Benson, 16 March 1908, Frank Williamson Benson Papers, Oregon Historical Society, Portland (hereafter cited as Benson Papers); for replacement of Van Dusen see J. L. Kruse to Benson, 17 February 1907; W. P. Andrus to Benson, 20 February 1907; H. G. Van Dusen to Benson, 23 February 1908; [Benson] to Van Dusen, 26 February 1908; John C. McCue to Benson, 7 March 1908; Benson to McCue, 12 March 1908; W. M. Cake to Benson, 13 March 1908; Van Dusen to Benson, 17 March 1908; Frank Seufert to Benson, 6 April 1908; Benson to Seufert, 4 May 1908, all in Benson Papers. Not everyone favored Van Dusen's dismissal. Gillnetters supported him to the end, and at least one fellow Republican cautioned against his removal to preserve party unity; Fish and Game Commission minutes, box 1, folder 2, ODFW Papers, p. 116; "Want Van Dusen Retained," *Morning Oregonian*, 16 February 1908, 7; Alma D. Katz to Benson, 7 February 1907, Benson Papers.

46. *Morning Oregonian* articles: "Will Oust Warden," March 11, 1908, 6; "Van Dusen Out, M'Allister In," March 26, 1908, 6; "New Fish Warden Is H. C. McAllister," March 26, 1908; March 27, 1908, 7; "Remarks on the New Fish War-

den and the Reasons for His Appointment," March 31, 1908, 8. McAllister proved no less partisan, and he soon found himself trapped by the same problems of political patronage as his predecessors; H. C. McAllister to Benson, 4 August 1908, Benson Papers. "Fish Warden To Move His Office," *Morning Oregonian*, March 29, 1908, 8.

47. For quotation see Dodds, "Rogue River Monopoly," 278–80; Dodds, *Salmon King*, 151–54.

48. "Protect Our Salmon [advertisement]," *Morning Oregonian*, May 31, 1908, 11.

49. "Last Word on Bill No. 332 [advertisement]," *Morning Oregonian*, June 1, 1908, 6.

50. *Morning Oregonian* articles: "Analysis of Fish Bills," February 25, 1908, 8; W. Hampton Smith, "River Fish Bills and the Oregon Initiative," March 1, 1908, Magazine section, 9; "Rival Salmon Bills," March 9, 1908, 6; "Ballot Lawmaking," May 29, 1908, 10; "Just a Pointer for Your Guidance Next Monday," May 30, 1908, 3; "Lest You Forget How to Vote Today on These Measures," June 1, 1908, 4; "A Little Tough on the Fish," June 4, 1908, 1.

51. *Morning Oregonian* articles: "Vote Down the Fishery Bills," May 14, 1908, 8; "Modify Fish Laws," May 25, 1908, 8; "Analysis of Fish Bills," February 25, 1908, 8.

52. *Oregon Fish Commission Reports* (1908), 130–33; (1909), 6.

53. "To Arrest Seufert Brothers," *Morning Oregonian*, September 13, 1908, A8; "Would Arrest M'Allister," *Morning Oregonian*, September 16, 1908, 12; *Congressional Reporter*, 60th Cong., 2d sess., vol. 43, 26; "States' Rights for Fisheries," *Morning Oregonian*, December 7, 1908, 6.

54. *Oregon Fish Commission Reports* (1909), 10–12; "Fishing Laws to Suit Two States," *Morning Oregonian*, January 31, 1909, sec. 1, 6; "Interstate Fish War Soon to End," *Morning Oregonian*, February 1, 1909, 1, 2.

55. *Oregon Fish Commission Reports* (1907), 30–31; (1908), 128–29. *Morning Oregonian* articles: "Central Salmon Hatchery," February 13, 1908, 7; "Guard Salmon Fry," September 2, 1908, 14; "Hatcheries Need Support," February 3, 1909, 18; "Salmon Hatchery for Bonneville," July 8, 1909, 11; "Big Hatchery to Open," November 9, 1909, 6; "Salmon Hatchery Dedicated Today," November 15, 1909, 9; "Land for Hatchery," September 21, 1907, 16. Leonard A. Fulton, "Spawning Areas and Abundance of Chinook Salmon (*Oncorhynchus tshawytscha*) in the Columbia River Basin—Past and Present," *United States Fish and Wildlife Service Special Scientific Report* 571 (Washington, D.C.: Government Printing Office, 1968), 23; Fulton, "Spawning Areas and Abundance of Steelhead Trout and Coho, Sockeye, and Chum Salmon," 32–34.

56. For vote totals, see abstracts of elections, Secretary of State Papers, Oregon State Archives, Salem.

57. Colleen J. Sheehy, "American Angling: The Rise of Urbanism and the Ro-

mance of the Rod and Reel," in *Hard at Play: Leisure in America, 1840–1940,* ed. Kathryn Grover (Amherst: University of Massachusetts Press, 1992), 78–92; Thomas L. Altherr, "The American Hunter-Naturalist and the Development of the Code of Sportsmanship," *Journal of Sport History* 5 (Spring 1978): 7–22; John F. Reiger, *American Sportsmen and the Origins of Conservation,* rev. ed. (Norman: University of Oklahoma Press, 1986), 25–49; Philip G. Terrie, "Urban Man Confronts the Wilderness: The Nineteenth-Century Sportsman in the Adirondacks," *Journal of Sports History* 5 (Winter 1978): 7–20.

58. Gordon B. Dodds, "The Fight to Close the Rogue," *Oregon Historical Quarterly* 60 (December 1959): 461–63, 464–66, 470–74; "Initiative and Referendum Measures," *Morning Oregonian,* November 3, 1910, 12; Morris S. Isseks, "History of State Administrative Agencies in Oregon, 1843–1937," Report on Projects O.P. 65-94-823 and O.P. 165-94-6052 Under Auspices of the Works Progress Administration (1939), typescript at Oregon State Library, Salem, 236; Courtland L. Smith, *Oregon Fish Fights* (Corvallis: Oregon State University Sea Grant College Program, 1974), 3; Courtland L. Smith, *Fish or Cut Bait* (Corvallis: Oregon State University Sea Grant College Program, 1977), 29; Joseph E. Taylor III, "For the Love of It: A Short History of Commercial Fishing in Pacific City, Oregon," *Pacific Northwest Quarterly* 82 (January 1991): 26–27.

59. William G. Robbins, *Hard Times in Paradise: Coos Bay, Oregon, 1850–1986* (Seattle: University of Washington Press, 1988); William Dietrich, *The Final Forest: The Battle for the Last Great Trees of the Pacific Northwest* (New York: Simon and Schuster, 1992); Anthony Nerboy, *The Columbia River Salmon and Steelhead Trout: Their Fight for Survival* (Seattle: University of Washington Press, 1980); Spurlock, "A History of the Salmon Industry in the Pacific Northwest"; J. E. Damron, "The Emergence of Salmon Trolling on the American Northwest Coast: A Maritime Historical Geography" (Ph.D. diss., University of Oregon, 1975); Willa Nehlsen, Jack E. Williams, and James A. Lichatowich, "Pacific Salmon at the Crossroads: Stocks at Risk from California, Oregon, Idaho, and Washington," *Fisheries* 16 (March–April 1991): 4–21.

60. Richard White, *The Organic Machine: The Remaking of the Columbia River* (New York: Hill and Wang, 1995), 105.

Nature's Industries

The Rhetoric of Industrialism in the Oregon Country

WILLIAM G. ROBBINS

[handwritten marginalia: See Second paper private timber mopped-out by 1940's]

In the conventional view, the material conditions of the late nineteenth-century American West presented a landscape filled with promise and opportunity, and a story line imbued with the notion of progress.[1] The Oregon country in particular, according to its boosters, was a land abounding in potential, a place where nature's wealth and human technical genius would combine to forge the good society, to provide decent, stable lives for citizens of all generations. The future, in that view, was full with the expectation of improvement, with the hope that in this special place the next generation would banish want and indigence. An effusive narrative line—pursued in travel and real estate brochures, commercial club and promotional pamphlets, and through the regional newspapers—celebrated the region's seemingly limitless opportunity. Those booming rhetorical devices were linked, of course, to very practical ambitions that envisioned the "commodification" of resources for human consumption, turning nature's wealth into personal wealth.

The transcendent vehicle for that transformation, the boosters argued, was a lush and abundant landscape in which nature would be put to work to benefit humankind. The entire Northwest, *Pacific Monthly* enthused in 1904, was a field laden with opportunity. Everything that nature could provide or the human imagination conceive was present in the region: "Beautiful and fertile valleys, glorious and majestic mountain and river scenery, wonderful forests, mines of gold, silver, copper, nickel, . . . rivers teeming with fish. . . . We have it; we are in possession of it—this garden spot, this land pregnant with hidden resources, possibilities that almost

[handwritten marginalia: I tend to think of our generation (the first to be so absorbed) but it's not true]

264

"Oregon's Easter Hat" (cartoon by Harry Murphy, *Oregonian*, 1909)

stagger the imagination, opportunities!!" The "material dialectic" of that world was centered in a burgeoning global capitalism, booming industrial development in the eastern United States, explosive economic growth in the Oregon country, and a sense of confidence that the future would bring rich material rewards. The great need of the moment, therefore, was to get on with the task of turning those natural advantages to personal gain.[2]

The narrative accounts prefiguring that remarkable period of change had already served up powerful metaphorical tools that ascribed meaning to conditions and circumstances in Oregon and the Pacific Northwest. It can be said with some accuracy that the rhetoric defining the relationship between culture and landscape, between human activity and environmental change, assumed a more assertive and confident—even arrogant—tone with the onset of the industrial era. The advent of stream power, expressed especially with the coming of the railroad, marked an increasingly more intrusive cultural presence in the region. Railroads were the main instrument in the expansion of industrial capitalism across the United States—vehicles, Alan Trachtenberg has argued, that "re-created American nature into 'natural resources' for commodity production." For regions of North America distant from metropolitan markets, the steam-powered locomotives were physical symbols of industrialism, of mechanization, visible representations of change—social, economic, political, and environmental.3

Long before the coming of railroads to the Oregon country, dreamers and other fanciful witnesses drew attention to the complementarity between the region's natural abundance and the symbols of industrialism. Peter H. Burnett, an early immigrant to Oregon and future governor of California, gave voice to the industrial potential of the country when he pointed to the "inexhaustible quantities" of timber along the Columbia River "just where the water power is at hand to cut it up." And in 1849, the seminal year of the California gold rush, the first newspaper published in the Northwest, the *Oregon Spectator*, underscored the important link between resources (timber) and water power: "With these forests the slopes of our magnificent mountains are densely covered. And down those mountain slopes . . . come tumbling . . . thousands of creeks and rivers affording endless hydraulic privileges." The *Oregon Statesman* made a similar comparison a few years later, praising both the enormous value of the lumber business to Oregon and the "immense" water power nearby. Those images, linking protoindustrial activities to rivers and streams, suggest an affinity between the machinery of production and the natural world of a particular place.4

The Pacific Northwest abounded in romantic and ambitious visionaries, promoters whose resourceful and imaginative accounts about "developing" the country knew few restraints. An early travel guide published in 1846, Overton Johnson and William Winter's *Route Across the Rocky Mountains*, reported signs of incipient industrial activity on the lower Willamette River. Such bustle and commotion, the guide suggested, was mere prelude to the building of "villages, towns, and cities, with massive walls and glittering spires." The authors looked forward to the time when "the powerful locomotive, with its heavy train, will fly along the rattling railway; when . . . the proud steamer will dash along the majestic river."5

A decade later, and in language especially suited to mid-nineteenth century Fourth of July oratory, Washington Territory's J. W. Goodell envisioned a future where "well cultivated farms adorned with fields of golden wheat" had replaced the region's forests, where the "hum of machinery" could be heard near every waterfall, and where the shrill whistle of steamboats echoed dockside as they discharged and received the freight of "flourishing towns":

Sounds like hell

> I behold large cities, with their numerous spires, glistening in the rays of the morning sun, their streets teeming with busy thousands, and their numerous wharves crowded with immense steamers and ships from all parts of the world, receiving and discharging their immense cargoes. I turn my eyes eastward, and behold an immense train of rail road cars thundering down the inclined plain of the Cascades.[6]

For Theodore Winthrop, Boston scion and traveler through the Northwest, civilized humankind had never experienced "a fresh chance of developing itself under grand and stirring influences so large as in the Northwest." His compatriot and fellow pamphleteer, Samuel Bowles, made special mention of the Willamette Valley as "the garden of Oregon," the present bulwark of its prosperity, "its sure security for the future."[7]

The Oregon press aggressively promoted efforts, especially in hinterland areas, to join the industrial realm with earthly abundance. "The progress of new countries depends, to a great degree, upon their railroads, and their connection with extensive railroad systems," *Willamette Farmer* argued in 1872. In the case of the Rogue Valley, the newspaper praised Jackson County officials for constructing bridges and roads long before the arrival of the railroad. Improvements in transportation, it contended, would promote the development of the area's unparalleled water power and mill sites whose abundance was "sufficient . . . to drive the machinery for the milling and manufacturing purposes of an entire State." This "extensive basin of unsurpassed fertility and loveliness," the *Farmer* exclaimed, had been "supplied by nature" with all the elements necessary to build a "dense agricultural, manufacturing and mining population."[8]

even in their own propaganda they don't see the conflict

The peripatetic David Newsom, who wrote promotional articles for several Northwest publications, was one of the most energetic and artful in linking the region's abundance with the development of manufactories. In an essay published in 1876, Newsom praised Oregon's industrial resources, the "vast coal fields" in its southwestern counties and the great fishery on the Columbia River. But the state's "great source of wealth, . . . little appreciated as yet," was its immense stands of timber and abundant water power. Newsom then outlined an industrial vision that would capitalize on the state's natural wealth: "Capital and brains are needed to utilize them, and [to] erect factories, machine shops, foundries, fisheries, ship yards, rolling mills, nail factories, woolen mills, etc., and to push our commerce to foreign lands."[9]

Still the area's largest-circulation newspaper as the nineteenth century drew to a close, the Portland *Oregonian* was equally enthusiastic and boastful about the industrial potential of the region. "It is the language of truth and not of exaggeration which describes the great Northwest," proclaimed its January 1 issue of 1890. From timbered seacoast to wheat fields east of the Cascade Mountains, Oregon offered commercial advantages that would truly astonish the world. Even in its still sparsely settled coastal valleys, "the smoke of the settler's hut and. . . the sound of the woodsman's axe . . . [indicate] that the reign of Civilization is at hand." But it was along the winding Willamette River—that "exhaustless storehouse of manufacturing power"—where cities and towns were using the "power of the river to light their houses, factories and streets, and to turn the mills that clothe and feed them." With its rich soils, endless mineral wealth, and unmatched scenery, the *Oregonian* concluded, "Oregon is America in miniature."

As the decades passed, promoters extended those early visions of an agrarian paradise and the region's industrial potential to embrace other enterprises, especially those associated with new, more intrusive forms of human activity. What the economists refer to as "economic development" first came to the Oregon country with the building of the great transcontinental railroads, transportation arterials that linked the region's natural abundance to riverine and oceanic highways and to the industrial centers of the East.[10] The influence of the new transportation technology reverberated everywhere—from the expanding acreages of wheat in the interior country, to the rich mineral lodes in northern Idaho and the Rossland district in British Columbia, and to the fir, cedar, and pine forests throughout the Northwest.

In truth, during the last quarter of the nineteenth century, eastern and foreign capitalists viewed the northern West as a magnificent investment opportunity, a promoter's paradise. More than any other factor, therefore, the heavily capitalized railroads marked the arrival of the industrial world[11] and the subsequent transformation and reordering of the regional landscape. Even in agricultural settings such as Oregon's Willamette Valley—a seemingly nonindustrial environment—railroads vastly expanded the volume of trade, especially in speeding the delivery of modern plows and reapers.[12] As historian Carlos Schwantes puts it, the emergence of industry in the American hinterland was "the child of the steel rail."[13]

What is most fascinating about this period is the rhetoric defining human activity and its relation to particular places—the ongoing dialectic between culture and nature; the idea that the destinies of people and natural systems were intertwined. In his now classic work, *Space and Place*, the geographer Yi-Fu Tuan observes that culture explains how people "attach meaning to and organize space and place," and that myths tend to flourish in the absence of precise knowledge.[14] A reading of the literature promoting the development of an industrial infrastructure in the northern West gives substance to Tuan's assertion.

The salutatory issue of *West Shore* in 1875 listed its publisher and editor as L. Samuel, recently arrived in the city of Portland. Until it ceased publication in 1891, the magazine was the most assertive and widely circulated promotional journal in the Northwest. By 1877 it was being distributed in thirty-two states and Great Britain. While *West Shore* paid special attention to the price of agricultural land in Oregon and Washington Territory and regularly carried a section dubbed "Information for Immigrants," Samuel's greatest enthusiasm was the region's commercial and industrial growth, especially the building of railroads. Indeed, when Portland celebrated the completion of the Northern Pacific Railway in 1883, Samuel published a forty-six page souvenir edition.[15]

In an early issue, *West Shore* recalled those "brave and enterprising men" of the 1840s who created a "broad, solid, enduring foundation" from an "unredeemed wilderness." The building of that "superstructure" enabled the Oregon country to provide a "wealth of breadstuffs to the nations of Europe," an accomplishment that won the region prominence as a producer "in quality as well as quantity." Those early immigrants, the magazine concluded, would never have anticipated the productiveness of the present moment: "our lumbering trade, our unequaled Salmon fisheries, and our growing and increasing manufacturing enterprises—Iron Mines, Iron Works, Woolen Factories, Machine Shops, Furniture Manufactories, Ship Yards, Flouring, Oil, Paper, and other Mills—and the very lucrative and extensive lines of ocean and river steam navigation." Two years later *West Shore* again boasted about the region's natural abundance: "Her wheat and wool, lumber, salmon and fruits, make up an aggregate of commercial resources which must be considered

nothing aesthetic
where were
the John
Muirs
?

extraordinary." An endless wealth of timber "stored up" for future wants and limitless quantities of salmon provided a perpetual source of revenue.[16]

Other contributors to *West Shore* underscored the importance of water power as the grand feature of the Oregon country—"natural power," as one writer put it, that existed in greater quantity than anywhere else in the United States. The magazine touted the manufacturing productivity of the Willamette River in Clackamas County (its six sawmills, woolen mill, tub and bucket factory, paper mill, and iron reduction works), which, along with its abundant water power, promised an even greater industrial presence. In promoting the timber resources of Clatsop County, *West Shore* pointed to the juxtaposition of "timber of the finest quality . . . with numerous streams to float it to market." The Portland-based publication praised agricultural Linn County in the heart of "the great Willamette Valley, the 'garden of the world,' " for its "easy access to markets" made possible because of its proximity to steamboats on the nearby river.[17]

West Shore repeatedly cited the need for investment capital to build industrial enterprises to take advantage of the region's endless sources of wealth. To realize that "undeveloped richness," the magazine insisted that the critical and essential ingredient was capital.[18] *West Shore*'s reasoning suggested, in part, that nature's industries left unadorned would leave the region vulnerable, a potential victim to exploiters from afar. Left unsaid in that equation was the power and influence of distant capital itself.

But it was the steam locomotive that most energized those who wrote for *West Shore*. In an essay extolling the natural blessings of the Oregon country—agricultural productiveness, unlimited water power, excellence in fruit growing, and potential for manufacturing—writer P. B. Simmons observed in 1879 that the region was "only waiting for the magic touch of the iron horse to make it the richest producing section in our country." Writers for *West Shore* were particularly conscious of the revolution that railroads would bring to logging and lumbering operations. Extending a rail line through northwestern Oregon's Columbia County, one author predicted, would bring forth the full promise of its "rich and varied natural resources," especially its abundant timber resources. The absence of rail lines to "sections where the finest of the commercial woods are most abundant," the magazine observed, "has retarded the growth of the lumbering industry."[19]

Waterways, too, were industrial arterials, providing natural routes for transporting the region's bounty to processing centers and then on to national and global markets. The Coquille River on Oregon's southern coast, according to *West Shore*, was "a most beautiful stream having very much the appearance of a natural canal." Once the rocks at the mouth of the river were removed, there would be no obstacles "to the carrying of the immense wealth of this region [timber] out to the markets of the world." Without the river corridor, the natural wealth of the area might "lie dormant for generations." Loggers, it should be noted, were among the first to impose an industrial-like regimen on waterways to "flood" timber down smaller creeks to major streams where logs were placed in booms and then rafted to mills.[20]

Of special importance to the region, *West Shore* contended, were the vast resources of coal and iron and "the great quantity of timber on every hand." Moreover, manufacturing in the Oregon country had barely made a beginning. But there was a solution to the problem of sending the raw products of nature out to world markets: promote local manufacturing facilities that would turn the region's timber and other primary materials into finished products *before* they were shipped to rail and ocean highways. "Why enrich the laborers of other States at the expense of our fellow-workers?" *West Shore* inquired. "Why stop the wheels of industry, when the skilled operatives are waiting at the doors?"[21] Although this Portland monthly was not the only publication promoting the development of the region's bounty, for a time it surpassed all others in its uninhibited boasting.

By the last quarter of the nineteenth century, industrial technology in the form of steam power had reached far beyond railroad locomotives and waterborne stern wheelers. The distant forces of an industrializing world—an expanding market demand for lumber and the increased mechanization of production processes everywhere—spurred the adaptation of the machine to timber operations. Although steam-powered sawmills had operated along the North Pacific slope since the 1850s, not until the 1880s were steam-driven machines adapted to hauling in the felled timber. The growing use of steam donkeys to yard and load logs vastly stepped up the pace of activity in the woods—and disturbance to forest ecosystems. Speed and productivity were part of the new industrial ethos, and the adaptation of steam power to logging increased the operators' control over both their labor force and a difficult natural environment.[22]

As early as 1884, only four years after California redwoods logger John Dolbeer patented the first steam-powered yarding machine, *West Shore* observed that industrial technology was replacing human and animal power in woods operations. Under the heading "Our Industries and Resources," the magazine reported that railroads and steam engines were replacing skid roads and bull teams in some logging operations. The new machines, one logger reported, were capable of hauling "logs from three to four . . . miles to river or bay, at no greater cost than ox teams have done it one or two miles." Twenty years later, Grays Harbor lumberman George Emerson made the classic appraisal of the steam donkey: "When one considers [that] they . . . require no stable and no feed, that all expense stops when the whistle blows, no oxen killed and no teams to winter, no ground too wet, no hill too steep, it is easy to see they are a revolution in logging."[23]

Steam power also promoted the integration of production and marketing systems: the movement of fleece to woolen mills, shipments of mineral ores to smelters and reduction facilities, and the transport of felled timber to sawmills. Steam-driven engines enabled producers to circumvent the forces of nature, especially in the ability to move natural objects turned into commodities through difficult terrain and against riverine and tidal currents. The production and marketing system of the Willamette Steam Mills, Lumbering and Manufacturing Company, located on the banks of the Willamette River in North Portland, was a prototype of sorts for the more expansive enterprises that emerged in the twentieth century.

The production system of the Willamette Steam Mills originated deep in a Douglas-fir forest somewhere up the Columbia River. Steam donkeys yarded the felled and bucked timber to railroad sidings where the logs were loaded on cars and hauled to water's edge. From that point the logs were floated into booms and rafted down the Columbia and up the Willamette to the company's large, modern milling facility, a plant capable of turning out 250,000 board feet of lumber every twenty-four hours. The company possessed, according to one source, "Exceptional shipping facilities": (1) access to the Northern Pacific Railroad, whose tracks passed through its lumber yard, and (2) deep water wharves that fronted on the Willamette River. The firm sent large quantities of lumber eastward by rail, and it shipped equally sizable cargoes into the Pacific to markets in California, Central and South America, the Hawaiian Islands, and the Orient. From beginning to end, according to West Shore, that system brought a remarkable transformation in the forests adjacent to the Columbia River, converting the products of nature "into cities, towns and farms."[24]

Celebrating the region's natural abundance and its unlimited potential to enhance the fortunes of the state, the Oregonian promoted agricultural progress (including the expansion of irrigated acreages), railroad building, unrestricted open-river transportation, mineral development, and literally anything that would redound to the "opening up" of Portland's tributary region.

The growing metropolis on the lower Willamette River, the newspaper boasted, was a natural community, in both a commercial and a physical sense. By rail, ocean, and river, Portland was accessible to a vast resource-rich tributary region to the east and oceanic highways to the west; its "advantages of position" signaled that its expectations for the future were invincible.[25]

Despite Portland's trading prowess, writers for the *Oregonian* constantly urged the local business community to do more that would lead to a broadly based manufacturing infrastructure. On one occasion the newspaper chided the city for being little beyond "a depot for exchange of goods produced elsewhere." It accused men of property and wealth of "store keeping" rather than developing the metropolis as a center of production. For the area to become more than a point of transfer, the business community had to develop local manufactures founded on its own raw-material industries. In that way, Portland would attract "the trade of all the surrounding country" and make adjacent communities tributary to its own commerce. "To build up an industrial empire upon the western slope," the paper urged Portland entrepreneurs to develop processing facilities, "the raw material for which can be produced upon our own soil." The world beyond the city held "every requisite" in the way of raw materials; therefore, with its ideal natural location at the crossroads of commerce, it would be wise for those with investment capital to act.[26]

Working up its own wool, tanning its own hides, and canning its home-grown fruit would provide the city with a manufacturing infrastructure and expand the radius of its influence in the hinterland. Advances in the city's manufacturing and industrial sector eventually convinced *Oregonian* writers that Portland deserved status as a true metropolis. As the decade of the 1880s drew to a close, the community's financial indexes showed a 73 percent increase in manufacturing production. "Nothing is so strongly indicative of the progress of a city as its factories," the local press boasted. Railroad passenger lists, the arrival of immigrants and tourists, and increases in trade were all signs of advance, but manufactures demonstrated a city's ability to provide jobs for a large population and to produce goods for local consumption and for shipment elsewhere. In fact, Portland's growth during the last two decades of the nineteenth century suggests a considerable expansion in local industrial activity. The city's population grew from 17,577 in 1880, to 46,385 in 1890, and then nearly doubled to 90,426 by 1900.

Portland's increasingly urban and industrial appearance by the turn of the century was at one with similar developments in other communities, most notably Seattle, Tacoma, and Spokane.[27]

The image the *Oregonian* projected for Portland's future embraced both natural and industrial symbols. "Nature could scarcely do more for a state than she has done for Oregon," the newspaper remarked on August 16, 1894, in celebrating the "wonderful diversification" of its resource industries. Because all natural routes of travel and transport led to Portland, the city was the pivotal center, the industrial and commercial depot for the vast area tributary to the Columbia. An August 11, 1900, *Oregonian* editorial urging citizens to "build up the industries and develop the resources of this region" discussed the influence of nature and culture in Portland's development: "Nature has done a great deal for Portland. The railroads have done a great deal more. But Nature and the railroads can't do it all. It is well enough to have influential friends, if we don't depend on them too exclusively; but a man must do something for himself. It is about that way with a community." What the Northwest needed, the editors insisted, were energetic and industrious people to till its valleys, shear its sheep, fatten its cattle, dig its mineral resources, and make "lumber out of its forests, shoes out of its hides, clothing out of its wool."

Despite the Portland business community's effusive rhetoric, an ambitious, even aggressive cultural strategy was increasingly evident in the more intrusive alterations taking place beyond the city. Those prescriptions involved a complex dialectic that was part of an expanding industrial presence that gained ascendancy during the 1890s. We might call this the industrial modeling of nature's wealth, instrumentalizing the outback, commodifying and integrating trees, fish, minerals, and the products of the soil into a larger design involving the global capitalist marketplace. That collective effort followed certain cultural imperatives—summarized brilliantly by Donald Worster—that viewed the natural world as capital, that obliged humankind to use that capital for self-advancement, and that assumed that the social order should promote the accumulation of personal wealth.[28]

The industrial construction and reconstruction of the Oregon country at the onset of the twentieth century reflects the influence of those values. The more imaginative among those articulating that new configuration envisioned a symbiosis of metropolis and countryside, cooperating to mutual advantage. Nature's boundless wealth would flow from hinterland to processing center and then via railroad and the great blue corridor of the Columbia to oceanic markets. Under that set of arrangements, wheat, beef, minerals, logs, and other raw materials followed the natural gradients of the Willamette and Columbia Rivers to Portland while goods and merchandise flowed outward from the city to lesser towns in the interior districts. In his study of Chicago and its hinterland, William Cronon argues that an "elaborate hierarchy of central places, from the largest metropolis down to the smallest town and most remote rural farm, existed to sustain this movement of goods and produce shuttling between city and country."[29] For the Oregon country, those expanding concentric rings of power also meant that distant and larger constellations of capital (and markets) heavily influenced the course of events in tributary territories, the material source of nature's industries.

The effects of the more advanced industrial transport technology—steam-powered locomotives, ocean-going vessels, and river steamers—strengthened Portland's already favored position in the exchanges between upriver resource communities and downstream metropolis. In addition to the attention it gave to the development of Portland's tributary area, the *Oregonian* also encouraged the city's business sector to expand its own manufacturing capacity, especially using local raw materials. It required only entrepreneurial effort "to build an industrial empire upon the western slope." Factories, according to one writer, indicated progress, stamped a community as a city, and provided employment in the making of "goods and wares for home consumption and for shipment to tributary country."[30]

Shortly after the climactic presidential election of 1896 between William McKinley and William Jennings Bryan, the *Oregonian* again boasted that Portland and its hinterland possessed "the essentials that go to make up a great industrial community." There was wheat to be ground, fruit to be canned, iron and coal seams to be worked, wool for clothing, and "untold quantities of timber to be converted into useful articles of commerce." Portland possessed the wealth, the enterprise, and the "unrivaled facilities" to take advantage of the raw materials close at hand and the markets within easy reach. The newspaper offered a utopian vision of a future industrial complex lining the banks of the Willamette River from its mouth to Oregon City, a stretch of twenty-six miles of riverfront where electric-powered factories would turn the productions of nature into finished goods. But while some concerned themselves with Portland's prospects as a manufacturing center, there were others whose imaginations embraced larger, more ambitious programs.

Railroads and other symbols of the industrial world became increasingly apparent everywhere in the Oregon country as the nineteenth century drew to a close. Because certain forms of the new technology—the telegraph and the steam-powered locomotive—encouraged and quickened the union of rural, resource-rich districts with urban centers, commercial organizations and an assortment of other enthusiasts took notice of those conditions to promote a more closely integrated economy. The potential for extending the influence of strategically located urban centers gave flight to a soaring prose and an expanding geography of commercial and industrial ambitions. Those aspirations were displayed regularly in a wide array of public forums.

"WHERE ROLLS THE OREGON," an *Oregonian* headline blared in the December 19, 1896, issue. "The mighty river [that] drains an empire" gave special advantages to the metropolis of the Northwest, benefits that would increase as the contours of the Columbia River and the landscape of the Oregon country were refashioned to suit the new industrial imperatives: "Every railroad built, every steamer launched, every foot added to the channels of the river, every manufacturing industry started, every building erected, every store opened, every dollar brought into the country . . . has added to the growth and prosperity of Portland." As for the great waterway itself, the recently completed Cascade Locks and Canal "improved" the river and "would be of inestimable benefit to the entire country." Employing the metaphor "an open river"—a slogan that became the rallying cry of the early twentieth century—the *Oregonian* article called for more improvements on the "water highway" to provide cost-effective competition to the rail carriers and to increase the overall capacity for goods shipped along the river corridor.

Promoters of both rail and water transportation in River City repeatedly argued that natural geographic features had preordained Portland's position as the preeminent commercial center in the Columbia River country. "All Roads Lead to Portland," the *Oregonian* proclaimed on July 3, 1899. Because "the great artery . . . which drains a vast region of rich and varied resources" followed the laws of gravity, logic and common sense suggested the importance of Portland. Even a casual glance at a map of the region, the newspaper contended, indicated how geography favored Portland: "As naturally as water run[s] down hill does the produce of the interior seek a market through Portland." In that sense, the city was a transfer point because of "natural conditions that were recognized when the town was established."

Fill the country beyond Portland with producers, the *Oregonian* of July 4, 1904, argued, and the city itself would benefit enormously. The promotion of that sense of interdependence between country and city, it suggested, should be the primary objective of Portland's investment community. The hinterland, with its "immense latent resources, which may be turned into wealth," was the true source of urban prosperity. Factories in the cities provided markets for the products of the countryside, and transportation lines in turn contributed to the productiveness of rural areas and advanced exchanges between the two sectors. In a bit of rhetorical overkill, the newspaper concluded: "The country will build the city—if you build the country."

There was much work to be done on the big river, especially removing the principal remaining "obstacle" to open commerce, the "wild stretch of river between The Dalles and Celilo." Removing that obstruction, according to the *Oregonian*, would make Portland "the great distributing point by water, as it is now the great distributing point by rail. All water highways, like all rail [roads] . . . have to come to the metropolis." For the local business community, the chief objective in opening the river to free navigation was the "area of productive country known as the Inland Empire, which is rich with all the resources that give wealth to the state." Overcoming the impediments of nature, according to that logic, required a twofold effort: (1) building a rail line on the Oregon side of the river through the difficult section between The Dalles and the Cascades; and (2) creating an efficient water passageway in the same section to expand commerce and protect against railroad monopoly. The open-river campaign, therefore, involved environmental alterations rooted in what its supporters deemed democratic and economic objectives.

Portland's commercial community worked tirelessly to correct nature's imperfections on the Great River and to improve the channels that linked the Willamette metropolis "with the productive country of the interior basin," stated the *Oregonian* of January 1, 1903. Building a canal system from The Dalles to Celilo would free the river "from the oppression of arbitrary and unnatural agreements between transportation agencies." Of the two great barriers to upriver traffic, that of the Cascade rapids had already been neutralized. Removing the last obstruction would enable goods to be transported along the natural corridor of the Columbia and provide shippers with an alternative to the "unnatural and costly route over the summit of the Cascade Mountains."

Organized business groups were especially active in pressing the "open river" campaign. The Portland Chamber of Commerce established an Open River Committee to respond to the frequently asked question: "How can relief best be given the people of the Inland Empire?" The committee's seemingly selfless response was to urge the building of a government canal between The Dalles and Celilo. To expand its lobbying effort with Congress, the committee met with representatives from eastern Oregon, eastern

Washington, and Idaho to form the Open River Association. To facilitate travel along the river, the two groups decided that first a portage railroad should be built to bypass the falls and rapids, and provide temporary relief from excessive railroad rates; and second, they should work for the completion of the canal and locks.[31]

Couched in rhetoric that suggested environmental change, the meanings attached to the open river campaign carried a commercial message: freeing traffic from economic monopoly and lowering the financial costs of travel by water. Both commercial and political discourse hinted that "natural" forces rather than federal regulation would provide a more effective means to curb monopoly influence. Reporting on a meeting of the National Rivers and Harbors Congress in 1907, Oregon governor George Chamberlain told the Portland chamber that the great waterways of the United States were "natural regulators of freight." In a direct reference to the work of the Open River Committee, Chamberlain observed that an open waterway would serve as "a law provided by nature to regulate the freights of a country tributary to it." With a Columbia River open and unobstructed from its mouth to its headwaters, there would be no need "to regulate freight rates, because the river itself will regulate it."[32]

As the great artery of commerce for the Northwest, the Columbia provided a "natural" passageway for tapping the wealth of the rich interior country while at the same time advancing the economic interests of Portland. If the city was to be a great commercial seaport and if the interior country was "to reach its proper development," the Portland Chamber of Commerce argued, then reasonable transportation rates had to be established between upriver shipping points and the city of Portland. An open river upstream and "a deep and safe channel to the Sea" were necessary to the unrestricted navigation of Northwest waterways. In its *Report on an Open River*, the chamber raised the issue of the city's future trading prospects, especially with the opening of the Panama Canal and the potential for an expanded trade with Pacific Basin countries. Only with a considerably enhanced water transportation infrastructure would Portland be in a position to take advantage of that potential continental and oceanic flow of goods and materials.[33]

The discussions that centered on improvements to navigation on the Columbia River offered complex and contradictory rhetorical messages, a confusing juxtaposition of the meaning of natural and unnatural that fused geography and economics into a larger industrial vision. The Portland business community talked about "tapping" into the resources of the "unoccu-pied" sections of the inland empire, thereby further enlarging the region tributary to the river and by extension to the city of Portland. Shortly after the turn of the century, the newly organized Portland Board of Trade ac-tively pursued several agendas: (1) promoting railroad projects throughout the interior country; (2) advertising the region's agricultural production; and (3) lobbying the federal government to continue its canal-building efforts on the mid-Columbia River.

Because the telegraph, telephone, and railroad had revolutionized com-merce in Oregon, the Portland Board of Trade announced in a 1902 promo-tional pamphlet its intention to advertise the city as a manufacturing and commercial center, the mark of "every civilized community." Portland's situation was advantageous because it had mountains nearby filled with precious metals, streams to be harnessed for power, rich soil and ideal clima-tic conditions, and inexhaustible forests to supply the construction needs of the nation. All of this combined "to make the Pacific Northwest a country of the greatest opportunities of any in the world." The board urged Congress to retain in the current "Rivers and Harbor Bill" funding for improved navigation on the Columbia River. The immense resources of the interior would be brought to market "by the cheap transportation . . . afforded by . . . an open river."[34]

New urban rivals for commercial supremacy in the Pacific Northwest prompted a heightened sense of promotion and boosterism among Portland bankers and the Board of Trade at the turn of the century. When the Klondike gold rush boomed the Seattle economy and helped it recover quickly from the depression of the early 1890s, the Portland business commu-nity moved aggressively to reassert its preeminence as the leading city in the region. The most elaborate example of Portland's resurgence was the city's sponsorship of a commemorative commercial fair in 1905, the Lewis and Clark Centennial Exposition. Civic leaders, especially the local business community, saw the exposition as an international advertisement, heralding the promise that Portland and its hinterland held for prospective settlers and investors.[35]

The most ambitious circular promoting the development of the Oregon country was the *Portland Board of Trade Journal*, subsequently appearing under a number of titles, including *The Chamber of Commerce Bulletin*. As the opening of the Lewis and Clark Exposition approached in 1905, the board celebrated Oregon's virtues in its monthly publication: "No where in the world is there such a land of promise and opportunities as in the State of Oregon. She has countless store of mineral wealth hidden in her broad bosom awaiting the touch of capital to convert it into material tangible wealth. . . . [S]he has the soil, climate and all other conditions unsurpassable that guarantees the successful pursuance of every industry." To prospective visitors to the exposition, the publication observed: "Nature has blessed the section of which Portland is the center with lavish prodigality." Such references to turning the natural world to account in the marketplace and similar rhetorical ploys were stratagems dating from the earliest published observations about the region. However, there was a new buoyant, aggressive, and even strident tone to the commercial literature published in the early twentieth century.[36]

Jefferson Myers, president of the commission in charge of the Lewis and Clark Exposition, hinted to local audiences that the celebration would bring many thousands of visitors, "the best class of immigration," and that those who made the trip might find themselves a new home. Oregon alone, he said, had "more native underdeveloped resources than any other commonwealth within the United States." Its immense forests, its mines barely past the stage of discovery, and its fisheries were "only producing a small part of the revenue" of which they were capable. What the state required, according to the commission president, was the "industry, ambition, and wealth" to turn those resources to its advantage. To the *Oregonian*, the exposition represented even more, "an appeal to the country," as well as to provide a means to concentrate attention on the Pacific states "and upon their vast and yet undeveloped resources." The Portland fair, it believed, would be a true exhibition of nature's wares; it would allow the region to show its wealth in the "products of field, forest, mine and sea."[37]

From a civic and commercial standpoint, the Lewis and Clark Exposition, open from June 1 to October 15, 1905, was a striking success, totaling 1,588,000 paid admissions with another 966,000 attending through courtesy passes. The *Oregonian* called the exposition "a great financial success," one that "surpassed every expectation." The event drew the attention of the entire nation to the region, and in the succeeding months and years was certain to contribute "to the advantage, development and progress of the Northwest." Urban historian Carl Abbott calculates that the exposition earned for the organization's stockholders a 21 percent return on their investments. "Portland put itself in the mainstream of American boosterism with its decision to stage the exposition," he concludes. In an editorial opinion of 1906, the *Oregonian* provided a summary commentary: "The

Lewis and Clark Exposition officially marked the end of the old and the beginning of the new Oregon."[38]

The growing industrial presence in the Oregon country at the turn of the century accelerated and advanced powerful word symbols that linked the natural abundance of place with an increasing technical ability to manipulate that world to personal advantage. An aggressive, expansive, optimistic booster rhetoric characterized the period—a discourse steeped in a self-confident capitalist ethos that saw unlimited wealth in transforming nature's abundance into commodities to be trafficked in the global marketplace. In a more specific sense, the literal and figurative meaning of the rhetoric of industrialism was expressed in terms of nature's industries: that is, enterprises seeking to profit from the region's magnificent forests, the rich soils in the valley bottoms, the mineral riches that underlay the interior mountains, and the seemingly limitless multitudes of salmon that plied its numerous waterways. The end result of those collective efforts, the literature assured, meant public benefits in the form of improved living conditions and general prosperity for all citizens.

But in its more substantive meaning, the uninhibited booster discourse of the late nineteenth and early twentieth centuries was merely an extension of earlier narrative forms. From the beginning of the Euroamerican presence in the region, a new commercial ethos was set loose on the land, a set of beliefs and a core of values that viewed the natural world in terms of its commodity potential with the objective of turning that natural abundance to advantage in distant markets. That already robust and expansive rhetoric became increasingly more aggressive as the nineteenth century drew to a close. The grand design and ambition argued in those proposals urged the systematic and orderly development of the region's unparalleled natural wealth. Collectively, it was word play that implied an increasingly intrusive industrial influence on the landscape of the Oregon country. The degree and magnitude of environmental manipulation suggested in that literature would be effected in the coming decades.

NOTES

1. For a further elaboration of this idea, see Donald Worster, "Nature and the Disorder of History," *Environmental History Review* 18 (Summer 1994): 2.

2. *Pacific Monthly* 11, no. 1 (January 1904): 65. Worster argues that this com-

plex material dialectic is a constantly shifting reference point, reflecting changes both in the world of nature and in the human expectations of nature ("Nature and the Disorder of History," 2).

3. Alan Trachtenberg, *The Incorporation of America: Culture and Society in the Gilded Age* (New York: Hill and Wang, 1982), 19 and 57.

4. "Documents," *Oregon Historical Quarterly* 3 (December 1902): 422; *Oregon Spectator*, October 4, 1849; and *Oregon Statesman*, July 3, 1852.

5. Overton Johnson and William H. Winter, *Route Across the Rocky Mountains* (1846; reprint, Fairfield, Wash.: Ye Galleon Press, 1982), 42 and 69.

6. Olympia *Pioneer and Democrat*, July 18, 1856.

7. Theodore Winthrop, *The Canoe and the Saddle*, ed. John H. Williams (1862; Tacoma: Franklin-Ward Company, 1913), 210. Samuel Bowles is quoted in the *Oregon Statesman*, November 6, 1865.

8. *Willamette Farmer*, June 28, 1869, and February 24, 1872.

9. *West Shore* 1, no. 6 (January 1876): 1.

10. Frances Fuller Victor, *All Over Oregon and Washington: Observations on the Country* (San Francisco: John Carmany and Company, 1872), 67.

11. This point is made in Olivier Zunz, *Making America Corporate, 1870–1920* (Chicago: University of Chicago Press, 1990), 39–40.

12. *West Shore* 6, no. 2 (February 1880): 39.

13. Carlos A. Schwantes, "The Concept of the Wageworkers' Frontier: A Framework for Future Research," *Western Historical Quarterly* 18 (January 1987): 43.

14. Yi-Fu Tuan, *Space and Place: The Perspective of Experience* (Minneapolis: University of Minnesota Press, 1977), 5 and 85.

15. J. D. Cleaver, "L. Samuel and the *West Shore:* Images of Changing Pacific Northwest," *Oregon Historical Quarterly* 94 (Summer–Fall 1993): 170–89.

16. "Oregon—Past and Present," *West Shore* 1, no. 4 (November 1875): 1–2; and 3, no. 3 (November 1877): 41.

17. *West Shore* 1, no. 10 (June 1876): 5; and 14, no. 8 (August 1888): 415.

18. *West Shore* 1, no. 6 (January 1876): 1; 2, no. 5 (January 1877): 85; and 2, no. 12 (August 1877): 223.

19. P. B. Simmons, "Oregon as Seen by a Philadelphian," *West Shore* 5, no. 1 (January 1879): 25; 15, no. 3 (March 1889): 152; 16, no. 229 (October 25, 1890): 173.

20. *West Shore* 1, no. 6 (January 1876): 9, 11; and no. 10 (June 1876): 5; 2, no. 8 (April 1877): 150; 5, no. 1 (January 1879): 25; and 9, no. 6 (June 1883): 128.

21. *West Shore* 6, no. 8 (December 1880): 315; 10, no. 5 (May 1984): 136.

22. Richard A. Rajala, "The Forest as Factory: Technological Change and

Worker Control in the West Coast Logging Industry, 1880–1930," *Labour/Le Travail* 32 (Fall 1993): 73–85.

23. *West Shore* 10, no. 3 (March 1884): 75; and George H. Emerson, "Logging on Grays Harbor, *The Timberman* 8 (September 1908): 20.

24. *West Shore* 14, no. 8 (August 1888): 410.

25. *Oregonian*, January 2, 1888.

26. *Oregonian*, October 2, 1884, and January 2, 1888.

27. *Oregonian*, January 1, 1889; and Carlos A. Schwantes, *The Pacific Northwest: An Interpretive History* (Lincoln: University of Nebraska Press, 1989), 191–92.

28. Donald Worster, *Dust Bowl: The Southern Plains in the 1930s* (New York: Oxford University Press, 1979), 6.

29. William Cronon, *Nature's Metropolis: Chicago and the Great West* (New York: Norton, 1991), 310–11.

30. *Oregonian*, January 2, 1888; and January 1, 1889.

31. *The Chamber of Commerce Bulletin* 3, no. 3 (September 1904): 1; and 3, no. 8 (February 1905): 9.

32. "Address by Governor Chamberlain," *The Portland Chamber of Commerce Bulletin* 7, no. 2 (February 1907): 35–37.

33. Portland Chamber of Commerce, *Report on an Open River* (Portland: Chamber of Commerce, 1906), 3–5.

34. *Columbia River Basin Journal* (Portland: Board of Trade, 1902), 12–13.

35. Carl Abbott, *Portland: Planning, Politics, and Growth in a Twentieth-Century City* (Lincoln: University of Nebraska Press, 1983), 33–34; Schwantes, *The Pacific Northwest*, 216–17.

36. *Portland Board of Trade Journal* 1, no. 2 (March 1905): 5–6.

37. *Oregonian*, May 31, 1903, and January 1, 1904.

38. Abbott, *Portland*, 44; and *Oregonian*, October 14 and 15, 1905, and October 14, 1906.

PART IV

GENDER IN THE URBAN WEST

Lighting Out for the Territory
Women, Mobility, and Western Place

VIRGINIA SCHARFF

Places are interesting, worth studying on their own terms. The way *spaces,* those unbounded expanses of planetary terrain, get made into *places*— meaning-laden, bordered areas that themselves help to define human beings as insiders or outsiders—seems worthy of examination.[1] What can we learn from the creation of elaborately, yet incompletely bounded places, like western cities, out of topographic spaces, through processes of material and cultural production, inscription, and interaction?

Making "western place" an object of examination requires the investigator to hold still for a while, to take up a position and a limited viewpoint. We may pretend to stand everywhere and nowhere at the same time when we describe places and the things that happen in and around and through them, but of course we don't. The ingenious devices of language enable us to cloak our prose and our point of view in the garb of neutrality, exteriority, and objectivity. When we begin to speak about the terrains we survey, we use strong yet remarkably flexible rhetorical strategies to construct geographies. Since historians wish to account for human presence, we also construct ethnographies, telling stories in the same fashion as the ethnographer Vincent Crapanzano describes: His [sic] "place in his text is purely rhetorical. It is deictically, or perhaps better, pseudo-deictically constructed. It is impossible to fix his vantage point. His is a roving perspective, necessitated by his 'totalistic' presentation of the events he is describing. His presence does not alter the way things happen or, for that matter, the way they are observed or interpreted. He assumes an invisibility that, unlike Hermes, a god, he cannot have."[2]

Ungodlike though we late twentieth-century humans are, we do get around. Holding still, as frequent flyers know, may not be characteristic of people in our time; for most people, it has never been possible in any strict sense. Thus the job of figuring out places requires noting the geographical mobility of humans whose activities construct places, as well as the mobility of those of us who do the describing. Representing people in place requires finding out how they got there, how long they intend to stay, why they do or don't stay, where else they go, and how they think about what they've done and where they've been and where they are going. We need also to know how their mobility affects their understanding of who they are and what they do.3

But we must somehow account for our own point of view. The decision to make (western) place an independent variable in a historical inquiry fixes the observer's field of view without confining her or him rhetorically. Taking up the position of observer, I imagine myself, in the manner of Christopher Isherwood's non-ingenue Sally Bowles, as a camera. But much has changed in the three-quarters of a century since Sally danced through the smoke of Weimar Berlin. I fancy that I am a stationary video camera, always on, much like the "Cloud Cam" used at one of Albuquerque's local news stations, endlessly photographing the sky over the Sandia Mountains, so that the weather woman can spend thirty seconds of air time in front of footage of clouds rolling in and out over the range and the city. Or, perhaps I am one of those surveillance cameras that, as Mike Davis reminds us, peer down from steel traffic stanchions set in cement throughout Los Angeles, always on the lookout for suspicious characters. Those cameras are sinister or reassuring, depending on your point of view.4

But, like most people, I am not fixed in place. I see the things I see because I happen to be at the right (or wrong) place at the right (or wrong) time. In this sense, all contemporary observers are like George Holliday, the fellow who was trying out his new video camera, one early morning in March 1991, when some Los Angeles police officers finished off a car chase by arresting African American male motorist Rodney King across the street from Holliday's house. In most cases, there will be a lapse of time, and a production of distance, between when we do the observing, and recording, and when we think about what it means and tell somebody else. And as more time and motion passes, the meaning of what we saw is repeatedly reconfigured. Holliday's footage appeared to mean something very clear when it was aired, again and again, in the days immediately after the beating. It quite evidently took on different meanings to the Simi Valley jury that viewed it repeatedly, often in slow motion or freezing the action. And its meaning was again reconfigured when thousands took to the streets of Los Angeles after the officers who struck the blows were acquitted, with a fourth transformation to come when another camera recorded another beating, this time of a white man, in the civil disorders that followed the verdict. Each of those who saw and interpreted Holliday's video adopted the ethnographic, or pseudodeictic, stance. Viewers brought to the event ideas and experiences only incidental to the place it occurred, and made knowledgeable judgments, for example, about the significance of the participants' race. I cannot recall anyone, at the time, suggesting that gender also constructed the event, but I would wager that the documented beating of Rodney King would have taken on very different meanings and consequences had he been female.

The Holliday video, or any such recording, demonstrates that even when observers choose not to move around, and instead take a stand for temporary, specific reasons, what we see through the camera lens is an almost unfathomably kinetic image of place. The clouds and the cars and the people move in and out of scope, seemingly randomly. But the operations of clouds and cars and people are not random, though just as surely their movements respond to contingencies in their spatial and temporal paths. People move deliberately, if not always willingly. They set themselves in motion with particular objectives in mind, generally with a measure of choice about changing their paths, though always constrained in ways both known and unknown to them. The movements of bodies in space, indeed, are components in turbulent and complex systems that are very hard to figure out.[5] Thus it is difficult to say, from a fixed point of view, where anyone or anything has come from, and where it's going, or why.

For western historians, to insist on the primacy of place is to act as if everything and everybody we might study can be framed by the West, understood in geographical terms, for the purpose of this essay on "power and place," as a region. Here it may be objected that, as historians, we are not simpleminded about places. We inevitably take time seriously, and assume that places change as time passes. But even a time-lapse Landsat series of photographs of the trans-Mississippi region couldn't make sense of the historical experiences of the people who have moved across, through, in, and out of the place—who indeed construct what the place *is* with their seemingly chaotic presences and absences.

Western historians have themselves described and analyzed how processes and persons, whose origins and ends are far beyond the physical borders of this place, matter deeply for what we've called the West. To take but one obvious example, markets include places outside whatever gets called the West at any given moment. "West" is itself a relative term, *defined with reference to* some other place or force or set of places or forces. For example, historians have examined the relation of the West to external "markets"—London or Paris for furs; England or "the East" for timber; the world for irrigation-dependent grains and fruits and vegetables; Chicago, itself "hog butcher to the world."[6]

Thus doing western history always means moving, rhetorically, in and out of the West, from an Olympian and indisputably mobile point of view, which also claims to know and describe the location of the West. Sometimes the historian gestures, in deictic fashion, at some space and calls it "West." Sometimes, she or he moves and looks and points elsewhere. To the extent that the pseudodeictic posture persuades the audience, those people and things that appear only when they cross the narrator's path play minor roles in the service of a master narrative. Those things that they cause to happen, and that happen to them in places and times distant from the narrative path, become invisible and irrelevant to the story of western history.

Women whose life paths have entered, or crossed, or been encompassed by the trans-Mississippi region have appeared, in the main story of the West, as minor, transient characters. But the narrative of women's history has a different geography and ethnography, mapping places by following women's thoughts and actions. Sometimes these geographies and ethnographies intersect, but they are not coterminous. As a historian of women, particularly women automobile drivers, my own relation with western history has been affectionate but ambivalent, sometimes ironic, sometimes admiring, sometimes patronizing, sometimes fleeting and retrospective. I've zoomed through the discourse of western history like a freeway traveler, choosing the off-ramp convenient to my purposes, getting back on, perhaps, later, for different reasons. And I've cruised the scholarly domain of western history like a shopper looking for a parking place at the mall; I'll park here for a while, do some specific business, then pull out and go elsewhere. If my metaphor strikes you as bourgeois, I am guilty as charged. But I don't think bourgeois academics are the only people who have experienced The West, or Western-ness, as a partial, discontinuous, and sometimes voluntary category of experience.

Speaking only from my acquaintance with the histories of many different kinds of women (but mostly, middling European American women), I've never believed that any woman's experience could be explained fully by being framed as "Western." I've researched the lives and actions of white women who migrated, as wives, from the East and the Midwest to mining boomtowns in Wyoming after the Civil War, of suffragists in and outside the West, and of unmarried professional women who took positions at fledgling western universities in the 1880s. I've looked at the highly mobile life of Wyoming's Nellie Ross, the first woman governor in U.S. history. I've studied women (again, mostly Anglo) who drove cars in Los Angeles in the 1920s, and women drivers since that time, an increasingly diverse group ethnically and economically. I've given thought to the voyages of indige-nous women and overland trail migrants, and of myself and my colleagues who get paid to teach and write in universities today. I've studied the lives and creations of women of various ethnicities, ages, and class positions who painted in the West between 1890 and 1945. And I've thought about all kinds of women who live in western cities like Albuquerque right now.[7] The more I've thought about it, the less I've believed it possible to describe any women as captives to something totalized as "the West."

Women like English professor and black civil rights activist Jo Ann Gibson Robinson prove my point. In 1955 and 1956, as a young faculty member at Alabama State College, Robinson played a leading role in orga-nizing and maintaining the Montgomery bus boycott, one of the most dra-matic successes of the civil rights movement. The boycott was largely the product of women's movements, both spatial and political. Immediately upon hearing of Rosa Parks's arrest, Robinson and her colleagues in the Montgomery Women's Political Council gathered together, planned, publi-cized, and carried off a one-day protest, and ultimately organized hundreds of drivers into a carpool lasting thirteen months. African American citizens of Montgomery, as well as some white Montgomeryites, female as well as male, defied segregation by driving each other, and by walking. In 1960, Robinson and other activists were blacklisted by the Alabama legislature, and she left the state, eventually moving to California. There, she taught in the Los Angeles public school system, bought apartment buildings, remained dedi-cated to social justice. Jo Ann Robinson lived and worked in and shaped Los Angeles for decades, but her life can hardly be said to be circumscribed by the West.[8] For such mobile women, as James Clifford put the matter in a different context, "Their history was a series of cultural and political trans-actions, not all-or-nothing conversions or resistances." Or, to quote a group of distinguished but highly disorderly "Western women's historians," as they considered the matter late one night at a conference in Massachusetts a few years ago, "We Mae West; then again, we may not."[9]

Let me return to my parking lot metaphor. Suppose we think of the West as a bounded region, paved and repaved with the products of human thought and action, in at least that regard similar to a parking lot. Actually, there are plenty of people who think the West has *become* a parking lot, but that is an issue for another time. There is no reason to assume that women, whom I distinguish here from men by virtue of rather small biological divergences that get turned into rather larger cultural differences, are the only ones moving in and out of parking spaces. But movement in our parking lot is shaped in significant ways by gender, among other things. If you go to the mall during most business hours, you'll see (big surprise) more women than men. Lots of preschool children accompany those women, suggesting that a particular group of women is probably overrepresented in the mall population. Somewhat mysteriously, you will also see lots of teen-agers (and what *are* they doing there during school hours?). Similarly, gen-der norms, as well as age and class and racial or ethnic positions, have shaped the movements of people who have come into, lived in, or left the trans-Mississippi region. And the social landscape of our mall/parking lot configuration is in no small measure a product of its inhabitation by already gendered (and racialized, and class-positioned) human beings.

Movement, in turn, reconfigures gender ideas and practices. Mall parking lots today are full of women drivers, behaving, often enough, in highly unladylike fashion. Mining boomtowns of the nineteenth century were pre-dominately male, but they also provided settings for men and women to act outside and against conventional masculinity and femininity. Prairie and Great Plains farming regions have had relatively equal sex ratios, signifying a development ethos that assumed the presence of both men and women in families. But the hard work and isolation of farm life inspired new forms of cooperation and mobility. In the early twentieth century, towns like Juarez and Tijuana, on the south side of the border between the United States and Mexico, were disproportionately populated by women and children, as male family members crossed the border to work in the United States and sent for the remainder of the family later. In each case, and in all cases, the gender composition of these places, and access to physical mobility that is itself gendered in complicated ways, are critical components of the workings of social and ecological systems.[10]

The United States today is a nation of people in motion. But not everyone is expected to move around, or to stay put, on equal terms. The power to move independently, to go where one wants, and to feel secure in going or, in many cases, in *staying*, is a privilege of dominant social groups: men, whites, the rich. And yet all kinds of people who aren't supposed to do so, move around, or stay put where they aren't supposed to be: teenagers in the mall, women drivers downtown, migrant farmworkers, for example.[11]

Numerous scholars have looked at how control over spatial mobility and stability has been contested according to race and ethnicity and class. I want to focus here on the spatial politics of women's history, as women's history engages with western places. The fact that some of the bodies that move through western space are female matters for the persons living in those bodies. It also matters for such places as Albuquerque and Los Angeles and other western cities. It even matters for men. Indeed, it matters on a much larger scale, and at a much deeper level, because when women move, they contest structural assumptions about gender that are remarkable for their forcefulness in a staggering variety of social settings. I would even venture that control over mobility is a form of power crucial to the constitution and disruption of the hierarchical social structures we recognize, for example, as race, class, and gender.[12]

Mobility is gendered in at least three ways. The first has to do with freedom of bodily movement. The second entails access to places. The third involves personal safety. These gendered aspects of mobility are sometimes complementary, sometimes contradictory. I will take each aspect in turn, and illustrate how it has been enacted and contested in historical practice.

Freedom of bodily movement—as intimate and basic as the unencumbered raising of one's arm, or placing one foot in front of the other, or as collective and technologically mediated as commuting across town to a job or flying to Seattle on an airplane—has in many times and places been a vehicle of male privilege. Women who moved too freely—like the bull-whacking, trouser-wearing Calamity Jane, or like the Mexican women of the Southwest who wore short skirts and danced fandangos—contested power-laden gender conventions.[13] As I have written in *Taking the Wheel*, women who have claimed the power of driving automobiles as far and as fast as men are entitled to do have, for more than a century now, challenged American gender norms, and been called to account for their actions. As feminist critics have long pointed out, nothing in American history better symbolizes the impetus to contain women's actions in space than female fashions, from nineteenth-century whalebone corsets, bustles, and floor-length skirts, to the bound-and-gagged look achieved by rubber girdles, harness brassieres, and cinch-waist dresses in the fifties, to the footbinding spike heels and liposuction-inspiring spandex miniskirts in last month's *Vogue*. Men who complain about having to wear ties have a tiny inkling of what it means to be a woman, and encouraged (or obliged) to wear clothing that constricts and restricts movement to the point of making it hard to breathe, talk, or walk.

The way clothing constrains movement is obviously gendered. And spaces are themselves structured by this heavily mediated movement. Thus the streets of western towns and cities, in an era of horse traffic, were more hospitable to men wearing pants than to women whose skirts dragged along the ground. Navigating crowded trolleycars posed more of a problem for women in long dresses and big hats than for men in less ponderous garments. Women riding in early open automobiles looked more like wrapped packages than hardy travelers out for an adventure. Those of us today who choose to get around in high heels and tight short skirts are far less in charge of our legs and feet, and more vulnerable to physical violence, than are persons wearing clothing designed for freedom of movement. The woman lawyer, dean, or account executive who strides through the city in a business suit and a pair of Reeboks makes a gendered statement about power, as well as about comfort.

If the freedom to move is one aspect of the gendering of mobility, unequal access to places is another. Such inequality can be enforced in many ways. One, of course, is legal, as exemplified by de jure segregation which has operated, in the American West as well as the South, more often along racial than sexual lines. Another is customary, as in the largely unwritten, generally observed rules governing male and female access to spaces, such as topless bars in the North Beach section of San Francisco. Custom pushed to shove may, of course, become law, as in the sex segregation of Rotary Club meetings until the 1970s, or the males-only rules governing the membership of the Bohemian Club. In Kansas City, Kansas, at the turn of the century a local ordinance made it illegal for "any unattended female to parade the public streets of this city at night, or to congregate on the street, or other place, or to wander abroad in the night time, or to be found about the streets or public places of the city, or to be found about stores or other places at late hours without lawful business and without giving good account of themselves." Unequal access to spaces, in all these examples, gives men privilege and power over women. Where women have chosen to contest such inequality—in lawsuits against the Rotary Clubs, in topless clubs where dancers develop rules governing where customers may and may not put parts of their bodies, or perhaps by riding the streetcar from Kansas City, Kansas, across the border into Kansas City, Missouri—they have done so at risk to themselves, with much to lose or gain.[14]

Another way to maintain unequal access to spaces along gender lines is to subject the excluded persons to threat of bodily harm if they violate rules of access. Thus women who walk alone at night on the streets of Albuquerque or Berkeley or Seattle or El Paso contest presumptions about who ought to be allowed free access to the city, and they do so at substantial personal peril.[15]

The process of making western places out of spaces thus entails the operation of gender as an ordering (but, I shall argue, potentially contradictory) system of beliefs and practices. In fact, without understanding the gender relations at work, it is impossible to make substantive sense out of events in any locale that has become (or ceased to be) a place deemed western. Women's history, which has pioneered the use of gender as a category of analysis, assuredly has this much to say to western history.[16]

At the same time, as much as I want to affirm the usefulness to western historians of looking at gender, I have become increasingly suspicious of the notion that the main value of women's history has been to demonstrate the significance of gender as a historical force in all people's lives.[17] First, women's experiences are not explicable strictly in terms of gender. Race and class and age and a host of other cultural and material factors assuredly matter. And *every* woman acts, at times, against and outside the strictures of femininity. Moreover, whatever is wrong with western history cannot be fixed by focusing attention, in fresh and exciting ways, on masculinity alone. We need to understand gender as a force in history, but we will never understand how gender operates in the West until we know far more about women's history.[18]

And so I insist on taking a critical view of the usefulness of both western place and gender as circumscribing categories. Women's history perpetually contests and escapes and transforms these categories, and indeed the material realities that arise from them, in part because women's bodies move through space. Therefore, I would advocate a historical project to put women's experiences at the center of a dynamic interaction with the "West" (understood, in synechdochic fashion, as Place) and with Culture (presenting itself in truncated brief, today, as Gender).[19]

Women have propelled their bodies through spaces that have become western places in knowledgeable, and not always compliant, ways. That movement—let's call it female mobility—has had significant consequences not just for western history but for the history of the nation, and for relations across political borders. Physical mobility itself is a historically gendered phenomenon—gendered masculine, to be specific—in most places and times with which I am familiar. But this is not to say that women have never moved on their own. Dolores Huerta has traveled the length and breadth of California, and the nation, organizing farmworkers. Emily Post, the epic arbiter of manners, drove across the country. Even Gidget had her own car. But when such actions are seen as neither temporary nor aberrant, they begin to look disorderly. When women move around independently, they violate gender at a structural level, becoming actual forces of disruption and potential agents of historical transformation. The editor of the automobile trade journal *Motor* magazine put it this way in 1927: "Every time a woman learns to drive—and thousands do every year—it is a threat at yesterday's order of things."[20]

It is also the case that gender, understood as a system of power relations we might call, simplistically, "patriarchy," puts people in double binds that are resolvable only when the system shifts to redefine a cultural opposition in new terms. Thus, while mobility and masculinity have been considered coterminous in these patriarchally structured times and places, women may sometimes find themselves *obliged* to move around in order to fulfill their duties as subordinates. Compulsory mobility is, of course, imposed on the basis of race and class too, but here I want to discuss the ways in which being made to move is a mark of sex. Under conditions of economic, political, and technological transformation, women may not only be allowed to move around, they may have to do so. But they had better do their moving in ways that are seen as beneficial to men.[21]

Consider those forerunners of today's women drivers, the women who migrated westward on the overland trails. These women have become symbols of a retrograde, Eurocentric women's history, and their story certainly does not exhaust the possibilities of women's history in their time and place, as many Native American and Mexican women would have been happy to point out.[22] But the overland women's experience remains worthy of study for reasons including insight into their part in expanding the empire of the United States. Most of them carried along a sense of their obligations as wives and mothers who took vows at marriage to obey their husbands. Their domestic duties on the journey entailed extraordinary expenditures of motion and energy—gathering buffalo dung for fuel, packing and unpacking kitchen equipment, carrying babies and tired children along the trail. Every time they washed a diaper in a creek or threw another buffalo chip on the fire, they transformed their immediate environs, and made travel the next day possible. Women's knowledge, labor, and motion were thus critical to inscribing the trail across the continent. But the movement of women migrants was hardly a threat to male authority; if anything, they resisted domination by *refusing* to move, for example, when a child took sick, or when the dead had to be buried.[23]

How about more recent women in motion? Have twentieth-century women drivers, like those who fill up our mall parking lots, pursued mobility in ways similarly calculated to reproduce men's social and economic dominance? I'm not quite sure. Certainly, many social commentators of the early twentieth century regarded women's presence at the wheel as a profoundly scary thing. And some feminists of the period saw the automobile as a powerful tool of emancipation. But by the time of the 1929 stock market crash, most women who drove did so in the service of family obligations—to shop, to do other errands, to chauffeur husbands and children. Nonetheless, women do, and did, use the auto in ways that contest men's control of their time and movement, whether they are running away from violent husbands or cruising for burgers in daddy's T-Bird (or better still, in a T-Bird of their own).

Women's use of cars has transformed urban space in ways we are only beginning to understand. I have argued elsewhere that women drivers in Los Angeles in 1920 were among the forces that catalyzed suburbanization in that city.[24] Likewise, "postsuburban," multinucleated urban configurations (like the Los Angeles Metropolitan Area in general, Orange County as a particular example) are in part products of the needs and actions of American women who daily shuttle between home, paid job, childcare center, grocery store, dry cleaner, and other places where they do the work of consumption, production, and service. Women who make their rounds in today's car-culture suburbs trace, and maintain, the suburban sprawl that enriches real estate developers and enrages urban planners. The proliferation of strip malls, fast food outlets, mega-supermarkets, and discount stores may not appeal to us aesthetically, but, for hard-pressed women stretching their time and their work across American cityscapes, these establishments represent efficiency masked, trivialized, and feminized as convenience. Conversely, where women do not venture forth on their multiple daily journeys, our suburban commercial landscapes, and the investment and profits they embody, are endangered. Think of the sinister boarded-up strip malls of overbuilt Houston, or the endless "for sale" signs in Aurora, Colorado, in the late 1980s.[25]

To the extent that women have contested restriction of their power to move, to claim access to male-dominated spaces, and to enjoy safety as they go—or stay—as they choose, they have been agents of historical transformation. Some who have claimed mobility have done so in a consciously politi-

cal way, sometimes more on grounds of race than sex. Such women knowl-
edgeably and strategically claimed rights on behalf of an oppressed group,
like the wealthy African American philanthropist Mary Ellen Pleasant, who
insisted in the 1860s on her right to ride the public horsecars in San
Francisco; or, of course, like Jo Ann Robinson and Rosa Parks.[26] But many
others claimed the freedom to move around as individuals, only later, if
ever, asserting that they had made new opportunity possible for women
when they hitched rides into uncharted terrain.

Consider Texas rock legend Janis Joplin. This immensely gifted woman,
who died horribly at the age of twenty-seven, lives on in her songs. In her
time of fame, she was a heady and troubling emblem of disorderly women in
motion. The entry for her in the 1970 edition of *Current Biography* noted,
"In performance Janis Joplin constantly moves." Two years earlier, *Vogue*
had called her "a magnetic moving fireball." Her tour manager and friend,
Bobby Neuwirth, recalled more than twenty years after her death: "People
tried to tell her to slow down, but that was like trying to tell a B-29 to stop
its propeller." A writer for the trade magazine *Cashbox* described her as "a
kind of mixture of Leadbelly, a steam engine, Calamity Jane, Bessie Smith,
an oil derrick, and rot-gut bourbon funneled into the twentieth century
somewhere between El Paso and San Francisco." She told a reporter for the
New York Times: "Man, I'd rather have 10 years of superhypermost than live
to be 70 by sitting in some goddam chair watching TV."[27]

It is possible to read Janis Joplin's life as a series of risky, ever-widening
attempts to move freely through space (and finally, perhaps, to leave her
body itself behind). Joplin was a singer, but she was also a mover. When
she went from Texas to the Haight-Ashbury, she became the female em-
bodiment of a counterculture devoted to spontaneous embrace of sex,
drugs, and rock and roll. Hitchhiking west in search of fun, freedom, and
sympathy, she found people like herself, and people who wanted her to do
what she was so good at doing: singing the blues. At the height of her fame,
after her triumphant appearance at the Monterey Pop Festival, after she
had become a superstar with a psychedelic Porsche, a life devoted to rock
music, a legendary appetite for sex, Southern Comfort, and heroin, and a
coterie of people who depended on her to keep their lives going, she
observed: "No guy ever made me feel as good as an audience. . . . Like, I
don't think I'd go off the road for love now, to live with a guy, no matter
how good. Yeah, it's the truth. Scary thing to say, though, isn't it?"[28] Too
scary, after all.

This essay is not the place to retell the life of Janis Joplin. But I would like to ask the reader to act like a camera, a moving one, and picture the kinetic, young, frustrated Janis Joplin poised for flight, at the moment before takeoff.

As a desperately talented, overweight teenage girl in the 1950s, Joplin experienced the confines of feminine fashion in a visceral way, and she never looked or moved the part. Millions of girls reacted to similarly difficult situations by trying to conform, or by seeking to draw as little attention to themselves as possible, to hold still and hope for the best. Not Janis. She decided to be one of the boys. She climbed the water tower and drank beer with them and sang songs at the top of the tower. The boys got a car and she went with them across the river, to rough blues bars in Louisiana where they ended up slam-bang drunk and got into fights. It would have been very hard for Joplin to decide, at that point in her life, to fly solo. She needed the boys to help her get around. But she paid a heavy price, moving so far from the geographical and gendered realms of respectability that she found herself cast out of proper Port Arthur society.

The most important thing Janis Joplin ever did was to *get out* of Port Arthur. She ran away from home the first time, at age seventeen, and got as far as Houston. Later ventures took her to Los Angeles, but she kept coming home to make a go at being a good girl. Only when she discovered, while a student at the University of Texas in Austin, that she could really sing, was she able to make the break with the place she experienced as a prison. Sure, she could sing, and the crowds at the local folkie coffeehouse loved her performances. But when campus wits voted her "Ugliest Man on Campus," she split.

This reaction to social excommunication in Texas in the early 1960s was made possible by a burgeoning network of telephone lines, interstate highways, nationwide bus routes, and scheduled commercial airline flights, not to mention truckers and others willing to pick up strangers who thumbed a diesel down. It was also made possible by a national network of people who thought music was a way of life, many of them women of her age, setting out for places far from their hometowns. And by her own desperate, but courageous, determination to move to a new, less miserably oppressive place. Janis Joplin was not any parent's idea of a role model, but she both inspired and represented a huge movement of young women away from home, into peer communities, into uncharted terrain. Without such women's movement, there would have been no sexual revolution, no counterculture, no Women's Liberation. Like Huck Finn, Janis and her contemporaries lit out for the Territory. It was risky. The Territory would never be the same.

NOTES

1. On this issue, see Anthony Giddens, *A Contemporary Critique of Historical Materialism* (Berkeley: University of California Press, 1981); Edward W. Soja, *Postmodern Geographies: The Reassertion of Space in Critical Social Theory* (London: Verso, 1989); Akhil Gupta and James Ferguson, "Beyond 'Culture': Space, Identity, and the Politics of Difference," *Cultural Anthropology* 7 (February 1992): 6–23.

2. Vincent Crapanzano, "Hermes' Dilemma: The Masking of Subversion in Ethnographic Description," in *Writing Culture: The Poetics and Politics of Ethnography*, ed. James Clifford and George E. Marcus (Berkeley: University of California Press, 1986), 53.

3. An excellent example of such a study is Roger Rouse, "Mexican Migration and the Social Space of Postmodernism," *Diaspora* 1, no. 1 (1991): 8–23.

4. Mike Davis, *City of Quartz: Excavating the Future in Los Angeles* (New York: Vintage, 1992), 221–63; especially photos, 225, 245.

5. Which is not to say that social scientists, and hard scientists, and even literary critics don't try. Heisenberg's famous uncertainty principle is the emblematic statement of the difficulty of understanding bodies in motion. Currently, chaos and complexity models address the problem of how to understand seemingly random events. For ingenious attempts to connect the insights of chaos models in science with contemporary strategies in fiction and literary criticism, see N. Katherine Hayles, *The Cosmic Web: Scientific Field Models and Literary Strategies in the Twentieth Century* (Ithaca: Cornell University Press, 1984); and Hayles, *Chaos Bound: Orderly Disorder in Contemporary Literature and Science* (Ithaca: Cornell University Press, 1990).

6. On this subject see, for example, William Cronon, *Changes in the Land: Indians, Colonists, and the Ecology of New England* (New York: Hill and Wang, 1983); Cronon, *Nature's Metropolis: Chicago and the Great West* (New York: Norton, 1991); Donald Worster, *Rivers of Empire: Water, Aridity, and the Growth of the American West* (New York: Pantheon Books, 1985).

7. Virginia Scharff, "The Case for Domestic Feminism: Woman Suffrage in Wyoming," *Annals of Wyoming* 56, no. 2 (Fall 1984): 29–37; Scharff, "The Independent and Feminine Life: Grace Raymond Hebard, 1861–1936," in *Lone Voyagers: Academic Women in Coeducational Universities, 1870–1937*, ed. Geraldine J. Clifford (New York: Feminist Press, 1989), 127–45; Scharff, "Of Parking Spaces and Women's Places: The Los Angeles Parking Ban of 1920," *National Women's Studies Association Journal* 1, no. 1 (September 1988): 37–51; Scharff, "Gender and Western History: Is Anybody Home on the Range?" *Montana* 41, no. 2 (Spring 1991): 62–65; Scharff, "Else Surely We Shall All Hang Separately: The Politics of Western

Women's History," *Pacific Historical Review* 61, no. 4 (November 1992): 535–55; Scharff, "Make-Believe and Graffiti: New Mexico Families Since 1940," in *Contemporary New Mexico, 1940–1990*, ed. Richard W. Etulain (Albuquerque: University of New Mexico Press, 1994), 91–118; Scharff, "Feminism, Femininity, and Power: Nellie Tayloe Ross and the Woman Politician's Dilemma," *Frontiers* 15, no. 3 (1995); and Scharff, "Women Envision the West, 1890–1945," in *Independent Spirits: Women Painters of the American West, 1890–1945*, ed. Patricia Trenton (Berkeley: University of California Press, 1995).

8. Jo Ann Gibson Robinson, *The Montgomery Bus Boycott and the Women Who Started It: The Memoir of Jo Ann Gibson Robinson* (Knoxville: University of Tennessee Press, 1987); Virginia Scharff, "Getting Out: What Does Mobility Mean for Women?" paper presented to the Symposium on Re-Envisioning the West, sponsored by the Clark Library, UCLA, and the National Endowment for the Humanities, January 1994.

9. James Clifford, *The Predicament of Culture: Twentieth-Century Ethnography, Literature, and Art* (Cambridge: Harvard University Press, 1988), 342.

10. The literature on mining towns and farm regions is vast. See, for example, Paula Petrik, *No Step Backward: Women and Family on the Rocky Mountain Mining Frontier, Helena, Montana, 1865–1900* (Helena: Montana Historical Society Press, 1987); Elizabeth Jameson, "High Grades and Fissures: A Working Class History of the Cripple Creek, Colorado Mining District, 1890–1905" (Ph.D. diss., University of Michigan, 1987); Susan Lee Johnson, " 'The Gold She Gathered': Difference and Domination in the California Gold Rush, 1848–1853" (Ph.D. diss., Yale University, 1993). On farming regions, see Katherine Jellison, *Entitled to Power: Farm Women and Technology, 1913–1963* (Chapel Hill: University of North Carolina Press, 1993); Mary Neth, *Preserving the Family Farm: Women, Community and the Foundations of Agribusiness in the Midwest, 1900–1940* (Baltimore: Johns Hopkins University Press, 1995); also Virginia Scharff, *Taking the Wheel: Women and the Coming of the Motor Age* (New York: Free Press, 1991), 144–45. On border towns, see George J. Sánchez, *Becoming Mexican American: Ethnicity, Culture, and Identity in Chicano Los Angeles, 1900–1945* (New York: Oxford University Press, 1993).

11. Scharff, "Of Parking Spaces and Women's Places"; Juan Roman Garcia, *Operation Wetback: The Mass Deportation of Mexican Undocumented Workers in 1954* (Westport, Conn.: Greenwood Press, 1980); James N. Gregory, *American Exodus: The Dust Bowl Migration and Okie Culture in California* (New York: Oxford University Press, 1989); Benny Andres, "Race Relations in Imperial Valley, 1900–1920" (M.A. thesis, University of New Mexico, 1993).

12. Historians have identified the notion that physical mobility is a masculine prerogative as well as a masculine trait, continually breached by women's actions, in

various cultural settings. See, for example, Margot Liberty, "Hell Came with the Horses: Plains Indian Women in the Equestrian Era," *Montana: The Magazine of Western History* 32, no. 3 (Summer 1982): 10–29; Christine Stansell, *City of Women: Sex and Class in New York, 1789–1860* (New York: Knopf, 1986); Sarah Deutsch, *No Separate Refuge: Culture, Class, and Gender on an Anglo-Hispanic Frontier in the American Southwest, 1880–1940* (New York: Oxford University Press, 1987); Joanne J. Meyerowitz, *Women Adrift: Independent Wage Earners in Chicago, 1880–1930* (Chicago: University of Chicago Press, 1988); Scharff, *Taking the Wheel*; Dorothy Ko, *Teachers of the Inner Chambers: Women and Culture in Seventeenth-Century China* (Stanford: Stanford University Press, 1994).

13. "Calamity Jane," in *Encyclopedia of the American West* (Memphis: Zenda Publishing, 1996); Deena J. Gonzalez, "La Tules of Image and Reality: Euro-American Attitudes and Legend Formation on a Spanish-Mexican Frontier," in *Building with Our Hands: New Directions in Chicana Studies*, ed. Adela de la Torre and Beatriz M. Pesquera (Berkeley: University of California Press, 1993), 75–90.

14. Ordinance quoted in Donna L. Cooper Graves, "Gender and the Geography of Crime: Criminal Activity in Kansas City, Kansas, 1890–1920" (Ph.D. diss., University of Kansas, 1994). Graves cites a report that "very young women were frequently seen boarding the streetcars to ride across the state line and participate in the pervasive sexual commerce of Kansas City, Missouri" (p. 298).

15. Catharine R. Stimpson et al., eds., *Women and the American City* (Chicago: University of Chicago Press, 1981); Dolores Hayden, *Redesigning the American Dream: The Future of Housing, Work, and Family Life* (New York: Norton, 1984).

16. Karen Anderson, "Western Women: The Twentieth-Century Experience," in *The Twentieth-Century West: Historical Interpretations*, ed. Gerald D. Nash and Richard W. Etulain (Albuquerque: University of New Mexico Press, 1989), 99–122.

17. The emblematic statement of this view is Joan Wallach Scott, "Gender: A Useful Category of Historical Analysis," in her *Gender and the Politics of History* (New York: Columbia University Press, 1988).

18. Here, I take issue with Susan Lee Johnson, " 'A Memory Sweet to Soldiers': The Significance of Gender in the History of the 'American West,' " *Western Historical Quarterly* 24, no. 4 (November 1993): 495–518, from a position similar to that argued by Christine Stansell, "A Response to Joan Scott," *International Labor and Working Class History* 31 (Spring 1987): 28–30.

19. My thinking here bears the influence of John Toews, "Intellectual History After the Linguistic Turn: The Autonomy of Meaning and the Irreducibility of Experience," *American Historical Review* 92, no. 4 (October 1987): 879–907. For a critique of Toews's argument, see Joan W. Scott, "The Evidence of Experience," *Critical Inquiry* 17 (Summer 1991): 773–95.

20. On Dolores Huerta see Margaret Eleanor Rose, "Women in the United Farm Workers: A Study of Chicana and Mexican Participation in a Labor Union, 1950–1980" (Ph.D. diss., University of California, Los Angeles, 1988). Emily Post, *By Motor Car to the Golden Gate* (New York: D. Appleton, 1916). Quotation from Scharff, *Taking the Wheel*, 117.

21. See Maria Elena Lucas, *Forjada Bajo el Sol / Forged Under the Sun: The Life of Maria Elena Lucas*, ed. Fran Leeper Buss (Ann Arbor: University of Michigan Press, 1993).

22. For a critique of ethnocentric women's history, see Antonia I. Castañeda, "Women of Color and the Rewriting of Western History: The Discourse, Politics, and Decolonization of History," *Pacific Historical Review* 16 (November 1992): 501–33.

23. John Mack Faragher, *Women and Men on the Overland Trail* (New Haven: Yale University Press, 1979); Julie Roy Jeffrey, *Frontier Women: The Trans-Mississippi West, 1840–1880* (New York: Hill and Wang, 1979); Lillian Schlissel, *Women's Diaries of the Westward Journey* (New York: Schocken Books, 1982).

24. Scharff, "Of Parking Spaces and Women's Places."

25. Rob Kling, Spencer Olin, and Mark Poster, eds., *Postsuburban California: The Transformation of Orange County Since World War II* (Berkeley: University of California Press, 1991); Sandra Rosenbloom, "Why Working Families Need a Car," in *The Car and the City: The Automobile, the Built Environment, and Daily Urban Life*, ed. Martin Wachs and Margaret Crawford (Ann Arbor: University of Michigan Press, 1992), 39–56; Ann R. Markusen, "City Spatial Structure, Women's Household Work, and National Urban Policy," in *Women and the American City*, ed. Stimpson et al., 20–41.

26. On Pleasant, see Helen Holdredge, *Mammy Pleasant* (New York: G. P. Putnam's Sons, 1953); Paula Giddings, *When and Where I Enter: The Impact of Black Women on Race and Sex in America* (New York: Morrow, 1984); Lynn M. Hudson, "A New Look, or 'I'm Not Mammy to Everybody in California': Mary Ellen Pleasant, a Black Entrepreneur," *Journal of the West* 32, no. 3 (July 1993): 35–40.

27. The best place to start, among numerous Janis Joplin biographies, is Myra Friedman, *Buried Alive: The Biography of Janis Joplin* (New York: Morrow, 1973); *Current Biography*, 1970, 209–11; *Vogue*, May 1968, 214; *Entertainment Weekly*, October 2, 1992, 72. *Cashbox* writer quoted in *Current Biography*, 211. Michael Lydon, "The Janis Joplin Philosophy: Every Moment She Is What She Feels," *New York Times Magazine*, February 23, 1969, 39.

28. Lydon, "The Janis Joplin Philosophy," 44.

Contributors

RICHARD WHITE is professor of history at Stanford University. His latest book is *Remembering Ahanagran: Storytelling in a Family's Past* (1998).

JOHN M. FINDLAY is professor of history at the University of Washington, Seattle, and Managing Editor of *Pacific Northwest Quarterly*. He is the author of *Magic Lands: Western Cityscapes and American Culture After 1940* (1992).

JAMES P. RONDA is the H. G. Barnard Professor of Western American History at the University of Tulsa. A specialist in the history of the exploration of western North America, he is the author of *Lewis and Clark Among the Indians* (1984), *Astoria and Empire* (1990), *Revealing America: Image and Imagination in the Exploration of North America* (1996), and *Voyages of Discovery: Essays on the Lewis and Clark Expedition* (1998). He is currently writing a book about trading-post communities in the American West.

JAMES F. BROOKS is assistant professor of history at the University of Maryland, College Park. His monograph *Captives and Cousins: Slavery, Kinship, and Community in the Southwest Borderlands, 1680–1880,* is forthcoming from the Omohundro Institute of Early American History and Culture (University of North Carolina Press).

JOHN LUTZ is assistant professor at the University of Victoria, in British Columbia. His research focuses on aboriginal-nonaboriginal relations in the Pacific Northwest, and he has written articles for the *Journal of the Canadian Historical Society* and the *Journal of the West*. He is currently revising his Ph.D. dissertation, "Work, Wages and Welfare in Aboriginal–Non-aboriginal Relations in British Columbia, 1849–1970," for publication.

KEVIN ALLEN LEONARD is assistant professor of history at Western Washington University. He is currently completing a book manuscript, "The Battle for Los Angeles: Race, Politics, and World War II," for the University of New Mexico Press. He has also begun work on a study of racial politics in the Cold War West.

WILLIAM DEVERELL is associate professor of history at the California Institute of Technology. He is currently working on a book about ethnic relations in Los Angeles from 1850 to 1940. He is the author of "Privileging the Mission over the Mexican: The Rise of Regional Identity in Southern California," which appeared in the recent volume *Many Wests: Place, Culture & Regional Identity*, edited by David Wrobel and Michael Steiner. He has an essay in *Over the Edge: Remapping Western Experience*, edited by Blake Allmendinger and Valerie Matsumoto (1998).

DOUGLAS FLAMMING is associate professor of history at the Georgia Institute of Technology, where he serves as director of the Center for Society and Industry in the Modern South. His first book, *Creating the Modern South: Millhands and Managers in Dalton, Georgia, 1884–1984*, won the 1992 Philip Taft Labor History Prize. His current book project is titled "A World to Gain: African Americans and the Making of Los Angeles, 1890–1940."

CHRIS FRIDAY is associate professor of history and director of the Center for Pacific Northwest Studies at Western Washington University. Friday's research and teaching focus on Asian American labor and immigration as well as broader constructions of race in the Pacific Northwest and American West.

HAL ROTHMAN is professor of history at the University of Nevada–Las Vegas, where he edits *Environmental History*. He is the author of *Devil's Bargains: Tourism in the Twentieth-Century American West* (1998), *The Greening of a Nation? Environmentalism in the U.S. Since 1945* (1997), and numerous other works. He was featured in "Las Vegas" on the A&E network.

PAUL W. HIRT is associate professor of history and American studies at Washington State University, Pullman, and the author of *A Conspiracy of Optimism: Management of the National Forests Since World War Two* (1994). He is also editor of a collection of essays on Northwest history titled *Terra Pacifica: People and Place in the Northwest States and Western Canada* (1998) and coeditor, with Dale Goble, of an interdisciplinary collection of essays titled *Northwest Lands, Northwest Peoples* (1999).

JOSEPH E. TAYLOR III teaches western and environmental history at Iowa State University. His publications on the social, cultural, environmental, and scientific history of Pacific salmon fisheries include *Making Salmon: An Environmental History of the Northwest Fisheries Crisis* (1999). He is currently writing a biography of the Colorado congressman Edward Thomas Taylor.

WILLIAM G. ROBBINS is Distinguished Professor of History at Oregon State University, where he teaches courses in western American and environmental history. He is the author of several books, including *Colony and Empire: The Capitalist Transformation of the American West* (1994) and *Landscapes of Promise: The Oregon Story, 1800–1940* (1997).

VIRGINIA SCHARFF is the author of *Taking the Wheel: Women and the Coming of the Motor Age* (1991) and the coauthor of *Present Tense: The United States Since 1945* (1991) and *Coming of Age: America in the Twentieth Century*. She is currently working on a book about women, mobility, and the West. She is associate professor of history at the University of New Mexico.

Index

Lewis, Meriwether. *See* Lewis and Clark Expedition
Lewis and Clark Centennial Exposition (Portland, 1905), 279–81
Lewis and Clark Expedition, 4, 5–10
Linnaeus, Carolus, 63–64
livestock: in New Mexico borderlands economy, 33, 35–38
Lockheed-Vega company, 92–93
logging. *See* timber industry
Los Angeles: importance of, in West, 91–92; growth of, 1880–1930, 118–19; and Rodney King, 288–89; women in, 291
Los Angeles Railway: and employment discrimination against African Americans, 94–96

McGroarty, John Steven, 123, 124
McLoughlin, John, 12–13
Meinig, D.W., x–xi
men: and wives in New Mexico borderlands economy, 31–33; white, and Indian wives, 65–68; roles of, among American-born Chinese and among Nisei, 153–54; and mobility, 292–95, 296–97
Mexican Americans, 99, 164. *See also* Latinos; Mexicans; New Mexican settlers
Mexicans: images of, among white boosters in Los Angeles, 123. *See also* Latinos; New Mexican settlers
missionaries, 14–15
Mission Play, The (McGroarty), 123–24
"mixed-bloods": legal status of, in British Columbia, 72–74
Myer, Dillon S., 98–99

Native Americans. *See* Indians
nature: and Los Angeles boosters, 119, 125–26; "managing," in national forests, 206–209, 216–27; managing, in salmon fisheries, 233–34; and economic development in Oregon, 264–66
Navaho Indians, 25–42. *See also* Diné Ana'aii
"neo-natives": identity of, and western tourism, 178–80, 190–91, 197–98
New Mexican settlers, 25–49
New Mexico: borderlands political economy, 23–25, 33–39
Nisei: and sports, 144–45, 153–54; and Japanese language school, 148; effect of Pacific War on, 147–48, 157–59; as "pioneers," 150, 153; effect of World War II on identity of, 161–63. *See also* Japanese Americans
North West Company, 11

Oregon: Indians and non-Indians in, 3–20; timber industry in, 205, 210, 271–73; competition with Washington state over salmon fishery, 239–40, 246–47; boosterism in, 264–81
overland trail, 296–97
Owen, Robert C., 125

place: and mobility, 289, 292–95; and western American history, 287–90; as defined by tourism, 177–80; defined, x. *See also* spatial analysis
Portland, Oregon: and an economic hinterland, 272–81; growth of, 273–74. *See also* Lewis and Clark Centennial Exposition; Oregon